FOREIGN OPERA AT THE LONDON PLAY.

In the early nineteenth century over forty operas by foreign composers including Mozart, Rossini, Weber and Bellini were adapted for London playhouses, often appearing in drastically altered form. Such changes have been denigrated as 'mutilations'. The operas were translated into English, fitted with spoken dialogue, divested of much of their music, augmented with interpolations and frequently set to altered libretti. By the end of the period, the radical changes of earlier adaptations gave way to more faithful versions. In the first comprehensive study of these adaptations, Christina Fuhrmann shows how integral they are to our understanding of early nineteenth-century opera and the transformation of London's theatrical and musical life. This book reveals how these operas accelerated repertoire shifts in the London theatrical world, fostered significant changes in musical taste, revealed the ambiguities and inadequacies of copyright law and sparked intense debate about fidelity to the original work.

CHRISTINA FUHRMANN is a Professor in the Department of Music at Ashland University. Her publications include articles in *Nineteenth-Century Music Review* and *Gender, Sexuality and Early Music* and a volume on *Romanticism and Opera*. Her critical edition of Henry Bishop's adaptation of *The Marriage of Figaro* was published in 2012.

CAMBRIDGE STUDIES IN OPERA

Series editor Arthur Groos, *Cornell University*

Volumes for Cambridge Studies in Opera explore the cultural, political and social influences of the genre. As a cultural art form, opera is not produced in a vacuum. Rather, it is influenced, whether directly or in more subtle ways, by its social and political environment. In turn, opera leaves its mark on society and contributes to shaping the cultural climate. Studies to be included in the series will look at these various relationships including the politics and economics of opera, the operatic representation of women or the singers who portrayed them, the history of opera as theatre and the evolution of the opera house.

Published titles

Opera Buffa in Mozart's Vienna
Edited by Mary Hunter and James Webster

German Opera: From the Beginnings to Wagner
John Warrack

Johann Strauss and Vienna: Operetta and the Politics of Popular Culture
Camille Crittenden

Opera and Drama in Eighteenth-Century London: The King's Theatre, Garrick and the Business of Performance
Ian Woodfield

Opera Liberalism, and Antisemitism in Nineteenth-Century France: The Politics of Halévy's
La Juive
Diana R. Hallman

Three Modes of Perception in Mozart: The Philosophical, Pastoral, and Comic in *Cosi fan tutte*
Edmund J. Goehring

Landscape and Gender in Italian Opera: The Alpine Virgin from Bellini to Puccini
Emanuele Senici

Aesthetics of Opera in the Ancien Régime, 1647–1785
Downing A. Thomas

The Puccini Problem: Opera, Nationalism, and Modernity
Alexandra Wilson

The Prima Donna and Opera, 1815–1930
Susan Rutherford

Opera and Society in Italy and France from Monteverdi to Bourdieu
Edited by Victoria Johnson, Jane F. Fulcher, and Thomas Ertman

Wagner's Ring Cycle and the Greeks
Daniel H. Foster

When Opera Meets Film
Marcia J. Citron

Situating Opera: Period, Genre, Reception
Herbert Lindenberger

Rossini in Restoration Paris: The Sound of Modern Life
Benjamin Walton

Italian Opera in the Age of the American Revolution
Pierpaolo Polzonetti

Opera in the Novel from Balzac to Proust
Cormac Newark

Opera in the Age of Rousseau: Music, Confrontation, Realism
David Charlton

The Sounds of Paris in Verdi's *La traviata*
Emilio Sala

The Rival Sirens: Performance and Identity on Handel's Operatic Stage
Suzanne Aspden

Sentimental Opera: Questions of Genre in the Age of Bourgeois Drama
Stefano Castelvecchi

Verdi, Opera, Women
Susan Rutherford

Rounding Wagner's Mountain: Richard Strauss and Modern German Opera
Bryan Gilliam

Opera and Modern Spectatorship in Late Nineteenth-Century Italy
Alessandra Campana

Opera Acts: Singers and Performance in the Late Nineteenth Century
Karen Henson

Foreign Opera at the London Playhouses: From Mozart to Bellini
Christina Fuhrmann

Foreign Opera at the London Playhouses

From Mozart to Bellini

Christina Fuhrmann

Ashland University

CAMBRIDGE
UNIVERSITY PRESS

University Printing House, Cambridge CB2 8BS, United Kingdom

One Liberty Plaza, 20th Floor, New York, NY 10006, USA

477 Williamstown Road, Port Melbourne, VIC 3207, Australia

314-321, 3rd Floor, Plot 3, Splendor Forum, Jasola District Centre, New Delhi - 110025, India

79 Anson Road, #06-04/06, Singapore 079906

Cambridge University Press is part of the University of Cambridge.

It furthers the University's mission by disseminating knowledge in the pursuit of education, learning and research at the highest international levels of excellence.

www.cambridge.org
Information on this title: www.cambridge.org/9781108722117

First published 2015
First paperback edition 2018

A catalogue record for this publication is available from the British Library

Library of Congress Cataloging in Publication data
Fuhrmann, Christina, author.
Foreign opera at the London playhouses: from Mozart to Bellini /
Christina Fuhrmann, Ashland University.
        pages   cm. – (Cambridge studies in opera)
Includes bibliographical references and index.
ISBN 978-1-107-02221-8 (Hardback : alk. paper)
1. Opera–England–London–History–19th century.   2. Musical theater–England–
London–History–19th century.   I. Title.
ML1731.8.L7F84   2015
792.509421´09034–dc23   2015013724

ISBN 978-1-107-02221-8 Hardback
ISBN 978-1-108-72211-7 Paperback

CONTENTS

FIGURES

ACKNOWLEDGEMENTS

This book would not have been completed without the assistance of many individuals. Darrell Berg first sparked my interest in the field and Bruce Carr generously shared his work in this area. My colleagues and students at Ashland University supported my research. A semester of sabbatical leave and several summer grants gave me time to work on the project. Jeff Pinkham tirelessly sought out interlibrary loan items, Alexander Sanchez-Behar graciously read drafts, Stephanie Sikora performed several excerpts from these adaptations and Fatima Imani Smith provided research assistance. Several librarians aided my research, most especially Peter Horton at the Royal College of Music and Bradley Short at the University of Washington in St Louis. At the Oberlin College Conservatory of Music, members of my writing group helped me refine my ideas and my prose: Sarah Gerk, Jared Hartt, Charles McGuire, Jan Miyake and James O'Leary. Roger Parker graciously invited me to present a workshop for his European Research Council project, Music in London, 1800–1851, and I am grateful to him and his research fellows for their insightful comments. David Kennerley and Jan Smith generously shared their thesis work. Especial thanks go to Alison Mero and Jennifer Oates, who read substantial portions of the manuscript in its final stages and answered last-minute queries. I also thank my parents, who instilled a love of opera in me from a young age; my mother also graciously lent her artistic talents to the cover of this book. Finally, I thank my husband, Christopher Borgmeyer, who broke all records for patience and support.

In the nineteenth century, operas experienced constant revision, translation, alteration and variation. Librettists often adapted plays or novels, composers revised their scores and singers ornamented their lines and inserted favourite substitute arias. Operatic excerpts headlined concerts and publishers' catalogues overflowed with arrangements of popular opera tunes. When operas travelled to new countries, changes could be particularly exhaustive. Perhaps the best example is in early nineteenth-century London. Numerous operas were adapted for the London playhouses, where audiences heard them alongside Shakespeare, melodrama and pantomime (see Appendix 1). Operas by composers such as Mozart, Rossini, Weber, Auber, Boieldieu, Meyerbeer and Bellini appeared in English, with spoken dialogue instead of recitative. British adapters often radically transformed libretti and freely cut, recomposed and replaced musical numbers.

Negative rhetoric has hampered scholarly exploration of these adaptations.[1] The primary reason for distaste stems from a competing strand of nineteenth-century musical life: canon formation. Scholars such as Lydia Goehr and William Weber argue that the late eighteenth and nineteenth centuries saw the rise of the 'fixed work', reproduced faithfully to create a canon of masterpieces.[2] As new ideals of canonicity emerged, change drew condemnation. Contemporary critics such as Leigh Hunt, William Ayrton and Richard Mackenzie Bacon began to refer to operatic adaptations as defacing, mutilating and vulgarising the original. Such attitudes continue to influence scholarship. *Grove music online* refers to the adaptations of one of the most prominent British composers, Sir Henry Rowley Bishop, as 'mutilations', while *An Oxford companion to the Romantic age* states that the original operas were 'ferociously hacked about'.[3]

Scholars have, however, begun to recognise the centrality of change to opera. Mark Everist, Philip Gossett, David Levin, Roger Parker and Hilary Poriss have explored adaptation, revision, substitution and re-staging.[4] Literary scholars have conducted theoretical studies of adaptation.[5] The vast source materials for British theatre music have also begun to receive more attention, both from theatre historians such as Tracy C. Davis and Jane Moody and from musicologists such as Rachel Cowgill, Gabriella Dideriksen, Alison Mero and Deborah Rohr.[6] Finally, exploration of British adaptations is aided by work on operatic life in the United States, where many London adaptations were exported.[7]

Such work invites a return to these adaptations with a fresh perspective. Past disparagement has obscured the central role they played in London musical and theatrical life. They intertwined with debates about repertoire, class and nationalism. They both arose from the lack of laws governing international copyright and helped accelerate efforts by composers and publishers to control the pan-European distribution of opera. And, although these adaptations are often seen as opposed to canonisation, they in fact contributed to the move towards fidelity – the term contemporaries most often used for adherence to the original work. The early decades of the nineteenth century represent a crucial transition between the late eighteenth century, when pastiche prevailed, and the Victorian era, when translation largely replaced adaptation.[8] During this brief window of time, adaptations were important catalysts of change. They helped foster the ubiquity necessary for canonical status, since they were the first and sometimes only way in which many listeners came to know foreign operas. They gradually helped to bridge aesthetic divides between native and continental opera, as London audiences became more familiar with the latter. Finally, adaptations were a locus for critical debates about the nature and desirability of fidelity, which helped to shape the rhetoric of canonicity.

THE CONTEXT FOR ADAPTATION

Adaptation dominated London theatre in the early 1800s.[9] Many stage works reworked or revised pre-existent stories. The adapted foreign operas discussed here appeared alongside adaptations of French and German plays, dramatisations of novels by favourite authors such as Sir Walter Scott and 'updated' versions of older plays. Even Shakespeare's plays were altered. Thomas Bowdler's infamously censored *The family Shakespeare* was published in 1818, giving rise to the term 'bowdlerisation', and stage productions rarely followed Shakespeare's original text without change.[10] Contemporaries most commonly referred to these practices as 'adaptation', although they also used 'translation', particularly if the original was followed closely. Terminology was by no means fixed, however, and contemporaries used many expressions, including 'version', 'selection', 'arrangement' and 'olio'. Sometimes they simply referred to a 'production' or 'opera', which obscured distinctions between original and reworking.

Why was adaptation so prominent? Linda Hutcheon has theorised various reasons, several of which apply to this context. First was simply the 'enormous demand for all kinds of stories'.[11] London playhouses employed the repertory system, which featured a large number of new and revived pieces, all on double or triple bills. A theatre might produce as many as ninety separate works during a nine-month season. Even given that many of these were revivals, there was a huge need for new productions. Second was the 'obvious financial appeal'.[12] With no official government subsidy and no 'tryout' venues, London theatre managers preferred proven successes to untested new works. Since copyright law was far from solidified, adaptation was frequently the cheapest, speediest way to find new productions. This prompted many theatres to produce competing adaptations of the same original, which increased the importance of adaptation; changes were necessary to differentiate one version from the next and to entice audiences to yet another manifestation of the same story. Finally, adaptation could 'expand the audience' of each theatre.[13] At its heart, operatic adaptation stemmed from a desire to capitalise on the elite lure of opera in theatres that were not exclusively devoted to the genre.

In some ways, however, these adaptations do not fit current theories. Today, Hutcheon writes, adapters often wish to 'interpret [the] work' and 'take a position on it'.[14] This tends to be the current preferred view of the adapter, as a kind of author redefining the original in artistically driven ways. David Levin, for example, urges opera directors to embrace 'strong readings' of opera, which are 'surprising . . . asserting some distance from prevailing and predictable accounts. A weak reading fails to do so, tending instead to . . . reproduce the work's prevailing aesthetic identity.'[15] While much recent scholarship urges a move away from a sacrosanct work, the ideal of authorial vision – located in adapter if not author – still seems too important to relinquish. Nineteenth-century adapters do not fit this aesthetic. They did wish to 'reproduce the work's prevailing aesthetic identity', as this identity was novel and potentially profitable. Their changes stemmed more from a need to suit the work to its new context, to bridge divides of taste and practicalities of performance, than to stamp it with their own vision. This divergence helps to explain why nineteenth-century adaptations have suffered from a kind of double jeopardy. Modern detractors of adaptation find the practice disturbing in all time periods, while modern supporters value adaptation for reasons removed from nineteenth-century values.

Different views of adaptation primarily stem from different relationships to the canon. In the early nineteenth century, adaptation was one of many fluid practices that assisted the relatively new process of canonisation. In the early twenty-first century, fidelity is the norm and original works have been heard thousands of times. Rather than helping to establish a canon, adaptation is now often intended to disestablish it, to refresh long-canonised works. Speaking of the most common modern type of operatic adaptation, *Regieoper*, in which visual elements are typically altered while the score is retained intact, Richard Taruskin observes, 'The boredom of endlessly reproducing fetishized texts is what invites, and even demands, the compensatory excesses of *Regieoper*.'[16] Although the same word is used for adaptation both then and now, these practices' divergent contexts and motivations make it problematic to equate them.

Adaptation was not, however, a universally accepted practice in the nineteenth century. On the contrary, it received severe contemporary criticism, as it intertwined with some of the most contested aspects of London theatrical culture: repertoire laws and conventions; the perceived decline of the native drama; and the rise of interest in fidelity and its legal sister, copyright. The very existence of adapted opera at the playhouses stemmed from a complex and antiquated set of repertoire regulations.[17]

In 1662, Charles II issued patents to Sir William Davenant and Thomas Killigrew for the exclusive right to produce drama. Until 1843, these patents resided with Covent Garden and Drury Lane – the 'patent theatres' – located a few steps away from each other in a densely populated theatrical district, near the Strand and across from Waterloo Bridge. These theatres possessed the exclusive privilege of performing 'legitimate' drama, which essentially meant spoken drama in English. Opera, meanwhile, was the preserve of a theatre founded in 1705 and known variously as the Queen's Theatre, the King's Theatre and Her Majesty's Theatre, depending on the monarch. This theatre, located farther west than the patent theatres, in Pall Mall, primarily performed opera in Italian and French ballets. It was often known as 'the opera house' or 'the Italian opera house'. Licences and agreements in 1707 and 1792 prevented the patent theatres from encroaching on this house's repertoire and vice versa.

Numerous other theatres tried to challenge these three houses' supremacy, but only the Haymarket or 'Little Haymarket' succeeded in obtaining a patent, in 1766, for summer performances, when the other theatres were closed.[18] Theatres without such patents, known as the 'minor' theatres, were spread throughout the city, both near the patent theatres and in less salubrious locales, and operated on yearly licences regulated by acts of 1737 and 1755.[19] These 'minor' theatres – as opposed to the 'major' theatres, Covent Garden and Drury Lane – were allowed to perform only 'illegitimate' drama. This was an ambiguous term that essentially meant productions focused on music and spectacle rather than speech.

London theatre may therefore seem to fall into neat packages of legitimate drama, illegitimate drama and opera, with music a crucial definer among these types. In fact, music played an ambiguous role, at once maligned and desired. Long-held prejudices fashioned music as effeminate, irrational and opposed to the British character. James Boaden mourned that 'music triumphantly reigns over the subject reason of the country' and Henry Redhead Yorke railed against music as 'corruption, effeminacy, execrable fooleries and sing-song lullabies'.[20] Richard Leppert explains that 'the musical gentleman by his interests and actions semiotically deconstructed ... the definition of gender upon which both the society and the culture ultimately depended. It is this, I believe, which justified the phenomenal attention devoted to the control of music in English society.'[21] London's theatrical system was in a sense built on these prejudices. The most prized houses of the national drama, the major theatres, had a patented right to speech, while music was relegated either to the foreign productions at the King's Theatre or to the realm of spectacle and show at the minor theatres.

In reality, however, music fascinated theatre audiences and pervaded every venue and virtually every performance. All three types of theatre envied their neighbours and made increasingly bold incursions across repertoire lines. The minor theatres tried numerous inventive methods to outwit repertoire restrictions, with few legal repercussions, while major theatres frequently turned to 'illegitimate' genres filled with music in order to stay solvent. Opera was a particularly desirable commodity. In 1832, for example, William Dunn, secretary and treasurer to the committee that owned Drury Lane, asserted that they would have been able to ask £4000 or £5000 a year more in rent had they been able to perform Italian opera.[22] The operatic adaptations studied here stemmed from the desire of the major and minor theatres – the playhouses – to challenge the King's Theatre's operatic domain. By the late 1820s and 1830s, foreign operas regularly appeared at all three types of theatre.

Music thus pervaded playhouse productions, but in a distinctive shape born of these circumstances.[23] Despite music's popularity, speech remained central. Many pieces featured only isolated musical numbers or, like melodrama, focused on instrumental accompaniment rather than vocal music.[24] Even operas mixed song and speech; with the exception of Arne's *Artaxerxes*, few British operas were sung throughout. Furthermore, while native operas featured plentiful music, they still tended to privilege speech. Leading male characters frequently did not sing at all and vocal music functioned primarily as an ornament, not as a participant in the action.[25] Only a handful of native singers received the training and encouragement necessary to compete with the foreign stars at the King's Theatre, although this changed in the second quarter of the nineteenth century. Playhouses' orchestras and choruses received mixed reviews and additional musicians and rehearsals were often needed to tackle challenging works.[26] Adapters of foreign opera thus had to reconcile a chasm between the typical shape of continental opera and its form on the playhouse stage. Still, the effort seemed worthwhile in order to capitalise on the popularity of foreign opera without breaking repertoire laws.

While some contemporaries struggled to maintain rapidly collapsing repertoire distinctions, others wished to abolish the theatrical patents altogether. Anti-patent rhetoric drew much of its force from larger economic and political issues. Davis describes the patent monopoly as 'directly analogous' to monopolies granted to companies such as the English East India Company and the theatre became an important site for advocating a laissez-faire policy.[27] The patent theatres also seemed to hoard power and use it unwisely, much like the government and the unpopular King George IV. Eugene Macarthy linked theatrical and political oppression, claiming 'the arrogant and despotic edicts of a Theatrical Oligarchy have roused the honest and indignant feelings of the English heart, which swells with a natural and instinctive hatred of tyranny and oppression'.[28] It is no coincidence that the first bill to eliminate the theatrical monopoly reached Parliament in 1831–2, at precisely the same time as the Reform Bill, which advocated less corrupt and more widespread political representation. The Reform Bill passed, but theatrical reform failed in the House of Lords. For some, this solidified the idea of an entrenched aristocracy resisting the change demanded by the broader populace. Repertoire restrictions were not lifted until 1843, as part of a larger shift towards free trade that included the repeal of the Corn Laws in 1846.[29] By that point, however, generic boundaries had become so contested that theatrical reform was almost a formality.

Whether they supported the patent system or not, most contemporaries agreed that the national drama was declining. A pervasive rhetoric described Shakespearean drama as a height from which theatres had fallen. The stage no longer attracted the greatest writers of the day, such as Wordsworth or Byron.[30] Instead, the foreign, musical and spectacular seemed to overrun theatres. Thomas James Mathias mourned:

> When Novels die, and rise again in plays:
> No Congress props our Drama's falling state,
> The modern ultimatum is, 'Translate'.[31]

Contemporaries most often blamed decline on the large size of the patent theatres, which had rebuilt on a grander scale both in the late eighteenth century and then again after fire destroyed both houses in 1808–9. John Payne Collier summarised the prevailing view:

> I think the great theatres have owed their present condition partly to their magnitude, partly to the representations that have taken place at them, and partly to the difficulty of hearing, understanding and enjoying representations of a more regular and legitimate character. In fact it all resolves itself into magnitude.[32]

These houses were not necessarily larger than other London and continental theatres.[33] Nonetheless, the size argument proved pervasive because it aptly symbolised the complex factors implicated in decline. The image of a huge theatre, dependent on large receipts for its survival, mirrored the gradual move from aristocratic to public patronage. While this freed artists in some respects, it dangerously equated artistic and financial worth. Patrick Brantlinger summarises: 'Literature and the other arts, emancipated ... from aristocratic patronage and repression, were emancipated through the processes of commodification.'[34] Greed seemed the catalyst of decline. Some drew parallels between managers' focus on whatever would earn the most money and the prostitutes who solicited clients in the audience. One of Drury Lane's proprietors exclaimed, 'What would a theatre be without the girls? ... morality and profit can't go hand in hand in our Theatres.'[35] Some contemporaries feared he could as easily have said artistic worth and profit.

Class issues lay at the root of these concerns. London theatres were divided into three sections: boxes, pit and galleries. At the patent theatres, prices for these sections remained fairly constant through the first few decades of the nineteenth century: seven shillings for a box; three shillings sixpence for the pit; two shillings for the gallery; and one shilling for the upper gallery. Patrons could enter later in the evening for half

price tickets. Contemporaries viewed these regions as strictly stratified, as James
Robinson Planché described:

> Ye belles and ye beaux
> Who adorn our low rows,
> Ye gods, who preside in the high ones;
> Ye critics who sit
> All so snug in the pit
> An assemblage of clever and sly ones.[36]

Although audiences of the period still await systematic study, Jim Davis confirms these
basic divisions: 'Audiences comprised a cross section of society: the more aristocratic,
fashionable and affluent patrons in the boxes; intellectuals, less affluent gentlemen
and professionals in the pit; tradesmen and their wives in the middle gallery and
servants, footmen and sailors among the inhabitants of the upper gallery.'[37]

These classes jostled uneasily together. One writer complained in 1821, 'Half a
century ago ... the prosperity of a theatre depended mainly on people of rank, and
a critical Pit ... All this is swept away by the enlargement of the theatres, and the
immense alteration produced by the commercial intoxication of the last thirty years.'[38]
As the playhouses began to spiral out of the control of the educated elite, wealthy
patrons retreated.[39] Actor and manager Charles Mathews noted: 'if [the fashionable]
are asked whether they have been at Covent Garden or Drury Lane, they say, "Oh
dear, no! I never go there, it is too low!"'[40] Playhouse managers tried to lure these
patrons back, and adaptations of the same operas that played at the opera house – seen
as an upper-class preserve – were clearly meant to attract them. Yet, such appeals
had to be subtle. When John Philip Kemble re-opened Covent Garden in 1809 after it
had been destroyed by fire, he deliberately tried to attract the elite; he raised prices,
erected more private boxes and hired foreign opera star Angelica Catalani. The violent
'old price riots' that erupted forced Kemble to retract these changes and showed
managers that they could not cater so blatantly to a moneyed clientele.[41]

Swinging to the opposite extreme and gratifying gallery attendees, however, also
drew criticism. Many contemporaries thought these patrons lowered the collective
taste of the playhouses. Gallery audiences encored 'low, vulgar song[s]', and were
'at the beck of specious and showy charlatanism'.[42] One author stated baldly, 'our
dramatic public is always likely to be ignorant, whilst all classes are admitted to
the same entertainment'.[43] Bringing such patrons into the fold of elevated taste took
on an urgent tone in light of the riotous tendencies that lay uncomfortably close to
the surface of Georgian life. Riots against the Corn Laws, attacks or planned attacks
in the late 1810s and 1820s on the unpopular Prince Regent, later George IV, and
agitation surrounding the Reform Bill in 1832 led to anxiety about the potential power
of disaffected masses.

Who, then, was supposed to guide theatrical taste, and how could they do so? Jacky Bratton, Rachel Cowgill and Jennifer Hall-Witt have argued that the 'middling' classes – the 'critical Pit' – fought to assume this role.[44] They did so through a powerful public channel, for the critics of the expanding press were predominantly middle class.[45] Such critics possessed both considerable bias and influence, often through corrupt connections with theatre managers. Critic Leigh Hunt scoffed that 'what the public took for a criticism on a play was a draft upon the box-office, or reminiscences of last Thursday's salmon and lobster-sauce'.[46] Of course, Hunt here vaunted his own objectivity, which was hardly unassailable. Critics were not simply managers' minions, however; they were individuals with strong views and an effective conduit for transmitting them. Although all reviews were anonymous, most critics' identities were an 'open secret'.[47] Men such as William Ayrton, Richard Mackenzie Bacon, John Payne Collier, William Hazlitt and Hunt both reflected and shaped public opinion. Some, such as Ayrton and Bacon, were prominent in London musical life and edited groundbreaking musical journals – *The Harmonicon* and the *Quarterly Musical Magazine and Review*, respectively – to promulgate their agenda of improving musical taste. Others, such as Hunt and Hazlitt, were part of the 'Cockney' writers, so named because of their radical politics and middle-class background, and utilised theatrical and literary criticism to effect social and political reform.[48] Still others approached opera from a primarily literary angle and even confessed ignorance of music. *The Athenaeum* explained, 'Our duty is with theatrical, not operatic criticism, and music only comes to us incidentally, through the former medium.'[49] Literary-minded critics like Collier therefore focused on preserving legitimate drama and sometimes relegated music to a corrupting influence.[50]

Despite often-conflicting views, the majority of these critics agreed that the national drama desperately needed rescuing from a state of decline. Bratton even suggests that they engendered this idea: '"the decline of the drama" was a concept generated in the press and in critical writing of the period for the particular purposes of a newly ascendant hegemonic faction, the literate (and overwhelmingly male) middle classes, whose project was to recapture the stage ... for the exclusive transmission of their own voice'.[51] They primarily sought to do this by undermining the 'event-oriented' theatrical model, in which the audience focused on favourite performers and the experience of attending the theatre. Instead, they advocated a 'work-oriented' model, in which the goal of attendance was to hear, with rapt attention, a specific piece.[52] With this model, critics hoped to shield works from commercialism and mass judgment, to impose aesthetic and social control through theatrical taste. Such goals merged seamlessly with canonicity. Weber discerns that 'Because the great master-works were thought to stand above the money-making side of musical life, they could help society transcend commercial culture.'[53] The battle against dramatic decline was therefore also the battle for fidelity.

In numerous respects, adaptation fell on the wrong side of these debates. On a practical level, it ran counter to expanding copyright law, the legal underpinning of the canon. In Britain, copyright laws began in 1710 for print culture, but only gradually expanded into the fluid sphere of performance. Only in the 1830s, for example, did authors win rights to performances beyond the original theatre and in the 1880s to performances beyond the original country, although attempts at establishing international copyright began in the 1830s.[54] While some foreign composers tried to control adaptations of their works, as shall be seen with Ries and Meyerbeer, adapters could still profit fairly freely from others' originals. In 1828, *The Athenaeum* bristled, '[adapters] talk with the utmost complacency of the success of *their* piece (!!) and remorselessly appropriate the profits arising from the disfigurement and destruction of a work'.[55] The financial motivation for copyright – and the challenge posed to it by adaptation – is clear.

Operatic adaptations also strayed from the purported repertoire of the patent theatres in all three of their most basic aspects: they were adaptations; they were musical; and they were foreign. Although adaptation pervaded virtually all theatres, it was often viewed as a specifically minor theatre activity. At the edge of the law, minor theatres frequently used adaptation to present popular major theatre pieces in new versions that could just barely escape legal repercussions. As Jane Moody argues, adaptation was tainted with illegitimacy: 'The spectre of adaptation rapidly became synonymous with the impossibility of curtailing illegitimate representation.'[56] Adaptations of operas were even more troublesome. When major theatre managers imported pieces that featured music, they abandoned their patented duty to maintain the legitimate, spoken tradition of native drama. Additionally, such adaptations drew the major theatres closer not only to musical, illegitimate fare, but also to the King's Theatre, with its foreign operas sung by foreign stars. This appeared inimical to theatres that were supposed to uphold native drama, as well as to native composers and any hope of a national operatic tradition. British composer and adapter Bishop spoke of the harsh personal and financial consequences of the culture of adaptation:

> with the situation into which I have been thrown by the system now pursued by the Theatres (from the patronage of whatever is foreign only) it is with utmost difficulty we can manage to get together day after day the bare means to live! ... Heaven knows I tried every nerve to [write an Opera for publisher Thomas Mackinlay], but foreign music, and all that was foreign, was the cry![57]

Adaptation also challenged burgeoning canonical ideals by testing the nature of fidelity. Most fundamentally, adaptation exposed the slippery nature of the original. Opera composers often created several versions and revisions, which derailed a sense of a fixed original. As Parker reasons, 'Considered at all closely, almost all operas become problem works so far as establishing a definitive text is concerned.'[58] The original libretto was itself frequently an adaptation of a tale known in other forms. The story of the barber of Seville, for example, was not confined to Rossini and Sterbini's opera, but crowded alongside remembrances of Beaumarchais' play, its British adaptation and Paisiello's opera. Adaptations were therefore often part of a continuum of retellings, of which the opera was only one manifestation.

Compounding this issue was the fact that few listeners would have had access to a reliable original. Some heard these works performed abroad and retained vivid but not always accurate memories of them. Others first heard them at the King's Theatre, where music directors often made changes to the score, interpolated divertissements between acts or performed only individual acts of popular operas. Listeners could also consult published scores, but a full original orchestral score was less frequently available than piano–vocal arrangements, excerpts, variations and fantasias. Popular foreign works also frequently appeared in multiple adaptations in London – most memorably with eight separate productions of *Der Freischütz* in 1824 – which tended to obscure the original in a sometimes bewildering abundance of versions.

Even when critics felt confident in comparing original to adaptation, they often found that fidelity did not equal worth. When adapters significantly altered a revered original, critics could espouse a strict rejection of change. *The Atlas* exclaimed of Bishop's adaptation of *Le nozze di Figaro*, 'What has been gained by defacing, mutilating, and vulgarizing so perfect an opera?'[59] Usually, however, there was a considerable grey area. Few critics objected to or even remarked on the translation of foreign operas into English or the use of spoken dialogue in lieu of recitative. Many critics actively encouraged adapters to interpolate pieces from the same composer's other operas. Reviewing an adaptation of *Die Entführung aus dem Serail*, Ayrton suggested that 'It were much to be wished, that all the deficiencies had been supplied from Mozart's less known works'.[60] Still others thought changes were necessary to improve musical taste. The *Journal of Music and the Drama* applauded Bishop's adaptation of *Figaro*, citing his 'zealous and honourable ambition to enrich and improve the music of his native stage'.[61] Assessments varied widely depending on the perceived worth of both original and adaptation. Outraged at Eugène Scribe's changes to Sir Walter Scott in *La dame blanche*, Collier protested that 'if the music were to be sacredly preserved, there is no reason why equal homage should be paid to the ignorance and incongruities of the French writer'.[62] Change was often preferable to fidelity if it produced a better result. *The Times* suggested that an adaptation of Winter's *Das unterbrochene Opferfest* be curtailed, since 'Apple-pudding is an excellent thing; but a man might be fed with too large a quantity of it – especially, if he had to eat through a heavy crust before he came to the apples.'[63]

These conflicting responses speak to the messy reality of the canonical process, as critics struggled to assess and even define fidelity. They also underline that, while adaptation seemed to derail canonicity, it was also its helpmeet. Michael Dobson explains:

> many of the plays upon which Shakespeare's reputation . . . is now most squarely based . . . were in practice only tolerated in the theatre in heavily revised versions, even while that very reputation was being established. This coexistence of full-scale canonization with wholesale adaptation . . . has long been regarded as a quaint paradox . . . [but] adaptation and canonization, so far from being contradictory processes, were often mutually reinforcing ones.[64]

Such reinforcement occurred in three primary ways. First, as Everist describes, adaptations were often the primary means by which operas gained the ubiquity necessary for canonical status. 'To hold that the position assumed by the work today was won by that work itself, unchanged and monumental, is to misunderstand one of the more important bases of the music history of the nineteenth century.'[65] Operas had to be drastically altered to suit the London playhouses, yet only with such changes could opera appear there at all. Adaptation brought operas to audiences who may not otherwise have ventured to the opera house and in some cases offered important London premières. Second, adaptation was not a static process. The influx of foreign operas diminished the divide between native and continental taste that had prompted changes in the first place, such that adapters could afford to challenge their casts and listeners with increasingly faithful productions. Finally, adaptations prompted critics to develop a rhetoric against change; despite inconsistency and hypocrisy, their overriding desire for fidelity helped lessen adapters' freedom. London adaptation therefore changed drastically within a short timeframe. Substantial alterations of the late 1810s gave way to far more faithful versions by the early 1830s. London in the early nineteenth century provides an unusual glimpse into the workings of the canonical process, fraught with contradiction and ambiguity, but nevertheless a force for considerable change in theatrical and musical life.

OPERA ADAPTED FOR LONDON

This book explores operatic adaptation in London through a study of almost twenty imported operas from 1814 to 1833. A picture of these adaptations must be assembled from numerous sources. In a few cases, there are no extant sources for the libretto or score, but a basic picture can be constructed from playbills and newspaper advertisements and reviews. Most adaptations are documented by at least a manuscript libretto, since all theatres had to submit their plays to the Lord Chamberlain's office for censorship, a requirement that stood until 1968.[66] Within the theatre, patrons could purchase word books, which contained only the text for the musical numbers; many but not all of these survive. Finally, libretti of popular adaptations were published, occasionally in multiple editions well after the première.

In many cases, only libretti sources are extant and an idea of the music must be pieced together by comparing adapted and original libretti. In other cases, manuscript and printed sources for the score are available, but these were virtually never complete. Published scores were not intended to preserve organic wholes for posterity, but to profit from sales of popular theatre pieces to the large domestic market. Publishers offered either a few isolated pieces or a 'complete' score that contained only the most popular numbers. In both cases, scores were always piano–vocal. Ayrton, noting jealously that full orchestral scores regularly appeared in France, complained, 'with us only detached pieces from operas, and these for one voice, or two at the utmost, have any chance for a remunerative sale'.[67]

Manuscript scores were orchestral, but not complete. This is due to adapters' working procedure, observable in Bishop's adaptations of Boieldieu's *Les deux nuits* and Rossini's *La gazza ladra*. Bishop obtained a manuscript or printed version of the original score, onto which he wrote small changes, new English text and cuts. In a separate manuscript score, he wrote added pieces, new orchestral parts and numbers that were changed too much to write onto the original score. Typically, only this manuscript score survives. The one deviation from this procedure was Bishop's adaptation of *Robert le diable*, which was re-orchestrated from piano–vocal sources and for which we therefore have a full, complete manuscript score. In the few cases where the original score with the adapter's emendations survives, we can know exactly which original source was used. Otherwise, an educated guess must be made based on the scores that would have been available at the time. Whenever multiple sources for an adaptation survive, they differ from each other, sometimes substantially. This reflects the continual process of change that took place from rehearsal through première and subsequent performances. Adaptations are therefore difficult to pinpoint, as they must be pieced together from numerous sources, virtually all incomplete and varying from each other.

Reception of these adaptations is similarly problematic. Contemporary opinion is disproportionately well represented by newspaper reviews, which exist in abundant, readily accessible supply. Memoirs and letters are also available, but they rarely discuss particular adaptations in as much depth. Audiences' views are ephemeral, glimpsed only through the occasional memoir, reports of audience behaviour in the press and ledgers and playbills that indicate the profits and runs for each piece. This book therefore does not pretend to represent all contemporary feelings about adaptation, which must await future work. Rather, one aim of this study is to explore the reactions of the press, not as unproblematic records of all contemporary opinion, but as the beliefs of one of the most well-documented and influential segments of society. Critics' approaches to adaptation exemplify both changing attitudes and deeply ambivalent responses, as reviewers grappled with the future of the native stage and what role both operatic adaptation and fidelity should play on it.

Chapter 1 traces the rise of adaptation by examining two versions of Boieldieu's *Jean de Paris* in 1814. The Drury Lane version represents the typical use of foreign opera in the past, as part of the predominant pastiche culture. The adapters liberally altered the libretto, discarded the entire score and interpolated new numbers. At Covent Garden, in contrast, a new approach emerged. The adapters stayed close to the libretto and vaunted their preservation of Boieldieu's score, of 'the' work. 'Preservation' still entailed liberal cuts and interpolations to bridge the divide between native and continental conceptions of opera, but the adaptation represents a new, more faithful approach to foreign opera that was to dominate subsequent decades.

Chapter 2 explores an even more ambitious foray into imported opera. In 1817–19, Covent Garden directly competed with the King's Theatre with Henry Bishop's adaptations of *Don Giovanni*, *Il barbiere di Siviglia* and *Le nozze di Figaro*. Although these operas were vaunted as 'by' Mozart and Rossini, Bishop significantly altered them, cutting, recomposing or replacing much of the music and making important roles, namely Don Giovanni and Count Almaviva, completely spoken. Many of his changes derived from other versions of the same tales, demonstrating that adapters had to contend with multiple 'originals' besides these operas. His alterations also indicate crucial differences between native and continental operatic taste. Critical reception varied, since assessments of adaptation often hinged on assessments of the original. Rossini was viewed with some suspicion and adapters' changes therefore did not seem particularly problematic. Mozart, in contrast, was considered less malleable, although some critics were willing to excuse changes as necessary stepping stones to improved taste.

In the early 1820s, operatic adaptation waned and it appeared that perhaps it had been a passing fad. This changed in 1824 with the stunning success of *Der Freischütz*, which was adapted by eight different London theatres in four months. As Chapter 3 discusses, the triumph of Weber's opera marked several important turning points. It exploded already tenuous divisions between major and minor theatres, as both types of theatre mounted their own versions. Tellingly, the King's Theatre did not join them. The rise of German Romantic opera, as well as grand opera a few years later, helped weaken the King's Theatre's hegemony of Italianate opera and opened an avenue to operatic success for the more flexible playhouses. The multiple versions of *Der Freischütz* also helped close gaps between continental and native taste. Adapters felt emboldened to include more of its 'scientific' score than most thought the British audience would accept, and many critics hailed the work as a significant step forward in musical taste. Finally, the opera's success led to an unusual playhouse commission for a foreign composer, for *Oberon* in 1826. This set a precedent for foreign composers to become more involved in London performances of both adapted and original works.

After *Der Freischütz*, operatic adaptation changed from occasional novelty to repertoire staple. Chapters 4, 5 and 6 explore the uneven trajectory adaptations travelled in the following decade. Chronological order is loosened in favour of groupings by composer and nationality, which often impacted adaptations' reception. Chapter 4 traces attempts to find a German successor to Weber, with adaptations of Marschner, Ries and Spohr. Contemporaries struggled with these operas' quintessentially 'German' traits. At times this learned music, performed increasingly faithfully, appeared to fulfil predictions of an improved post-*Freischütz* musical landscape. At others, reviewers rejected the German style as un-dramatic and inimical to native taste. Regardless, fidelity was now firmly entrenched. An attempt to return to pastiche practice in an adaptation of Spohr's *Der Alchymist* – with selections from five other Spohr operas – backfired, effectively ending freer approaches of the past.

Chapter 5 discusses how these newly shrinking boundaries for change impacted adaptations of Mozart and Rossini operas in the late 1820s and 1830s. Adaptations of *Die Entführung aus dem Serail*, *Così fan tutte*, *La gazza ladra* and *Guillaume Tell* offer an informative contrast to the Mozart and Rossini adaptations of only a decade earlier. Adapters now retained the bulk of the challenging scores, even when it lessened their income. Changes were still accepted, but only in circumscribed areas, primarily the libretto and lengthy ensembles. The idea of fidelity to a composer's oeuvre rather than a specific work also emerged as an acceptable middle ground between change and preservation. Debates about Mozart and Rossini continued, but now with less clear-cut oppositions; critics struggled to assess Mozart's more obscure, less popular operas, while Rossini surprised critics with what seemed a new, more learned style in *Guillaume Tell*.

Although few critics assessed *Guillaume Tell* as a grand opera, other examples of the genre garnered intense interest. As explored in Chapter 6, adaptations of the latest Parisian hits, Auber's *La muette de Portici* and Meyerbeer's *Robert le diable*, signalled a new landscape for both theatrical competition and copyright. Theatrical boundaries all but disappeared as all types of theatre – major, minor and opera house – vied for the London premières, on a far more equal footing than previously. The battle for *Robert* became especially acrimonious as Meyerbeer attempted to confine production of his opera to the King's Theatre, guarded his performance materials from the other theatres and publicly protested when they mounted productions freshly orchestrated from the available piano–vocal scores. Copyright, while not yet legally binding across national borders, became the subject of intense debate. Critics confronted particularly thorny issues of fidelity, including how much control composers should have over their own works, how integral orchestration was to a work's identity and how valuable fidelity was, since the most faithful version of *Robert* was not the most successful. Overall, critics struggled with whether grand opera, dedicated to the sensational, scenic and musical, was truly beneficial for the native stage. Desires for fidelity collided uncomfortably with its practical manifestations.

Chapter 7 provides a snapshot of adaptation in 1833. In this year appeared a scrupulously faithful 're-adaptation' of *Don Giovanni*, an adaptation of Bellini's *La sonnambula* featuring foreign star Maria Malibran and perhaps the most successful adaptation of the period, of Auber's *Gustave III*. These adaptations demonstrate the new landscape of operatic adaptation. Opera house and playhouse had become so close in repertoire and in fidelity that the playhouses could produce an adaptation of *Don Giovanni* considered more faithful than the King's Theatre and import one of the biggest foreign stars – Malibran – to sing in a relatively unchanged version of *La sonnambula*. *Gustave III*, meanwhile, underwent more change with less protest. This showed that change was still accepted to works less known or less valued. Criticism was also typically swept aside in favour of success, as the spectacular ball scene helped fuel an astounding initial run of over one hundred performances. While ambiguity thus still surrounded operatic adaptation, on the whole adaptations were no longer the peripheral, heavily altered products of the late 1810s, but often remarkably faithful performances of foreign operas that had moved to the core of the playhouse repertoire.

Adaptation lay at the heart of seismic changes in early nineteenth-century London. Adapted foreign operas accelerated the breakdown of repertoire boundaries among major theatre, minor theatre and opera house. Adaptations activated deep-seated concerns about the abandonment of legitimate, national drama in favour of the foreign and the musical. They appeared at once to drag the patent theatres down to the lower social level of the minor theatres and to ape the frivolous upper classes at the opera house. Adaptations also seemed to undermine burgeoning ideals of canonisation as they subverted developing copyright laws and placed value on performer over author and immediate context over transcendent work. At the same time, however, adaptations seemed a laudable indicator of improving musical taste. As celebrated foreign operas appeared in increasingly faithful form, long-maligned divides between continental and native opera began to dissolve. Ironically, the same adaptations that seemed to accelerate decline also seemed to signal hope for an improved future, one in which an attentive audience accepted challenging operas in virtually whole form. These adaptations have slipped from history primarily because of their challenge to the canonical norm, yet they were perhaps one of the most important conduits through which that norm was achieved. Adaptation was a fluid process, one in which original and new context collided, with significant implications for both.

1 | A tale of two Boieldieus

Foreign opera was not new to the London playhouses in the early nineteenth century, but the way in which it was presented was. In the eighteenth century, foreign opera appeared as part of a pervasive culture of pastiche. For instance, when Charles Dibdin reworked Monsigny's *Le déserteur* for Drury Lane in 1773, he cut half the original score, supplied several numbers himself, borrowed two pieces from Philidor and rewrote many of the pieces he retained.[1] Native operas had a remarkably similar shape. One of the most dominant theatre composers of the late eighteenth century, Stephen Storace, regularly borrowed approximately half of his scores from pre-existent sources. *The haunted tower* contains original compositions alongside material from his own opera, *Gli equivoci*, pieces by six other composers and the popular tune 'The roast beef of old England'.[2] Pastiche thus permeated both imported and native operas, and fidelity to one original was rarely a focus.

In the early nineteenth century, this culture shifted. As Curtis Price observes, pastiche 'was on a collision course with the growing recognition in Great Britain of originality in music, or rather the protection of music as intellectual property, manifest in the emerging concept of music copyright'.[3] Drama gradually moved away from a fluid, ever-changing performance 'owned' as much by performers and adapters as authors. Jean Marsden perceives that expanding print culture 'made drama a product of the page as well as the stage'.[4] Theatrical culture began to focus on a specific work, fixed in one form in print, belonging exclusively to the author and increasingly protected by copyright law.[5] This process was hardly immediate, however, and adaptation played an important intermediary role. Adaptation melded freedom and respect, bringing 'the' work to audiences, yet with the alterations necessary to suit it to playhouse standards.

Nowhere can the clash of old and new approaches to foreign opera be seen better than in November 1814, when Drury Lane and Covent Garden presented two separate productions of Boieldieu's *Jean de Paris*. At Drury Lane, Samuel James Arnold and Charles Edward Horn continued patterns of pastiche. Horn discarded Boieldieu's score entirely in favour of a few of his own selections and Arnold significantly rewrote Saint-Just's libretto to highlight his star performers. At Covent Garden, Henry Bishop and Isaac Pocock followed a new direction. Although they still introduced plentiful changes, they remained much closer to the original. These two 'Boieldieus' demonstrate the legal, financial and theatrical contexts that prompted adapters' work and the difficulties adapters faced when suiting foreign operas to their performers and listeners. Their vastly different solutions juxtapose old and new, as pastiche began to wane in favour of adaptation.

OPÉRA COMIQUE AND THE BRITISH STAGE

Jean de Paris did not appear in isolation, but arose in a context that Michael Burden describes as engrossed in 'adaptation, re-interpretation and competition'.[6] The rival adaptations of *Jean de Paris* were not as much about Boieldieu's opera as they were about a continual, acrimonious battle over French imports. At the end of September 1814, Drury Lane manager Arnold had planned an adaptation of Pixérécourt's melodrama *Le chien de Montargis*, but Covent Garden managers Henry Harris and John Philip Kemble scooped him and produced their version first. Additional competition arose from a minor theatre, the Royal Circus (later known as the Surrey). There, Thomas Dibdin brought out his own version of *Le chien de Montargis* a week after Covent Garden, amidst a bill that featured 'evolutions' and 'equilibriums' on a tight rope and a 'stud of horses'.[7] Stung by Covent Garden's win in the race for *Le chien de Montargis*, two months later Arnold deliberately undermined Covent Garden's planned production of *Jean de Paris*, producing his version eleven days before theirs. Clearly, as the *Morning Post* noted, this was meant as retaliation; Covent Garden had 'stole a march' on Drury Lane with *Le chien de Montargis* and the 'compliment has been very happily returned'. (See Appendix 2 for review citations).

Such intense competition sprang from a liminal moment between pastiche and fidelity. Mining foreign pieces had always been financially attractive for theatres without government subsidy. As interest in a fixed original and a revered author grew, utilising isolated numbers from foreign works gave way to a desire to import popular foreign pieces relatively whole. While specific works therefore acquired increased value, copyright law did not yet accord them increased protection.[8] No law required theatre managers to obtain permission from a foreign author to import their work, nor even to pay for anything other than a score and libretto, which were often widely available in print. No law prohibited multiple theatres from performing the same work, again with no additional payment to the original author. Managers could therefore profit from interest in originality with minimal cost. Of course, many authors litigated against this state of affairs, and convention and public opinion sometimes mattered more than law, but many managers took advantage of legal loopholes and laxities. Conversely, the presence of copyright law for printed publications within Britain meant that each theatre wished to produce its own distinct version to publish for profit. Paradoxically, the rise of canonicity thus encouraged the spread of adaptation.

Both foreign authors and native adapters suffered as a result. British playwrights and composers, paid similarly for adapted or original pieces and often working under time constraints, had to put aside Romantic ideals of original genius. Horn blamed such a state of affairs for crushing Bishop's initial promise: he 'showed an original talent and style for composition . . . But . . . he had to compose, select and adapt for whatever was put before him, and that, at times, with such rapid succession that he was obliged to select from the French, Italian and German composers without ceremony . . . The managers of theatres generally thinking a composer was like a carpenter or scene painter.'[9] Original authors did not fare much better. Frenchwoman Flora Tristan decried this system after a visit to London in the 1830s: 'Since international law in Europe protects only material property, products of the mind go undefended; extradition is demanded for the thief who has stolen a pair of scissors, but he who has plundered the thought of others carries his head high . . . whereas the real author frequently dies of hunger in a garret.'[10]

As Tristan protested, France proved the most fertile ground for these originals, given its geographical proximity and thriving theatrical and musical life. London managers sent agents to Paris or maintained them there to adapt the latest works and some free agents settled there, hoping to sell new adaptations to London managers.[11] Bishop travelled across the channel in the summer of 1814 and obtained both *Le chien de Montargis* and *Jean de Paris* for Covent Garden.[12] His diary indicates that he attended several performances, including *Le chien de Montargis*, met Boieldieu and other composers and purchased various unidentified scores, *Jean de Paris* presumably among them. This system resulted in a deluge of French works in London. Allardyce Nicoll calculates that 'Fully one-half of the plays written between 1800 and 1850 must have been suggested by Parisian models, and many were literally adapted by English authors.'[13]

These practices helped collapse repertoire divisions. *Le chien de Montargis* was a perfect example. Pixérécourt's piece, in which a dog and mute boy help solve a murder, was properly an 'illegitimate' piece that should only have appeared at the minor theatres, but instead it proved popular at both major and minor theatres. Such slippage between legitimate and illegitimate ignited the prevalent rhetoric of the decline of native drama. *The Times*, clearly referring to the Pixérécourt adaptation, complained that 'Dogs and horses are doubtless fine animals, yet simple staring is the least permanent of human delights; and the unhappy exile of every thing stimulative of *human* excellence had left . . . but slight difference between Covent-garden and Sadler's Wells.'[14]

Despite such rhetoric, major theatre managers found foreign imports too appealing to relinquish. Opéra comique proved an especially desirable import for the major theatres because their competitors were either uninterested in or unable to compete for the genre. London's one opera house, the King's Theatre, certainly felt the allure of France, but their interest focused on the French ballets performed alongside the main opera, which was almost exclusively Italian, serious and all-sung.[15] Opéra comique, with its amusing plots and spoken dialogue, did not seem worth the trouble to translate. Meanwhile, minor theatres may have been confined to illegitimate (and hence musical) fare, but most of them did not possess sufficient musical resources to mount full-scale operas. They competed with the major theatres for French melo-dramas such as *Le chien de Montargis*, but not yet for opera; no competing version of *Jean de Paris* appeared at the minor theatres. Opéra comique therefore occupied a kind of limbo in London theatrical life: too elevated for the minor theatres, not elevated enough for the opera house. Its spoken dialogue, amusing plots and accessible musical style fit well with major theatre repertoire, however, and managers imported a steady stream. The appearance of competing versions of *Jean de Paris* was therefore charac-teristic of a theatrical culture heavily dependent on adaptation as a whole, and on adaptation of opéra comique in particular.

TRADITION: *JEAN DE PARIS* AT DRURY LANE

This particular competition was different, however, because it pitted older and newer approaches to foreign opera against each other. At Drury Lane, Arnold and Horn followed the older, freer path. Arnold retained only the core plot of Saint-Just's libretto. The Princess of Navarre travels to the castle of her brother, the king, to choose a husband. The son and heir of Philippe de Valois of France is interested, but wishes to ascertain her character. He disguises himself as humble 'Jean de Paris' and contrives to meet her at a country inn along the way. The princess is alerted to his disguise and decides to play along, teasing him by saying she has already made her choice. In the meantime, these events throw both the avaricious innkeeper and the princess's gluttonous seneschal into a comic tizzy. In the end, Jean reveals his identity, the princess accepts his proposal, and all ends joyously.[16] Arnold kept this basic framework, but altered it to suit his star performers. Meanwhile, Horn discarded Boieldieu's score in favour of a few of his own musical pieces. Arnold and Horn did not adapt *Jean de Paris* as much as create a new piece based on the same theme, one that could both thwart Covent Garden's production and suit the performer-centric nature of the London stage.

The *Monthly Theatrical Reporter* suggested that Arnold and Hawes had cut Boiel-dieu's score for practical rather than musical reasons: 'the desire to *forestall* Covent-Garden ... induced the Manager to divest it of its operatical dress, as the time would not admit of the necessary preparations, and drilling'. Without Boieldieu's music, Arnold could bypass any need to acquire the score or to spend time rehearsing it. The small amount of music Horn added could have been composed and prepared quickly. Adaptation was not simply about an isolated original work and how it might best be brought to the native stage. Rather, it was sometimes a crafty tool to evade the need to acquire performance materials and to win the race for the earliest première.

Perhaps because of time constraints, the music Horn added is minimal and entirely instrumental. The only music that reached print was a 'grand pastoral ballet'.[17] The libretto, however, contains several additional instrumental cues: 'trumpets' play as the princess enters; a 'flourish' accompanies Jean's exit; 'music' plays as the princess prepares to enjoy the banquet; and 'a lofty flourish' accompanies the final tableau.[18] Similar indications pepper playhouse libretti and denote brief snatches of instrumental music that accompanied stage action. While such music could play a significant dramatic role, particularly in melodrama, Horn's music for *Jean de Paris* probably formed an unobtrusive aural backdrop, underlining the protagonists' royal status and complementing the visual display of the banquet scene.

At Drury Lane, *Jean de Paris* thus became a play with music rather than an opera. Consequently, Arnold expanded the dramatic portion to fill the time freed by cutting the music and to highlight his cast. He enlarged the role of the innkeeper, whom he changed into the popular stage Irishman, played by a specialist in the role, John Johnstone.[19] As Arnold hoped, Johnstone made such a hit in the character that the *Monthly Theatrical Reporter* stated, 'The success of this dramatic trifle is principally attributable to the rich, inimitable humour and archness of Mr. JOHNSTONE, in the character of the Irish landlord . . . In parts of this description he has not his equal on the stage.' Arnold also added a sub-plot that mirrored the main storyline and highlighted another star performer, Fanny Kelly, in the role of Olivier. In the original, Olivier is Jean's male servant, but Arnold transformed the character into a woman in male disguise. Olivier is now the seneschal's daughter, who has adopted male attire to follow her beloved Theodore (another of Jean's servants) in defiance of her father's disapproval. In the end, she, like Jean, reveals her disguise and her father accepts the match. Interestingly, this entire sub-plot did not exist when the play was submitted to the Lord Chamberlain for censorship on 22 October, a little over a week before the première. Reviews of the first night mention it, though, so it must have been added at the last minute.

This new trouser role not only highlighted Kelly in a character type for which she was famous, but stirred up all the titillation and controversy that made such roles so popular. As recent scholarship has suggested, the ambivalence that greeted trouser roles pointed to broader concerns. Women playing men raised uncomfortable possibilities: of women abandoning the domestic sphere to invade public, masculine space; of the proposition that masculinity was not inherent, but an outward construct that could be assumed or removed at will; and of a disconcerting distortion of gendered desire, as women wooed each other, albeit dressed as members of the opposite sex, and as male audience members turned an eroticised gaze to other men, albeit men played by women.[20] Such roles also strengthened already pervasive stereotypes of actresses as sexually suspect; their display of their talents to any ticket purchaser seemed a short step from the actual prostitutes who frequented the theatres.[21]

These issues, at once disturbing and appealing, made the cross-dressed Olivier a focal point of Arnold's *Jean de Paris*. Some found Kelly's calculated sexual display too aggressive, a deliberate manipulation of the male gaze that upended clear gender divisions. *The Times* cautioned

> Miss KELLY is certainly a clever girl, and of course can scarcely be blamed for taking the shortest way to her object ... Her dress was *par excellence* masculine. It might, however, be suggested ... that if this exhibition of form and feature had betrayed a little more of feminine prejudice, it might have been forgiven. Modesty is a weakness of an order not severely visited on a young female. Miss KELLY's dress was even more masculine than that of the men; her display left nothing for the imagination; and ... we suggest a more cautious application for the time to come to the admiration of her audience.

The reviewer wished Kelly would remain more firmly in the feminine sphere, unable to adopt male dress convincingly. Kelly apparently further derailed convention by not submitting to male desires offstage. The *Monthly Theatrical Reporter* hinted as much, writing 'certain hypercritics ... affect to take alarm at some alleged contempt of moral fitness ... but what there is so peculiarly indelicate, in the dress of Miss KELLY, as Olivier, ... surpasses our limited powers of apprehension. Miss KELLY, from what little we have seen of her – (and *our* knowledge of performers extends *solely to their professional* character) is a very pleasing interesting actress.'

Arnold sought a middle ground for the role, flirting with its ambiguities but in the end firmly denying them. Lorezza, the innkeeper's daughter, develops a crush on Olivier, thinking him a man. When she sighs of love a bit too ardently, Olivier protests 'I never was in love with any woman in my life: – nay, what's more, I never shall be; and what's more still, I never *can* be! It's quite out of the question, and not at all in my way.'[22] Reviewers were quick to second this protest, although in the process, like Arnold, they also called attention to it. The *Monthly Theatrical Reporter* noted, 'The circumstance of *Olivier's* male disguise occasions some *equivoque*, and makes an impression (which however the discovery of her real sex soon does way) upon the soft heart of the landlord's young daughter.' Despite the criticism she received, Kelly clearly knew how to profit from the naughty appeal of the trouser role, and Arnold how to maximise opportunities for his performers in *Jean de Paris*.

Arnold and Horn's *Jean de Paris* followed eighteenth-century views of opéra comique as malleable material to be moulded freely into the best shape for its new context. Competition played into their decision to discard Boieldieu's score and use music minimally. New and altered material focused on star performers, Johnstone and Kelly, who delighted audiences with their specialty roles. Drury Lane's *Jean de Paris* demonstrates the continued centrality of performance to the London theatrical experience, a centrality that often overrode any sense of a fixed work or the dominance of the author's artistic vision. As Gerard Langbaine observed in 1691, this meant that 'all Foreign Coin must be melted down, and receive a new Stamp, if not addition of Mettal, before it will pass currant in *England*, and be judged *Sterling*'.[23] Arnold and Hawes continued this alchemical tactic.

A NEW PATH: *JEAN DE PARIS* AT COVENT GARDEN

At Covent Garden, Pocock and Bishop presented a new type of adaptation, one that foregrounded the original even while substantially altering it. The publication materials emphasise reliance on the original. In his advertisement to the libretto, Pocock announced, 'Those who wish to know how much I am indebted to the original of this Piece, or how little the original is indebted to me, must peruse the opera of "Jean de Paris", written by Mons. Saint Just.' Both libretto and score highlighted Boieldieu. Pocock noted that 'the Music . . . is composed by Boieldieu, and considered the most successful that has been heard for some time on the French stage'.[24] Similarly, the title page of the score proudly displayed Boieldieu's name, though in slightly smaller font than Bishop's, and carefully noted that the score was 'composed and partly selected' from the French composer's opera (see Figure 1.1).

Yet, Pocock and Bishop still made extensive changes. Bishop cut half of Boieldieu's numbers, considerably slimmed and altered many of the remainder, added a few instrumental pieces and wrote eight new vocal pieces, although four of these were cut before or soon after the first performance.[25] Most of Pocock's changes were conceived in tandem with Bishop's; he split the comic innkeeper into two roles, one spoken and one sung, embellished the spoken half of the role, rearranged several musical numbers and created new dramatic situations for interpolated numbers. Bishop and Pocock's *Jean de Paris* thus offered a blend that typified operatic adaptation in the 1810s and early 1820s: a strong desire to bring the original to London but an equally strong need to change it to suit the new context.

Given the free pastiche approach that permeated London theatre, why would Bishop and Pocock attempt even a modicum of fidelity? While deeper shifts towards a canonical model underlay the decision, competition and homage were the most immediate motivations. Covent Garden could combat Drury Lane's speedier version only by offering some novelty. In this case, Boieldieu's score, and Covent Garden's greater musical resources to perform it, formed their main draw. Although competition was narrowing the gap, Covent Garden still had a reputation for greater visual and aural display than its fellow patent theatre. Where Arnold had decided on a spoken version partly because few of his biggest stars could sing well, Covent Garden boasted two young, capable male singers (John Sinclair and John Duruset) as Jean and Olivier, respectively, the attractive Sarah Matthews as Lorezza and Catherine Stephens as the princess. Stephens had debuted at Covent Garden the previous year and soon became

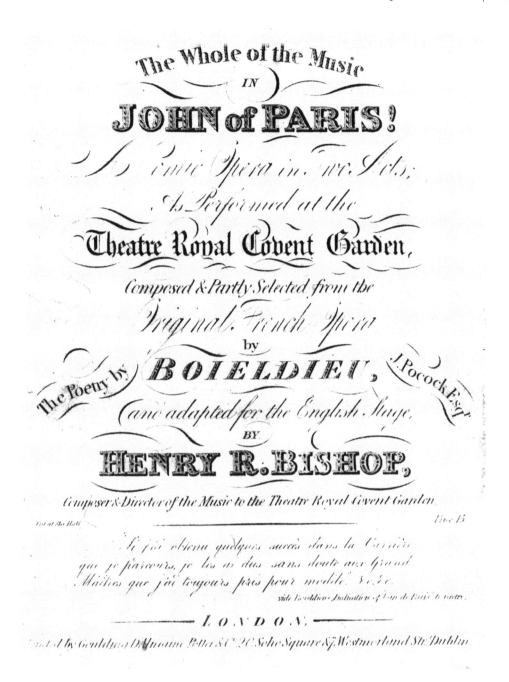

The Whole of the Music
IN
JOHN of PARIS!

A Comic Opera in Two Acts,
As Performed at the

Theatre Royal Covent Garden,

Composed & Partly Selected from the

Original French Opera
by
BOIELDIEU,

The Poetry by   J. Pocock Esqr

(and adapted for the English Stage,
BY
HENRY R. BISHOP,

Composer & Director of the Music to the Theatre Royal Covent Garden.

LONDON.

Figure 1.1 Title page, Bishop, arr., *Jean de Paris*

one of the most celebrated British stage singers. Change was thus not the only tool in theatrical competition; greater fidelity could also attract audiences to a tardy version.

Bishop took advantage of his superior musical resources to fulfil what seems to have been a personal interest in Boieldieu's work. Bishop met Boieldieu in 1814 and on a subsequent trip in 1816, when he dubbed the composer 'the Mozart of France' and praised his 'great knowledge, fire, and genius'.[26] Bishop may have been eager to pay homage to his colleague. The idea of homage may seem odd in an adaptation so altered, but departure and reverence need not be mutually exclusive. William Lockhart has argued that the worth of nineteenth-century keyboard arrangements stemmed from 'the ideal of the original – the notion that arrangements provided direct access to source compositions'.[27] Pocock's description of Bishop's work concurs with this idea. Pocock lauded the 'masterly manner in which ... Bishop, has executed the arduous task of selecting and adapting those parts which were thought most valuable, [which] has been approved by the auditors in a way that leaves me nothing to praise'.[28] Far from lazily stealing Boieldieu's works, Bishop is presented as engaging in a taxing labour of love to acclimate Boieldieu to his new context. Alterations were not arbitrary or capricious; rather, as Mark Everist observes, adapters often acted as a 'mediating agent' in the 'junction' between the work and its new context.[29] Adaptation could be a path to fidelity rather than an obstacle.

If these factors encouraged fidelity, others obliged departure. Bishop and Pocock's work can perhaps best be viewed in the etymological sense of the word adapt, which Daniel Fischlin and Mark Fortier point out is derived from *adaptare*, or 'to make fit'.[30] Bishop and Pocock sought to 'fit' *Jean de Paris* to a context entirely unprepared to accept the opera in its original form and an audience as yet largely uninterested in the origin of its amusements. Librettist James Robinson Planché emphasised the continuing primacy of effective performance: 'If the public are amused, they come – if they are not, they stay away, without caring one farthing whence that which they like or dislike is derived.'[31] As Katherine Preston observes of similar practices in the United States, which often imported these adaptations, 'At this time, "adapting" meant making these operas closer in musical style to English comic operas.'[32] Bishop and Pocock therefore sought to 'fit' Boieldieu within playhouse parameters.

The first issue was simply length. As seen in the playbill for the Covent Garden première of *Jean de Paris*, the work appeared on a typical multiple bill, alongside *A day after the wedding*, a comic interlude about marital strife, and *Timour, the Tartar*, a popular melodrama (see Figure 1.2). British adapters therefore virtually always engaged in what Julie Sanders calls the 'editorial' side of adaptation, 'trimming and pruning'.[33] Even though Boieldieu's opera is not excessively lengthy, Bishop cut the longest numbers, including most of the ensembles, significantly slimmed the pieces he did retain and kept his own interpolations to modest dimensions.

More thoroughgoing changes were required to address the rift between music and drama at the playhouses. As noted in the introduction, long-held suspicions of music as effeminate and frivolous led Britons to believe that their character was essentially opposed to music. The most highly prized form of theatre was 'legitimate' or spoken drama. Music appealed, and a good song could 'electrify the audience, and [be] a great

THEATRE ROYAL, COVENT-GARDEN
This present SATURDAY, Nov. 12, 1814.
Will be presented a New Comick Opera, *in two acts,* called

JOHN of PARIS.

The OVERTURE, SONGS, &c. entirely new.
The rest of the Musick selected from *BOIELDIEU* – the whole composed & adapted by Mr. *BISHOP.*
The new SCENERY painted by Mess. *Phillips* and *Pugh*
The Decorations by Mess. *Saul* and *Bradwell.* The Dresses by Mr *Flower* and Miss *Egan.*

John of Paris by Mr. SINCLAIR,
The Grand Chamberlain, Mr. TAYLOR, Vincent, Mr. DURUSET,
Pedrigo Potts (Landlord of the Inn) by Mr. LISTON,
Gregory, Mr. TREBY, Philip, Mr TINNEY,
Domesticks, Mess. Crumpton, Everard, Lee, Linton, Montague, Watson, &c.
The Retinue of *John of Paris,* Mess. I. Brown, J.Taylor, I Terry, Tett, S.Tett, Williams, &c.
Suit of the Princess, Mess. Baker, Banks, Batt, W. Chapman, Goodwin, Griffiths, Thurston, &c.

The Princess of Navarre by Miss STEPHENS,
Rosa by Miss MATTHEWS,
Attendants on the Princess, Mesdames Carew, Findlay, Norman, West
Peasants, Mesds. Coates, Corri, Grimaldi, Herbert, Hibbert, Iliff, Leaver, Ward, Whitmore, &c.

INCIDENTAL DANCE,
By Monf. SOISSONS, Mrs. PARKER,
Miss BRADWELL. Miss WORGMAN,
Mess. Brown, Goodwin, Grant, Heath, Louis, Piatt, Powers, Sarjant, Yarnold.
Mesdames Bologna, Boyce, Bradwell, Heath, Louis, Ryall, Sexton, Standen, Watts.
Misses Goodwin, P. Goodwin, Hatgood, Herbert, Shotter, F. Shotter, Thurston,
Books of the Songs, &c to be had in the Theatre, price 10d *and of Mr.* MILLER, *Bow-street.*
After which, an Interlude called

A DAY after the WEDDING.

Col. Freelove, Mr. JONES, Lord Rivers by Mr. CLAREMONT,
James, Mr Atkins, John, Mr Louis,
Lady Elizabeth Freelove, Mrs GIBBS, Mrs Davies, Mrs. EMERY.
To which will be added *(with renewed Splendour)* the Melo-Dramatick Romance of

TIMOUR, THE TARTAR

Timour by Mr. FARLEY,
Agib, Master CHAPMAN, Oglou, Mr. FAWCETT,
Abdalac Mr. King, Bermeddin Mr. Treby, Octar Mr. Jefferies, Orasinin Mr. Howell
Kerim, Mr. RICHER, Sanballat, Mr. BLYTHE, Captain of the Escort, Mr. DAVIES
Selima by Miss MATTHEWS, Litka by Mrs. LISTON,
Zorilda by Mrs. H. JOHNSTON,
Tartars,
Mess. Banks, Brown, Edgecombe, Goodwin, Grant, Griffiths, Heath, Jeffkins, Louis
Macdonald, Powers, Sarjant, Sibley, Thurston, Yarnold, &c.——Mesd. Bradwell,
Bologna, Heath, Louis, Ryall, Sexton, Standen, Watts.
Georgians,
Mess. Andrews, Bath, Cooper, Cordell, W. Davies, H. Davies, Fagan, Hall, Harris,
Hodson, Holford, Kelly, Lane, Paul, Smith, Tate, Turpin, Williams, Wright, &c.
Printed by E. Macleish, 2, Bow-street.
Vivant Rex & Regina.

The Publick are respectfully informed that

Miss O'NEILL

performed the character of ISABELLA (for the second time) to an audience, whose
numbers, and whose rapturous expressions of delight, admit not of increase, and
that she will repeat it on every *Friday*—the part of BELVIDERA on every
Wednesday—and JULIET on every *Monday* till further notice.

₊ Mr. KEMBLE's

Nights of performing will be on Tuesday and Thursday next.
₊ *No Orders can be admitted.*

On *Monday,* will be performed SHAKSPEARE's Tragedy of ROMEO and JULIET.
Romeo by Mr. CONWAY, Mercutio by Mr. JONES,
Juliet (8th time) by Miss O'NEILL.
On *Tuesday.* will be revived *Massinger's* Play of A NEW WAY TO PAY OLD DEBTS.
Sir Giles Overreach by Mr. KEMBLE, Wellborn by Mr. CONWAY, Marall, Mr. TERRY
Lady Allworth by Mrs RENAUD, Margaret by Miss S. BOOTH.
On *Wednesday,* OTWAY's Tragedy of VENICE PRESERVED.
Jaffier by Mr. CONWAY, Pierre by Mr. YOUNG,
Belvidera by Miss O'NEILL, *Being her* 9th *appearance in that character.)*
On *Thursday,* the Tragedy of The REVENGE. Zanga by Mr. KEMBLE.
On *Friday,* (3d time) *Southern's* Tragedy of ISABELLA. Biron, Mr. YOUNG.
Isabella by Miss O'NEILL, *(Being her* 3d *appearance in that character.)*

Figure 1.2 Playbill for Covent Garden for 12 November 1814

support to the piece', but the amount and function of music had to be carefully regulated.[34] All-sung opera rarely succeeded. Recitative seemed unfit for the English language, which John Payne Collier felt '[did] not, without great difficulty, wind itself into the sinuosities of music'.[35] The sheer amount of music also taxed listeners. As Edward Sterling quipped, 'Mere opera is too luscious a feast; its very sweetness cloys; but a song in a comedy is like a glass of champagne during dinner – it is a *bon bouche* in itself, and it wets the appetite for the luxuries that are to follow'.[36] The one exception, Arne's all-sung *Artaxerxes*, ran throughout the period, but for much of it in an adaptation with spoken dialogue.[37] Most native operas contained a mixture of song and speech and many featured important roles that were completely spoken.[38]

When music did appear, it typically paused rather than forwarded the action. Comprehension was partially at issue. The word books sold in the theatre, which contained only the text of the musical numbers, underline the importance of the text and imply that the music might obscure it otherwise. On a deeper level, music represented the foreign 'other' too strongly – and the upper classes who preferred it – to supersede the rational speech that the 'middling classes' found more congruent with their character. Richard Mackenzie Bacon, even as he advocated musical knowledge, still expressed the typical view that while 'The Italians depend almost wholly on the effect of the music, we blend the other . . . attractions of intricate plot, dialogue, scenery, and show with the music. In a word, we are not yet nationally speaking musical enough to melt down our other senses and faculties into the one reigning delight of combined melody and harmony.'[39] Planché blatantly linked music to the foreign and the elite: 'a dramatic situation in music was "caviare to the general", and inevitably received with cries of "cut it short!" from the gallery, and obstinate coughing or other significant signs of impatience from the pit'.[40]

The principle of separate spheres for plot and score permeated Bishop and Pocock's changes. This is most evident in their split of the role of the innkeeper into two characters, one sung and one spoken. At both Covent Garden and Drury Lane, adapters immediately identified the innkeeper as the most important comic character in the piece and both employed their best comedian in the role. Johnstone at Drury Lane was pitted against one of the leading comic actors of the day, John Liston at Covent Garden. Pocock added extra scenes and comic dialogue for Liston, who amused the audience so much that the *Monthly Theatrical Reporter* quipped '*Heraclitus* himself, were he to resuscitate, and witness Liston's performance, in this character, might find it no easy matter to preserve his serious look.' But, although Liston apparently had 'a good ear for music', 'he had no voice'.[41] This may not seem a problem, since Boieldieu's innkeeper had no solos and only a few ensembles. Yet, Liston was better able to charm his way through a solo than to do the harder musical work of blending in an ensemble. A new character, musical waiter Philip, therefore opportunely pops in for the ensembles but does not speak. Drastic as this alteration is, it is worth noting that Bishop still retained the innkeeper's music, even at the expense of dramatic congruity. It was not simple disinterest in Boieldieu's music that led to the split sung and spoken roles, but the clash between preserving the score and suiting the conventions and performers of the playhouses.

The rift between song and action also informed Bishop's approach to Boieldieu's longer ensembles. Bishop began ambitiously, retaining the opening introduction and the following trio. Here, however, the divide between French and British taste was not great. These ensembles are relatively short, they contain little action and the ensuing spoken dialogue repeats the plot information for any who did not catch it musically. Bishop more drastically altered Boieldieu's most complex ensemble, the act one finale. The French original follows a fairly standard alternation of what opera scholars have termed 'kinetic' or action-based sections and 'static' or contemplative ones.[42] The loosely structured opening sections (Allegro vivace and Allegretto) fluidly respond to the action, as Jean and the seneschal argue over who will book the inn and Olivier announces the princess's arrival. A slower, more lyrical section ensues (Maestoso), in which the princess appears and sings a solo with ensemble about her journey. Another kinetic section follows (Recitative – Allegro spiritoso) as the princess, much to the seneschal's dismay, accepts Jean's invitation to dinner. The act concludes with a musically exciting but dramatically static conclusion (Più Allegro), as everyone expresses dismay or delight at the situation. As was typical, almost the entire final section repeats. Bishop and Pocock worked to separate music and drama. Pocock added spoken dialogue later in the piece that repeated the essential plot information. Bishop kept all sections, but cut most heavily in the kinetic ones, discarding some-where between 70 and 90 per cent of them. The more lyrical set pieces, on the other hand, he only diminished by about 50 per cent. The whole became slimmer and more focused on static centrepieces in the midst of brief action.

Boieldieu's solos proved equally troublesome. In London, solos highlighted celebrated singers onstage and expanded the show's earning power offstage through sheet music sales. Boieldieu's *Jean de Paris* offers only three solos that are not part of larger ensembles. These primarily take place within the action, sung while other characters are present and often interrupted by interjections from these characters. Bishop cut all of Boieldieu's solos and added six new ones, one each for Olivier, the seneschal, the princess and Lorezza and two for Jean; Lorezza's and one of Jean's were, however, cut before or soon after the première. Pocock reworked the libretto to ensure that the majority of these solos took place when the character was alone onstage and featured generalised lyrics, not particular to the plot. This encouraged encores, which contemporaries viewed as clear indicators of a show's success, and encouraged the transition from stage to concert hall and parlour.

Bishop's new solos conformed to the three types most prized on the British playhouse stage: the comic song, the bravura and the ballad. Boieldieu's one comic solo is sung by the seneschal, a rather bumbling official more intent on food and pride than duty. In the French opera, he sings an entrance aria in which he commands that all follow his orders and that dinner be served. Boieldieu paints the character with fussy turns, pompous dotted rhythms and ostentatious leaps. The aria meanders through a free form that includes brief interjections from Pedrigo and Lorezza (Ex. 1.1a). Bishop's new aria for the seneschal, in contrast, takes place in act two, after the seneschal has spoken to the princess and heard that she will accept Jean's dinner invitation despite his protests. Alone onstage, he sings an Allegro patter song as he bursts with anger (Ex. 1.1b). No other characters interject and the aria follows a straightforward rondo

Example 1.1a 'Qu'a mes ordres ici tout le monde', Boieldieu, *Jean de Paris*, mm. 41–59

Example 1.1a (cont.)

form. While the vocal range is as large as in the original aria, Bishop's repetitive, stepwise lines are easier to sing, the seneschal does not have to sustain lengthy high notes and the challenge lies primarily in spitting out the words quickly enough. As Bishop hoped, the performer, a Mr Taylor, sold the song to an appreciative crowd. The *Monthly Theatrical Reporter* related that it 'drew down thunders of applause, and notwithstanding its fatiguing difficulty, was tumultuously *encored*'.

Example 1.1b 'My anger, my anger will choke me', Bishop, arr., *Jean de Paris*, mm. 29–40

Both Boieldieu and Bishop assigned some of their most challenging music to the prima donna. Boieldieu included a substantial, taxing solo section for the princess in the act one finale, the majority of which Bishop retained. Bishop still felt the leading lady needed more music, however, as well as a more easily extractable solo. He therefore added one in the traditional placement for a prima donna's aria, the opening of act two. Alone, the princess sings passionately about how time cannot erase the childhood affection she feels for Jean. Bishop's new aria begins with a brief recitative, replete with dramatic dotted rhythms and several 'ad lib' opportunities. The body of the piece is in ABA form. The A section begins modestly, with bouncy rhythms and a relatively simple melody. Towards the end it intensifies, as the princess climbs ever higher, peaking on a c''' and then erupting in a cadential torrent of demisemiquavers. The B section follows the pattern of simplicity moving to complexity; three times the princess begins a simple phrase that gives way to a relentlessly long, melismatic closing passage, with the latter increasingly difficult each time. Bishop provides an alternate, lower line for amateur performers at home (Ex. 1.2). The difficult line sung in the theatre is included, however, such that sheet music purchasers could marvel at and perhaps try to recreate the abilities of the new star soprano, Stephens. The aria concludes with a repeat of A that doubtless contained one of the most expected types of 'adaptation' in opera: added embellishment.

Although Stephens was well equipped to navigate Bishop's treacherous coloratura, she excelled more at the most beloved solo type on the playhouse stage: the ballad. Bacon commented on both Stephens' proclivity for the genre and its inherently national character: 'we infer the peculiar bent of her talent towards ballads and songs of simple declamation – in a word, towards that particular style which is generally esteemed to be purely English'.[43] Indeed, the ballad lay at the core of early nineteenth-century British opera. A simple strophic song that emphasised limpid, poignant melody, the ballad figured prominently in virtually every musical stage production of the time.[44] The most celebrated ones inundated the sheet music market and each principal singer generally demanded one. Henry Phillips, for instance, insisted on one in *The mountain sylph* in 1834 because 'the ballad had . . . become a necessary appendage to all my representations, and a ballad I must have'.[45]

Bishop catered to the popularity of ballads with four new ones, one for Olivier, one for Lorezza and two for Jean, although Lorezza's and one of Jean's appear to have been omitted in performance. Olivier's new ballad, 'The girl that I love', is an archetypal example of the genre (Ex. 1.3a). The text, a general rumination on the power of love, makes little sense for the character, who is not involved in any love story. It is, however, well calculated for easy extraction for the sheet music market. The piece is a concise thirty-two measures, employs a leisurely pace of Larghetto con amore, follows a simple strophic form and remains within a clear, predictable harmonic framework. The vocal line is undemanding, with a moderate range and primarily stepwise motion. It offers a basic template that could be stripped to lyrical simplicity or decorated with further ornaments as the singer's ambition dictated. A greater contrast could hardly exist between this unassuming miniature and Boieldieu's original solo for Olivier. There, in a number almost five times as long as Bishop's, Olivier describes his master's mode of travel to Lorezza and Pedrigo, who make brief interjections. The form is loose and largely non-repetitive and the vocal line focuses on onomatopoeic imitations of the sounds of Jean's travel (Ex. 1.3b).

Example 1.2 'No, never, no!', Bishop, arr., *Jean de Paris*, mm. 69–96

As these examples show, Bishop consistently avoided what was long, complex and immersed in the action in favour of what was brief, accessible and extractable. This helped fulfil a practical need for sheet music sales, which were vital to a show's success and provided composers with a significant source of income. It also points to

Example 1.2 (cont.)

irreconcilable differences between opéra comique and native opera at this time. Despite the similarities of spoken dialogue, light-hearted plots and tuneful music, the two genres still diverged in the amount, placement and function of music. Yet, Bishop clearly desired to present as much of Boieldieu's score as possible. He may have adapted Boieldieu's score heavily, but he did not cut it entirely like Horn or mix multiple authors in a pastiche approach. Instead, he and Pocock sought a new path, one that highlighted the original, not through strict preservation, but through earnest effort to suit it for its new context.

JEAN DE PARIS VS JEAN DE PARIS

Drury Lane and Covent Garden waged an intense battle over *Jean de Paris* and in the process produced two starkly different versions. Who emerged victorious? In both numbers and critical opinion, Drury Lane's less faithful version won. It stretched to some thirty performances throughout the rest of the season, while its rival enjoyed only seventeen, although the opera did become a stock piece at both theatres for the next few years.[46] Reviewers almost unanimously sided with Arnold and Horn's

Example 1.3a 'The girl that I love', Bishop, arr., *Jean de Paris*, mm. 5–18

adaptation, and their reactions demonstrate the ambivalence that surrounded early attempts at fidelity.

The most problematic issue was the most fundamental one: did contemporaries have sufficient access to the original to be able to compare the adaptations to it? As Linda Hutcheon points out, the original must be known, otherwise 'we will not experience the work *as an adaptation*'.[47] Bishop insisted that his contemporaries could easily compare original and adaptation. Defending himself later against a charge by

Example 1.3a (cont.)

Girl that I ____ love, from the Girl that I ____ love, I ____

ne'er ____ can ____ de-part ____ from ____ the Girl that ____ I love!

François-Joseph Fétis that he had taken pieces from Boieldieu without attribution, he wrote, 'knowing that "foreign scores" are as obtainable by others as by myself, [I should not] have been so destitute of common sense as to venture a proceeding that I must be aware was open to immediate detection'.[48] Bishop was in fact guilty of the charge, however, since the published score listed Boieldieu's 'Le troubadour' as 'composed by Henry R. Bishop'. The fact that not a single critic remarked on this false attribution underlines how few actually knew the original. Unless patrons had travelled to France or possessed the musical and linguistic education necessary to peruse printed libretti or scores, they would not have been able to assess changes accurately.

Example 1.3b 'Lorsque mon maitre est en voyage', Boieldieu, *Jean de Paris*, mm. 52–62

Lack of knowledge did not, however, stop comparisons. Reviewing the Covent Garden production for the *Morning Chronicle*, William Hazlitt reasoned that 'in both Theatres we suspect that they have taken freedom with the original. We do not know the French piece, but are sure that the French hotel-keeper would not have talked of soup at the top and fish at the bottom.' *The Times* rather unfairly surmised, 'From not having seen the composition in its primal state, we cannot say whether the Frenchman's labours have been wisely omitted; but Mr BISHOP, a good and somewhat tasteful fabricator of choruses, is unfortunate in songs; and we strongly fear Monsieur BOILDEAU [*sic*] might ... think himself ill treated in the substitution. The music in general is passable and no more.' One of the most crucial facets of adaptation was therefore missing: what Hutcheon describes as the 'constant oscillation between [the adapted work] and the new adaptation'.[49] For many patrons, the 'oscillation' appears to have been between the two British versions, or between these and an imagined picture of the French original. Fidelity had become important enough to comment on, but not important enough to ascertain precisely.

Unfortunately for Bishop and Pocock, few critics yet had much interest in their new, more faithful aesthetic. Some even derided attempts at fidelity. Writing in *The Examiner*, Leigh Hunt scoffed:

> Covent Garden ... has determined to bring out this ... piece with the superior attraction of the original French music. Tremendous menace! as if French music had any peculiar charms; they had better at once bring over one or two French singers, and improve the musical taste of Englishmen, by teaching them to sing through the nose ... the French ... are, in fact, a less musical people than the English.

Hunt's xenophobic rancour is hardly surprising, given the almost constant military tensions between the two countries. Hunt also wrote this tirade while in prison for libelling the Prince Regent and may have rankled at his own confinement while the national stage committed the anti-patriotic sin of continual French importation.[50]

Though few critics echoed Hunt's sentiments quite so strongly, a thread of distaste at the betrayal of the national stage to lightweight foreign pieces runs throughout reviews. Most did not voice direct protests, but referred to *Jean de Paris* with ingrained modes of describing – and dismissing – the French. In reviews of the Covent Garden adaptation, Hazlitt dubbed the work a 'dramatic trifle', the *New Universal Magazine* a 'bagatelle'. Others more explicitly tied the adaptations to dramatic decline. The *New Monthly Magazine* remarked that if Drury Lane's version showed 'the public taste, we shall be under the necessity of wishing that our theatres were completely closed, and their companies disbanded to follow a better occupation'. Similarly, the *Theatrical Inquisitor* launched into a long diatribe about Covent Garden's degraded state: the managers 'vitiated the popular taste, and degraded the national character by a succession of wretched buffooneries that ought only be tolerated in a barn ... If such repeated insults to the public understanding are to be met by tame acquiescence, the cause of the Drama is lost.'

The reception of the two versions of *Jean de Paris* demonstrates both how far London theatrical culture was from embracing the canonical ideal in 1814 and how many pitfalls lay in store for fidelity. Few reviewers possessed access to the original and most assessed the productions *as* productions, not as adaptations.

Drury Lane's version, with Johnstone as the quintessential comic Irishman and Kelly in her controversial, alluring trouser role, overrode any greater fidelity at the rival house. Finally, fidelity to a foreign – especially a French – work, and to a musical one, did not seem desirable for theatres that were supposed to promote national, legitimate drama.

Both music and French works appealed too much, however, for managers to abandon them. If the experiment of a more faithful *Jean de Paris* did not prove overwhelmingly successful, Hazlitt suggested it was worth pursuing:

> More pains and cost have been bestowed on this piece than it will be thought by many to be worth; but it affords us another specimen of that species of acting music which is common to the Italian and French stage, and in which we are as yet deficient. There are those who think that it is not possible to describe the action of a plot, in sing-song . . . It must be owned, however, that there are great beauties in compositions of this kind . . . We should be glad to see the best of the French dramas of this kind produced on our stage, as pleasing variety to our dramatic entertainments.

Here, we see the beginning of what was to become a common rhetoric surrounding adaptation. Although some decried foreign opera as not 'worth the pains and cost', others saw British taste as 'deficient', particularly in the 'acting music' that prevailed in continental opera. Adaptation could provide a kind of 'halfway house' on the road to greater musical refinement and hence fidelity. The contest between the two Boieldieus in 1814 was won by the older style of adaptation, which in fact had no Boieldieu at all. It was Bishop and Pocock's new approach, however, that would predominate in succeeding decades.

2 | The pippin and the pineapple: Rossini and Mozart

In 1817, Covent Garden managers Thomas and Henry Harris made an audacious move: they performed *Don Giovanni*, adapted by Henry Bishop and Isaac Pocock. This directly competed with the King's Theatre, where William Ayrton had produced the London première only a month previously.[1] Never before had the playhouses so clearly encroached on the King's Theatre's repertoire. The experiment succeeded and the adapted *Don Giovanni* became a stock piece for the next decade. Emboldened, Bishop and the Harrises brought out two further operatic adaptations in direct competition with the King's Theatre: *Il barbiere di Siviglia* in 1818 and *Le nozze di Figaro* in 1819. Covent Garden's *Il barbiere* came out only one season after the King's Theatre London première. Although their *Figaro* lagged some seven years behind the King's Theatre, they did challenge the opera house's 1819 revival. Opening on 6 March 1819, the Covent Garden *Figaro* preceded the King's Theatre revival by three days and then was played intentionally on Tuesday and Saturday nights – the only nights the King's Theatre performed – such that the two *Figaro*s competed directly. Operatic adaptation had entered a new phase. No longer on the periphery of operatic life, with pastiches or light opéras comiques, the playhouses ventured into its centre: the major Italian-language works performed at the King's Theatre.

Looking back in 1851, George Hogarth summarised both the importance and the ambivalent reception of this novel move:

> These pieces were so mutilated, and so full of interpolations to suit what was then considered the taste of an English audience, that they gave but a faint notion of the originals. But the public was captivated by the graceful and beautiful strains of the great foreign masters, and by the charming manner in which they were sung by Miss Stephens. By introducing these pieces ... Bishop created a demand for foreign dramatic music, and gave rise to the practice which has prevailed ever since, of supplying the English stage, to a considerable extent, with the musical productions of Italy, Germany, and France.[2]

Hogarth touches on two important facets of this new phase of adaptation. First, while Bishop clearly wished to bring as much of the originals to his audience as possible, he did drastically alter them to accord with what his audiences already knew of the opera's models, whether the Beaumarchais plays or the Don Juan legend, and to bring continental opera scores more in line with playhouse abilities and tastes.

Second, Hogarth expresses an ambivalent attitude that would become increasingly common. He begins by terming these adaptations 'mutilations', but then concedes that the audience enjoyed the 'graceful and beautiful strains' of the 'masters' and that Bishop 'created a demand for foreign dramatic music'. On one hand, altering operas that were more prominent and more linked to the King's Theatre than the typical *opéras comiques* aroused critical backlash. These adaptations provoked the vigorously anti-adaptation criticism that was to prompt more faithful renditions in the future. On the other hand, many critics recognised that opposition to alterations was not clear cut. Critical assessments ultimately hinged not only on fidelity, but on adapters' intent, the effectiveness of their adaptations and the perceived quality of the original. This was especially true when the composers adapted were as different as Mozart and Rossini. Ayrton wittily encapsulated the contemporary viewpoint: 'As to a competition between Rossini and Mozart, was there ever a competition between a pippin and a pine-apple?'[3] Changes to a revered figure such as Mozart met with a significantly different critical reaction than those to the newly popular Rossini. Bishop's ambitious foray into the King's Theatre's repertoire thus set the tone of much adaptation to follow. His changes were necessary to reconcile a vast divide between continental and native norms. Meanwhile, critics struggled with their own reconciliation, between the ideal of fidelity and its messier practical application.

MELODRAMATIC MOZART: *DON GIOVANNI*

Writing for the *British Stage*, Thomas Kenrick claimed that 'The wonderful success of "Il Don Giovanni" at the Opera House, has induced the Covent Garden Managers to bring forward nearly a fac-simile of it.' (See Appendix 2 for review citations.) Kenrick stressed the fidelity of the adaptation in order to protest the 'piratical mode of conduct' of detracting from the King's Theatre production. The adaptation was, however, hardly a 'fac-simile' of *Don Giovanni*. Bishop, working with Pocock, his *Jean de Paris* librettist, made both Don Giovanni and Donna Elvira completely spoken roles, cut over half of Mozart's numbers, reassigned several others, curtailed the finales and added two pieces from *Die Zauberflöte*.[4] Yet, Bishop interpolated only one piece of his own, an instrumental Bolero. As with *Jean de Paris*, he clearly wished to bring Mozart's opera to his audience, but had to make significant changes to do so. The result was a *Don Giovanni* that moved away from opera towards the popular genre of melodrama. The dramatic weight shifted to the spoken title role, which underlined ingrained links among speech, power and masculinity on the London stage. The music served two essential melodramatic functions: ornamental vocal pieces and dramatically important instrumental accompaniment. Finally, Pocock nudged the morally troublesome plot towards melodrama's comforting opposition between good and evil.

Perhaps the most striking change for modern listeners is the spoken Don Giovanni. Yet, this was not a unique choice. Karen Ahlquist has documented that the leading male spoken role featured in virtually all operas at the playhouses in the first quarter of the nineteenth century.[5] Why would the title character of an opera not sing? On the surface, this simply seemed a question of casting. The *Mirror of the Stage* wrote 'to the long list of female singers ... every hour is adding fresh candidates for musical celebrity – but it is very rare indeed that we have to record the success of a male vocalist'.[6] Likewise, few possessed the elusive ability to sing *and* act. Hogarth declared 'it has been all along an impediment to the improvement of the English opera, that our singers have not been actors, nor our actors singers'.[7] The *Theatrical Inquisitor* sighed 'The change is not advantageous, but as they could not compel Charles Kemble [the Don Giovanni] to sing, it was unavoidable.' The stratification of theatre casts fostered this – tragedians like Kemble at the top, comedians and singers lower on the pay scale. Yet, the choice was hardly 'inevitable'. Kemble could not be forced to sing, perhaps, but the Ottavio, John Sinclair, had played the title role in Bishop's *Jean de Paris*, and the Masetto, John Duruset (Olivier in *Jean de Paris*), was praised for his 'rare union of vocal accomplishment and histrionic ability'.[8] True, Sinclair was a tenor, but transposition was widely accepted at the time.[9]

Reviews of Sinclair and Duruset reveal deeper reasons why they were not cast. Sinclair was a 'pure tenor, with an unusually fine falsetto', but some derided him as 'The prettiest man upon the stage' and felt he used his falsetto 'too unsparingly, to the production of a feminine expression'.[10] Duruset drew similar rhetoric. Kenrick, describing actors with Shakespearean quotations, assigned him one from *Twelfth night*:

> ... they shall yet belie thy happy years,
> That say thou art a *man*: Diana's lip
> Is not more smooth and rubious: thy small pipe
> Is as the Maiden's organ, shrill and round:
> And all is semblative a woman's part.[11]

Ingrained connections between music and femininity thus coloured perceptions of male singers and may have steered otherwise talented men away from the profession. When the sensual sound of music emanated from a male throat, and particularly when it reached into the falsetto used for higher notes, it disturbingly distorted gender distinctions. Leigh Hunt mused, 'Women have carried the palm out and out, in acting, singing, and dancing. The pleasurable seems more the forte of the sex ... When the men are sweet, they either seem feeble, or ... have execution without passion.'[12]

A stereotypically masculine figure such as Don Giovanni seemed unfit for this ambiguous territory, not only because of his gender but also because of his class. Tellingly, Kemble was not the only actor who could not sing. Neither could the Leporello, John Liston, who had been excused from musical duties as Pedrigo in *Jean de Paris*. In the adapted *Don Giovanni*, however, he sang the famous catalogue aria, as well as one ensemble, even though Kenrick felt 'the deficiency in his voice [was] wofully apparent'. The master thus remained free of feminising influences while the servant had to shoulder them as best he could.

The spoken Don Giovanni also played into Pocock and Bishop's overriding concern to move the opera closer to melodrama. The word 'melodrama' has several meanings and music scholars often refer to it as a genre in which text is recited to musical accompaniment. In nineteenth-century theatre, it denoted a dramatic genre that featured an intense struggle between clearly delineated forces of good and evil.[13] Melodramas relied on blatant rhetoric, mute gesture, wordless action and spectacular stage effect. They sometimes featured villains whose inability to sing marked their separation from society, and the spoken Don Giovanni fits this tradition. Musically, melodrama focused less on vocal music than on melodramatic music, or brief snippets of instrumental accompaniment that heightened stage gesture and action.

Bishop and Pocock saw in *Don Giovanni* an opera that could be easily moved in a melodramatic direction. Mozart and Da Ponte's work already possessed some key features of melodrama. There is an exciting sword fight to whisk audiences into the action, an eerie, speaking statue and a spectacular illustration of the demise of evil, as Don Giovanni descends into hell. It is no coincidence that in the nineteenth century, when the scenically spectacular conclusions of melodrama thrilled audiences, it became common to cut the final ensemble.[14] Pocock expanded these melodramatic kernels. He refashioned the overall plot into a leaner trajectory, more focused on climactic points of conflict than leisurely musical embellishment or secondary plot lines. Act one led swiftly from exciting sword fight to thwarted seduction of Zerlina to confrontation with Ottavio, with no musical detours for Elvira, Anna or Ottavio. In act two, Pocock telescoped the opening seduction attempt and cut Masetto's beating and the characters' berating of Leporello. This allowed him to focus on the rising action, from the stony handshake to the breathtaking conclusion, unmitigated by the moralising close.

Bishop crafted a similarly lean score that accorded with the typical placement, function and style of music in melodrama (see Table 2.1). In melodrama, as in most genres on the playhouse stage, vocal music was primarily meant as a relief from the action, which was lodged primarily in speech. Bishop therefore foregrounded static solos and duets and either cut lengthy, kinetic ensembles or retained only brief, lyrical portions of them. He also weighted the vocal music towards act one, creating a natural dramatic acceleration in act two that propelled the plot to its spectacular conclusion.

Melodrama also tended to divide the cast into heavily musical characters, completely spoken roles and a few minimally musical parts. Bishop distributed the music accordingly. Less dramatically vital characters, especially Zerlina and Masetto, shoulder much of the music, as does the romantic male lead, Ottavio. As noted above, Elvira and Don Giovanni do not sing and other characters, such as Leporello, sing only occasionally. One unusual feature of Bishop's adaptation is the lack of a maximally

Table 2.1 *Placement of music in Bishop, arr.,* Don Giovanni

Overture (Mozart's Overture)

Act I

Scene i	Four indications for melodramatic music
	Aria, Ottavio ('Deh vieni alla finestra')
Scene ii	Two indications for melodramatic music
	Duet, Anna and Ottavio ('Fuggi, crudele, fuggi!')
Scene iii	Duet and chorus, Masetto and Zerlina ('Giovinette che fate all'amore')
	Duet, Masetto and Zerlina ('Là ci darem la mano')
Scene iv	Aria, Leporello ('Madamina, il catalogo è questo')
	Quartet, Anna, Leporello, Maria,[1] Ottavio (from act one finale)
Scene v	Two indications for melodramatic music
	Aria, Zerlina ('Batti, batti, o bel Masetto')[2]
	Ballet music (from act one finale)
	Septetto, characters unspecified[3] (from act one finale)

Act II

Entr'acte ('Der Vogelfänger bin ich ja', *Die Zauberflöte*)

Scene i	Two indications for melodramatic music
	Aria, Masetto ('Fin ch'han dal vino')
	Aria, Zerlina ('Vedrai carino')
Scene ii	Two indications for melodramatic music
Scene iii	Duet, Ottavio and Zerlina ('Bei Männern, welche Liebe fühlen', *Die Zauberflöte*)
Scene iv	Seven indications for melodramatic music, at least two from act two finale
	Chorus of demons (probably from act two finale)[4]

[1] Maria is a new servant character added to sing Elvira's line in this quartet and perhaps in other ensembles.

[2] Placed in quotation marks in the printed libretto and therefore probably cut in performance.

[3] This piece is in the printed libretto but not in the manuscript libretto or printed score. Although the character names are not listed, the dramatic context suggests that these were Anna, Masetto, Ottavio, Zerlina and perhaps Maria and another new servant character, Lopez.

[4] This piece is in the printed libretto but not in the manuscript libretto or printed score.

musical prima donna; Anna sings only one duet and a few ensembles. This stemmed more from the available cast than typical practice. Bishop only had one stellar female singer available, Catherine Stephens (the Princess in *Jean de Paris*). He cast her as Zerlina, where she could charm with what *The Times* called 'her forte ... in soft and simple airs'.[15] Only in the following year, when Maria Dickons returned from the continent and sang in adaptations of *Il barbiere* and *Figaro*, could Bishop include the vocal pyrotechnics his audience enjoyed. The loss of the virtuoso female role was not acute, however, as most vocal music in melodrama featured simplicity and lyricism. Consequently, Bishop retained only, in the *Morning Chronicle*'s words, 'the least elaborate and most popular pieces in the Italian Opera by MOZART'.

In melodrama, music and action combined not in vocal but in instrumental music. Concise instrumental passages known as melodramatic music delineated characters and heightened wordless scenes of action. As seen in Table 2.1, Pocock's libretto contains nineteen such indications for 'music'. Unfortunately, melodramatic music rarely appeared in published scores and it is therefore not certain whether Bishop used his own or Mozart's material. The latter seems probable, however, since the *Morning Chronicle* reported that 'a few of the most difficult choral pieces in the original Opera were executed by the orchestra only, as an accompaniment to the pantomimic scenes'.

The opera's conclusion gives us a sense of the possible provenance and function of this music.[16] The entire scene is almost completely spoken in the adaptation, save the chorus of demons, but seven indications for melodramatic music appear. Two of these are extant in the score, in a section at the end that contains several instrumental pieces. Since few specific indications tie these pieces to the libretto, their placement and use can only be approximated. The 'grand march' and 'banquet dance' are, however, based on the tunes Mozart quoted in his finale and therefore were probably used as follows. The *'burst of Music'* that *'introduce[s] the Company'* was probably 'the grand march', to the tune of 'Non più andrai'. As Don Giovanni sits down to dinner with his guests, Bishop's 'banquet dance' was probably heard, based on Mozart's excerpt from *Una cosa rara*. In both cases, Bishop cut all vocal lines.

Unfortunately, none of the remaining music is in the score, but one can reconstruct how Bishop may have used Mozart's finale, vocal lines removed. When Don Giovanni orders Leporello to answer the door, music is heard again. Bishop may have drawn from mm. 363–70 of Mozart's finale, in which a gradual ascent in the strings, lurching upwards chromatically, leads to Leporello's terrified cry. Leporello returns to announce the statue's arrival, and there is more music as Don Giovanni *'draws his Sword, and takes the light from the trembling hand of* Leporello'. Bishop may have used Don Giovanni's forceful response, mm. 398–406, as he resolutely arpeggiates the F major triad. Music accompanies the statue's entrance and music is again heard as the statue, completely mute, refuses food and drink. These cues probably utilised Mozart's solemn Andante, beginning in m. 433, with its memorable, stentorian lines for the statue. Music continues as the statue extends his hand, which Don Giovanni takes, then *'shrinks back and groans'*; Mozart sets the same action in mm. 516–23. A chorus of demons – whose text fits Mozart's disembodied chorus, m. 563 on – sings as Don Giovanni *'reels, and falls – Fiends arise from various parts, and on an immense rock of burning matter, with Serpents twining amidst a vivid red flame, which ascends in the centre'*. These impressive moments in Mozart's finale, shorn of vocal lines, could have intensified Don Giovanni's spectacular collision with his fate – opera could have metamorphosed into melodrama.

This was certainly the case in the adapted libretto by Pocock. Although *Don Giovanni* possesses many congruencies with melodrama, it does not conform completely to the genre's clear moral divisions. Giovanni is hardly the typical stalwart melodramatic hero, unsullied by moral failings; he creates the damsel in distress rather than rescuing her and refuses to admit his wrongs. Yet, he is not a true villain either. He aims more to please himself than destroy others and his victims often seem drawn to their victimiser. Kenrick felt Don Giovanni was not 'sufficiently vicious to call for the remarkable punishment he receives' and joked that if a similar fate met all such sinners, 'we should have our friends carried off by dozens, and see . . . daemons capering about at the corner of every street'. Such moral ambiguity disturbed some critics. The *New Monthly Magazine* cast the issue in nationalistic terms. While such a subject might suit 'the meridian of Seville', it was shocking that 'a piece so gross . . . could possibly be tolerated in the British metropolis'. Reviewing the King's Theatre's *Don Giovanni*, Richard Mackenzie Bacon suggested that the poles of good and evil be more clearly divided. Speaking of the seduction of Zerlina, he counselled: 'we hear a scream and a decided change of musical sounds, without guessing the cause; this attempt of the seducer should be told in a very conspicuous and predominant manner'.[17]

Pocock recast the tale in this more 'conspicuous' rhetoric. His Leporello, for example, offers not only a comic foil to Don Giovanni but also a moral one. Da Ponte already began this, as his Leporello points out that 'the life [Don Giovanni is] leading is that of (*into his ear, loudly*) a scoundrel'.[18] The British Leporello expands this line of reasoning. When Don Giovanni defends his actions, asking 'do I not gather every blossom that the spring of youth puts forth?', Leporello retorts 'Yes, but the fruit will be remorse.'[19] Pocock also forged the common melodramatic link between low class and high moral standards. Pretending to speak to a fictitious master, Leporello asks, 'think you, because you are a man of quality, with straight limbs, and a fair presence . . . that you are at liberty to go it as you do, without an honest man daring to give you your own? Then, learn from me, who am only your lacquey.'[20] The British Leporello thus acquired attributes of the simple, lower-class character in melodrama who, bumbling but good at heart, acted as a kind of moral barometer.

Pocock also attempted to strengthen the closest character to a hero in the opera, Ottavio. The original Ottavio is passive and ineffectual. He is outraged at the attack on Anna and the death of her father, yet is unable to avenge him and must wait a year to marry Anna. In the adaptation, Ottavio is still a weak foe. On the British stage, where speech often equalled masculine power, the fact that Ottavio absorbs much of the musical responsibility, including some of Don Giovanni's music, augments his passivity. We first meet him, for example, relieving Don Giovanni of musical responsibility – and in the process retaining one of the most appealing numbers of the opera – by singing 'Deh vieni alla finestra' to Anna. He then inadvertently enables Don Giovanni's seduction of Anna by revealing that their secret signal is a whistle. Don Giovanni promptly steals the whistle and uses it to gain access to Anna.

Pocock did, however, inch Ottavio in a more stalwart direction. For example, a new *tableau* at the end of act one takes the original Ottavio's brandished pistol to a new level of courageous, if ultimately ineffectual display:

[Don Giovanni] *stands in the midst, laughing at* [his opponents'] *rage, and braving their threats –* [Ottavio], *towards the close, breaks from* [Anna] *and* Elvira, *and attacking* Don [Giovanni], *is disarmed –* Elvira *rushes between them, and arrests the blow of* [Don Giovanni] *– Tableau.*[21]

In an added scene in the next act, Ottavio begins legal proceedings against Don Giovanni and bravely assumes responsibility for Zerlina's safety. Finally, Ottavio never presses his marriage suit with Anna, nor does she ask him to wait another year; Pocock simply does not elaborate on their status. Ottavio ultimately remains powerless in the adaptation, but he is slightly more courageous, more in control and less dependent on Anna's decisions.

As a foil to both villain and hero, melodrama relied on a virginal female whose patient purity eventually overcame evil. Pocock moved all female characters closer to this ideal. Donna Elvira, now a completely spoken role, attempts to redeem Don Giovanni. She warns him 'Oh, let me save you from ... the wrath of heaven! E'en now, the fatal bolt is launched at thy devoted head – already I behold the dark abyss opening to swallow thee in fires.'[22] Meanwhile, Pocock's Anna serves as a penitent example of the perils of moral indiscretion. She bewails 'O! [Ottavio], our fatal passion has destroyed [my father]: but for our imprudent assignation, he had still lived!'[23] She also receives subtle moral cleansing. In the opera, one does not know how far Don Giovanni carried his seduction, since, when the opera opens, Leporello has been waiting for an indefinite time. In the adaptation, the audience sees Don Giovanni enter Anna's apartment and exit only a few lines later, not enough time for significant indiscretion. Finally, Zerlina, whom the *Morning Chronicle* called 'an abominable coquette' in a review of the King's Theatre production, evinces a newly moral streak.[24] At first attracted to Don Giovanni, she later resolutely fends off his advances. In her defence, she employs a central message of melodrama, that inner worth means more than the outer trappings of rank or wealth: 'tho' humble in my station, I have learnt to prize the heart of an honest youth, beyond all the splendour of exalted infamy'.[25] Lacking music, Don Giovanni cannot charm her with the seductive strains of 'Là ci darem la mano', which are instead given to Masetto and Zerlina and thus redirected within conjugal boundaries.

Bishop and Pocock's changes are a kind of commentary on the chasm between continental opera house and London playhouse, even as the very appearance of *Don Giovanni* at Covent Garden sprang from an ambition to bridge that chasm. Bishop and Pocock primarily constructed that bridge by bringing opera closer to melodrama. The centrality of speech to the playhouses is evident in the spoken Don Giovanni, whose dramatic importance and virile power alike were unsuitable for music on the native stage. Vocal music shrank to a handful of static numbers, apportioned primarily to less dramatically vital characters and weighted towards the beginning of the work. Melodramatic music, meanwhile, heightened the action and helped drive the plot to its stunning conclusion. The refashioned libretto corralled Da Ponte's unruly cast into a stricter division of hero, villain, comic foil and virtuous heroine. The goal of the production was not, however, simply to offer yet another melodrama, but also to capitalise on the popularity of Mozart's opera at the King's Theatre. Bishop therefore ensured that the most popular numbers of *Don Giovanni* appeared, supplemented with some of the favourite tunes from *Die Zauberflöte* and largely free of interpolation. As with *Jean de Paris*, he turned away from pastiche practice of the past to offer as close an echo of the opera house as his venue's different aesthetic would allow.

'AN AGREEABLE OLIO': *IL BARBIERE DI SIVIGLIA*

In 1818, Covent Garden brought out what Kenrick described in the *British Stage* as 'an agreeable Olio, under the title of "The Barber of Seville," compounde[d] of the incidents of Beaumarchais' Comedy, and Rossini's Opera'.[26] The score's title page indicated that the adaptation was 'Partly Selected from Paesiello [*sic*] & Rossini's Highly celebrated Operas Partly Composed & the whole Arranged Altered & Adapted ... by Henry R Bishop'. Such descriptions underline an essential facet of nineteenth-century adaptation: foreign operas were frequently themselves adaptations of other sources, all considered equally 'original'. Librettists Daniel Terry and John Fawcett relied heavily – even verbatim at times – on George Colman and Samuel Arnold's English version of Beaumarchais' play, *The Spanish barber*.[27] As Katherine Preston observes, adaptations were often not so much of an opera as of a combination of opera and play, or 'plays regenerated from operas'.[28] In addition, there was another operatic model: Paisiello and Petrosellini's 1782 setting of Beaumarchais. The Paisiello had been frequently performed at the King's Theatre and the one number Bishop drew from it ('Saper bramante') had been excerpted in both Burgoyne's *The heiress* and Dibdin's *Haroun Alraschid*. When Rossini's *Il barbiere di Siviglia* appeared at the King's Theatre, Hunt viewed it as an adaptation, and a poor one at that: 'the author's having taken up an opera ... which had already been composed by so fine a master as PAISIELLO, was not a piece of ambition in the best taste, or a very promising symptom of excellence. We expected that we should find little genius exhibited ... and ... we were not disappointed.'[29] Rossini's opera was itself an 'olio' of sorts, for he had recycled the overture and 'Una voce poco fa', which appeared in both *Aureliano in Palmira* and *Elisabetta*. Change had also begun to creep into Rossini's opera: the lesson scene was becoming an accepted locus for substitution and the difficult 'A un dottor della mia sorte' was often replaced by Romani's 'Manca un foglio'.[30] As Philip Gossett states, 'there is no one correct text for most Rossini operas'.[31]

Such a dense continuum of retellings destabilised the authority of Rossini's opera, as the *Morning Chronicle*'s description of the adaptation demonstrates:

This piece, though introduced in a new form, is not original. It was first brought forward in France, and afterwards adopted in Italy. – At a subsequent period it was produced on our own stage by the elder COLMAN; and the only novelty it could boast on the last night was, we believe, an alteration from three acts into two, with some changes in the dialogue, the preservation of part of the music of PAESIELLO [*sic*] and ROSSINI, as performed at the Opera-house, the introduction of some new music by Mr. BISHOP, and of a few songs . . . The circumstance, however, which most probably attracted the numerous audience . . . was the first appearance of Mrs. DICKONS [as Rosina] . . . She distinguished herself . . . in a new bravura, the composition of Mr. BISHOP.

No indignation arises from the adapters' free patchwork of their own work with Colman, Paisiello and Rossini. Change is seen as a welcome novelty, necessary to enliven the well-worn tale and showcase the return of celebrated soprano Dickons. The implication is that the jumble of original materials should be fashioned into whatever format best suits its new context. Accordingly, Bishop kept less than half of Rossini's numbers – many substantially changed and others reassigned in order to accommodate a completely spoken Count Almaviva – and added six new numbers, most of his own composition.[32] The resulting 'olio' was an *Il barbiere* better suited to playhouse ideas of gender, comedy and the intersection of music and drama.

As with *Don Giovanni*, Bishop and his librettists more firmly separated music and gender. While this was most obvious in the spoken Count Almaviva, Rosina also emerged as more morally and musically congruent with British heroines. In Rossini and Sterbini's opera, Rosina defies numerous conventions: she is hardly the epitome of pure, virtuous femininity; she sings only one aria; and she falls into a contralto range. The British adapters sought to conform Rosina better to playhouse expectations. Bishop augmented her one solo with two more and transposed the role to a soprano. While librettists Terry and Fawcett could not completely eliminate her sly cunning, they moderated and redirected it.

The adapters retained the most unabashed celebration of Rosina's wiles, 'Una voce poco fa', but with a slightly softened text (see Table 2.2). Rather than relying on her own intellect ('I'll sharpen my wits . . . I'll be clever') and gleefully anticipating her 'triumph', the British Rosina fashions herself more as a victim. She is willing to 'die to have [her] way', but only if prompted by 'tyrant sway'. She gives comforting assurances of her 'docile' and 'meek' nature and seeks simply to trade one master for another; she will replace the 'tyrant' with 'sweeter bonds'. The aria, however, remained relatively intact musically. This might suggest that audiences heard the assertive musical message of Rosina's mischievous roulades rather than the subtly altered text. Bacon, however, reviewing the score of the adaptation for the *Quarterly Musical Magazine and Review*, mused that 'the different sentiments to which the English translator has had recourse, while the same music has been employed with great effect we think, is a proof that its expression is not of any certain application'. After all, the aria had been sung by Arsace as

Table 2.2 *'Una voce poco fa'* compared to *'Tyrant, soon I'll burst thy chains'*

Sterbini	Fawcett and Terry
A little while ago,	Tyrant, soon I'll burst thy chains,
A voice resounded in my heart,	Sweeter bonds than thine to prove;
My heart that is already wounded,	Passion's voice thrills thro' my veins,
But Lindoro will heal it.	Waking all my soul to love.
Yes, Lindoro will be mine.	With mild and docile air,
I swear that I will triumph.	And playful as a lamb,
My guardian will disapprove,	Never was gentler fair
So I'll sharpen my wits.	Than all confess I am.
In the end, I'll be clever	Doves not more meek appear,
and I'll be happy.	If none [provoke] or chide.
Yes, Lindoro will be mine,	But if with tyrant sway[,]
I swear that I will triumph.	My mind they seek to fix,
I am responsible, I am respectful,	I'd die to have my way; –
I am obedient, gentle, loving,	A thousand wayward tricks
I can be ruled and I can be guided,	And subtle wiles I'd play,
But if you hurt me	'Ere they my will should guide.[1]
I will be a viper with a hundred ways to	
Stop and make a fool of you.	
Yes, I will triumph.	

[1] Fisher, ed., *The barber of Seville*, pp. 64–5 and *The barber of Seville; a comic opera*, p. 16.

he readied himself for battle in *Aureliano in Palmira* and by Queen Elizabeth as she looked forward to seeing her beloved in *Elisabetta*. Bacon points to an essential, if troubling, facet of adaptation: music's slippery meaning enabled adaptation, as composers and adapters alike could easily re-appropriate old music to new ends.

Bishop's two new solos for Rosina served diverse ends. The first interpolated number, 'An old man would be wooing' (which replaced 'Contro il cor' in the music lesson scene) offered an unusual combination of musical sweetness, textual cunning and integration with stage action. Bacon claimed that the piece was based on a 'Venetian air'. While I have not been able to confirm this, the small melodic range, clear antecedent-consequent structure and catchy 6/8 metre adhered to the simple, folk-like qualities prized on the playhouse stage (see Ex. 2.1a). This is not, however, a standard British ballad. It begins with twelve measures of a virtuosic piano introduction designed to showcase Dickons' instrumental abilities – the sheet music even labels the piece 'the celebrated piano forte song'. It is also enmeshed within the action. In the first stanza of the strophic form, Bartolo begins to doze as Rosina warbles about how 'May and December can never agree'. In the second and third he falls asleep as Rosina sings of how the youth presses her hand and steals a kiss, respectively, but in each case awakens abruptly as the Count acts out the lyrics. Musical contrast heightens the stage

Example 2.1a 'An old man would be wooing', Bishop, arr., *Il barbiere di Siviglia*, mm. 13–20

action. The beginning of each verse portrays the cautious lovers, *pianissimo, più largo* and with plentiful fermatas after each tentative phrase, perhaps as they peep at Bartolo to make sure he still sleeps. When he awakens, sudden fortissimo chords, an acceleration to *più presto agitato* and a frantic piano accompaniment paint the action (see Ex. 2.1b).

Some critics noticed that Rosina in essence orchestrated daring physical contact. Bacon suggested that the text be changed for publication, as it 'does not accord with received notions of the delicacy appertaining to the manners of English women'. The number proved a hit, however, eliciting one of the few encores onstage and numerous sheet music publications throughout Britain and the United States. When framed within an accessible musical style and tied to amusing stage action, such risqué behaviour apparently seemed ameliorated.

Rosina's final new aria was more conventional. It provided one of the most beloved, anticipated types of solo at playhouse and opera house alike: the bravura showpiece. 'Una voce poco fa' of course already fulfilled this type. In his new piece, Bishop followed a similar pattern of plentiful vocal fireworks within a multi-partite structure. Given the importance of the adaptation as a showpiece for the newly returned Dickons, however, and given the expectation that leading female roles would shoulder a disproportionate

Example 2.1b 'An old man would be wooing', Bishop, arr., *Il barbiere di Siviglia*, mm. 60–80

amount of the music, another bravura seemed necessary. Bishop added it in the same location where Rossini later inserted a new aria for Joséphine Mainvielle-Fodor.[33] After Bartolo manages to convince Rosina that the Count has misled her, Rosina agrees to marry Bartolo out of anger and Bartolo exits. A leading lady alone onstage after she has learned disturbing information seems a perfect location for an aria, but Rosina utters only one line of recitative. This is where both Bishop and later Rossini inserted their new arias. Adaptation was therefore not always incongruent with a composer's own instincts for revision. In this case adapter may even have aided composer, since the score of

Example 2.1b (cont.)

Bishop's adaptation was published before Rossini added his aria.[34] Any connection ends there, however, and the two arias are clearly independent compositions.

Bishop's solo begins with a dramatic opening recitative in which Rosina forcefully shuns her former love. She then sings a more poignant Moderato grazioso

Example 2.2 'Away, deceiver!', Bishop, arr., *Il barbiere di Siviglia*, mm. 96–110

wondering 'how couldst thou so treach'rous prove?' As she warms to the topic, the simple melody becomes increasingly embellished by agile vocal ornamentation. After a brief return to the opening recitative, Rosina launches into an Allegro agitato, in which she pronounces her determination to leave Lindoro for ever with an impressive array of sustained high notes and streams of melismas. In the sheet music, Bishop allowed consumers to marvel at Dickons' abilities but also provided several alternative, slightly easier versions for domestic use (see Ex. 2.2). The lengthy demonstration of vocal force not only showcased Dickons but also tempered Rosina's spunk with moral righteousness. Rosina is not plotting to overthrow her legal

Example 2.2 (cont.)

guardian, but expressing the more morally acceptable rage of a spurned lover. Bishop, Terry and Fawcett thus nudged the irrepressible Rosina in a more conventional direction, focused more on vocal than histrionic talents, more on self-righteous anger than impish rebellion.

Just as the adapters tried to refashion the Count and Rosina into a purer hero and heroine, they also moved Bartolo closer to playhouse comedy. The Bartolo (John Fawcett) was one of the librettists, so he ensured that the part fitted his abilities. Like most British stage comedians, Fawcett was a specialist who delighted the audience with ad lib puns and physical comedy; if any music was heard, it took the form of simple, strophic comic songs. Even though he was called 'the best *buffa* singer on the English stage', Fawcett exhibited quite different musical strengths from his continental counterparts.[35] Hunt remembered

> Fawcett had a harsh, brazen face, and a voice like a knife-grinder's wheel. He was all
> pertness, coarseness, and effrontery, but with a great deal of comic force; and whenever he
> came trotting on to the stage . . . and pouring forth his harsh, rapid words, with his nose in
> the air, and a facetious grind in his throat, the audience were prepared for a merry evening.[36]

Fawcett therefore deserted the punishing patter singing of 'A un dottor' for easier ground, as did most Bartolos. He did not, however, choose the typical substitute, 'Manca un foglio'. Instead, Bishop crafted a new solo, 'Womankind', to show off Fawcett's strengths (see Ex. 2.3).[37] The fact that the solo appears only in the printed sources, and not in the earlier manuscript ones, suggests that it was a late addition, probably inserted at Fawcett's request. The typical simplicity of the comic British stage song reigns. The song is strophic, with each strophe in an ABA' pattern and each section made up of an antecedent–consequent pair of phrases. The text for each A' section repeats, forming a refrain. The range spans only an octave and, save for one flourish, the text setting is syllabic. Unencumbered by difficulty, the singer could freely milk the comic potential of the misogynistic lyrics. One can imagine Fawcett, in a style perhaps more akin to musical theatre than opera, whining out a nasal note on 'woman*kind*', sighing out the high note on 'life's vexations' or landing with a gleeful accent on 'slaves'. As with so much on the playhouse stage, comedy depended more on acting than music.

Bishop crafted new solos not only to highlight individual performers and character types, but also to counterbalance what contemporaries saw as one of Rossini's greatest faults: reliance on lengthy ensembles. A letter to the editor of the *Quarterly Musical Magazine and Review* mused, 'It is singular that Rossini should have derived almost his entire stock of reputation from concerted pieces, and should have written scarcely half a dozen airs that are known.'[38] This was a particular liability for a stage that did not welcome musico-dramatic fusion and that relied on sheet music sales. As Ayrton noted, pieces 'of the concerted kind . . . will hardly cover the expenses of engraving and paper'.[39] Bishop therefore cut, curtailed or reworked virtually all of Rossini's ensembles.

Example 2.3 'Womankind', Bishop, arr., *Il barbiere di Siviglia*, mm. 1–40

Example 2.3 (cont.)

His approach to the act one finale – in which the Count, pretending to be drunk, barges into Bartolo's home and manages to slip Rosina a note – exemplifies his methods. When reviewing the King's Theatre production, Ayrton deemed the finale 'quite *à la Mozart*, and that is the highest commendation', but recommended that it 'should be curtailed; the subject is too much spun out, and becomes at last enfeebled by frequent repetition'.[40] Bishop complied, keeping only 325 of the original 685 measures. His cuts fell into three basic types. First, he wrote new, shorter sections in place of others. In the first

Allegro, for example, he replaced mm. 212–85 with thirteen measures of similar material and mm. 322–58 with three measures. Second, Bishop cut any repetitive, easily excised material. For instance, he jettisoned the entire repeat of the concluding stretta (mm. 490–590). Finally, he eliminated or replaced sections saturated with action. This often coordinated with removing the non-singing Count from the finale. In the adaptation, the Count's part, as he drunkenly demands his billet, took place entirely in speech. Fiorello then entered, also disguised as an inebriated soldier, and sang the Count's music. In the opening Marziale, therefore, Bishop cut measures that contained banter among the Count, Rosina and Bartolo (mm. 49–72 and 87–175), much of which had already taken place in speech in the adaptation. To make up for this lost material, Bishop wrote 43 new measures in place of mm. 49–72, into which he inserted the comedy of the yawning and sneezing servants, repeated from an earlier scene and set to new music. Bishop thus replaced the most vital action with speech and delegated musical comedy to the servants' easily understandable physical distress.

The finale posed not only musical but also textual challenges. In his review of the adaptation for *The Times*, Edward Sterling pondered, 'The songs and duets of Rossini always appeared to us inflexibly Italian, and his finales seemed to defy mutability.' Early nineteenth-century writers felt convinced that Italian led naturally to song, English naturally to its absence. Ayrton expressed the common view: 'It is universally allowed that the Italian language is more sonorous, more harmonious, and of more easy utterance, than any other modern tongue.'[41] Voicing the typical flip side, John Payne Collier stated that English '[did] not, without great difficulty, wind itself into the sinuosities of music'.[42] Rossini's penchant for patter singing must have made the language gap appear especially unbridgeable. Bishop did not cut the sections of rapid-fire diction entirely, but tried to ameliorate them. First, he cut repeats so that the difficulty had to be surmounted only once. Second, he slowed the tempo. The first Vivace section is Moderato in Bishop, the second Allegro. He also rewrote the first Vivace section in 2/4 rather than 4/4, which appeared less daunting on the page and provided more anchoring downbeats. More drastic slowing occurred in the Marziale, where the most difficult line – Bartolo articulating a new syllable for every semi-quaver – Bishop calmed to quavers.

Word choice is crucial in sections of quick diction, and Bishop and his librettists diverged both from straight translation and Sterbini's rhyme scheme to assist their performers (see Table 2.3). Although the number of syllables is the same, the English rhyme scheme is simpler: each line ends with '-inning' before the concluding 'drown'd'. The singers have not only fewer rhymes to remember, but fewer words. For the new section starting m. 590, Sterbini wrote new text, but Terry and Fawcett repeated previous lines. Finally, in the most obvious simplification, on a long stretch of triplets starting in m. 614, Terry and Fawcett replaced four lines of Italian text with a simple (if not entirely meaningful) melisma on 'all'. Bishop, Terry and Fawcett thus 'bent' the 'inflexible Italian' with cuts, slower tempi and simpler text setting.

Table 2.3 *'Ehi, di casa' compared to 'Hollo! house, here'*

Rossini and Sterbini	Bishop, Fawcett and Terry
m. 460 on	**m. 257 on**
Mi par d'esser con la testa	What confusion with the dinning
In un'orrida fucina,	Round my giddy head is spinning
dove cresce e mai non resta	No one ending each beginning
delle incudini sonore	No one ending each beginning
l'importuno strepitar	All in rage and clamour drown'd
m. 590 on	**m. 278 on**
Alternando questo e quello	What confusion with the dinning
pesantissimo martello	What confusion with the dinning
alternando questo e quello	Round my giddy head is spinning
pesantissimo martello	Round my giddy head is spinning
alternando questo e quello	No one ending each beginning
pesantissimo martello	No one ending each beginning
fa con barbara armonia	Each beginning, each beginning
muri volte rimbombar.	All in rage and clamour drown'd
E il cervello, poverello	All–
già stordito, sbalordito	–
non ragiona, si confonde	–
si riduce ad impazzar	–
E il cervello, poverello	What confusion with the dinning
già stordito, sbalordito	Round my giddy head is spinning
non ragiona, si confonde	No one ending each beginning
si riduce ad impazzar	All in rage and clamour drown'd
m. 644 on	**m. 294 on**
E il cervello	All in
si riduce ad impazzar	Rage in rage and clamour drown'd
m. 658 on	**m. 300 on**
E il cervello, poverello	All in rage and clamour drown'd
si riduce ad impazzar	All in rage and clamour drown'd[1]

[1] Fisher, ed., *The barber of Seville*, pp. 89–90 and *The barber of Seville; a comic opera*, p. 29.

While Bacon pitied the 'unfortunate man … whose brains were tasked to find syllables of tolerable meaning' for the piece, he ultimately felt that Italian comic ensembles were 'as untranslatable as the point of an epigram'. In fact, Rossini's *Il barbiere* was in many ways 'untranslatable' in its complete form for the playhouses in 1818. Bishop did not have the vocal depth available and the opera defied too many ingrained playhouse conventions. The opera was not, however, the only original, and many Londoners saw the Rossini opera as another version of a tale already known through Beaumarchais and Paisiello. There was therefore little need to privilege Rossini as more 'original' than the others and Bishop, Terry and Fawcett melded together the most attractive and suitable portions of all *Barbers*. The resulting 'olio' offered both the familiar core of Beaumarchais' play and the allure of musical excerpts from the King's Theatre's repertoire.

MOZART'S MUSIC AND BEAUMARCHAIS' WORDS: *LE NOZZE DI FIGARO*

In 1819, Bishop followed advice that he had received five years earlier, after he had adapted *Jean de Paris*. Reviewing *Jean de Paris*, William Hazlitt had suggested that 'Mozart's music [in *Le nozze di Figaro*] [be] adapted to a good translation of Beaumarchais' words'.[43] This is precisely what Bishop did in order to compete with the King's Theatre's revival of Mozart's opera.[44] As Hazlitt intimates, Mozart and Beaumarchais were considered equally original and Bishop created a conglomerate of the two. Working unusually as his own librettist, Bishop relied heavily on Thomas Holcroft's well-known 1784 adaptation of the French play, still staged in the 1810s. He included Holcroft's plot changes (for instance, the entire Marcellina sub-plot disappears) and lifted long stretches of dialogue verbatim.[45] To this story Bishop wed approximately half of Mozart's numbers, cut all music from Count Almaviva, interpolated several of his own pieces and included music from *Don Giovanni*, *Così fan tutte*, *Idomeneo* and Rossini's *Tancredi*.[46] Such extensive changes obscure Bishop's desire to bring as much of Mozart's score to his listeners as possible. He initially retained four pieces in the manuscript libretto that he was obliged to cut before the published sources appeared: the overture; 'Cosa sento!'; 'Aprite presto aprite'; and 'Ricevete, oh padroncina'. He also drew from Mozart's other operas whenever possible and expended considerable effort to rewrite rather than replace several numbers. As he later defended himself, 'my sole object . . . was to improve the national taste for opera by rendering English audiences more familiar with truly dramatic music . . . To receive an instalment, seemed better than nothing.'[47] Bishop thus tried to bring as much of Mozart's music to his audience as possible through the most effective means: by joining its most appealing excerpts with Beaumarchais' familiar words.

Already at the outset of the opera, Bishop found that the best way to interest his listeners in Mozart was not through strict fidelity. He initially began his adaptation with Mozart's overture, but withdrew it after the first few nights. Presumably this was due to its difficulty, but the new overture he substituted also presented his listeners with a more familiar picture of Mozart. After an opening section by Bishop full of dotted notes and flourishes, the new overture featured a march (no. 8) from *Idomeneo*, 'È amore un ladroncello' from *Così fan tutte* and 'Fin ch'han dal vino' from *Don Giovanni*.

This patchwork approach mirrors how most consumers would have come to know *Figaro* in London. Londoners looking for sheet music of *Figaro* in 1819, for example, could have purchased, among others: 'the favourite Guaracha dance' from the King's Theatre's ballet version of 1811; 'When the banners of glory are streaming' from *The prisoner* and 'When the banners of England' from *The slave*, both re-workings of 'Non più andrai'; a piano 'capriccio' that contained 'favourite airs' from *Figaro* and *Don Giovanni*; 'Se vuol ballare' with nine piano variations; and individual publications of numbers such as 'Crudel! perchè finora', 'Che soave zeffiretto' and 'Non so più cosa son, cosa faccio'. True, a few complete piano–vocal scores were available, and the King's Theatre production performed in the 1810s was relatively faithful.[48] Yet, British consumers enjoyed Mozart in a wide variety of forms and in some ways Bishop's adaptation offers another 'arrangement' of *Figaro*. As the title page of the score states, it is 'partly Selected from Mozart, partly Composed, and the whole Adapted . . . and Arranged from the Score by Henry R. Bishop'. When operas were primarily disseminated in fragmented, altered form, Bishop did not so much depart from Mozart's original as continue established patterns of operatic consumption.

One established pattern that drove many of Bishop's changes was the divide between song and speech on the playhouse stage. This not only resulted in a spoken Count Almaviva but also led Bishop to discard, alter or replace all of Mozart's lengthy ensembles. Yet, Bishop also wished to wean his audience from their dislike of kinetic music. His divergent approaches, at once bowing to convention and challenging it, can be seen in his treatment of the finales. He could avoid the act three finale altogether since, following Holcroft, he combined acts three and four into one. Mozart's act four finale, which stretches to over 500 measures and encompasses the entire denouement, Bishop did not feel able to keep. Rather than discarding it altogether, however, he retained its most lyrical, appealing moment, the trio for the Count, Figaro and Susanna (mm. 275–334), placed earlier in the action and with Antonio singing the Count's part. Anxious as Bishop was to retain Mozart's score, he may have also considered keeping the final chorus of the act four finale. Apparently, however, he found this brief, rousing call for rejoicing unsuitable. In his only departure from Mozart's oeuvre, he turned to Rossini's finale to *Tancredi*, 'Fra quai soavi palpiti', to end his adaptation. In some ways, this substitution added a sheen of modernity to *Figaro*. Rossini's popularity was growing and Bishop could scoop the King's Theatre, which did not produce *Tancredi* until one year later. Bishop's motivations were probably, however, more old-fashioned. The Rossini is a vaudeville finale, a simple, strophic piece that alternated passages for soloists with a choral refrain. This format had originated in France and in fact one concluded Beaumarchais' play. Bishop's bow to this tradition underlines how London adapters continued to rely on France and opéra comique, even as they strove to enter new, Italian territory.

In the finales to the other two acts, however, Bishop stretched convention. In the act two finale, for example, Bishop paved the way for musical action with speech. First, the entire scene of Antonio entering inopportunely and insisting he saw someone jumping out the window happens in dialogue. Then the garrulous Antonio returns and essentially repeats his objections, this time in song. Here one senses the pedagogical impulse that Linda Hutcheon perceives as one goal of adaptation.[49] Just as Bishop had done with the act one finale of *Il barbiere*, he first offered what was familiar (action in dialogue), then slipped in the unfamiliar (action in music). Perhaps he hoped to prove to his audiences that they were capable of enjoying this 'instalment' of action in music.

Following similar motivations, Bishop added a finale to act one. Rather than conclude with an aria – 'Non più andrai' – as Mozart had done, he combined part of this aria with various portions of ensembles from *Così fan tutte*, namely its act one finale and 'Di scrivermi ogni giorno'. Why would Bishop add a finale when his audiences preferred arias? And why meld Figaro's aria with *Così fan tutte*? Both popularity and obscurity provide some answers. 'Non più andrai' was exceptionally popular in London. It was interpolated into other playhouse productions such as Storace's *The iron chest*, published in multiple arrangements, played as a favourite march for military bands and frequently performed with extensive embellishments by star soprano Angelica Catalani. Such popularity meant both that Bishop had to include this number in his *Figaro* and that he had to avoid entrusting it entirely to his Figaro, John Liston. Liston (who had played Leporello and the innkeeper in *Jean de Paris*) was more comedian than singer and could hardly compete with the likes of Catalani. Bishop therefore wove a portion of the famous aria – enough to satisfy fans of the piece, not too much to tax Liston – among selections from *Così fan tutte*. Here, obscurity helped. *Così* would not appear at the playhouses until a decade later and had been infrequently performed at the King's Theatre since its London debut in 1811. As Hilary Poriss has observed of aria insertion practice, singers typically chose substitute arias from less well-known operas, since these were less linked to a familiar original.[50] Bishop followed a similar approach, banking on unfamiliarity with *Così* to help bolster *Figaro*. Adding a finale in a context averse to extended ensembles was thus in fact a savvy move that shielded Liston while introducing listeners to more Mozart.

As 'Non più andrai' illustrates, Bishop had to rework not only Mozart's ensembles but also his solos. Just as Mozart's ensembles challenged playhouse audiences' tolerance for musico-dramatic fusion, his arias transgressed expected conventions. *Figaro* luxuriates in fourteen arias, with one for virtually every character and many involved in the action. Bishop cut all but four of these (not counting 'Non più andrai') and added six others. This brought *Figaro* closer to the ideal layout of solos for a British opera: the leading upper-class male role (the Count) did not sing; the closest character to a sensitive young male lead (Fiorello, brought in from *Il barbiere di Siviglia* to sing some of the Count's music) gained a new solo; the comic male characters sang one solo each (a new comic number for Antonio, a much-altered 'Se vuol ballare' for Figaro); the trouser role, Cherubino, more for an actor than a singer, was reduced to one solo (a reworked 'Non so più cosa son, cosa faccio'); arias for minor characters Barbarina, Bartolo, Basilio and Marcellina fell away owing to plot changes and overall abbreviation; and the main female roles acquired the most musical weight, with three solos each for Susanna and the Countess. The Countess lost all of her original solos and instead sang two by Bishop and appropriated 'Voi che sapete'. Susanna also sang two new arias by Bishop and only one of her original arias, a heavily reworked 'Venite inginocchiatevi'.

Bishop's new, recomposed and reassigned arias brought *Figaro* more in line not only with native musical conventions, but also with moral ones. One of the most striking examples is Cherubino. Bishop transferred the charming, lyrical 'Voi che sapete' to the Countess. In the early 1800s, popular arias accrued meaning less from their original dramatic situation than as transcendent melodies infinitely transformable for new contexts. 'Voi che sapete' held an especially tenuous connection to Cherubino. John Ebers, director of the King's Theatre in the early 1820s, said the aria could be sung by Susanna, the Countess or Cherubino, depending on the circumstances, and was 'incidental to the character.'[51] The 1811 London première of *Così fan tutte* interpolated the aria for Guglielmo and the 1812 King's Theatre première of *Le nozze di Figaro* gave both of Cherubino's arias to Susanna.[52] Moving the aria was so common that, in 1822, Thomas Massa Alsager found it 'a distinction of rare occurrence' when it was sung by Cherubino.[53] Some of this 'distinction' arose because the aria accorded so well with one of the most prized genres of the playhouse stage, the simple, lyrical British ballad. Such numbers typically fell only to the most prominent singing roles and Cherubino did not appear to merit such a prime piece. Bishop's Cherubino, for example, a Miss Beaumont, excelled at acting but had not been chosen for her vocal abilities. The *Theatrical Inquisitor* enthused that she 'looked the character most charmingly; and acted it with very great spirit', but Kenrick complained in the *British Stage* that she sang 'miserably'. On the British stage, a popular, ballad-like piece like 'Voi che sapete' did not belong to a lesser role nor to an actor-singer such as Beaumont.

Cherubino's other aria – 'Non so più cosa son, cosa faccio' – did not carry the same baggage. Bishop therefore retained it, but in a substantially altered form that reworked Cherubino's character (see Ex. 2.4). In the original, Mozart pliantly depicts Cherubino's hormonal bewilderment. Cherubino can barely wait for the orchestra before bursting in. A hint of a regular rondo at the beginning crumbles in the face of Cherubino's consuming passions. His melodies disintegrate into brief, abortively melodic outbursts, the tempo drastically dips at the thought of no confidante for his ardour and the aria ends abruptly. Bishop's re-composition creates a Cherubino more in control. His Cherubino does not rush in after a few beats, but instead patiently waits for ten measures of added orchestral introduction. His melody, decorated with ornaments, calmed from Allegro Vivace to Allegro Moderato and tidied with two measures of orchestral closure, emerges less as mad rush than pleasant filigree. As the aria progresses, Bishop's more staid Cherubino fulfils the promise of a rondo that Mozart's page abandons. Bishop discards most of the end of the aria in favour of a repetition of the opening melody and an orderly orchestral close.

Example 2.4 'O this love 'tis a passion so pleasing', Bishop, arr., *Le nozze di Figaro*, mm. 1–26

Cherubino's new English text mirrors this more sedate score (see Table 2.4). Additional rhyme – aaab instead of aabc – makes the text more predictable and highlights the one non-rhyming word: 'love'. Da Ponte's fluid Italian text is slowed down by a rather lurching, consonant-heavy translation that is especially awkward at the upward leap on 'delightfully'. The meaning of the text also shifts. Instead of feeling beset by wild passions, Bishop's Cherubino is 'delightfully teased' by love. After each verse he returns to the rather objective query, 'who could exist without love?' While Da Ponte's Cherubino barely knows what could make him tremble in every woman's presence, Bishop's character seems perfectly aware of the vicissitudes of love.

Bishop may well have wished to contain Cherubino, who transgresses numerous dividing lines. Cherubino capitalises on the liminal moment between boyhood and

Example 2.4 (cont.)

manhood to cast aside norms of decorum, class and (as a trouser role) gender. Although Bishop kept Cherubino's oversexed outlook, he relieved it of much of its impropriety. In the dialogue surrounding 'Non so più', for example, Bishop carefully purged sexual innuendo from Cherubino's references to the Countess, even though Da Ponte had already cleansed much of this from Beaumarchais. Cherubino does not, as in

Table 2.4 *'Non so più cosa son, cosa faccio' compared to 'O' this love!'*

Da Ponte		Bishop
Non so più cosa son, cosa faccio,	What is this feeling, this mysterious yearning,	O' this love! 'tis a passion so pleasing,
or di foco, ora sono di ghiaccio,	One moment freezing, the next moment burning?	To my soul so delightfully teasing,
ogni donna cangiar di colore,	Each woman I see makes me turn pale,	In my heart either burning or freezing,
ogni donna mi fa palpitar.	Each woman I meet makes my heart pound.	Yet who could exist without love!
Solo ai nomi d'amor, di diletto,	The merest mention of love's sweet delight	All the day some fair maiden delights me,
mi si turba, mi s'altera il petto,	Gives my trembling heart a delicious fright.	Each fond glance I bestow she requites me,
e a parlare mi sforza d'amore	Love's fearsome power, or its least detail –	And her eye, then, so kindly invites me!
un desio ch'io non posso spiegar.	They threaten and tease me, thrill and confound!	O', who could exist without love!
Non so più cosa son, cosa faccio...	What is this feeling, this mysterious yearning ...	O' this love, &c.
Parlo d'amor vegliando,	I speak of love in my sleep,	When at night to my pillow retreating,
parlo d'amor sognando,	I speak of love till I weep ...	Ev'ry pulse is with extasy beating,
all'acque, all'ombre, ai monti,	To the streams, to the shadows, to the mountains,	While in dreams the past joy I'm repeating,
ai fiori, all'erbe, ai fonti,	To the flowers, to the meadows, to the fountains,	Oh, who could exist without love!
all'eco, all'aria, ai venti,	To the echo, to the air, to the breeze	Oh, this love, &c.[1]
che il suon de' vani accenti	Which carries my exquisite disease,	
portano via con sé.	Carries it off and away ...	
E se non ho chi m'oda,	And if no one listens, well,	
parlo d'amor con me.	I talk about love to myself!	

[1] McClatchy, trans., *Seven Mozart librettos*, pp. 304–5 and Bishop, *The marriage of Figaro* ... (London: John Miller, 1819), p. 8.

Da Ponte, envy Susanna for being able to 'dress [the Countess] each morning, undress her each night'. He more primly wishes he too could 'be always near her!'[54] Similarly, he cannot summon the courage to ask the Countess directly about love, as Mozart's page does with 'Voi che sapete'. Instead, Susanna sings a new ballad for him, 'Ne'er can the rose'. Bishop also downplays the gender confusion in Susanna's 'Venite inginocchiatevi', in which Susanna disguises as a woman a male character who is played by a woman impersonating a man. Before the aria even begins, Bishop trivialises

Cherubino's cross-dressing by making it a harmless game of dress-up. The Countess dismisses the plan of disguising Cherubino, since he might be discovered – in other words, since a man could never truly be mistaken for a woman. Susanna therefore puts female clothes on him simply to see how he would have looked.

Cherubino's transformation encapsulates in miniature Bishop's approach to *Figaro*. Focus shifted from song to speech, characters walked narrower moral paths and musical numbers adhered better to expected conventions. As with *Il barbiere*, Bishop leaned heavily on Beaumarchais for the core spoken drama. Mozart's opera he treated as it often was in the sheet music marketplace: as a collection of individual numbers to cut, reassign and recompose to suit his performers and patrons. In the process, however, Bishop also challenged his listeners to accept more music, and more dramatically important music, than they typically enjoyed. In 1810s London, the route to accustom playhouse audiences to Mozart was not through complete fidelity, but through a combination of Mozart's music and Beaumarchais' words.

THE PIPPIN AND THE PINEAPPLE

In 1814, *Jean de Paris* fitted so smoothly into established traditions of importing opéra comique that few critics paused to consider fidelity to Boieldieu carefully. With *Don Giovanni*, *Il barbiere* and *Figaro*, however, Bishop wandered into different territory. He challenged the core of opera in London – the King's Theatre – and adapted composers at the forefront of musical life. The critical stakes were therefore higher and reviewers' reactions exemplify the complex, often contradictory assessments of adaptation in the early nineteenth century.

Some critics advocated a complete rejection of change. The *Theatrical Inquisitor* stated, 'Whenever [*Il barbiere di Siviglia*] has been departed from it has been decidedly for the worse.' Hunt, writing in *The Examiner*, called the adapted *Don Giovanni* 'a wretched burlesque' that was 'barbarously mutilated'. Such statements tapped into burgeoning ideals of canonicity. Already in 1815, E.T.A. Hoffmann had described *Don Giovanni* in terms of unassailable organic unity: 'Each of the wonderful sounds ... is mysteriously subsumed into the whole, like rays of light refracted into a single focus. So it is that *Don Giovanni* will always appear mangled and mutilated if it is not given according to the original score.'[55] Many critics depicted change as an inevitably lowering process of this immutable masterpiece, motivated by poor performers, pecuniary concerns and audiences on the lower end of the social spectrum. Bacon felt that Bishop's interpolated ballad for Fiorello in *Il barbiere* was 'levelled rather to the genius of the singers at Vauxhall, than calculated to raise and refine the taste of the audience at the first of English theatres'. Such concerns tied into the larger rhetoric of theatrical decline. For critics, who largely belonged to the middle class, the idea of a theatre in which artistic worth was determined by the applause of a large, socially heterogeneous audience seemed to prostitute art to commerce. Adapters who altered revered masterpieces appeared to facilitate such decay.

Many critics, however, saw opportunity as well as danger in adaptation. Several years later, 'M' in the *Quarterly Musical Magazine and Review* advised managers rather condescendingly to 'endeavour to please the enlightened instead of astonishing the vulgar part of their audience, and they will find them both more constant in their attendance, as the latter are certain to drop insensibly into the taste of those who are better informed'.[56] In this view, the 'vulgar' would follow better taste if they were led to it by their social superiors. Adaptation thus possessed a potentially pedagogical function. The *Journal of Music and the Drama* declared fulsomely of *Figaro*, 'A zealous and honourable ambition to enrich and improve the music of his native stage, constituted Mr Bishop's only object in bringing forward the sublime compositions of Mozart, nor can we suppress our cordial approbation of so spirited and intelligent a measure.' Along the lines of modernised versions of classics in recent years – such as Baz Luhrmann's *Romeo and Juliet* – these adaptations seemed a useful 'halfway house' to lure new audiences to a finer taste. Writing approvingly of the Adelphi Theatre interpolating Mozart and Rossini arias into their entertainments a few years later, Hunt declared, 'While so many of the most beautiful compositions that genius has produced, are unknown except to the Opera and professional circles, it would add vastly to the public taste and amusement, if the Adelphi practice were more extended.'[57] As Hunt suggests, adaptation exposed a far broader audience to Mozart and Rossini than may otherwise have heard him.

An equation between more foreign music and higher native taste was, however, not quite so simple. Music was, after all, the defining feature of 'illegitimate' drama, which was considered inimical to the preservation of the legitimate, national drama. Far from honoured masterworks, these operas could seem interlopers on the spoken dramatic tradition. Theatre historian John Genest described *Figaro*, for example, as 'little more than [Holcroft's] Follies of a Day degraded to an opera'.[58] The fact that these operas were foreign deepened concerns, as Hunt related of the adapted *Don Giovanni*:

> when an attempt was made by some rash over-weening enthusiasts to *encore* the
> enchanting airs of Mozart . . . the English disdaining this insult offered to our native talents,
> *hissed* – in the plenitude of their pampered grossness, and 'ignorant impatience' of foreign
> refinement and elegance, they hissed! We believe that unconscious patriotism has something
> to do with this as well as sheer stupidity; they think that a taste for the Fine Arts, unless they
> are of British growth and manufacture, is a sign of disaffection to the Government.

Strict rhetoric against the decline of the native drama backfired, for audiences could turn patriotic ire indiscriminately towards anything foreign or musical, even Mozart opera.

Lumping all originals – and therefore all adaptations – together raised another thorny issue. Just as rejecting any foreign incursion into the native stage meant rejecting Mozart, insisting that fidelity be applied to all originals implied that all composers were equal. And critics decidedly did not view Rossini and Mozart as equal, as demonstrated by Ayrton's comparison to a pippin and a pineapple, quoted earlier. Mozart was already beginning to acquire his current canonical status. Alsager wrote of an 1818 King's Theatre revival of *Figaro*, 'If we can imagine a being to whom by long habit music has become a language, the depositary of the purest breathings of genius, that being is Mozart, and his *Figaro* is the most striking example.'[59] In contrast, Rossini was new to the operatic scene and two complaints that dogged him throughout his career emerged: his style was too facile, designed to dazzle the multitude and fatten his purse rather than impress the connoisseur; and haste made him unoriginal, reusing the same tricks and even the same material. Ayrton judged that 'Rossini, in becoming rich, has also become fond of money, and even indolent . . . in some of his later productions, there are not to be found more than one or two original passages; all the rest is little more than a new arrangement of old ideas.'[60] Rossini thus posed two problems – the commercialisation of taste and the devaluing of originality – that were precisely what canonisation meant to alleviate. Critics struggled to find an appropriate stance to adaptations of such dissimilar composers, cleverly encapsulated in Ayrton's pun. Just as 'apples' and 'pineapples' seem similar linguistically, but are vastly different in flavour and geographic origin, so did adapted Rossini and Mozart opera seem to be similar entities, but with different implications for musical taste.

This division had interesting ramifications for the reception of adaptation. For instance, Bacon did not view Bishop's changes to *Il barbiere* as proof of Bishop's inadequacy, but of Rossini's:

> we are inclined to doubt whether there be enough of ability in the entire original to justify any very considerable estimation of the composer's merits, or sufficient to warrant the transfer to the English stage. The latter question will, perhaps, be settled at once by our remarking, that the English selector has been able to use only six pieces . . . there must be obviously a greater reliance elsewhere for attraction than upon the music of Rossini.

From this perspective, adaptation functioned as a kind of judgment on the original work, culling only what was of sufficient worth to transfer to the new context.

Extending this attitude would have implicated Mozart, whose *Figaro* and *Don Giovanni* were similarly slimmed. Reviewers therefore pursued another rhetorical tack. Hunt, though despairing of the audience's reaction to *Don Giovanni*, insisted that 'Almost every thing else was against it, but the music triumphed.' After all, had it *not* triumphed, would that imply that Mozart's genius was not strong enough to survive the transplant? Ironically, embracing a canon could entail embracing changes to that canon. In the early nineteenth century, awash with excerpts, transcriptions and adaptations, a work's ability to mutate was crucial to its longevity. The *Theatrical Observer* explained of *Figaro* that 'The strongest proof . . . of the intrinsic merit and excellence of the piece proceeds from the variety of languages into which it has been translated; under each of which transmigrations, notwithstanding the difference of popular feeling, it has been a decided favourite.' Canonicity was achieved not by an unchanging work, but by a work that could withstand change.

The essentially contradictory nature of adaptation emerges. On one hand, it seemed to degrade masterpieces, on the other to garner new audiences and raise taste. Changes might be a comment on the failing of the original or a compromise for the failings of the new context. And foreign opera might bolster native drama or accelerate its decline. Divergent approaches to Mozart and Rossini underline that adaptation was not as simple as deeming all change bad, all fidelity good. Much depended on the effect of the adaptation, the spirit in which it was proffered and the perceived worth of the original adapted, whether common pippin or prized pineapple.

In the early 1820s, it seemed that operatic adaptation was passé. The adaptations of the 1810s continued to enjoy a few performances each season, but no new adaptations appeared from 1821 to 1823. This drought ended in the summer of 1824, when a minor theatre, the English Opera House, chanced a production of Weber's *Der Freischütz*. Immediately, a craze for the opera erupted. As detailed in Appendix 1, no fewer than seven other London theatres offered their own adaptations within the next four months.

These proliferating versions represented a turning point in London operatic life. The playhouses vaulted to the forefront of important continental operatic developments, as they presented the London première of an important new German work. The King's Theatre, entrenched in Italianate, all-sung repertoire, did not respond until 1832, when a travelling German troupe performed *Der Freischütz*, although there were rumours of a production in 1825.[1] If 'intransigence' against adaptation had prevailed, as Mark Everist remarks of a similar situation with *Der Freischütz* in France, Weber's opera would have been kept out of 'musical and dramatic thinking' for a generation.[2] The minor theatres, which had not showed great interest in adapted opera in the past, now became serious contenders. *Der Freischütz* proved an ideal entry point into foreign opera because its melodramatic plot and catchy score suited their repertoire. Their success prompted them to become increasingly competitive in this arena. Weber's opera also challenged Britons' aversion to the fusion of music and drama. Initially, adapters made significant changes to *Der Freischütz*. By the last few adaptations, however, the familiarity of the opera emboldened adapters to dare a previously impossible level of fidelity. Many critics hailed *Der Freischütz* as the dawn of improved native musical taste. Others, however, expressed ambivalence at its specifically German features, which fuelled debates about the nature of German music and drama. Regardless, *Der Freischütz*'s popularity was so staggering that imported opera became firmly entrenched in the playhouse repertoire. As George Herbert Rodwell phrased it, 1824 was the year when 'the flood-gates of foreign music were thrown open'.[3]

THE PATH TO *DER FREISCHÜTZ*

With hindsight, contemporaries found it difficult to believe that the playhouses had not produced *Der Freischütz* earlier. In 1833, Edward Holmes castigated Henry Bishop as 'a very child in deciding upon the fit and unfit, to command success', citing as evidence that he 'gave it as his opinion that the *Freischütze* [*sic*] would never succeed here'.[4] In the early 1820s, however, several factors made operatic adaptation as a whole seem undesirable. Issues of personnel and management thwarted adaptation. This was especially true at Covent Garden, which had been almost solely responsible for operatic imports thus far. In 1817, John Philip Kemble, manager since 1803, retired, leaving the reins mainly to Thomas Harris and his son Henry. It was precisely from 1817 until 1820, when the elder Harris died, that Bishop's ambitious adaptations of Mozart and Rossini appeared. After Harris' death, the theatre disintegrated into a series of lawsuits among the multiple shareholders of its patent, culminating in bankruptcy proceedings in 1829.[5] 1820 was also the year when soprano Maria Dickons, who had shouldered the most difficult roles in *Il barbiere di Siviglia* and *Le nozze di Figaro*, retired. The leading singers of the early 1820s, Ann Maria Tree and Catherine Stephens, were certainly accomplished, but not sufficiently so for Covent Garden to continue to mimic the King's Theatre's repertoire, which at this time focused almost entirely on the challenging roulades of Rossini.[6] In 1822, Kemble's brother Charles assumed management, along with shareholders John S. Willett and John Forbes, and ousted Henry Harris with the promise of an annuity. In the same year, two prominent performers in these adaptations, John Liston and Catherine Stephens, moved to Drury Lane, apparently as a result of contract disputes.[7] By 1824, Harris sued the management for not paying the annuity and in the same year Bishop left for the rival house. Such a hostile managerial environment alienated personnel and seems to have proved unfavourable for imported opera.

Managers may also simply have turned to more lucrative possibilities. The longest initial run for an operatic adaptation was twenty-one performances for *Don Giovanni*, a respectable but modest number. In the early 1820s, other avenues seemed more promising. For a brief moment, one was native opera. Bishop's *Clari* (1823) stretched to forty-eight performances in 1823–4, thirty–one in 1825–6 and its most popular number, 'Home sweet home', became an enduring hit. The most profitable fad was for Sir Walter Scott adaptations. Some forty adaptations appeared at London theatres between 1810 and 1827, over half within the period 1820–4.[8]

No wonder, then, that the opera that finally ended this lull was *Der Freischütz*, which matched the craze for Scott's dark, Gothic tales. Germany had long been seen as an incubator for the bizarre and supernatural. Scott himself called it perhaps the only 'country or language' where 'the FANTASTIC mode of writing – in which the most wild and unbounded license is given to an irregular fancy', could have 'made its way'.[9] German imports had already appeared in the 1790s, with a period of 'German-mania' for plays by such authors as August Friedrich Ferdinand von Kotzebue.[10] The early 1820s saw the rage for wild, Teutonic tales continue, as translations of German ghost stories and E. T. A. Hoffmann tales appeared in print and several theatres staged the Faust legend.[11] Weber's *Der Freischütz* fitted effortlessly with these works' legendary, macabre flavour. As Michael Tusa explains, *Der Freischütz* appealed largely because it satisfied what contemporaries considered quintessentially German:

> The qualities of *Der Freischütz* that nineteenth-century audiences and critics identified as German (and thus helped to make it so overwhelmingly popular from the outset) were the particulars of the opera: the Bohemian forest village setting; the folkloric, natural, and supernatural elements of the story; the uncomplicated faith of the heroine Agathe and the benevolent Eremit; and the folk-like simplicity of much of the music.[12]

Londoners soon showed interest in *Der Freischütz*, but managers only gradually contemplated staging it. Approximately a year after the opera premièred in June 1821, Boosey brought out a score of the opera and in 1823–4 *The Harmonicon* featured articles about Weber and sheet music excerpts from *Der Freischütz*.[13] The tale on which the libretto was based appeared in translation in 1823, as 'The fatal marksman', and a play of the same name appeared at the Coburg Theatre in February 1824.[14] Sir George Smart performed the overture at the Philharmonic concerts around the same time, and its popularity apparently helped encourage theatres to perform the opera.[15] In 1822–3, Barham Livius travelled to Germany, visited Weber and obtained scores of *Der Freischütz* and *Abu Hassan*, intending to adapt and sell them to the patent theatres. By November 1823, Covent Garden manager Charles Kemble had Livius' adapted libretto, prepared with Washington Irving, but apparently they could not agree on a price. Kemble also may not have been satisfied with the adaptation, since James Robinson Planché was later brought in to revise the work.[16] Trepidation about the opera's success also caused delay. At a read-through of the opera to determine whether the work should be produced at the English Opera House, one of the performers, Henry Phillips, remembered that 'some thought it in parts too hideous, others that the music was wild and extravagant, and would never suit the English taste'.[17] Nevertheless, newspapers reported a forthcoming production at Covent Garden as early as January 1824 and in June it was even stated that the theatre intended to hire Weber as music director.[18] They delayed too long, though. The English Opera House produced the 'hideous' work in July 1824, when the patent theatres were closed for the summer season, and Covent Garden could not retaliate until their theatre re-opened in October. By then, virtually every theatre in London had brought out their versions and *Der Freischütz* mania was widespread.

THE LONDON PREMIÈRE

The theatre that captured the London première of *Der Freischütz*, the English Opera House, was a minor theatre that occupied an interesting limbo between major and minor theatre offerings. Manager Samuel James Arnold interpreted the centrality of music to 'illegitimate' theatre to mean that he could stage operas. Contemporaries found this an odd use of the term, as William Ayrton expressed: 'in defiance of common sense, operas only are allowed to be heard'.[19] Only luck allowed Arnold to create this loophole in the meaning of illegitimate. His father had unsuccessfully attempted to obtain a licence for opera and musical entertainments in 1792. In 1809, however, Drury Lane burned down and the company moved to the English Opera House until their theatre was rebuilt in 1812. Apparently as a result of his generosity and his involvement in Drury Lane as manager and author (he had adapted *Jean de Paris*), Arnold managed to retain a licence for musical works at the English Opera House. In 1815–16 he became so optimistic that he rebuilt the English Opera House on a lavish scale, with an array of private boxes clearly geared towards a higher class of clientele than typically frequented minor theatres. The patent theatres managed to have Arnold's privileged licence revoked for this audacity, much to his financial despair. Thereafter he remained, like all minor theatre managers, dependent on the vicissitudes of patent theatre managers and licensers. He succeeded, however, in keeping his operatic ambitions alive. He performed Covent Garden's adaptations of Mozart and Rossini at the English Opera House in the early 1820s and with *Der Freischütz*, he began to compete with the patent theatres for important premières of both foreign and native operas.[20]

Der Freischütz offered an ideal opportunity to move from copier to leader. Like Arnold's theatre, the opera fell somewhere between legitimate and illegitimate fare. It featured the spoken dialogue utilised at both major and minor houses and even included an entirely spoken role, Samiel. The wild, supernatural plot of Kind's libretto and the sensational Wolf's Glen scene resonated with the melodramas and Gothic dramas that were supposed to be the purview of the minor houses, but that crept into the major theatres as well. Weber's score was far more complex than the usual minor theatre production, but it also offered ample catchy tunes. Arnold, along with composer William Hawes and librettist W. McGregor Logan, was therefore able to retain the opera in a far more complete form than previous adaptations.[21] For the first time, Hawes did not cut any numbers, even lengthy, kinetic ensembles of the type usually discarded (see Table 3.1).[22] He did, however, alter, reassign or rearrange several of them and added four solos and two duets.[23] Most notably, he and his librettists made Caspar a spoken role and delegated his music to a new character, Rollo. The English Opera House adapters thus both conformed to and challenged playhouse norms.

Hawes sought to preserve and expand the most appealing portion of Weber's score: the catchy strophic numbers, which some scholars have seen as part of Weber's indebtedness to *opéra comique*.[24] These numbers were especially attractive because many thought they had been drawn from German folk tunes. Ayrton wrote, 'Those who have heard the beautiful national melodies, which are so frequently sung in every part of Germany ... will agree, that *Der Freischütz* is not *original*, at least, so far as melody is concerned.'[25] Such tunes tapped into the enormous popularity of 'national melodies'

Table 3.1 *Weber's* Der Freischütz *compared to adaptations at the English Opera House, Covent Garden and Drury Lane*

Weber Der Freischütz	English Opera House[1]	Covent Garden[2]	Drury Lane
Overture	Retained[3]	Probably retained	Retained
Act I			
Introduktion 'Viktoria, der Meister soll leben!'	Retained	Probably retained	Retained
Terzett mit Chor 'O! diese Sonne' Max, Cuno, Caspar, Chorus	Retained; Rollo sings Cuno's line	Probably altered and moved to the end of act one	Retained
Walzer, Rezitativ und Arie 'Nein! länger trag' ich nicht die Qualen' Max	Retained	Probably retained	Retained
Lied 'Hier im ird'schen Jammerthal' Caspar	Retained; sung by Rollo[4]	Retained; sung by the First Hunter and moved to II ii	Retained
Arie 'Schweig, schweig' Caspar	Retained; sung by Rollo	Cut	Retained
Act II			
Duett 'Schelm, halt' fest!' Agathe, Aennchen	Altered; later cut	Probably retained	Altered
	Solo added for Agathe, based on Weber's 'Lied der Hirtin', Op. 71 No. 5[5]		
Ariette 'Kommt ein schlanker Bursch gegangen' Aennchen	Altered	Probably retained and moved to I ii	Retained
Szene und Arie 'Wie nahte mir der Schlummer' Agathe	Retained	Retained	Retained
	Duet added for Aennchen and Max, based on a German melody[6]		
Terzett 'Wie? Was? Entsetzen!' Agathe, Aennchen, Max	Altered	Probably altered	Altered
	Solo added for Max, based on a German melody		
Finale Die Wolfsschlucht	Retained	Probably altered	Retained
Act III			
Entre-Akt	Retained	Unknown	Cut
	Solo added for Max, based on a German melody[7]	Solo added for Max; origin unknown[8]	Chorus added[9]
Kavatine 'Und ob die Wolke' Agathe	Retained	Probably retained	Retained
Romanze, Rezitativ und Arie 'Einst träumte' Aennchen	Altered	Cut	Altered
Volkslied 'Wir winden dir den Jungfernkranz' Chorus	Retained	Probably retained	Retained

Table 3.1 (*cont.*)

Weber *Der Freischütz*	English Opera House[1]	Covent Garden[2]	Drury Lane
Jägerchor 'Was gleicht wohl auf Erden' Chorus	Retained; moved to beginning of act three Solo added for Agathe, based on a German melody Duet added for Max and Agathe, based on a German melody	Probably retained	Retained
Finale 'Schaut, o schaut!'	Altered	Portion retained as duet for Max and Agathe in III i	Altered

[1] This table is based on the printed piano–vocal score published by the Royal Harmonic Institution. Other sources for the adaptation diverge somewhat, especially the score published by Cramer, Addison, and Beale c. 1841, which may represent a later, more faithful version. Various alterations were also made in subsequent performances, as discussed in *The Harmonicon*, September 1824, 174.

[2] Only three numbers of Livius' score are intact. All other comparisons are based on the libretti sources and therefore 'probably' is used.

[3] 'Retained' indicates that a number was kept with no to little change, 'altered' that it was kept with more substantial changes.

[4] The libretto lists Rollo as the singer for this and the following aria. The score announces that the pieces were sung by Mr Phillips, who played Rollo, but lists the character as Caspar.

[5] This solo, along with the new solo for Agathe in act three and the new duet in act three, were not in the original adaptation but were added soon after, in the middle of August, when Catherine Stephens succeeded Miss Noel as Agathe. Agathe and Aennchen's duet was also cut at this time.

[6] This is only in the manuscript libretto (crossed out) and was probably cut before performance.

[7] Different text for this solo exists in the manuscript libretto, printed libretto and printed score.

[8] A chorus of hunters is also added, but is in the manuscript libretto only and probably was not performed.

[9] In the score, this is 'Hymn to the virgin' by Bishop. The manuscript and printed libretti instead use an unattributed chorus, 'Jubilate! Jubilate!'

from various countries around the world, which offered an enticing aural 'other' placed reassuringly within familiar harmonic and formal frameworks.[26] They also marked *Der Freischütz* as quintessentially German, which fed fascination with exoticism and *couleur locale*. Hawes therefore not only kept numbers such as the Bridesmaids' and Hunters' choruses scrupulously intact, but added six new, similar numbers. To extend the German folk flavour of the score, Hawes drew these works either from Weber's other compositions or from unidentified German melodies.[27] Here emerges an interesting development in fidelity. In his review of the adaptation for *The Harmonicon*, Ayrton protested that 'any additions . . . should undoubtedly have been made from Weber's own works'. (See Appendix 2 for review citations.) It was not the fact that Hawes had added numbers that troubled Ayrton, but that they were not all by Weber. This attitude would inform many adaptations from the mid 1820s to the late 1830s. Adapters cultivated fidelity to a composer more than to a work and in the process echoed the kind of self-borrowing or substitution that composers themselves often employed.

Weber's score was not, however, all catchy, strophic numbers, nor did his use of spoken dialogue mean that he separated all music and action. Much of his score presented the other side of German musical style, learned, serious and recondite. Tusa notes how *Der Freischütz* encapsulated both accessible and abstruse facets of German music: 'Weber's aesthetics and compositional style modeled early nineteenth-century concepts of "Germanness" – stereotypes like simplicity, depth, naturalness, thoroughness'.[28]

Clearly determined to present as much of Weber's score as possible, Hawes did not cut these numbers, but altered many of them drastically. The trio 'Wie? Was? Entsetzen!', for example, Hawes transformed from an extended conclusion for II iii to a brief, lyrical moment within the scene. Weber's trio begins with two dramatic sections, first Allegro and then Vivace con fuoco, in which Agathe and Aennchen express horror that Max plans to enter the Wolf's Glen, moves to a gentle Andantino in which the lovers say farewell and ends with a brisk Allegro vivace as the ladies exhort Max to caution and he hurries out. To downplay the ensemble's dramatic significance and to avoid its abrupt changes of mood, extended contrapuntal passages and dearth of lyricism, Hawes severely curtailed it and placed it in the midst of the dialogue. Hawes retained only the first and third sections. At the mention of the Wolf's Glen, Agathe began the trio with Weber's agitated Allegro. After only 28 measures, however, as opposed to 141 in the original, Hawes moved to the affectionate Andantino farewell, skipping over the entire Vivace con fuoco. Hawes ended the ensemble here, in this sweet, lyrical vein, instead of continuing to the agitated Allegro vivace. In addition, Max did not exit directly after the ensemble, but participated in further dialogue that contained the essential plot information. The scene ended not with Max's rushed exit, but with his calm farewell to Agathe in a new ballad based on a German tune. Instead of one, culminating, complex musical outburst, therefore, Hawes offered two brief, lyrical miniatures that relieved rather than heightened the action.

A desire to separate action and music also prompted the most striking alteration: the split of Caspar into two roles, a completely spoken Caspar and his new singing confidante Rollo. As noted in previous chapters, this provided the prominent, spoken male role that featured in both native operas and adaptations. Henry Phillips, the first Rollo, identified casting difficulties as the cause for the split: '[Caspar] was considered of importance as an acting part, and the music most important and difficult. No doubt seemed to exist but that I was the person to sing it; but I was too young and inexperienced to act it. So, as a last resource, they resolved to cut Caspar in two, and create me Rollo, his companion.'[29] Caspar went to George John Bennett, an actor who had aspired to tragic Shakespearean roles but found a better niche in melodrama, especially 'terrific personages'.[30] Nevertheless, Catherine Jones observes that Caspar's new lines echo Shakespearean and Faustian language, linking the role with the tradition of legitimate drama.[31] It was not that Phillips could not act at all, therefore, but that he could not act to the high standards expected of prominent actors in legitimate drama. This did not mean, however, that the music was considered completely expendable, nor that such roles always had to be divided. In fact, there is no Rollo in the manuscript libretto, which was submitted to the Lord Chamberlain's office for censorship on 29 June, only a few weeks before the première on 22 July. The adapters clearly thought until the last minute that they could keep the role as is. Even once the split was made, Hawes preferred the dramatic awkwardness of the Rollo character to discarding the music. As Phillips described, both acting and music were considered 'important', so important that separate specialists needed to assume each.

This was especially true since Hawes kept both of Caspar's challenging arias relatively intact. In particular, 'Schweig, schweig' paints a menacing picture of Caspar's evil. Weber's fluid form swings from a supple, recitative-like vocal line to intimidating, virtuosic runs and concludes with a reminiscence of the shrill piccolo flourish from Caspar's previous aria, 'Hier im ird'schen Jammertal'. Richard Mackenzie Bacon observed in the *Quarterly Musical Magazine and Review*, 'With respect to the voice part it cannot fairly be said to be vocal. The succession of half tones is so continual, that the best trained voice may be gravelled by the attempt.' While the aria is an effectively chilling portrait of Caspar, it hardly accords with the simple ballads beloved on the British stage, nor does it even suit the bravura tradition, which tended to be formally straightforward and focused on more formulaic vocal pyrotechnics. The fact that Hawes did not cut a single measure of this demanding aria testifies both to his desire to bring the opera to London in as complete a form as possible and to the value he placed on a performer able to tackle such a piece.

Hawes further challenged playhouse norms by retaining the Wolf's Glen scene virtually verbatim. This scene seems to violate all that British playhouse audiences held dear. Weber's lengthy score flits from one idea to the next, rarely offering any sing-able tunes and following only the form of the dramatic action itself. Yet, this scene, retained in its entirety, was crucial to the work's success in London. Sheer visual display accounted for much of its appeal. The *Theatrical Observer* called the scene 'decidedly the *ne plus ultra* of the terrific' (see Figure 3.1). It thrust viewers into a gory world of nocturnal creatures and supernatural monsters, experienced more vividly in an unusually darkened auditorium.[32] Such a scene tapped into the rage for dark, super-natural tales, capitalised on the popularity of novelties such as the phantasmagoria and fitted seamlessly with the visually sensational genre of melodrama.[33] The affinity to melodrama also helped audiences accept the kinetic music. Bacon perceived that 'The clear distinct train of association which is kept up throughout ... and [the music's] power in awakening those emotions, which are appropriate to every various situation in the scene, raise it to the highest rank as melo-dramatic music.' Here, Bacon means

Figure 3.1 Title Page, Hawes, arr., *Der Freischütz*

the kind of fluid instrumental passages that intertwined with action in melodrama. Playhouse audiences may have been averse to extended, action-based ensembles, but they were well familiar with melodramatic music. This familiarity, coupled with the entrancing visual display, helped them embrace Weber's fluid setting.

The English Opera House adaptation of *Der Freischütz* was both ambitious and cautious. Despite concerns that the music might be too 'wild and extravagant' for British taste, Hawes did not cut any numbers. He challenged audiences to accept long ensembles, fluid arias and, especially, the confluence of music and action in the Wolf's Glen scene. But he compensated for this by trimming most of the longest pieces, extracting them from the action and splitting the dramatically important role of Caspar into acting and singing characters. Hawes also significantly expanded the most appealing aspect of Weber's score: the simple, tuneful numbers imbued with the allure of an idyllic German folk culture.

MELODRAMATIC WEBER: MINOR THEATRE ADAPTATIONS

Emboldened by the English Opera House's successful foray into adapted opera, three other minor theatres – the Royal Amphitheatre, the West London Theatre and the Surrey – squeezed *Der Freischütz* onto their roster within the next two months.[34] These houses could not hope to mimic Arnold, Logan and Hawes' ambitious presentation of almost the entire score. With fewer musical resources and no privileged history, as the English Opera House had, of quasi-legitimate offerings, they exploited the one convergence between *Der Freischütz* and their usual fare: melodrama.[35] Bacon realised that *Der Freischütz* seemed almost more suited for this genre than opera, at least on the British stage. Its plot was 'of the most romantic and mysterious nature, such indeed as no English dramatist would I conceive venture to produce to his countrymen in any other way than as a melo-drame of dumb-show'. Certainly, *Der Freischütz* conformed to several key requisites of melodrama: the picturesque setting; the devoted romantic pair threatened by a demonic villain; and, especially, the colossal visual portrayal of evil in the Wolf's Glen scene. *Der Freischütz* was not fully melodramatic, however, and minor theatre adapters refashioned the work to suit the even more spectacular extremes their patrons relished.

The most crucial divergence between melodrama and Kind's libretto occasioned the most change: the lack of a spotless hero. Max weakly submits to the lure of the magic bullets and his conflict centres more within himself than with the villain. Mark F. Doerner argues that a layer of adaptation had already taken place; Kind had himself conformed the original tale to more melodramatic standards, rendering Max a less vacillating hero and strengthening the opposition of good and evil.[36] Minor theatre adapters went even further. Most radically, for the Royal Amphitheatre J. H. Amherst completely eliminated Max's submission. He removed the temptation of the trial shot by dispensing with it at the beginning; Caspar wins, but Max simply has to wait before marrying Agathe rather than losing her altogether. Max ventures to the Wolf's Glen not to cast bullets, but to return a favour Caspar paid him. Amherst moved temptation away from the trial shot and towards the common melodramatic lures of wealth and status. In the glen, Caspar entices Max with visions of rank and riches. Unlike Kind's Max, however, this hero heeds his mother's ghost, who spells out melodrama's valuation of inner worth over outer riches: 'sell not thy soul for wealth or honours which must perish: hold fast thy faith; lift thy thoughts from earth to heaven'.[37] Amherst thus eliminated the main reason for Max's weakness – his desire for the magic bullets – and substituted a didactic example of virtue triumphing over vice.

Other adapters took more circuitous routes to fulfil melodrama's need for incorruptible virtue. At the Surrey, for example, Edward Fitzball kept the trial shot and Max's equivocal behaviour, but added a trial of Agathe's virtue. Caspar, needful of additional victims besides Max, lights on Agathe. Beholden to Caspar for past assistance, Agathe at first agrees to aid him. When the evils of the satanic compact he wishes her to sign with his blood become too evident, however, she refuses: 'I would beg, suffer, perish, to repay an act of kindness; but a thousand and a thousand times will I undergo death, rather than subscribe to an act from which nature and religion teach me to recoil.'[38] Incorruptible feminine virtue featured in many melodramas, often, as here, to expiate the sins of less steadfast characters.

To throw the purity of hero and heroine into greater relief, adapters also deepened Caspar's villainy. Added claps of thunder, flashes of lightning and withered flowers accompanied his evil deeds. Utilising the transparent rhetoric of melodrama, new text more clearly spelled out his depraved desires. Amherst's Caspar, for example, gleefully anticipates how he will 'urge [Max] to accept the magic bullets which I'll pilfer from him, trample on his bleeding bosom, and before his aching eyes clasp shrieking [Agathe] to my marble heart'.[39]

In melodrama's didactic universe, such evil always proved its own punishment. All of these versions more emphatically stressed the wages of sin, most spectacularly with new endings that foreground Caspar's demise. Kind's original conclusion mitigates several important messages of melodrama. Kind dispenses with Caspar's downfall quickly and devotes most of the finale to the Hermit's ruminations. The Hermit not only diverts attention from Caspar's ruin, but lectures that all are susceptible to vice, that forgiveness is essential and that much of the blame must fall to the societal convention of the shooting contest. These Christian ideals characterise good and evil too relatively for the polar extremes of melodrama. Adapters therefore redirected the denouement towards Caspar's ghastly downfall. The Hermit's lines either disappear or drastically decrease. Max's transgression draws little attention. Instead, Caspar's horrific sufferings viscerally underline the consequences of sin. The end of John Kerr's version, for example, epitomises melodrama's blend of the sensational and the didactic:

> *[Caspar] fires, as he supposes, the sixth bullet – suddenly a whirlwind ensues – the forest is scattered to the earth, and a dreary glen opens to the view, in the midst of which [Samiel] is beheld on his sable charger . . . [Samiel] fires at [Caspar], who is engulphed in the earth, surrounded by demons and torturing fiends . . . [Ottokar], in pantomime, expresses that the fate of [Caspar] must ever afford an example to mankind, that vice, though it may triumph for a period, is ever certain of meeting dreadful punishment.*[40]

In melodrama, these stark oppositions of good and evil often received relief and reinforcement from comic, simpleminded but ultimately moral characters. All three of these versions lightened the original with such characters. Kerr added entirely new comics: a pair of clueless servants, Tregora and Zenza, and a drunk huntsman, Roberto. The other two adaptations enlarged the closest approximation of a comic role in the original: Kilian. Adapters expanded the simple huntsman into one of the two comic types prevalent in British melodrama: the traditional fault-ridden but good-hearted comic and the innocent simpleton who instinctively discerns good from evil. At the Surrey, Kilian provides comic relief with his simpleminded tactlessness and hopelessly inflated self-image. His bumbling attempts to partake in the shooting contest and to console Agathe display the comic's risible ineptitude: '[Max's] going to be hanged, but you can't help that you know ... but don't you cry; there are plenty who will be glad to have you; I will if you'll wait till [Aennchen's] dead.'[41] At the Royal Amphitheatre, in contrast, Amherst's Kilian abandons low comic for wise fool. The other characters pity him as 'poor foolish [Kilian]', yet his moral barometer immediately distinguishes hero from villain and his machinations deprive Caspar of the magic bullets at the end.[42] He exults at Caspar's demise:

> [CASPAR]: ... No, it cannot be; yet [Max] is unhurt, – and o'er my heart a mortal sickness comes. It must be, I have lost my sixth strong magic bullet; am I foil'd by fiends from nether hell. Who has done this deed?
> [KILIAN]: I, [Kilian]! the fool and lunatic ... Thy cowardice and treachery in provoking [Max] 'gainst infernal odds is furnish'd by a fool.[43]

Unfortunately, scores are not extant for these productions, but it is clear that the minor theatres offered far less music than their better-equipped competitors. The West London libretto contains no vocal numbers, only indications for 'music', or instrumental, melodramatic accompaniment. It is unknown whether these were drawn from Weber's score or newly composed. The other two versions contain similar indications, but also seem to have retained a few of Weber's most popular, accessible numbers, such as the overture and the Hunters' and Bridesmaids' choruses. Even this much, however, was considered a novel draw. The Royal Amphitheatre playbill advertised 'the Original Music & Celebrated Overture by the Popular German Composer, CARL MARIA VON WEBER *Which engages the Assistance of a largely encreased Orchestra, and many additional Choristers*'.[44] Fitzball, in his preface to the Surrey adaptation, attributed any success of his version to 'the harp of Weber', whose 'thrilling, grand, and horrific chords had the power to throw over the whole of my poor compound an air of re-animating, stormy, awful grandeur'.[45] Minor theatre adapters may have drastically curtailed Weber's score, but they simultaneously vaunted its presence, desirous of even a portion of opera's cultural cachet.

These versions of *Der Freischütz* began a pattern that was to expand in succeeding decades. Minor theatres increasingly competed with major theatres for the latest operatic hits, not in operatic form, but in melodramatised re-imaginings of the libretto adorned with the most popular, accessible musical extracts. The power of the original paradoxically entailed its alteration, as even those theatres least musically equipped for foreign opera sought to capitalise on its growing appeal.

'STALE AS MACKEREL A MONTH OLD': MAJOR THEATRE ADAPTATIONS

In November 1824, the *European Magazine* exclaimed, '*Der Freischütz*, after going the round for several months of all the theatres in London, has actually been brought out at Drury, when it is as stale as mackerel a month old, and when every body is almost sick of the very name of it!' Because their seasons did not begin until the autumn, Covent Garden and Drury Lane were obliged to bring up the rear. Their renditions seemed especially repetitive, since performers who had already appeared in the English Opera House adaptation filled several principal roles.[46] Although it was typical for patent theatre performers to seek summer engagements at minor and provincial theatres, there had not been quite as close a correlation between major and minor theatre casts before. In addition, Drury Lane adapters George Soane and Henry Bishop and Covent Garden adapters Barham Livius and James Robinson Planché pushed the opera in the same melodramatic direction as their minor theatre competitors.[47] For those who bemoaned the decline of legitimate drama into the illegitimate realm of spectacle and sound, this seemed an especially blatant example.

Nevertheless, these 'stale' versions enjoyed stunning success. The Covent Garden ledgers demonstrate how the adaptation almost singlehandedly erased crippling debts.[48] At Drury Lane, the opera stretched to seventy-two performances in the first season, an unprecedented number that was almost double the usual longest run of the season. Partially, success stemmed from these theatres' superior resources. Both houses augmented their orchestra and chorus for the occasion. Their renowned scenic departments plumbed the horrific possibilities of the Wolf's Glen scene until, as *The Examiner* described of Drury Lane, 'the conceptions of *hellish* Breughell [*sic*] are almost exhausted'.[49] Both also attempted to keep as much of Weber's score as possible but still had to make several changes. Their efforts underline the importance of fidelity as a marketing strategy, demonstrate what was still considered too challenging for their audience and represent important breakthroughs in both fidelity and taste.

As in previous versions, the patent theatre adaptations nudged hero and villain towards the starker extremes of melodrama. At Covent Garden, Livius, finding Kind's Max 'a feeble undecided character; half saint, half sinner', created the most spotless melodramatic hero yet.[50] His Max not only spurns Caspar's magic bullets, but refuses to enter the Wolf's Glen at all. At first tempted by the sure shots, Max is jolted back to his senses as he recognises the implications of his decision:

> CASPAR ... What, dost thou still hesitate ... So that the gift be good, what matters it whether from spirit good or evil – from heaven or from hell?
>
> [MAX] (*Starting at the last word.*) Ha! I wake as if from a dream ... I spurn thy proffered services! All magic aid, if such there be, I scorn! On heaven and honest skill I rest my hopes, nor seek, by juggling arts, to cozen fortune.[51]

Typical of the just universe of melodrama, Max's fortitude results in regained shooting skill. Meanwhile, Caspar ensnares not Max but foolhardy Kilian.

In his preface, Livius claimed purely moral motives for the change: 'Various objections having been taken against the German drama, especially with reference to poetical justice, and to the moral, the author ... has been induced to vary considerably from the original.'[52] This statement suggests that fidelity was beginning to be viewed as a requisite, something whose absence required explanation. Fidelity also served as a convenient screen for Livius' more pressing motivation: to conform Max to a more melodramatic aesthetic. Given the link between melodrama and illegitimacy, Livius was careful to distance his major theatre adaptation from any taint of minor theatre motives.

If the Covent Garden adaptation offered the purest hero, the Drury Lane version concentrated on the most tortured villain. Soane added a new scene devoted to the inner torments that often rack melodrama's miscreants. Cuno implores Caspar to forsake evil: 'the old man kneels to you – prays to you ... deny your master! return to heaven!' Eventually, Caspar relents and attempts to enter the church. Samiel, however, foils him in visually stunning fashion: 'As [Caspar] *approaches the entrance, a broad flash of light passes across it, and* [S]AMIEL *stands before him.* CASPAR *rushes back with a cry of horror. A wild burst of wind closes the glass doors.* CASPAR *sinks to the ground.'*[53]

Spectacular as it might have been, the scene ran afoul of the censor. In 1824, George Colman had succeeded John Larpent as licenser of plays. Colman had been a risqué playwright but became, to everyone's surprise, a severe censor, particularly in religious matters.[54] Whereas Larpent had let 'devil' and 'damned' appear in *Il barbiere di Siviglia* and *Le nozze di Figaro* without comment, Colman struck 'damn' and even 'for heaven's sake' from *Der Freischütz*. No wonder, then, that he objected to the religious references that saturated this scene. Bertram calls Caspar's attention to 'the sounds of Easter morn', urges him 'onward to the church' and reminds him of 'the solemn pledge, once spoken by the lips of heaven ... Mercy to all sinners! Salvation to all that would be saved.'[55] Colman allowed the premise of the scene, but demanded a complete rewrite that eliminated all direct religious references. Soane bowed to these objections and rewrote the scene twice, a process that helped delay Drury's production to last place.[56] Theatres, however, usually paid lip service to the censor on paper and then produced the offending original onstage, since the censor rarely checked up on his directives in practice.[57] It is possible that this happened with the offending scene in Soane's *Der Freischütz*, since it appeared in the printed libretto, objectionable material reinstated.

While major theatre adapters joined their minor theatre competitors in making the libretto more melodramatic, they attempted to distance themselves with more faithful scores. At Covent Garden, Livius asserted in his preface that his 'chief attention and anxiety' was 'to preserve [the score] entire and uninjured'.[58] Yet, he made Caspar a completely spoken role, dropped Aennchen's and Caspar's second solos, added a solo for Max, heavily abridged most of the ensembles and rearranged several numbers (see Table 3.1). Clearly, Livius wanted to capitalise on the growing importance of deference to the original author, but his alterations pinpoint the places where he felt he had to conform the opera to British expectations. Keeping Caspar a spoken role underlined the continuing link between dramatic importance and speech. The slimmed ensembles also attested to this aesthetic. This can be seen especially well in the lengthy finale to the opera. Livius did not use Weber's finale to end the opera, but instead fulfilled melodramatic conventions with a scenically stunning tableau as the Wild Huntsman drags Caspar off to an ignoble demise. Yet, he did not discard all of Weber's finale. A portion served as a duet for Max and Agathe at the end of III i, rectifying the unusual lack of a lovers' duet in the original. Ensembles were not always to be shunned, though. One commentator felt that the final number in act one, Caspar's 'Schweig, Schweig', 'though a powerful piece for stage effect, [was] not . . . as well adapted for the conclusion of an act as a concerted piece or a chorus'.[59] To supply the more familiar ensemble at the end of the act, Livius cut the aria and transplanted a slimmed version of the trio and chorus 'O! diese Sonne' from the middle of act one to its end. Overall, Livius' 'preservation' of Weber's score demonstrates the boundaries of fidelity. As long as the score's recognisable core was retained, however rearranged or reassigned, its more obscure fringe could be cut, slimmed or augmented to suit the new venue.

Yet, this fluid view of fidelity was beginning to harden. The popularity of *Der Freischütz* laid the groundwork for greater fidelity. At Drury Lane, Bishop, emboldened by the success of a score many had thought too abstruse for British taste and in desperate need of novelty as he brought up the rear, paid more than lip service to fidelity (see Table 3.1). True, Bishop added a chorus for the new scene, in which Caspar attempted to repent, and slimmed Aennchen's second solo and several of the ensembles. Yet, in some instances he swept aside ingrained British conventions in order to remain faithful to the original. He did not, like Hawes, add any of the limpid ballads that formed the core of British opera. He retained all of the ensembles thought to be so antithetical to playhouses' separation of music and drama, many with only modest cuts. Bishop even preserved Weber's protracted finale, which had drastically shrunk or disappeared in all previous adaptations. He did cut approximately a quarter of it and, as with *Figaro*, relieved the music of dramatic responsibility; the characters sing mainly of an impending storm, and then conduct the true business of the denouement in speech. Compared to other versions, however, which had discarded or retained only a small fraction of the finale, this was a huge step towards fidelity. Bishop took his biggest leap with Caspar. Spoken in all other London adaptations, at Drury Lane he reassumed his original music. Karen Ahlquist locates this moment as a crucial turning point away from the prominent male spoken role, not only in adaptations but also in native opera.[60]

The patent theatre adaptations thus offered a mixture – of legitimate and illegitimate, of fidelity and departure. Unfortunate timing made them followers rather than leaders of the minor theatres, a situation that would recur as the minors recognised the appeal of imported opera. Major theatre adapters' use of similar casts and melodramatic tactics in the libretto made their versions appear even closer to their competitors. Pressure therefore fell on the music to differentiate their versions. As it increasingly would, fidelity became a tool in theatrical competition. Both patent theatres stayed closer to Weber than previous adaptations and, at Drury Lane, Bishop strikingly broke with convention to include more music, more immersed in the drama. The saturation of *Der Freischütz* adaptations assisted him. While not every patron would have seen every production, the mania for *Der Freischütz* was such that most had probably seen more than one version, read the details of various adaptations in the newspapers and heard excerpts from the opera in the street, ballroom or salon. As Benjamin Walton has written of the proliferation of dramatisations of the William Tell story in France, 'the versions ... seem to merge into an amalgam that can accommodate variation without much altering the overall impression'.[61] Building on familiarity, adapters could leap to a novel level of fidelity.

SCIENTIFIC OR HORRIFIC?

The success of *Der Freischütz* in London hinged on its German character.[62] Musically, this entailed not only charming, folk-like music but what critics came to see as the essence of German art music: the 'scientific' traits of learned scores based more on counterpoint and harmony than melody. Reviewing the London première, Bacon encapsulated these persistent tropes:

> there are in the elaboration of the accompaniments ... marks of the national [German] preference for instrumental over vocal effects ... the absence of melody except in occasional short traits, the chromatic structure of the voice parts, which are far more instrumental than vocal ... all these are not less nationally characteristic. These to all ears, except German ears, are drawbacks and great drawbacks.

Bacon confined interest in such traits to Germans, who enjoyed a reputation as a particularly musical nation. Ayrton proclaimed, 'There is no country in the world, not excepting Italy, where the people have a more general taste for music, than Germany.[63] In contrast, Britain was widely considered hostile or at least apathetic to music. The preface to one libretto of the English Opera House adaptation of *Der Freischütz* stated 'it is ridiculous to call the *English* a musical nation'.[64] Many critics therefore did not think Weber's opera would find a welcoming audience in London. In a review of the English Opera House adaptation, the *Literary Gazette* predicted, 'We much doubt if there be a single Air that is likely to become popular ... however scientific it may be ... our tastes are "wide as the Poles asunder".'

In what seemed a breakthrough in national taste, however, the British embraced Weber's music. In his review of the English Opera House adaptation, Bacon quoted 'a very philosophical musician' who found it 'curious to observe the astonishing mutability of taste respecting vocal music, which the English public are now ... seen to display'. This led several writers to predict a halcyon future for native taste. Ignoring the elimination of the music at most of the minor theatres (which were in any event rarely reviewed), the *Morning Chronicle* felt the opera's success at Covent Garden proved that 'the English nation [is] much further advanced in a knowledge of the harmonic art than people abroad, and many persons even in this country, are inclined to allow'. Ayrton crowed that *Der Freischütz*'s success demonstrated 'the taste of the middling classes for what is really good in music'.[65] His focus on the 'middling' classes not only conveniently eliminated consideration of the less elevated audiences at most of the minor theatres, but sent a clear message to the upper classes at the King's Theatre. While they ignored *Der Freischütz* and ran after Rossini, widely viewed as the Italianate antipode to learned German music, their social inferiors were upstaging them by welcoming meaty music at the playhouses.[66]

Some reviewers felt less sanguine. Bacon saw *Der Freischütz* not as an operatic triumph but as yet another melodramatic, foreign piece that usurped Britons' support for native opera. Noting that King George IV patronised *Der Freischütz* at both patent theatres, Bacon complained:

> in truth music has by no means the importance in our musical drama that should appertain to it. Nothing proves this more strongly than the attractiveness of the German melo-drame. Nor can it be otherwise until ... a portion of that patronage which has been ... dedicated to the planting and maintaining a theatre for an Italian, be addressed to the establishment and support of an English opera ... till this be done, our stages are not likely to exhibit any thing beyond the same anomalous jargon of dialogue and song ... which ... effectually stops the progress of national taste.[67]

Bacon pinpointed the central problem of aspiring British opera composers: the lack of a theatre dedicated to native opera. Wealthy patrons and royalty alike focused their musical interests on foreign opera at the King's Theatre. The playhouses offered the only potential venue for native opera, but they were meant to be dedicated to legitimate drama and therefore largely relegated music to a subsidiary role. Now, with the popularity of foreign imports at the playhouses, already slim opportunities for native operas diminished further.

Other critics agreed that *Der Freischütz* spoke less to musical triumph than to melodramatic encroachment. The vaunted love of music seemed merely a veneer pasted over the seamy truth of sensational appeal and financial gain. The *London Magazine* protested, 'We are beginning to get very sick of this very good music, – or rather of the fuss that is made about it by those who, under the pretence of doing honour to the genius of Weber, and of fostering the musical taste of the country, are paying only the most rigid attention to the galleries, and to the silver that is caught from the lovers of melo-dramatic effect.' It is no coincidence that this was a review of the Drury Lane production, for this theatre seemed especially linked to theatrical decline. From 1819 to 1826, it was managed by Robert William Elliston, who had begun as a prominent manager of minor theatres. As Jane Moody describes, the advent of Elliston, who had so long undermined the major theatres as a minor theatre manager, seemed to spell the doom of legitimate drama:

> Elliston's arrival marked a cultural and social watershed: the dramatic *ancien régime*, in which managers and committee members had originated predominately among . . . the gentry, aristocracy, old theatrical dynasties, and Parliament, was suddenly overthrown by a man whose capital had been acquired by producing illegitimate drama . . . Drury Lane was now in the hands of a watchmaker's son, a ruthless modern cultural entrepreneur.[68]

Der Freischütz, having gone the rounds of virtually every minor theatre, appeared at Drury Lane directly after the run of *The enchanted courser*, an 'equestrian melo-drama' that borrowed a horse troupe from a minor theatre.[69] Many lumped opera and horses into the same disturbing trend of theatrical decline.

Concerns congregated around Kind's libretto. The *European Magazine* vividly described it: 'The music that is scattered through "Der Freyschütz," adorns it pretty much in the same way that pearls would a dunghill.'[70] The plot sparked concerns not only about melodrama, but, more broadly, about German drama and Romanticism. The 1790s had seen a craze for German drama, especially of the sensational, Gothic variety. As Moody observes, this fashion coincided ominously with the French Revolution: 'German drama seemed to offer a seditious blueprint for the disintegration of an aristocratic, Christian political state.'[71] The fact that both patent theatres were rebuilt on a larger scale in the 1790s to entertain larger – and by extension more socially diverse – audiences awakened fears of a kind of cultural echo of the French Revolution, with elite desires washed away by the masses' purchasing power.

Concerns of class shaded into concerns of gender. Critics deprecated Germanic and Gothic works alike as 'popular, feminized, and unnatural' and some reviewers specifically linked *Der Freischütz* with the feminine.[72] The *Theatrical Observer* stated that, at the English Opera House, 'when the house is re-lighted [after the Wolf's Glen scene] many a fair face betrays some remaining symptoms of alarm at the terrific objects that have been presented'. Similarly, letters to the editor of the same paper – most likely fabricated – protested both that the darkened theatre meant that 'many a pretty face, therefore goes without its just tribute of admiration' and that a husband 'positively [couldn't] think of taking [his] wife to either of the houses in her present situation'.[73] Women, the newspaper reassured its readers, were the only ones truly affected by such spectacle, yet exposure to it could undermine their traditional roles as either mothers or objects of the male gaze.

Rejection of the feminised, sensual nature of these Teutonic tales in some ways spoke to a broader rejection of Romanticism. Scholars have questioned an uncomplicated relationship between German Romanticism and *Der Freischütz*, but many contemporary reviewers interpreted the work in this light.[74] In a review of the Covent Garden adaptation, for example, *The Drama* protested:

> we have no honest liking for the German drama ... our reason is too stubborn to submit
> to *all* the monstrous demands that are made upon it ... A German dramatist is never at
> rest but when he is harrowing up our feelings: ... his *sublimity* always reaches above 'the
> seventh heaven,' and his *horrors* have no fathom ... we must feel with his heroines through
> all their extremes ... Now, we have really no fondness for all this wildness and
> extravagance ... we could never brace ourselves up to the relish of so much emotion.

The writer posited a specifically German propensity for the supernatural and the spectacular that flew against 'stubborn reason' and in essence feminised the viewer, who '*must* feel with his *heroines* through all their extremes'. The very attributes the critic resisted are thus those most frequently allied with Romanticism – the sublime, the horrific, the extreme. On the London stage, such traits resonated uncomfortably with illegitimate drama and helped vex the opera's reception.

Given such mixed responses to *Der Freischütz* itself, it is not surprising that fidelity to it evoked similar ambivalence. A handful of reviewers supported strict adherence to Weber. Writing in *The Harmonicon*, Ayrton stated approvingly, 'After this piece had already been ... brought before a London audience in a mutilated state, it was judicious in the managers to give a new character to it here [Drury Lane], by restoring its primitive form.' The *European Magazine* chastised adaptation of a different sort: singers' ornamentation. Speaking of Catherine Stephens' performance of Agathe at the English Opera House, the critic wrote that 'though liberties may be taken with the works of certain of our English composers (and, perhaps, with benefit to them) they are not to be rashly attempted upon the *chef d'œuvre* of a great German master'. Fidelity is reserved only for foreign masters, while ornamentation improves native works.

Few critics, however, insisted so stringently on fidelity. Partially, this was because fidelity was difficult to discern among the bewildering number of adaptations. This proliferation enabled Bishop to dare a greater level of fidelity, but it also weakened a sense of a fixed original. The fact that the German opera was itself an adaptation further complicated matters and several reviewers became mired in a confusing tangle of versions. Both Ayrton and the *Literary Gazette*, for example, attributed the happy ending to native adapters, when it was Kind who had provided a newly happy close to the original tale, in which Agathe is shot.[75] Similarly, some critics, apparently confused by the playbills, which indicated that Bishop had adapted the music, imagined that he had altered more than he had. The *Morning Chronicle* cautioned 'we cannot help thinking it a dangerous, if not an unnecessary experiment, to ... accommodate to the English ear, what the English ear has adopted with enthusiasm already'. This error persists today, as some scholars have described Bishop's adaptation as the most heavily altered.[76] Paradoxically, the sheer abundance of changes made them seem less prominent. *The Drama* referred to the massive changes at the Surrey as 'slight variation[s]' and *The Examiner* admitted of the Covent Garden adaptation, 'A little perplexity now and then occurs, in consequence of a portion of bustle among our summer associations, produced by these changes and transpositions, which in other respects, however, are of no great moment.'

Even when critics recognised the changes, they did not always approve of them. The *Literary Gazette*, for example, criticised Bishop's restoration of music to Caspar, preferring native convention to fidelity. While a sung villain might be 'highly gratifying to the lovers of harmony, [it] is nevertheless disadvantageous to its general interest, as singers are almost uniformly bad actors'. Other writers found adapters' changes superficial, made more for the sake of novelty and profit than for pressing structural reasons. Of the Drury Lane adaptation, the *Morning Chronicle* sighed, 'it was hardly worth while of the Theatres to go to the trouble of translating it each for themselves, unless the laws of copy-right obliged them to do so ... There are some diversities in the conduct of the fable not worth describing, especially as the interest is by this time worn out.' As noted in Chapter 1, while adapters could profit relatively freely from foreign works because no copyright extended across national borders, copyright of printed works within Britain encouraged each theatre to present a distinct adaptation. While some critics hailed widespread interest in *Der Freischütz* as evidence of improved musical taste, others worried about the implications of such wild, melodramatic fare for the native theatre.

AFTERMATH

Regardless of critics' concerns, *Der Freischütz* made an enormous impact on London operatic life. As George Hogarth summarised, 'no dramatic production ever made a more sudden, a greater, or a more lasting impression on the public'.[77] One of the most intriguing results was an unusual commission for a foreign composer to write for the playhouses: in 1826, Weber composed *Oberon* for Covent Garden. As an original work,

Oberon lies outside the scope of this study.[78] Its commission and Weber's subsequent visit to London are worth discussing briefly, however, as they offer an unusual opportunity to juxtapose original and adapted works.

When Covent Garden manager Charles Kemble and music director Sir George Smart visited Weber in 1825 to conduct negotiations for *Oberon*, they first had to extricate themselves from Weber's charges that he had not received payment for *Der Freischütz*. Livius had obtained a score of the opera from Weber, but apparently had never delivered the promised compensation.[79] Once Kemble assured him that he had sent the money and blamed Livius for not delivering it, 'Weber was perfectly satisfied ... Mr. Kemble proceeded to business ... by paying first what Weber demanded, namely, thirty pounds, for the score of *Preciosa* ... at parting I understood the agreement was made that he was to receive five hundred pounds for his new opera.'[80] Such negotiations reveal the fluid dealings that took place before international copyright laws, as well as the difference in cost between adapted (£30) and original (£500) work.[81] In fact, the cost for adaptations was often even less, since no records exist for any of the other seven London theatres who produced *Der Freischütz* even promising to pay Weber. No wonder that managers preferred to adapt rather than commission: the success of *Der Freischütz* must indeed have been powerful to prompt such outlay for *Oberon*.

Weber received not only the £500 but also £380 for conducting *Oberon* and portions of *Der Freischütz* at the oratorio performances at Covent Garden.[82] It is unclear, however, whether he saw a full performance of any of the London adaptations of *Der Freischütz*. Theatre managers seem to have been a bit shy of performing the adaptation in Weber's presence. Most of the minor theatres were closed, but Covent Garden avoided their adaptation altogether and Drury Lane offered only a handful of performances. Paul Bedford, who played Caspar at Drury Lane, related that Weber 'occasionally visited Drury Lane, to hear how we natives rendered his great conception' and complimented Bedford, but little other documentation exists.[83] There is evidence that Weber was planning a performance at Covent Garden for what turned out to be the day of his death, 5 June.[84] He wrote to his wife on 18 April, 'It's all talk now of giving a complete performance of *Freischütz* at Covent Garden. What gets me is that ... I shall have to chew over this opera again from the beginning. Indeed, the music is completely rehearsed, but the numbers need to be put in order again and the dialogue prepared.'[85] It is unclear whether Weber used Livius' adaptation, replacing the order Livius had rearranged, or whether an entirely new production, with fresh dialogue, was crafted. Certainly, he used his own score when conducting the excerpts at the oratorio performances, as Bacon observed: 'his own score differed materially from those hitherto used in this country'.[86] Unfortunately, while we know that Weber was angry at not receiving payment for Livius' adaptation, his reaction to the adaptations themselves is unclear.

What is certain is that Weber found Covent Garden unsuited to the type of opera he wanted to write in *Oberon*. Modern scholarship tends to view *Oberon* as a failure, the blame attributable to what Cyril Ehrlich and Simon McVeigh have called the 'degraded' state of the 'metropolitan stage tradition'.[87] Such condemnation stems from Weber himself, who famously wrote to the librettist of *Oberon*, Planché: 'The intermixing of so many principal actors who do not sing – the omission of the music in the most important moments – all these things deprive our "Oberon" of the title of an opera, and will make him unfit for all other theatres in Europe.'[88] Certainly, this accords with the kind of separation between music and drama discussed throughout preceding chapters. Still, *Oberon* was not a complete failure, nor was the only issue the British context. Rather, as with all of Weber's operas after *Der Freischütz*, the problem was that it did not deliver the same wild picture of Germany that audiences now craved. As a letter to *The Examiner* a decade later complained, bemoaning both the divergence between *Oberon* and *Der Freischütz* and the failings of native taste, 'If the causes of the success of *Der Freischütz* be analysed, I fear they might be traced to devilry, red and blue fire, the great owl, and *Tallyho* chorus. Without these adjuncts, would the piece have pleased our public? Certain grounds for a reply in the negative, I fear, may be found in the failure of *Oberon*.'[89] In attempting to suit *Oberon* for the British stage, Weber had failed to provide what audiences truly wanted: another embodiment of Germany as a land of the macabre. The importance of adaptation should not be overlooked, as the versions of *Der Freischütz*, however altered, produced more impact in London than an original work written specially for the city.

The very success of the *Der Freischütz* adaptations eventually lessened the need for adaptation. As the Duke of Sussex told Weber when he visited, *Der Freischütz* 'had created a veritable revolution'.[90] *Der Freischütz* altered virtually every aspect of London theatrical life. It unsettled the dominance of the King's Theatre in the operatic realm and helped erode boundaries between major and minor theatres. It demonstrated the potential for musico-dramatic fusion on the native stage, especially when Bishop retained a singing Caspar and most of Weber's lengthy ensembles. It sparked an unusual commission for a foreign composer to write for the playhouses. As George Biddlecombe observes, it influenced subsequent generations of native composers.[91] Most importantly, it engendered a glut of operatic adaptations. In the decade before *Der Freischütz*, a scant six foreign operas were adapted; in the following decade, over forty surfeited London playhouses, often in multiple versions. Such saturation gradually narrowed stylistic gaps between native and continental opera and rendered fidelity both more feasible and more desirable. As with *Der Freischütz* itself, however, subsequent adaptations continued to raise difficult questions: whether foreign opera elevated or lowered taste; whether fidelity produced a better result than adaptation; what financial and moral obligations adapters had to the original composer; and what the craze for opera meant for the future of native drama. Despite these uncertain implications, after *Der Freischütz* there was no return to a lesser role for adapted opera.

4 | The search for Weber's successor

In the wake of *Der Freischütz*'s success, playhouse managers scrambled to find another such hit. The most logical source, Weber's other operas, proved unsatisfactory. Adaptations of *Preciosa*, *Abu Hassan* and *Silvana* produced only modest results; the most popular, *Abu Hassan*, ran for a little over thirty nights and had a few revivals in subsequent seasons, but this hardly compared to the hundreds of repetitions of *Der Freischütz*. Even *Oberon*, written by Weber specifically for Covent Garden, could not equal *Der Freischütz*. Undaunted, managers spread their net to other German composers. Operas by composers such as Marschner, Ries and Spohr appeared from 1829 to 1832.

While none of these works became the elusive second *Der Freischütz*, they did precipitate several important changes in operatic adaptation. The minor theatres, emboldened by their success with *Der Freischütz*, became significant contenders for operatic adaptation, particularly the English Opera House, where most of these German adaptations appeared. The playhouses' focus on opera also challenged the King's Theatre. The latter largely avoided German-language operas until the early 1830s, and even then offered them only with a travelling German troupe rather than their regular company.[1] None of the works discussed in this chapter appeared there. Now that the playhouses began to compete aggressively for London premières of important, recent works, they negotiated more directly with living foreign composers, and their transactions illuminate the business aspects of adaptation. Finally, these adaptations demonstrate shifting boundaries of fidelity and taste. Operas by Marschner and Ries appeared in a remarkably faithful form, which challenged the role and style of music on the playhouse stage and in the process changed the shape of adaptation. When two competing adaptations of Spohr operas appeared in the early 1830s, one faithful, the other a pastiche, the outrage that greeted the latter demonstrated that the freedoms of only a decade earlier could no longer be taken with impunity.

Changing attitudes to adaptation played out against a backdrop of intense strife in the London theatrical world. In 1832, Parliament debated a bill to abolish the major theatres' patents for legitimate drama, which would have ended what many saw as theatrical monopoly. This resonated with the contemporaneous Reform Bill, which ostensibly reformed corrupt election procedures and extended the vote to more of the population.[2] As Katharine Newey argues, the impetus for both bills was to '[clear] out ... the accumulated injustices of outmoded aristocratic and corrupt practices of preferment and protectionism'.[3] Unlike the Reform Bill, however, which was passed in June 1832 after debate and riot, theatrical reform failed in the House of Lords. This exacerbated already rampant criticism of the major theatres and widespread concerns about the decline of native drama, especially given the financial and managerial troubles at both major theatres.[4] Drury Lane saw a series of managers bankrupt: former minor theatre manager Robert William Elliston in 1826; American Stephen Price in 1830; and amateur speculator Frederick Polhill in 1834. At Covent Garden, Charles Kemble struggled with expensive litigation among the multiple owners of the patent. By 1829, payments were so far overdue that a tax collector temporarily possessed the theatre and only public support rescued it. Pierre-François Laporte, manager of the King's Theatre since 1828, took over the theatre for one disastrous season in 1832–3, leaving the performers to fend for themselves before it ended.[5] The patent system seemed in desperate need of overhaul.

Imported German operas appeared at times a solution for these problems, at others an accelerant. Paradoxically, many critics embraced these foreign imports as signs of improving national taste. As explored in the previous chapter, German music acquired a reputation as erudite and substantive, a sober antidote to the more flighty Italian style prevalent at the King's Theatre. Critics interpreted the preponderance of German operas at the playhouses as a sign that their mainly middle-class patrons (including the critics themselves) had better taste than the elite frequenters of the opera house. The fact that these operas appeared in more faithful form also pitted a work-oriented approach at the playhouses against an event-oriented approach at the opera house, a dichotomy that scholars have argued was rooted in class conflict.[6] Just as the Reform Bill allegedly wrested control from the privileged, so too did these adaptations seem to claim opera for a broader audience.

A less optimistic view saw imported German operas as a symptom of the decline of legitimate drama. As foreign imports, these operas supplanted native works. As operas, and operas with increasing amounts of music intertwined with drama, they seemed to prove that the major theatres had abandoned legitimate, spoken drama. The fact that the minor theatres competed so successfully for these imports further fuelled the drive to abolish the patents and open the theatrical marketplace. German music also appeared less beneficial than critics at first supposed. At times it sounded learned and scientific, at others mannered and lacking in spontaneous genius. None of these operas proved as popular as *Der Freischütz*, and critics began to question the suitability of the German style for native audiences and for opera as a whole. German operatic imports largely dropped away after 1832. Nevertheless, the flurry of German adaptations in the late 1820s and early 1830s helped alter both musical taste and the acceptable boundaries for fidelity.

'A NEW EPOCH': GERMAN OPERA AT THE ENGLISH OPERA HOUSE

The most aggressive promoter of adapted German opera was the man who had introduced *Der Freischütz* to London: English Opera House manager Samuel James

Arnold. As described in Chapter 3, Arnold had long aspired to raise his theatre to the level of the majors. When the chance arose, he even tried to run the major theatres; his was one of several bids to lease Drury Lane after Elliston went bankrupt in 1826.[7] He lost to Price, however, and instead redoubled his efforts to make the English Opera House a serious contender for musical excellence. In the late 1820s, he and music director William Hawes offered an ambitious string of operatic adaptations (see Appendix 1). These were all London premières except for *Così fan tutte* and *Don Giovanni*, utilised many of the major theatres' performers during their 'off' summer season and focused almost exclusively on German composers. This remarkable run slowed only when fire destroyed the theatre in 1830.

The *Literary Gazette* hailed the English Opera House adaptations of the late 1820s as a 'new epoch in the history of [dramatic music] in this country'.[8] The reviewer explained how Arnold gave hope to those who thought theatrical decline could not be reversed:

> We have long been convinced, that the excuse of a manager being obliged to conform to the taste of the public, is an idle one ... Let those who doubt us look at the English Opera House. Half-a-dozen seasons ago, had any one been rash enough to produce upon its boards a foreign opera, in its original state, he would have paid the forfeit of his temerity ... and had Mr. Arnold been one of those said vulgar and selfish speculators, he might have gone on producing melo-dramas ... But Mr. Arnold ... cultivates and admires the fine arts generally, for love as well as for money ... to the astonishment of all London, audiences were found, and large ones too, who could patiently sit out ... finales having as many notes in them as a whole English opera contained previous to that period. Our gratitude to Mr. Arnold, and his zealous coadjutor Mr. Hawes, for ... the important victory they have achieved over the ignorance and prejudice of the mob, is great.[9]

Arnold and Hawes seemed to be fulfilling many critics' dream: they were creating a theatre in which artistic worth and financial gain were not mutually exclusive and in which a strong leader improved audience taste instead of bowing to it. The fact that this took place in a minor theatre bolstered those who fought to overturn the patent system.

New, also, were Arnold's demands on his audience, as he produced significantly more faithful adaptations. Leanne Langley separates these adaptations from preceding ones, which were 'mostly ... revivals of popular English plays with borrowed music', while Arnold presented 'versions of genuine continental operas'.[10] While this is a harsh assessment of Bishop's efforts with Mozart and Rossini, overall the English Opera House adaptations – including that of *Der Freischütz* discussed in the previous chapter – did constitute a new approach to foreign opera. Arnold's performance standard rivalled the major theatres and even the King's Theatre and he displayed a remarkable dedication to fidelity, even when it challenged ingrained British conventions.

NEGOTIATING FOR THE NEXT *DER FREISCHÜTZ*

While Arnold and Hawes adapted a variety of German operas, old and new, their best hope for a successor to Weber and *Der Freischütz* lay in the two most recent operas they imported: Ries' *Die Räuberbraut* and Marschner's *Der Vampyr*, both written in 1828 and adapted in 1829. Arnold and Hawes, perhaps influenced by Covent Garden's commission of *Oberon*, dealt directly with both composers in an effort not only to adapt their works but to publish them in London and to commission new works.[11] The commission for Marschner never came to fruition, but Ries did write *The sorceress* for the English Opera House in 1831.[12] Hawes, who also worked as a publisher, brought out scores of *Die Räuberbraut* and *The sorceress* and excerpts of *Der Vampyr*.

Foreign composers were thus increasingly involved in the adaptation and commissioning of their works for London. In the case of Ries, this involvement is unusually well documented and helps shed light on the business of adapting and publishing across national lines. Ries had lived in London from 1813 to 1824 before earning enough to retire to Germany, fulfilling the prevalent stereotype of the foreign musician who siphoned money away from London. He continued, however, to promote his music in London through his brother Joseph, a businessman and amateur musician who remained in the city.[13]

Ries' letters to Joseph demonstrate three intriguing facets of the business of adaptation. First, adaptations often made their way to a theatre via a network of people not officially employed there. For instance, a Charles Aders, London merchant and art collector, and his wife apparently negotiated with both major theatres to adapt *Die Räuberbraut*.[14] Second, they show how composers sometimes tried to utilise theatrical competition to their advantage. Ries' wife Harriet told Joseph:

> I am quite of opinion that the thing [*Die Räuberbraut*] should be offered to both [patent] houses at once – or we shall lose both – for I need not tell you the jealousies which have existed time out of mind between them, and as Ries has already written to Sir George [Smart], and I think we may depend upon his wish being serious of having it for Covent Garden, it will decidedly be right to give him the preference – but I think at the same time it might not be impolitic to add that the other house had made some advances.[15]

While some composers may have succeeded with this tactic, it backfired here. Neither major theatre took the opera and Ries' relations with Smart became strained.[16]

Finally, and most intriguingly, Ries' letters elucidate the role of publishing in adaptation, particularly when several countries were involved.[17] Ries instructed Joseph to offer Hawes the full score of *Die Räuberbraut* 'for use of the opera for 30 guineas – the copying alone costs four. Naturally, he may not have it engraved, but if he brings the thing out in performance, I will give him the privilege.'[18] Performance and publication were therefore both separate and intertwined. Hawes clearly wished to perform and publish the opera. Ries was willing to sell him the score for performance, but publication was a separate matter, allowable only if Hawes in fact performed it. Even then, any 'privilege' for publication was for a specific format only. Ries wrote to Peters, for example, about publishing the piano–vocal score of the opera, but freely noted that he was negotiating with Simrock and Schott to publish excerpts from it.[19] Similarly, he wrote an angry letter insisting that Hawes had the right to publish the overture only in piano arrangement, not in full score, which right Peters had.[20] Even the complete score could be parsed into separate sales to separate countries. He asked Joseph to suggest to Hawes 'that I will only give him the score for England? – Perhaps he then could speculate with publication &c &c, as he will, and I transfer to him alone all rights?'[21] Hawes could publish the entire piano–vocal score, but in Britain only. Additionally, Ries wrote several panicked letters to Joseph urging him to remind Hawes that the score could appear only at a certain time, in order to coordinate with publication by other publishers in other countries, and also that the title page had to include these publishers' names. Had this not happened, Ries seems to have feared both that the publishers with whom he had negotiated would rescind payment and that other, unscrupulous publishers would feel they could republish a score already available in print.[22]

Hawes' resistance suggests that he did not find these arrangements typical. Indeed, they represent a new phase of adaptation. Only because Hawes' adaptation followed Ries' opera so closely could Ries conceive of the publication as a 'British edition' of his opera. Only when the score was considered to represent Ries' work, albeit in English, could it be necessary to coordinate with publishers of the original opera. And only when British adapters aggressively sought the London premières of important new foreign operas did they find the original composers interested in supervising the adaptations and benefiting from their profits. With no international copyright laws yet in place, however, these transactions were not standardised. Ries' dealings with Hawes demonstrate the effort that was required and the miscommunications that arose as composer, adapter and publisher positioned themselves on unstable ground.

OF MISFITS AND MONSTERS

Die Räuberbraut and *Der Vampyr* seemed especially well suited for adaptation because they played into the latest theatrical crazes. They offered the legendary, lurid tales that so appealed in *Der Freischütz*, *Faust*, *Frankenstein* and the works of Sir Walter Scott. They featured a popular character type: the Byronic hero, a tortured but alluring social outcast. In *Die Räuberbraut*, this type is embodied in Roberto, who is forced to become a robber chief after he audaciously asks for the hand of the Count of Viterbo's daughter, Laura, and is exiled by the Count. When the Count is later pursued by political rivals, Roberto strikes a despicable bargain: he will save the Count, but Laura (in love with Fernando) must become the titular robber's bride. Last minute reversals – different in original and adaptation – save Laura from this fate. In *Der Vampyr*, the title character, known as Lord Ruthven, is less sympathetic, as his designs on virginal brides are purely murderous. He is a tortured soul, though, racked by his need for blood and obliged to sacrifice these brides to extend his term on earth. He is also thwarted, though not of his own volition. Stopped from marrying the heroine by her beloved Aubry, Ruthven is denied further time on earth and struck down by lightning.

Both libretti partook in multiple webs of retelling and adaptation. *Die Räuberbraut*'s libretto was initially written by Johann Joseph Reiff, but Ries became dissatisfied with it and asked Georg Döring to revise and complete it.[23] It is unclear whether either author had a specific model for the libretto, but it certainly partook in a long history of robber tales, of which Schiller's *Die Räuber* was the best-known example. London critics did not cite a specific model for *Die Räuberbraut*, but found tales of robbers 'old and uninteresting', reminiscent of half-remembered minor theatre productions.[24] Robbers still clearly captured public attention, though. In the autumn after *Die Räuberbraut*'s production at the English Opera House, both Covent Garden and Drury Lane offered new robber pieces, unconnected with Ries' opera: *The robber's wife* and the hugely popular *The brigand*, respectively.[25] Sometimes, theatrical competition was not for another version of the same opera, but for a fresh manifestation of a popular theme.

Der Vampyr, meanwhile, participated in a vogue for the undead.[26] While vampire tales had a long history, public attention was especially captured in 1819 by a short story, *The vampyre*, at first mistakenly attributed to Byron but in reality by his doctor, Polidori. Stage versions proliferated, many based on one of the first adaptations, Nodier's *Le vampire*. Two London versions of Nodier appeared in 1820, by James Robinson Planché for the English Opera House and William Moncrieff for the Coburg. Planché's version proved especially popular, so much so that Marschner's librettist, Wilhelm August Wohlbrück, used it as his source for *Der Vampyr*. Here is a perfect example of the kind of multi-layering that could take place with these adaptations: Wohlbrück's libretto is an adaptation of Planché's adaptation of Nodier's adaptation of Polidori. The layers become even denser, since Planché then adapted Wohlbrück's *Der Vampyr* for the English Opera House. The fact that Planché had therefore produced two adaptations of the same tale confused critics. They assumed that these were the same libretti, and the *Morning Post* even proclaimed, 'It would … be a work of supererogation to speak of the plot, which is precisely the same.' (See Appendix 2 for review citations.)

Neither Ries' nor Marschner's operas, however, were transferred to London in 'precisely the same' shape. With *Der Vampyr*, fidelity actually led to divergence. That is, Planché had been faithful to Nodier's adaptation in 1820 and he was again faithful to Wohlbrück's adaptation in 1829. Wohlbrück, however, had not been faithful to Nodier (or rather to Planché's adaptation of him), so Planché's two versions were not identical.

Planché did, however, introduce one important change to the German libretto: the setting. While Polidori's original tale took place in Greece and London, Nodier and Wohlbrück transferred it to Scotland. Planché had also used the Scottish setting in 1820, augmented with traditional Scottish tunes. For France and Germany, Scotland represented the distant land of Sir Walter Scott, Ossianic bards and arcane superstition. Blending vampires into this exotic setting seemed appropriate. London audiences, although equally enamoured with Scott, chafed at the indiscriminate mixture. Leigh Hunt protested that Scotland, while 'a country of superstition', was not associated with this particular superstition.[27] Planché, who built a reputation for realism in costume and sets, apparently regretted the choice he had made in 1820. When he adapted the German opera in 1829, the 'advertisement' for the word book – which seems to be by Planché himself – announced that the new adaptation would atone for his error and transfer the action to 'the Turkish Principalities and Transylvania, the head-quarters of Vampyrism'.[28]

Despite the allure of these tales, both Planché and the librettist for *Die Räuberbraut*, Edward Fitzball, felt they needed to be softened for a London audience. For instance, Roxana Stuart argues that Ruthven, the title character of *Der Vampyr*, is 'more viscerally disturbing' than in previous stage versions.[29] In need of three brides to extend his term on earth, he kills Janthe in the opening, murders Emmy offstage while her fellow villagers, unaware, sing a catchy drinking chorus and is barely stopped from killing the heroine, Malwina. Tempering this bloodthirsty path, Planché returned to Nodier's requirement that only one maiden be sacrificed. The British Ruthven, like the operatic figure he parallels – Don Giovanni – is not entirely successful with any of his conquests. Janthe escapes, and Ruthven's seduction duet with Emmy, which Thomas Grey compares to 'Là ci darem la mano', is cut, lessening his sexual power over his virginal female targets.[30] Emmy still dies, but not by the vampire's hand; rather, when her fiancé shoots the vampire, he also inadvertently wounds her.[31]

Similarly, Fitzball softened the ending of *Die Räuberbraut*. At the close of the original, Roberto is injured as he fights his rival, Fernando. Regretting his evil deeds, Roberto tells Fernando to take the robber's bride and then perishes onstage. In the adaptation, Roberto, after a lengthy struggle between guilt and desire, nobly cedes Laura to his rival and then suffers exile rather than death. Some of this may have stemmed from concern about censorship, particularly the death onstage, but it also speaks to divergent British and German conceptions of Romanticism. Richard Mackenzie Bacon, for example, found the subject of *Der Vampyr* intrinsic to the German landscape, writing in the *Quarterly Musical Magazine and Review* that it was 'sterile and gloomy, like many of the mountain paths on the shores of their own Rhine'. For native viewers, though, it was 'capable of exciting only the strongest physical disgust'. Given the proliferation of these sensational tales, Londoners clearly revelled in them more than Bacon wished to admit, but adapters still felt they needed to temper their violence.

A NEW STANDARD OF FIDELITY

With few exceptions, Hawes wed these libretti to closely preserved scores, setting a new precedent for fidelity. Between the two operas, he interpolated only one number, cut two and slimmed or reassigned others.[32] Some of what he retained suited British taste well. Both German operas contain plentiful catchy choruses for villagers or robbers as well as several accessible solos and duets for minor characters. But much of the music presented challenges that Hawes' listeners had not accepted in the past. Following the model of *Der Freischütz*, both operas abound in lengthy, polyphonic ensembles, adventurous, chromatic harmonies and free forms, moulded to the action. Hawes practised both reverence and departure, but with a far heavier dose of the former than had yet been attempted in these adaptations.

In *Der Vampyr*, for example, Hawes retained the title character's first aria, despite the fact that it did not conform to any of the beloved solo types on the British playhouse stage. In Marschner's aria, Ruthven exults that he has been granted an extended time on earth as long as he delivers the required victims. He describes graphically how he will blissfully suck blood from his victims' red lips and exult at their groans of terror. A fleeting sense of remorse overtakes him as he remembers his former human existence, but he throws this aside to return to the opening of the aria. Planché softened the text somewhat. He made Ruthven require only one victim and described his vampiric activities less shockingly. The general 'sweet sensation' and 'voluptuous feeling' of 'reanimation' is contrasted with the 'horrible thirst' that soon returns and the 'banquet gory' that must recommence as the vampire's 'fiendly frame' is seen 'feeding'.[33]

Hawes retained Marschner's tortured, demonic setting with only tiny changes, mainly adding alternate, lower notes for the amateur purchaser. This is remarkable, given the aria's length and difficulty and how little it suits the playhouse aesthetic. Marschner's form is fluid. It opens with a brief recitative, followed by a loose ABA form – with elements of recitative in the 'B' section – and a coda, *furioso*. The beginning sets the macabre tone, rife with chromaticism, dissonance and menacing trills (see Ex. 4.1a). The body of the aria is marked by harmonic instability, beginning in F major, moving fluidly through A♭ major and B minor at various points, and concluding in D minor. Ruthven's vocal lines, sung above dense orchestral activity, feature twisting chromatic movement, brief phrases, sudden leaps and maniacal laughter (see Ex. 4.1b). These features effectively portray the bloodthirsty, tortured title character. They also echo many of the elements London audiences had already enjoyed in *Der Freischütz*. Still, the aria is a significant departure from the types of solos that usually appeared at the playhouses. It offers neither the sweet lyricism of the ballad nor even the clear periodic structure and stable harmonic framework of the virtuosic scena. The fact that Hawes did not excise even one bar of this lengthy, challenging solo is striking.

Similarly, Hawes' treatment of the trio 'Dem Mann von Ehr' und Pflicht' in *Die Räuberbraut* contrasts with his approach to the trio 'Wie? Was? Entsetzen!' from *Der*

Example 4.1a 'Hah! Yet one and thirty days', Hawes, arr., *Der Vampyr*, mm. 1–10

Freischütz, discussed in Chapter 3 (see p. 77). Hawes had kept only a fraction of Weber's trio, carefully removing it from the action. In contrast, Hawes kept Ries' entire long, multi-partite ensemble. Granted, there was no need to remove Ries' piece from the action, as it is already static. Fernando, a soldier who has come to arrest Laura's father the Count, discovers the disguised Laura's identity due to the flightiness of her servant, Gianettina. The three sing a trio in which Fernando – in love with Laura – assures the anxious women that he will act honourably towards them and the Count. The piece is in fact dramatically extraneous, other than emphasising the connection between Fernando and Laura. Had Hawes taken a freer approach, he could easily have cut it entirely. Certainly, he would not have retained it complete a few years earlier. The opening section, Allegro ma non troppo, challenged playhouse listeners' preference for clear forms and simple harmonies. Ries moves freely from one melodic idea to the next, modulates frequently, liberally uses borrowed chromatic tones and dips into the minor mode to express the women's distress. The Andante is calmer and more static,

Example 4.1b 'Hah! Yet one and thirty days', Hawes, arr., *Der Vampyr*, mm. 58–69

but features fugal writing. The concluding Allegro molto contains plenty of harmonious singing in thirds and sixths, as well as some internal repetition, but it also utilises a rich harmonic language, with passing chromatic movement and a sudden recourse to a diminished seventh (see Ex. 4.2). While this trio certainly included appealing elements for London listeners, overall it qualified as the kind of 'scientific concerted music' that

Example 4.2 'Dear maid in me confide', Hawes, arr., *Die Räuberbraut*, mm. 125–42

Example 4.2 (cont.)

had been slimmed or eliminated in the past. The fact that Hawes retained Ries' entire trio, where he had drastically curtailed Weber's trio only a few years earlier, shows how ambitious he was to raise native taste.

Hawes was not so dedicated to fidelity, however, that he did not make several significant changes. These revolved mainly around a still-contentious area on the playhouse stage: the combination of drama and music. For instance, Hawes significantly slimmed the finale of *Der Vampyr* and in the process largely separated action and song. In Marschner, the finale encompasses the entire denouement. The wedding between Ruthven and Malwina is about to take place, as it must do before midnight if Ruthven is to extend his time on earth. Aubry chafes against the oath he swore to Ruthven not to reveal his identity and manages to delay the wedding past midnight. As Ruthven disappears in a bolt of lightning, Aubry finally can announce that he was a vampire. Malwina's father then agrees that she should marry Aubry and all rejoice. Hawes retained only a fraction of the finale. The chorus still rejoices at the beginning, but Ruthven's entrance and Aubry and Malwina's initial pleas that the wedding be stopped take place in dialogue. The finale then recommences as Aubry battles to save Malwina and continues through Ruthven's demise and the final jubilation, but with over one hundred measures excised. The word book reveals that Hawes cut further by the time the work was performed. In another parallel to *Don Giovanni*, Hawes eliminated the ebullient final chorus and instead ended with the vampire's thrilling demise. Hawes' ending is thus clearer and more concise, with less of the action in music, and offers a suitably horrific, melodramatic conclusion.

In *Die Räuberbraut*, Hawes separated speech and song even more strikingly. Reverting to a technique not used prominently since the adaptations of *Der Freischütz* in 1824, he split a leading role, the robber chief, into spoken and sung parts. Why did Hawes include such a drastic change amidst a context of fidelity? As with many of these splits in the past, casting provides the readiest answer. Ries' original presents an unusual and challenging distribution of voice types, since three basses are required. Robber chief Roberto, whose actions drive much of the plot, sings no traditional arias, but only ensembles and solo portions within the robbers' choruses. Meanwhile, Laura's father, the Count, is relatively powerless in the plot, able to do little more than bemoan his fall from political favour, yet he shoulders significant musical responsibility. A third bass is needed for the minor role of castellan Anselmo, who sings only in ensembles.

This atypical allocation of roles strained the English Opera House's roster, for they had only one accomplished bass-baritone, Henry Phillips.[34] Phillips had been deemed inadequate for the acting responsibilities of Caspar in *Der Freischütz* at the English Opera House in 1824 and had helped necessitate the split of Caspar into two roles. Since then, however, he had matured and regularly shouldered both acting and singing responsibilities, including the title roles in *Don Giovanni* and *Der Vampyr*. He therefore could have played either Roberto or the Count, but as he was the only singer who could manage the Count's music, Hawes placed him in that part. Phillips also probably would not have agreed to sing the aria-less role of Roberto, for he urged Hawes to add his one interpolation in these adaptations: an additional aria for the Count.[35] For the role of Roberto, Hawes probably did not wish to cast his other basses: Edwin Ransford, a raw, inexperienced performer, to whom he entrusted the musical half of the role only; or James Russell, who typically played comic roles and was cast as Anselmo. Instead, he chose a Mr Perkins, whose acting was clearly equal to the task. Edward Sterling lauded him in *The Times* for 'a degree of ability that would do honour to the boards of either of the winter theatres. The scene in which the bandit . . . resigns the hand of *Laura*, was admirably acted, and drew down plaudits from every part of the house.'

The decision to split Roberto's role was not as obvious, however, as having an actor and a singer who could not master each other's craft. The acting half of Roberto (Perkins) had sung small roles in other adaptations and could have attempted the music, while the singing half (Ransford) was not yet a particularly strong vocalist. *The Examiner* complained that he 'was particularly ingenious in scarifying the ears of all those who knew *sharp* from *natural*, or *natural* from *flat*'. The split role, therefore, seems to speak not only to casting but to a desire to widen the gap between active speech and contemplative song. The most crucial dramatic moments now take place in speech: Roberto's heroic ceding of Laura to Fernando expands from one line of recitative to several pages of impassioned dialogue. Roberto's remaining music, not central to an understanding of the character, transfers easily to a generic solo voice within the band of robbers. Overall, Hawes' approach combined ambition and compromise. The areas most entrenched in tradition, those related to effective casting and to the most challenging combinations of drama and music, he still had to alter. In other respects, however, Hawes far overstepped the usual boundaries for music at the playhouses.

THE NATURE OF GERMAN MUSIC

Reviewers unanimously viewed the adaptations of *Die Räuberbraut* and *Der Vampyr* as faithful versions of challenging German operas. Some saw this as gratifying proof of elevated native taste. The *Belle Assemblée* boasted, 'He who disputes our musical taste must visit the English opera, and witness *Der Vampyr*; he must see the interest with which Mr H. Phillips is heard, in passages of music not very familiar to English ears.' The *Morning Post* noted that, even on a second performance, when the musically knowledgeable listeners who flooded the première had given way to a more 'mixed audience', these patrons' appreciation 'exhibited a gratifying proof of the advanced general taste for such refined enjoyments'.

Others, however, chafed against these operas' challenge to the established play-house aesthetic. Even with the split of spoken and sung roles in *Die Räuberbraut*, John Payne Collier of the *Morning Chronicle* thought 'there is a vast deal of music in it, little story, and less dialogue; and the English public . . . are not yet, whatever they may be hereafter, qualified to enjoy such a performance to its full extent, or anything like it'. Edward Taylor counselled in *The Spectator*:

the finale [of *Die Räuberbraut*] contains too much dramatic action; and it would be improved by casting the greater part of it into dialogue, for, as sung, it savours strongly of the ridiculous. A battle is supposed to take place on the stage ... but both parties having to sing during the period of this event ... the battle is lost and won without ... moving a leg.

For some critics, Hawes' leap forward was too drastic, fidelity an offence to native sensibilities rather than a valued goal.

These conflicting responses tapped into broader concerns about the nature of German music. Virtually all reviewers had some praise for the attributes of German music by then widely acknowledged: complex harmony; preponderance of concerted numbers; and novel, dense instrumental accompaniment. The *Morning Post* pronounced *Die Räuberbraut* 'teeming with the beauties of harmony and instrumental effects' and *The Examiner* enthused about 'modulations ... of the most masterly character' in *Der Vampyr*. Nevertheless, both operas drew criticism for precisely these learned elements. Especially inexcusable was the most consistent lacuna in the German style: melody. The *Morning Post* pronounced *Die Räuberbraut* 'absolutely a blank' in melody, while William Ayrton in *The Harmonicon* found it 'the most glaring deficiency' of *Der Vampyr*.

This was especially troubling because most saw melody as not only the essence of the Italian style but also central to British music. Composer Charles Dibdin stated the common opinion: 'harmony is a Combination of Sounds upon the most mechanical Principles; and may be shifted, twisted and turned at Pleasure, without the smallest Fancy' while 'Melody springs from Genius'.[36] Such a description muddied definitions of Romanticism. Melody at times appeared the antithesis of Romanticism, a kind of superficial, aural candy for the masses that degraded aesthetic value. The *Dramatic Magazine* complained of *Die Räuberbraut* that 'the music is too scientific to please "the million", for one half of the frequenters of the theatre would be more gratified with "I'd be a butterfly" or "The fairest flower" than the most sublime compositions of Handel or Mozart'. At other times, however, melody seemed the essence of Romantic genius, an unfettered, subconscious expression removed from the workaday tasks of harmony and orchestration. Speaking of *Die Räuberbraut*, Ayrton in *The Harmonicon* pondered 'there is that which no science, or labour, or skill, can ... command, namely, the creative faculty – the power to invent – genius ... [the opera] is learned, past all doubt; but there is ... a dryness in it that does not look as if it had flowed from the mind in so spontaneous a manner as most great works.' Further, Collier linked musical science to imitation and melody to originality in his review of *Der Vampyr* for the *Morning Chronicle*: 'those portions where [Marschner] has condescended to work only upon melody were infinitely the freshest and the most agreeable ... while, on the other hand, in his labours after the scientific, he has thrust himself entirely into the *Der Freischutz* style'.

Increasingly, reviewers wished for a greater balance, between harmony and melody, German and Italian styles, foreign and native taste. *The Examiner* stood alone in claiming that Marschner had achieved this elusive blend in *Der Vampyr*: 'Music such as MARSCHNER'S is like a fine flower; its perfume and extrinsic qualities make an immediate appeal to the senses; but upon exploring the arcana of its mechanism, we observe artful construction, and fresh subject for admiring the MIND which gave existence to the beautiful creation.' Bacon acknowledged this mixture but denied that such a balance could be completely German. Instead, he interpreted the stylistic split in *Der Vampyr* as an unsuccessful attempt to marry German and Italian styles: 'we can distinctly trace a passage from one, and a passage from the other, whilst the composer's spontaneous ideas drop in now and then'. Confusion arose here, as Bacon found the patter singing in the drinking quartet particularly Italian – 'We could not have thought the German tongue capable of such treatment' – while Taylor, in *The Spectator*, dubbed the same piece 'in the style and spirit of several other German trinklieder'.[37] Were catchy, folk-like numbers like this, which had so appealed in *Der Freischütz*, which had seemed so quintessentially German, in fact more allied to Italianate melody? Critics found themselves in a bind, desirous of melody and accessibility but unable to place these elements within a picture of German music that had become focused on the learned and scientific. One of the reasons *Der Freischütz* had succeeded was that it had seemed to balance melody and science. That Marschner and Ries seemed unable to replicate this balance left many critics disillusioned.

Nevertheless, the English Opera House management described their 1829 season as a triumph for two goals: nationalism and improved musical taste. In stage manager George Bartley's farewell address of the season, he countered a 'general outcry' that 'nearly all our modern productions' are '*taken from the French*', boasting '"We have been English, Sirs," – (almost) "from top to toe"'.[38] Of nine new productions, he stated, only *Die Räuberbraut* and *Der Vampyr* were not native. Second, 'the manner in which those great operas have been performed, will be deemed to have . . . advanced another step towards exalting the character of Musical Drama in this country'. Chafing against the patent theatres' monopoly, Bartley suggested that had the English Opera House not been confined to the summer season, there would be 'no doubt' of the 'eventual benefit to the Science [of music] and its Professors'.

Bartley's claims were disingenuous. The English Opera House hardly offered only native works, and operas such as *Die Räuberbraut* and *Der Vampyr* enjoyed modest initial runs – slightly over ten nights – and mixed critical responses. Overwhelmingly, however, critics joined in Bartley's idealistic depiction of Arnold's efforts. Review after review hailed his spirit of enterprise. Even in an otherwise negative notice of *Der Vampyr*, Ayrton exclaimed, 'What a pity it is that the accursed principle of monopoly, which is ruining the large, the overgrown houses, prevents Mr. Arnold from having granted to him a licence that would enable him to make still greater efforts.' Not every imported opera at the English Opera House was perfect or popular. Yet, Arnold's and Hawes' dedication to learned music, faithful adaptations and high-quality performances demonstrated in many critics' minds what the native stage might accomplish were the patent system abolished.

THE BOUNDARIES OF FIDELITY: SPOHR OPERA IN LONDON

Despite (or perhaps because of) Arnold's direct challenge to the patent theatres' supremacy in adapted opera, he and patent theatre managers seemed to enjoy a mutual, if uneasy respect. Patent theatre managers did not offer competing versions of any of the operas Arnold adapted in the late 1820s and early 1830s save *Don Giovanni*, which they had adapted first. Covent Garden even transferred two of Arnold's adaptations to their stage – *La neige* and *Das unterbrochene Opferfest* – with full acknowledgement of their origin at the English Opera House. Patent theatre managers therefore largely steered away from German opera in the late 1820s, only returning in the early 1830s to a composer whose operas had not yet appeared in London: Spohr.

Spohr's influence in Britain was considerable. His *Times* obituary stated, 'Mendelssohn excepted, no great foreign composer in recent times has exercised so large a personal influence in this country as Spohr'.[39] Spohr visited Britain several times between 1820 and his death and numerous excerpts from his operas appeared in concert, particularly from *Faust* and *Jessonda*. The *Harmonicon* published a translation of his address to German composers in 1823 and a memoir of him in 1824.[40] His popularity peaked after the success of his oratorio, *Die letzten Dinge*, at the Norwich and Liverpool festivals in 1830 and at the Philharmonic Society in March 1831. The *Athenaeum* joked that London musical life was a 'labyrinth of Spohr – Spohr – Spohr – Spohr!'[41] Both Kemble at Covent Garden and Polhill at Drury Lane capitalised on this craze: *Zemire und Azor* appeared at Covent Garden in 1831, *Der Alchymist* at Drury Lane in 1832. These adaptations represent opposing approaches to fidelity. Sir George Smart presented a version of *Zemire und Azor* lauded for its faithfulness. In contrast, Henry Bishop's adaptation of *Der Alchymist* was a fascinating – but disastrous – throwback to pastiche practice. These opposing Spohr productions marked a turning point away from an unfettered approach to adaptation.

SPOHR VS. SPOHR

At Covent Garden, Smart was well placed to select an appropriate Spohr opera. A leading figure in London musical life and frequent conductor of the Philharmonic Society concerts, Smart knew both Spohr's works and the composer himself. He had already expressed interest in producing Spohr's *Der Berggeist* when he visited the composer in 1825.[42] Smart did not select this work, though, nor the operas most excerpted at the Philharmonic Society, *Faust* and *Jessonda*.[43] Instead, he appears deliberately to have chosen an opera that abjured ultra-Germanic traits: Spohr and Ihlée's *Zemire und Azor*. Based on the libretto of Grétry's *Zémire et Azor*, the opera tells the enchanting fairy tale of beauty and the beast.[44] It features the spoken dialogue playhouse audiences expected as well as several appealing ballads and choruses. One solo, 'Rose wie bist du', was so popular that Thomas Moore had already rather unscrupulously published it in his 'National melodies' as 'Rose of the desert'. As Clive Brown describes, the score of *Zemire und Azor* diverged from the typical German style: 'The opera contains some of Spohr's most charming melodic writing and some effective coloratura, influenced, Spohr admitted, by the popularity of Rossini.'[45]

Audiences may have appreciated a lighter work, but they also expected German operas to fit the fantastical, supernatural mould of *Der Freischütz*. Smart's and librettist William Ball's modest changes therefore enhanced the opera's magical, fairy-like qualities and their impressive scenic display. Several new spirit characters appeared and Ball split the opera into three acts rather than two so he could add a thrilling finale to act one, as the evil spirits view a vision of the heroes escaping in a chariot and raise a storm to thwart them. At the end of the opera, the evil spirit dies spectacularly; enveloped by a serpent, he sinks through the stage. Numerous critics admired the gorgeous visual effects, and *The Age* attributed much of the adaptation's success to 'beautiful scenery and capital machinery, together with the interpolated diablerie and witchery'.

A year later at Drury Lane, Bishop chose the darker tale of *Der Alchymist*, an adaptation by Spohr and Pfeiffer (under the pseudonym Schmidt) of a short story by Washington Irving, *The student of Salamanca*. The tale concerns an old alchemist in pursuit of the fabled philosopher's stone. Jealousy between villain and hero over the alchemist's beautiful daughter leads the villain to condemn the alchemist to the Spanish inquisition. Various machinations ensue, many involving a picturesque band of gypsies, and finally the alchemist is pardoned and hero and heroine united happily. Both Bishop and his librettists, Thomas Haynes Bayly and Edward Fitzball, significantly altered the original. Bishop cut half of Spohr's numbers in *Der Alchymist* and added seventeen pieces from five additional Spohr operas: *Der Berggeist, Faust, Jessonda, Pietro von Abano* and *Der Zweikampf mit der Geliebten*. Bayly and Fitzball added a comic character for John Harley, introduced a new, sensational explosion of the alchemist's laboratory and significantly expanded the starring role for Mary Ann Wood, née Paton. As *The Athenaeum* joked, the adapted *Der Alchymist* was 'a drama in three acts, written by two Englishmen, partly founded on a novel by one American, with music selected by a third Englishman, from six operas by one German'.

Bishop clearly viewed the multiple borrowings from Spohr as appealing. The word book proudly proclaimed that 'the whole of the music [is] composed by Louis Spohr' and listed all of the 'celebrated operas' from which Bishop 'selected'.[46] This evinces an intriguing blend of reverence and freedom. Bishop blithely disregards the unity of a particular work. Yet, he sees the proliferation of Spohr as an attraction rather than a drawback. There is also a sense of deference in Bishop's careful acknowledgement of his borrowings, especially since most of the operas were too obscure for contemporaries to have identified them otherwise. Bishop, who was involved in selecting excerpts of Spohr operas for the Philharmonic Society concerts, must have thought that he was assembling the perfect Spohr score, but he miscalculated.[47] While *Zemire und Azor* received twenty-one performances in its first season at Covent Garden, *Der Alchymist* lasted only three nights. Edward Holmes witheringly remarked in *The Atlas*, 'In one night it has established a claim ... to be considered the silliest, the worst, and the dullest opera of the day.'

The crux of the discrepancy was fidelity. Smart's approach to *Zemire und Azor* elicited extensive panegyrics. Taylor's in *The Spectator* is worth quoting at length, as it helps define the meaning of faithful adaptation in the early 1830s:

> It has been fortunate for the fame of this great artist [Spohr], that he has fallen into the hands of men who had sufficient musical knowledge to appreciate, and sufficient nerve to produce him to their countrymen unmutilated and undiluted ... Because, in some cases, it has been found necessary to make alterations in the English versions of foreign operas, every musical pretender thinks he has a licence to hack and hew the master-works of Germany and Italy ... Sir GEORGE SMART has used the pruning-knife most sparingly; and if a shoot has been cut off, it was only to engraft on the trunk one of greater vigour and beauty. He has set about his work ... with a sense of the responsibility which ... one would necessarily feel under the attempt to give life and reality to productions of a genius like that of SPOHR.

An 'unmutilated' work was therefore not one free of changes, but one in which the extent and intention of the changes struck contemporaries as appropriate. Smart made his 'sparing' alterations with a sense of respect for Spohr and out of a desire to improve the opera with superior 'grafts'. What were these changes, that Smart could make them and still be lauded for fidelity? He dropped a duet for Zemire's two sisters, excised Azor's second aria after the première since it proved too difficult for the tenor, John Wilson, rearranged some numbers and made numerous internal cuts to the lengthiest pieces.[48] An opera could therefore be modestly reduced in size, particularly if it proved ineffective in performance, and the placement of numbers was negotiable. Smart also interpolated two pieces: a duet from *Jessonda*, 'Lass für ihn, den ich geliebet', to replace the more difficult duet he had cut, and 'Brenne, Laterne' from *Faust* to provide the new act one finale. Here, Taylor did chastise Smart, who had mildly abridged the *Jessonda* duet, advocating 'the restoration of every missing bar'. Yet, Taylor did not protest the use of numbers from other Spohr operas.

Where Smart was able to make changes and still be praised for fidelity, Bishop's more radical approach activated an uncompromising anti-adaptation rhetoric. In the

Morning Chronicle, Collier protested that 'it is just as absurd to compose one Opera out of many, as it would be to manufacture a Tragedy by selecting speeches from some half dozen other productions of the same kind'. Taylor expostulated in *The Spectator*, 'SPOHR is not a writer at random, and his operas must not be treated as a collection of detached pieces. Every air or concerted piece is fitted to its appropriate place and character, and cannot be removed without injury to the structure.' This contrasts strikingly with only a little over a decade previously, when critics embraced Drury Lane's pastiche approach to *Jean de Paris* and felt lukewarm about Covent Garden's more faithful version. A free approach now risked violent protest and adapters became increasingly reluctant to chance this outcome.

Neither praise of *Zemire und Azor* nor castigation of *Der Alchymist*, however, were consistent or uncomplicated. *Der Alchymist* was not rejected simply because it was a pastiche. Although pastiche was waning, other isolated instances of the practice had not resulted in the same failure. No outrage had greeted *Native land* in 1824, which wove selections from Bishop, Rossini, Zingarelli and others into a new plot, or *The casket* five years later, which set Mozart excerpts to a libretto adapted from the French. Critics had not panned Michael Rophino Lacy's adaptation of *La cenerentola* in 1830, which had included music from *La cenerentola*, *Guillaume Tell*, *Armida* and *Maometto II*. Ayrton even felt the selections 'strengthened' an opera that 'could alone not have contributed enough to satisfy an audience unbiassed by fashion'.[49]

Why did *Der Alchymist* elicit so much more critical disdain than these other examples? Katharine Ellis' assessment of nineteenth-century adaptation in France applies here as well: 'Whether the practice was condoned or not depended largely on the audacity of the enterprise and the organic unity and status of the work in question.'[50] Certainly, Bishop's approach was audacious, particularly as he disconcertingly blended freedom and reverence. The compilers of *Native land* and *The casket* had not made any pretence of preserving one whole opera, but rather wed a mélange of music to new stories. Lacy's adaptation of *La cenerentola* was, however, fairly similar to *Der Alchymist* because it combined an adaptation of one opera with a selection from several. The reason *Der Alchymist* fared so much worse was probably the 'status' Ellis mentions. Rossini, with his dubious reputation for self-borrowing and mannerism, seemed open to change. Spohr, meanwhile, seemed a laudable, learned antidote to facile, showy music. Reviewing *Zemire und Azor*, the *Literary Gazette* counselled that 'the music of Spohr will not be fully appreciated on a first hearing; for it has neither the plain familiarity of the English ballad style, nor the sparkling brilliancy of Rossini's. But, in true simplicity, pure melody, and strong dramatic expression, no music of the present day surpasses that of Spohr.' Spohr, the reviewer felt, had inherited 'the mantle of Mozart'.

Not all critics, however, viewed Spohr so positively. Many found even the Italianate *Zemire und Azor* too Germanic for native taste. *The Athenaeum* felt that Spohr displayed typical German drawbacks: 'a scarcity of melody and simplicity, and a too great tendency to display learning, by creating difficulties for the sole purpose of surmounting them'. While others urged listeners to raise their taste to meet these challenges, this critic protested the exclusionary nature of such music: 'This may be all very well to the professional auditor – but why sacrifice the many to the few? The general listener, who goes solely for his amusement, either fails to have his attention arrested by such passages, or if he do attend to them, merely remarks at the end, "I dare say that may be very clever, but I don't like it."' *The Age* reflected even more cynically that 'The whole of the first act is inefficient, and if not relieved by beautiful scenery and capital machinery, together with the interpolated diablerie and witchery, would have overlaid the Opera.' The ambiguity that had greeted *Der Freischütz* persisted. German scores seemed at times salutary challenges that improved taste, at others times excessively dense works only tolerated because of sensational subject matter and display.

So divided were critics on Spohr's worth that some blamed him for *Der Alchymist*'s failure and even for Bishop's pastiche approach. *The Athenaeum* declared 'no opera of [Spohr's], as a whole, will ever be popular on our stage … Mr. Bishop must have felt this difficulty, or why did he ransack six operas to collect materials for one?' Even though Bishop cut the most involved, abstruse pieces and interpolated the most appealing ones, John Forster still felt *Der Alchymist* epitomised the drawbacks of German music. Writing for the *True Sun*, he complained 'It consists almost entirely of those rambling unconnected phrases, and those substitutions of science and harmony for feeling, which are fitter for instrumental voluntaries and fantasias, than for the composition of an opera.' A nationalistic slant informed this criticism: 'If Mr. Bishop were not an honest man … we should almost be tempted to think that he had brought together a set of Mr. Spohr's worst common-places, to show how inferior one of these trumpeted German composers could be to himself.' In this view, a poor original necessitated adaptation, while failure resulted from an original too poor to rescue.

Easy equations between fidelity and worth were complicated not only by the perceived quality of the original, but also the perceived quality of the adaptation. Taylor implied that *Der Alchymist* failed because Bishop had been too concerned about its effectiveness in performance. 'Much of this … is chargeable upon the singers. One is clamorous for a song here, another for a duet there; and each wants his or her part to be what is called "written up", no matter for the author's reputation, or the patience of the audience.' Bishop had abandoned a work-oriented approach, in other words, in favour of an event-oriented approach. Ironically, however, it was perhaps the very desire for a successful performance that resulted in a poor one. Bishop had included so much music to showcase his best singers and Bayly and Fitzball had introduced so many changes to highlight actors and machinists alike that the balance between music and speech became skewed and the plot virtually incomprehensible. Holmes joked in

The Atlas that 'characters came and went and no one knew what for – on all sides the people gave it up, like an impenetrable riddle at Christmas time'. Even the superlative performers for whom many changes had been made could not save the piece. Harley was hissed so assiduously that the *Theatrical Observer* related that the adapters cut his entire part in subsequent performances and Forster sighed that Mrs Wood 'wasted a great quantity of beautiful tones'. It was therefore not only the status of Spohr or the extent of Bishop's changes that influenced critical response, but the detrimental effect that these changes had on the performance. Even as critics panned *Der Alchymist* because it had not sufficiently respected Spohr's work, they did so primarily because it had not resulted in an effective performance.

Reactions to these two Spohr adaptations were also not only about fidelity, but what fidelity represented in the politically and theatrically volatile context of the early 1830s. Taylor, for example, utilised Smart's faithful *Zemire und Azor* to vaunt the worth of the middle class against the opponents of the Reform Bill:

> We have usually observed ... the execrable taste of the audience (the noisy part of it) who frequent the Italian Opera ... whereas, for the most part, the approbation of the Covent Garden audience was awarded precisely where it was deserved ... The superior discernment and more correct taste of the Covent Garden audiences must have been palpable to every musician; and it affords another proof of the increased knowledge and true refinement of the middle classes. Yes – as HORACE TWISS says, these persons are growing 'very dangerous', and have taken an odd notion of thinking, judging, and acting for themselves.

Twiss had recently made an unpopular statement against the middle classes during debates about the Reform Bill.[51] Taylor was clearly anxious to prove the superiority of middle-class playhouse listeners – and by extension voters – to the 'execrable taste' of their elite counterparts at the opera house. With a successful adaptation like *Zemire und Azor*, musical taste thus intertwined with political and social aspirations.

On the other hand, a flop like *Der Alchymist* seemed to epitomise the need for theatrical reform. Reviewing *Der Alchymist*, Collier wrote, 'In these times, when an outcry is raised that the Legitimate Drama is not only neglected, but deserted – that the Stage is at an end – that play-going is extinct, and so on, we can hardly regret, in a public point of view, that this new attempt directly out of the line of the legitimate drama, has failed.' *Figaro in London* added Polhill's poor management to the chorus of disapproval: 'Polhill's pockets must once more become martyrs to his want of taste, and his foolish ardour for theatrical speculation.' With the introduction of the theatrical Reform Bill only months away, disillusionment with the patent system and management mounted and a piece like *Der Alchymist* suffered from heightened scrutiny of the major theatres.

The varying fates of *Zemire und Azor* and *Der Alchymist* in London define the boundaries for fidelity in the early 1830s. Smart was extolled for fidelity despite cuts, rearrangements and interpolations from other Spohr operas. Bishop was denounced for a reversion to pastiche. In some ways, this spelled the end of pastiche practice and the triumph of desires for fidelity. Few adapters dared take so free an approach subsequently. In other respects, however, opposing views of these adaptations reveal the relativity of fidelity. There was no simple equation between change and failure. Rather, acceptance of adaptation hinged on the extent of adapters' changes, whether the adapter was considered respectful of the original, the perceived worth of the original and the effectiveness of the performance. Bishop in effect tested these boundaries and found the edge beyond which adapters could no longer tread. It is worth noting, however, that the end of pastiche did not necessarily signal the beginning of fidelity. *Der Alchymist*, at least, did not appear on the London stage again in the nineteenth century and the playhouses largely avoided Spohr opera until the 1840s–50s. Works that could not be effectively adapted within the narrower boundaries for change often simply slipped from the repertoire.

AN UNSUCCESSFUL SEARCH

From the sensation of *Der Freischütz* in 1824 to the catastrophe of *Der Alchymist* eight years later, playhouse audiences witnessed the London premières of numerous significant German operas. From one point of view, these signalled a heartening improvement of taste at the playhouses; all had premièred there rather than at the King's Theatre and all but *Der Alchymist* appeared in relatively faithful form. As tensions mounted surrounding the Reform Bill, some critics vaunted the learned qualities of German music as evidence of a sober respectability at the middle-class playhouses that put the capricious upper-class listeners at the King's Theatre to shame. The string of ambitious, unusually faithful adaptations at the English Opera House bolstered this attitude and increased hopes that, if theatrical reform passed in 1832, such enterprises could revitalise the declining native drama.

Yet, imported German operas disappointed in the one respect most important to managers: they did not replicate *Der Freischütz*'s fame. Rising optimism about the salutary effect of imported German opera was therefore tempered by increasing concerns. Easy equations between weighty German music and worth were complicated by feelings that the one key to Romanticism – spontaneous, natural genius – was antithetical to the laboured learning of many German works. Some also felt the preponderance of imported opera overran native drama rather than rejuvenating it. Londoners' deflated hopes for German opera echoed German composers' own experience, as their ambitious plans for native opera faded in the 1830s.[52] All of these factors lessened interest in new German operas, and by the middle of the 1830s managers essentially abandoned their search for another *Der Freischütz*.

Nevertheless, the influx of German operas in the late 1820s and early 1830s had a lasting impact on operatic adaptation. They helped set new standards for fidelity, as adapters challenged their listeners to accept more learned music and as critics denounced outright pastiche in *Der Alchymist*. Adapters had to recede further in the background, more subtly balancing complexity with popularity and adopting a more strategically respectful approach. The lessening divide between native and continental operatic taste also allowed managers to court foreign opera composers directly, which highlighted the problems of a legal system with no provision for international copyright. German opera may not ultimately have proved completely congruent with national taste, but the prevalence of both adapted German operas and German opera composers wrought significant changes on the shape of opera at the playhouses.

On 14 December 1827, Covent Garden performed Henry Bishop's adaptation of *Le nozze di Figaro*. On the surface, this was a normal event; Bishop's *Figaro* had been revived every season since its première in 1819. What happened at this performance, however, represents a turning point in London adaptations. Henrietta Sala as the Countess and Lucia Vestris as Susanna sang 'Che soave zeffiretto' to rapturous applause and a few lines of dialogue ensued. Vestris then stepped forward and the orchestra began Charles Edward Horn's 'I've been roaming'. The song had been advertised in the playbill as a draw, for it was one of Vestris' most popular hits.[1] Yet, even before Vestris began singing, protests arose. Vestris, piqued, left the stage, and only returned and finished the song when applause in some quarters demanded it.

Before Vestris performed *Figaro* again, on 1 January 1828, she addressed her public in the press.[2]

> Respecting the opposition to my introducing the admired song 'I've been roaming' into the opera of *Figaro*, I have only to state, that Miss Stephens, Miss Paton, Miss Tree, and other ladies, have introduced songs of their choice, there being no song by Mozart in the opera as originally produced on the English stage; and those composed by Mr Bishop for Miss Stephens are quite out of the compass of my voice . . . I have been permitted to introduce 'I've been roaming' in the same situation these last two seasons . . . with great success; and I must beg to call your attention to the circumstance of there being no opposition shown by the admirers of Mozart to 'What can a poor Maiden do?' – a song by the same author.

The sense of hypocrisy is palpable. Bishop had composed a new song for his Susanna and subsequent Susannas had substituted numbers to showcase their talents. The preceding spring, for example, Mary Ann Paton had sung 'Follow, follow o'er the mountain' in the part. Vestris had previously interpolated both 'I've been roaming' and another piece by Horn, 'What can a poor maiden do?' from *Philandering*, into *Figaro*, with no protest. She had sung 'I've been roaming' in four other pieces in the past two seasons, and her rivals at Drury Lane, Paton and Emma Sarah Love, had also used the song as a substitute number in other works that autumn.[3] Aria substitution was thus widespread, particularly in revivals. Vestris' public plea apparently drew sympathy. The next time she appeared in the role she refrained from singing the piece, but the *Theatrical Observer* related that the audience demanded it after the opera and Vestris complied 'with the most happy effect'.[4] Vestris did not press the matter further, however. Although she continued interpolation practice in general, she avoided singing Susanna for the rest of the season and, when she resumed it the following season, playbills did not advertise the offending piece.[5]

Never before had the London audience expressed its disapproval of adaptation so strongly or so publicly. Given the prevalence of interpolated numbers, why did this particular song elicit such rancour? One suspects that theatrical politics and scandal played some role. Vestris had won damages in a libel case the previous year against the publisher of the salacious *The adventures, public and private, of Madame Vestris*, which to some extent only heightened perceptions of her as risqué and rebellious.[6] Critics, however, ascribed the incident to loftier concerns of commercialism, fame, class and fidelity. They denounced aria interpolation practice as detracting from any sense of a fixed original. The *Morning Post* claimed, 'This evil is growing to such an extent that although the Managers may put a different title to their Operas ... they will soon all contain the same songs.'[7] This proved particularly problematic for a composer as revered as Mozart. The vivid contrast between Mozart's 'Che soave zeffiretto' and 'I've been roaming' – a quintessential British ballad, replete with charming melody, sentimental text and simple accompaniment – made painfully clear the chasm between continental and native taste (see Ex. 5.1). Richard Mackenzie Bacon decried the 'admixture of so light a composition amongst Mozart's music'.[8]

While interpolation practice weakened author and work, it strengthened singer and audience. 'B. W.' protested the close financial links between interpolation and success in a rebuttal to Vestris' letter: 'the oftener certain vocalists sing particular songs, the more they benefit by it. It is no wonder that such-and-such performers sing with pathos and *expression* such-and-such songs, when they have a *feeling* from every copy that is sold.'[9] 'I've been roaming' seemed an example of a theatre under performers' control and, by extension, under the control of those audience members who encouraged them. A 'dilettante' in *The Harmonicon* chastised manager Charles Kemble for a lack of 'judgment' as well as 'authority', since 'Singers always did, and always will do, such things, if not under proper control.'[10]

Class factored significantly. The 'dilettante' spiralled into an attack on a 'passive' public who allowed the theatres 'to be turned into bear-gardens' by claqueurs and 'half-witted, half tipsy, vulgar people', which 'deter[red] multitudes of decent, rational persons'. John Payne Collier specified that the initial dissenting voices against 'I've been roaming' came from 'the pit and boxes', i.e. the more expensive seating areas.[11] Vestris was only brought back onstage by 'the galleries' as well as some kinder pit patrons who pitied her. 'I've been roaming' thus agitated deep-seated concerns that control of the national theatres lay not in the hands of an educated, middle-class, author-centric model, but resided in the murkier territory of money, performers and unrefined audiences.

The public nature of this protest marked a new era in adaptation, one in which performers and adapters had to modify more subtly, aware that the boundaries for acceptable change were shrinking. This can be seen in adaptations of Mozart and

Example 5.1 Horn 'I've been roaming' mm 0–16

Andantino con amina

I've been roam-ing, I've been roam-ing, Where the mead-ow dew is sweet, And I'm

com-ing, and I'm com-ing, With its pearls up-on my feet; I've been roam-ing, I've been roam-ing, Where the

mead-ow dew is sweet, And I'm com-ing, and I'm com-ing, With its pearls up-on my feet.

Rossini in the late 1820s. Adaptations of *Die Entführung aus dem Serail* in 1827, *Così fan tutte* in 1828 and *La gazza ladra* and *Guillaume Tell* in 1830 represent the new face of adaptation. Adapters took a more careful approach than they had with Mozart and Rossini a decade earlier – not one that did away with change entirely, but one that focused and explained such change with greater care.

The more constrained arena for change signalled two important developments in London operatic life. Previously clear demarcations between London's playhouses and its one opera house disintegrated as all competed more directly for the same works, in more similar form. In addition, as the playhouses began to offer London premières of important works and more faithful adaptations in general, critics began to assess these less as adaptations than as new productions. Critical focus therefore shifted even more keenly than before to appraisals of Mozart and Rossini. Critics struggled to place Mozart's lesser-known, more problematic operas within an increasingly canonised image. Rossini was no longer the dubious new face of *Il barbiere di Siviglia*, but critics remained ambivalent about his merits, even with the new direction shown in *Guillaume Tell*. Throughout their responses to Mozart vs. Rossini, critics continued to employ a dichotomous discourse of German vs. Italian, ancient vs. modern, sober middle class vs. frivolous nobility or, in the memorable words of Leigh Hunt, 'roast beef' vs. 'the frothy evanescence of an Italian cream'.[12]

THE ABDUCTION FROM GREECE

When William Dimond and Christian Kramer adapted *Die Entführung aus dem Serail* for Covent Garden in 1827, they gave the London première of the opera.[13] They were able to scoop the usual home of important London operatic premières – the King's Theatre – because of both genre and class. The King's Theatre remained committed to a view of opera as Italian and all-sung, which increasingly placed them behind developments in German and French opera. They had considered performing *Die Entführung* in around 1818, but it did not appear there until 1866, in Italian with recitatives. Playhouse repertoire, however, easily accommodated Singspiel's spoken dialogue and light musical numbers. Many contemporaries also saw Mozart as antithetical to the frivolous, upper-class taste that seemed prominent at the King's Theatre.[14] Reviewing the adaptation for *The Atlas*, William Hazlitt asserted, 'All the operatic writings of [Mozart] have been long pronounced by the world of fashion [i.e. King's Theatre patrons] to be dull and stupid; and they have been ... effectually removed from our hearing.' (See Appendix 2 for review citations.) The appearance of *Die Entführung* at Covent Garden thus seemed evidence of a laudable, middle-class taste that welcomed the Mozart operas that the King's Theatre allowed to languish.

Die Entführung did not appear unchanged, however, and in fact the one aspect that has drawn most interest today drove most of the changes: exoticism. Mozart and librettist Gottlieb Stephanie's depiction of the Turkish 'other' has intrigued listeners and scholars alike.[15] In the early nineteenth century, however, repetition had worn such tales threadbare. In the *New Monthly Magazine*, Thomas Noon Talfourd sighed, 'The plot . . . is merely the old hacknied [*sic*] story of two Christian lovers in the power of a Mahometan autocrat.' Librettist Dimond, in his preface, felt that the libretto's 'doric simplicity' would no longer 'satisf[y] John Bull'.[16] Ralph Locke affirms that 'by around 1830 *alla turca* and its attendant dramatic types (e.g., the boorish tyrant) were becoming somewhat shopworn, tiresome to composers and perhaps increasingly predictable to audiences'.[17] Additionally, in light of Greece's struggle for independence from Turkey in 1821 to 1833, Turkey represented a different kind of 'other'. Dimond created a more complex, relevant brand of exoticism by transporting the tale to a Turkish-occupied Greek island. He also shifted the nationalities of the Western captives to Italian rather than Spanish and English. A new servant, Dr O'Callaghan, added a final layer of exoticism by bringing the beloved stage Irishman to Greece. Composer Kramer accordingly shifted the aural exoticism of the score. The clear dichotomy between Western and Turkish characters became more diffuse, as Mozart's 'European' numbers mixed with Turkish and Greek sounds.

The relocation of *Die Entführung* to Greece both updated views of Turkey and deliberately politicised the opera. In the late eighteenth century, as Nasser Al-Taee argues, Viennese 'memories of the Turkish threat and failed sieges of their city' created 'ambivalent feelings of animosity and attraction toward the Orient'.[18] The real political threat of Turkey had largely receded, however, and Thomas Bauman points out that Stephanie drew more on artistic than political viewpoints of the Orient.[19] In Dimond and Kramer's day, in contrast, Turkey represented a very real oppressor from which Greece struggled to gain independence. Western Europeans became invested in the conflict, which symbolised the liberation of the birthplace of Western (Christian) values from Eastern (Muslim) usurpation.[20] Many voluntarily joined the Greeks, most famously Byron, whose death in Missolonghi in 1824 spurred British involvement. In 1826, the fall of Missolonghi further ignited European sympathies for the Greeks and works such as *The siege of Missolonghi* at Astley's brought these horrors vividly to the public's attention. The year that *Die Entführung* appeared in London, 1827, represented a turning point. In October, Russia, France and Britain helped Greece achieve an important victory at Navarino. *Die Entführung*'s London première on 24 November capitalised on this success and on the prevailing sentiment, expressed by the *Theatrical Observer*, that Greece was 'at this moment the most interesting spot in the world'.

Given this backdrop, some of the adaptation's greatest draws were its stunning visual portrayal of a Grecian island and its new Greek characters. By all accounts, the sets (painted by David Roberts), lighting, machinery and costumes were magnificent. Talfourd enthusiastically described the 'succession of the richest classical pictures which could be imagined as belonging to a Greek island, adorned with the noblest remains of ancient art, and shown in the most delicious lights'. Such spectacle reinforced that Greece was simultaneously an ally against the Eastern enemy and itself an exotic locale. Audiences thus found double the voyeuristic pleasure, enchanted by the exoticism of both Turkey and Greece. Dimond's new Greek characters served as examples of the Western world's struggle against a threatening East. Aging proprietor Eudoxius provides a mouthpiece for Greek nationalism. He sighs that he possesses only 'a *slave's* fickle tenure on the soil of his free fathers' and remarks of the Greek

Table 5.1 Die Entführung aus dem Serail *vs.* The Seraglio

Mozart numbers cut from *The Seraglio*	Kramer numbers added to *The Seraglio*[1]
Aria, Osmin, 'Solche hergelauf'ne Laffen'	Semi-chorus for Greek villagers, 'Softly ply the muffled oar', cut after première
Aria, Belmonte, 'O wie ängstlich, o wie feurig'	Chorus with solo, Alexis, Greek villagers, 'Away, away, neighbour'
Marcia	Air, Alexis (Greek), 'Oh! mark yon vineyards rich in bloom'
Aria, Blonde, 'Durch Zärtlichkeit und Schmeicheln'	Air, Blonde, 'Come girls with smiling faces', possibly cut in performance
Aria, Pedrillo, 'Frisch zum Kampfe!'	Air, Belmonte, 'Constanza! once more to behold thee'
Aria, Belmonte, 'Wenn der Freude Tränen fließen'	Air, Doris (Greek), ''Tis when the garish sun has set'
Aria, Belmonte, 'Ich baue ganz auf deine Stärke'	Duet, Konstanze, Belmonte, 'Joy hath tears as truly flowing', possibly added after première
Aria, Osmin, 'O, wie will ich triumphieren'	Act two finale (Greek celebration), 'Hark! The joyous bells are ringing'
Duetto, Belmonte, Konstanze, 'Welch ein Geschick!'	Air, Belmonte, 'Love! Lift thy torch'
	Musical Situation, 'Plagues and furies!'
	Duet, Blonde, O'Callaghan, 'Come old and young'

[1] Two additional numbers, a duet for Doris and Alexis and a chorus of Greek girls, both presumably by Kramer, appear in the manuscript libretto and/or the printed libretto, but in no other sources. They were therefore probably cut before or shortly after the first performance.

ruins on the island: 'These monuments of former glory, are to the poor bondsman, the lonely evidence that his country *once* was free.'[21] Eastern villainy deepened. Osmin, already the core of Turkish wickedness in the original, now orders the Greek ruins to be destroyed in order to fill a ditch behind Selim's stable; the cradle of Western heritage becomes so much Turkish refuse.

To accommodate the additional Greek characters, Kramer added five new Greek numbers, alongside three additional arias, two duets and an ensemble for the other characters (see Table 5.1). These pieces stood somewhere between Mozart's division of West and East. Kramer blended the 'national' tunes popular at the time with broader musical tropes of exoticism. Early nineteenth-century audiences purchased reams of sheet music featuring tunes from various nationalities, domesticated with simple, westernised accompaniments. Kramer's new pieces contain the 'rustic' features common to such numbers. For instance, ''Tis when the garish sun has set', which Doris sings in anticipation of a night of rustic celebration, features a catchy tune, repetitive 6/8 rhythm and drone-like harmony (see Ex. 5.2a). Kramer embellished this simple core with some unusual elements. Grace notes and runs text paint 'crickets' and 'firegnats'; later, the metre changes and the key shifts abruptly from minor to major

Example 5.2a ''Tis when the garish sun has set', Kramer, arr., *Die Entführung aus dem Serail*, mm. 1–12

(see Ex. 5.2b). Such elements resonate with 'exotic' music as a whole. Eve R. Meyer has found grace notes, modal shifts and metre changes representative of Turkish music in *Die Entführung* and similar works.[22] In Kramer's adaptation, it was thus not only the Turkish 'enemy' who was portrayed with exotic sounds, but the 'good' Greek characters as well. The expansion of exotic elements was also present in Kramer's added orchestral parts, which displayed his skills as 'Master & Conductor of His Majesty's Band', specifically his wind band.[23] While a full score is not extant, Bacon gave an extensive description in the *Quarterly Musical Magazine and Review*. The timbral difference must have been striking; 'tromboni and triangle' increase the Turkish clangour in 'Singt dem großen Bassa Lieder' and 'rich and . . . voluptuous instruments'

Example 5.2b ''Tis when the garish sun has set', Kramer, arr., *Die Entführung aus dem Serail*, mm. 37–48

(especially the flute and clarinet) enrich virtually every number. While both Greek interpolations and lusher orchestral sounds increased the exotic allure of the score, they also diffused Mozart's stricter division of Western and Eastern sound worlds.

This diffusion is especially evident in changes to the comic characters. In Mozart's opera, the most explicitly exotic music devolves to Osmin. His arias, especially the famous 'Solche hergelauf'ne Laffen', encapsulate disruptive Eastern rage. Yet, none of these arias appeared in Kramer's score; only Osmin's three duets remained. Reviewers attributed this to the most likely culprit: the lack of an English *basso profondo* equal to Ludwig Fischer, Mozart's Osmin.[24] Yet, it also tied into a more significant shift in how comedy and exoticism interacted. Dimond added a completely new character who more comfortably combined wit and the 'other' for London audiences: the stage Irishman. This was Dr O'Callaghan, who became Blonde's lover, while Pedrillo became her brother. O'Callaghan not only highlighted a popular specialist in such roles, Tyrone Power, but also redirected comedy in a more familiar direction. The stage Irishman was an ubiquitous type who subsumed concerns about Ireland in a comfortably comic, stereotyped portrayal.[25] He frequently travelled to new locales – such as *The ninth statue; or, the Irishman in Bagdad* and *The middle dish; or, the Irishman in Turkey* – both as a kind of sacrificial explorer in new worlds and a comforting reminder of a well-known type in distant realms. O'Callaghan provided the rich brogue, loquacious speeches and sly jokes expected of such characters. Yet, he also symbolised Europe's unified support for Greece. He proclaimed that he was the 'countryman' of Sicilian Belmonte: 'Ar'n't both of 'em [Sicily and Ireland] islands, and united by the sea? so, that circumstance makes 'em the same country.'[26] O'Callaghan, like all playhouse comics, played a musically minimal role, as did Pedrillo, whose solos were cut or transferred to Blonde (she sings 'In Mohrenland gefangen'). In the adaptation, comedy therefore receded from the more frightening exotic figure (Osmin) to the more common 'other' (O'Callaghan) and from Osmin's virtuosic buffo singing to the physical and linguistic jokes of the London stage.

Dimond also sought to make Selim less foreign. Selim, spoken in the original, fitted well with the prominent, non-singing male character in native opera. Dimond renamed the character Pasha Ibrahim, presumably after the eponymous Turkish general who led campaigns against Greece. But, perhaps in an effort to negate the threat the real Ibrahim posed, Dimond drew his theatrical Ibrahim closer to Western roots. The Western heritage of Dimond's Ibrahim is explained earlier and in more depth by the added character Malek, a kind of Turkish father figure who rescued Ibrahim as a child from Turkish pirates. Dimond's Ibrahim is even more restrained in his advances to Konstanze and her defiant 'Martern aller Arten' is sung not to Ibrahim but to Malek, as she awaits punishment after the failed rescue attempt. Dimond found Ibrahim's pardon of the lovers inexplicable, 'springing out of no other very apparent motive than the necessity of finishing the Opera with a Chorus'.[27] He therefore increased Ibrahim's connection to the lovers by making him Konstanze's long-lost brother. While this change explained Ibrahim's magnanimity, it made his decision to remain an Islamic leader less plausible; Collier, writing in the *Morning Chronicle*, found it odd that Ibrahim retained the 'Mahometan faith'. Still, although Dimond stopped short of returning Ibrahim to Western Europe and Christianity, he left viewers with a satisfying fantasy of foreign lands ruled by Western-born leaders.

When Michael Kelly considered performing *Die Entführung* at the King's Theatre around 1818, he abandoned it because 'finding there were no finales, and it would be a musical heresy in this country, to add finales of any other composer, it was laid aside'.[28] Dimond states in his preface that Kelly referred the work to him, rightly imagining that the playhouses had more leeway to alter the original. Dimond and Kramer's adaptation then, altered as it was, was the only route by which *Die Entführung* could reach the London stage in the early nineteenth century; indeed, it was those very alterations that enabled it to be performed there. As Mark Everist has observed of French practices, adaptations did not destabilise canonical works as much as provide one of the only conduits through which they could remain part of the repertory.[29] In 1820s London, this meant updating Mozart and Stephanie's opera to suit musical tastes and current events. Kramer and Dimond abducted their characters from a different but equally compelling seraglio.

A NEW SCHOOL FOR LOVERS

There is perhaps no opera whose libretto has been altered as much as *Così fan tutte*. *Così*'s unsettling tale of partner swapping sparked numerous rewrites in the nineteenth century, of which German ones have been especially well documented. In Berlin in 1820, for example, Carl Alexander Herklots made the Albanians two new characters instead of the original lovers in disguise. In Berlin in 1846, Louis Schneider had the women recognise the disguise and only continue in fun. In Stuttgart in 1856, Bernhard Gugler had the 'new' couples – Fiordiligi and Ferrando, Dorabella and Guglielmo – love each other from the beginning.[30]

Samuel James Arnold, Hampden Napier and William Hawes' adaptation of the opera, as *Tit for tat, or the tables turned* for the English Opera House in 1828, followed suit. The sisters recognise first Despina, in her disguise as a doctor, and then the men and only play along to punish them. Arnold and Napier clearly found such a change necessary for moral respectability, although the opera had been performed at the King's Theatre since its London debut there in 1811 with no appreciable plot change. Even though King's Theatre audiences could read the libretto in Italian and English on facing pages, perhaps Arnold and Napier felt that having risqué ideas conveyed onstage in the vernacular caused more consternation. In contrast to the altered libretto, *Tit for tat* featured Mozart's score virtually intact. This accorded with Arnold's ambitious string of adaptations in the late 1820s, discussed in Chapter 4, in which he sought to best other theatres with his daringly complete versions of important foreign operas. The result was a combination that became prevalent at the playhouses in the late 1820s: an increasingly fixed score wed to a still malleable libretto.

Edward Holmes, in his review for *The Atlas*, deemed *Così* a 'delicious libel on the women'. In rewriting the plot, Arnold and Napier sought to eradicate both the libel and its deliciousness. Any hint of flirtatiousness or sexual desire disappeared. Already at the beginning of Da Ponte's libretto, Fiordiligi declares she feels mad and fiery, while Dorabella somewhat more chastely longs for marriage:

> FIORDILIGI: I am in the mood to do something quite mad this morning. I feel a sort of fire, a sort of tingling in my blood . . .
>
> DORABELLA: . . . I also feel something unusual stirring inside. I could swear that soon we'll hear wedding bells.[31]

Later, they playfully anticipate romantic dalliance in their duet 'Prenderò quel brunettino', concluding 'what pleasure, what fun I shall have!' And, while Fiordiligi suffers moral anguish in the face of Ferrando's advances, Dorabella's 'È amore un ladroncello' advises complete submission to Cupid; in the end, both sisters do just that. In the British adaptation, none of this occurred. When the sisters first appear, they do not speak of fires or tingling. The duet 'Prenderò quel brunettino' is sung to mock Despina by pretending they both desire the doctor, i.e. Despina in disguise. Dorabella does retain the original sentiment of 'È amore un ladroncello', since she is piqued that Fiordiligi feels she pretended to succumb too soon. Ultimately, though, only pretended infidelity occurs.

Arnold and Napier also mitigated Despina's corrupting influence.[32] Shocked when Despina suggests that, in the absence of their lovers, they 'make love as furiously as [they] can – if it was only for pastime', the sisters stalk out.[33] Despina therefore sings her callous 'In uomini! In soldati' alone. By the time she sings her equally conniving 'Una donna a quindici anni', the sisters have already found her out. Despina's challenge to class hierarchy also recedes. Her initial soliloquy vanishes and with it her pointed social critique; she no longer asks 'must I just smell [the chocolate] and not taste it? Don't I have an appetite like yours?' Instead, the sisters shame Despina when they force her to confess her role in the plot. They demonstrate their superior acuity, as they recognise the men in disguise and she does not. They oblige her to confess her greed in accepting Don Alfonso's bribe and elicit her contrite promise to 'do any thing now for the pure pleasure of being revenged upon Signor Alfonso'.[34] Finally, they remind her of the gratitude a servant owes indulgent mistresses: 'ungrateful girl – is it thus you repay our kindness who have ever treated you more as a companion, than as a servant'.[35] The sexual and social subversion of Da Ponte's late eighteenth-century plot ceded to more conservative pre-Victorian views.

Compared to these substantial alterations, Hawes kept the score remarkably intact. Only a few numbers were published, but the manuscript libretto and word book suggest he initially retained all of Mozart's pieces. Several, however, were cut during rehearsal: Ferrando and Guglielmo's first duet; the quartet 'La mano a me date'; and Ferrando and Fiordiligi's second arias. Hazlitt and William Ayrton reported that additional pieces disappeared after the première; in his review for *The Harmonicon*,

Ayrton noted the loss of 'Il core vi dono', while in *The Examiner*, Hazlitt remarked on the absence of 'Secondate, aurette amiche' and 'a beautiful scena or two'. The three extant published numbers – the opening trio, the quintet 'Di scrivermi ogni giorno' and Ferrando's 'Un' aura amorosa' – are virtually identical to the original. One aria appears to have been added: a ballad for Despina, included only in the word book. Its sentimental text about a pining lover, as well as its strict alternation of eight and seven syllable lines, suggest that it was a newly composed piece in the British ballad style. So many reviewers praised Hawes for not interpolating any numbers, however, that it is possible it was cut in performance or taken from a Mozart work I have not yet identified.

Such modest changes contrast sharply with the liberal rewrites of *Le nozze di Figaro* and *Don Giovanni* only a decade earlier, as well as with the adapted *Die Entführung* a year previous. They even show greater fidelity than the King's Theatre, which was typically viewed as presenting *the* opera to audiences, not an adaptation. The King's Theatre's 1811 London première had maintained the original plot, but cut over ten numbers, interpolated 'Porgi amor' and 'Voi che sapete' from *Figaro* and transferred 'È amore un ladroncello' to Fiordiligi.[36] Revivals at the King's Theatre retracted some of these changes, but Hawes still offered the fullest version of the score Londoners had yet heard.[37] To paraphrase the original subtitle, *Tit for tat* became a school less for lovers than for listeners.

THE RAGE FOR ROSSINI

While British adapters felt comfortable bringing more Mozart to their audience, they felt trepidation about the most popular foreign composer in 1820s London: Rossini. Rossini saturated up to 80 per cent of the King's Theatre's repertoire during the decade and was rapturously received when he visited London in 1823–4.[38] Yet, playhouse managers were slow to capitalise on this craze. *Il barbiere di Siviglia*, which had been adapted in 1818, was still revived, an un-staged version of *La donna del lago* was performed for the Lenten oratorios in 1823 and some of Rossini's numbers appeared in the 1824 pastiche *Native land*.[39] Not until 1827, however, did another full-length, staged adaptation of Rossini appear, when *Il Turco in Italia* was adapted for Drury Lane. A spate of Rossini adaptations followed soon thereafter: Michael Rophino Lacy adapted the pastiche *Ivanhoé* in 1829 and *La cenerentola* in 1830 (with music from *La cenerentola*, *Guillaume Tell*, *Armida* and *Maometto II*) for Covent Garden; and Bishop adapted *La gazza ladra* for Covent Garden and *Guillaume Tell* for Drury Lane in 1830.[40]

Playhouse managers' initial reluctance to follow Rossini mania stemmed from two main causes. First, they were occupied with another obsession, for which the King's Theatre offered no competition: Weber, whose popularity was explored in Chapter 3.

Bacon observed in 1825 that 'The English public may now be said to be falling under the dominion of two musical despots – Rossini rules us from the King's Theatre, whilst Carl Maria Von Weber asserts his empire from the great and little English play-houses.'[41] Given that *Der Freischütz*'s success sent managers in avid pursuit of imported operas, however, Rossini should have been a more obvious choice. The second barrier was difficulty. Maria Dickons had surmounted Rosina's challenging role in Bishop's adaptation of *Il barbiere di Siviglia* in 1818, but she retired in 1820, with few heirs apparent. Additionally, Bishop had been able to rework *Il barbiere* freely to accommodate his uneven vocal company; he could no longer alter with such impunity in the late 1820s. Occasionally a singer attempted the task, as did Fanny Ayton in the adapted *Il Turco in Italia*, but she received lukewarm reviews as 'an accomplished singer with an indifferent voice'.[42] The playhouses' renewed interest in Rossini in the late 1820s therefore coincided with the rise of a prima donna equal to his challenges: Mary Ann Paton. She was largely responsible for the string of Rossini adaptations in 1829–30, starring in *Ivanhoé*, *La cenerentola* and *La gazza ladra*. While Paton did not sing in the final Rossini adaptation of 1830 – *Guillaume Tell* – Drury Lane had a respected bass-baritone, Henry Phillips, equal to the title role.

These adaptations helped form a growing web of interconnections between the playhouses and the King's Theatre, defying barriers of repertoire and class. Virtually all of these operas appeared at both houses, with *Ivanhoé* the only exception. *La cenerentola*, *La gazza ladra* and *Il Turco in Italia* debuted at the King's Theatre in 1820–1 and were stock pieces there by the time the playhouse adaptations appeared. A ballet version of *Guillaume Tell* appeared two months before the Drury Lane adaptation. Unusually, several performers moved between opera house and play-house. Ayton sang in both *Il Turco in Italia* and *La gazza ladra* in 1827 at the King's Theatre before singing the former opera at Drury Lane. Vestris had made her London debut at the King's Theatre in 1815–16 before moving primarily to the playhouses and continued to sing isolated roles there in the 1820s, notably one of her signature trouser roles, Pippo in *La gazza ladra*.[43] Paton competed directly with Maria Malibran at the King's Theatre; both appeared as Cinderella in 1830, often on the same nights. Paton even performed the role at the King's Theatre the following year when she sang there briefly as a substitute. Another crossover could have occurred in 1833, when Alfred Bunn apparently offered Rossini 20,000 francs to write an opera for the playhouses, but this never materialised.[44] Prevalent stereotypes saw playhouse and opera house audiences as completely separate. Reviewing Drury Lane's *Guillaume Tell*, the *Theatrical Observer* stated that 'the frequenters of the National Theatres are not the frequenters of the Opera'. Still, audiences started to overlap and several reviewers remarked on the unusual number of fashionable patrons at the playhouse Rossini adaptations.[45] Boundaries of musical taste, class and nationality began to erode.

TRIUMPHS, SCANDALS AND THE PRIMA DONNA

Paton's involvement with these Rossini adaptations represented a pinnacle in her career as the playhouses' leading prima donna. After her 1822 London debut as Susanna in an adapted *Le nozze di Figaro*, she grew steadily in reputation and ability. She profited from Weber's ascendancy, singing Agathe in the first London *Der Freischütz* and creating Reiza in *Oberon*. Her performances in revivals of the adapted *Il barbiere di Siviglia* demonstrated her facility with Rossini and critics found her particularly suited to works by these foreign composers. Edward Sterling, for instance, referred to 'the immense superiority of advantage in which her talents are displayed in the Italian and German style'.[46] After a brief hiatus in 1827–8, owing largely to illness, she returned triumphantly in 1829–30 in the three Rossini adaptations listed above, which were clearly designed for her. Her success in *Ivanhoé* led Bishop to adapt *La gazza ladra* 'for the express purpose of introducing Miss Paton in the interesting character of [Ninetta]' and *La cenerentola* was apparently her suggestion as well.[47] As in so many European centres, prima donnas could dictate repertoire.

Prima donnas also often drew scandal, and Paton was no exception. In May 1824, she had secretly married Lord William Lennox in Scotland and delivered his child in March 1825. Within only a few years, the marriage deteriorated and rumours flew of an affair with her leading man in all of the Rossini productions, Joseph Wood. Already at the 1828 York Musical Festival, a satirical play hinted that she was pregnant by Wood, which may help explain her absence from the patent stages around this time.[48] The scandal climaxed during the run of *La cenerentola*, in May 1830. After a series of arguments in which Paton fled Lennox's house and Lennox accused Wood of harbouring her, Paton performed in *La cenerentola* at Covent Garden on 22 May. Although she asked the stage manager, George Bartley, to 'protect [her] from all interruption and annoyance', Lennox created a scene in the green room. Paton refused to return to his home and 'the trumpet tongue of slander' suggested she was living with Wood, particularly when Alfred Bunn engaged them to perform in Dublin that summer.[49] Paton obtained an annulment in February 1831 and a few days later married Wood; Bishop gave away the bride.[50]

Scandal intertwined with Paton's performances in these adaptations. First, each of her Rossini roles contained parallels between the personal and professional. In *Ivanhoé*, she played the scorned Rebecca, pursued by an unscrupulous nobleman but championed by the courageous Ivanhoe. In *La gazza ladra*, she was again wrongfully accused, pursued by a corrupt judge but loved by an upright farmer. *La cenerentola* found her in the title role, unfairly downtrodden by her family but rescued by the prince. Each fictional situation resonated with her tangled love life. *The Age* also suggested that collusion in the theatre led to discretion outside it: 'The *first* elopement of Lady William Lennox ... on Wednesday, May 19th [1830], was planned between herself and Wood during the performance of *Cinderella* [Lacy's adaptation of *La cenerentola*] on Tuesday, the 18th '.[51]

The personal even crept into the libretto. In *La cenerentola*, Lacy apparently added lines that referred to confusion surrounding Paton's name. Paton had been tardy in acknowledging her marriage to Lennox and therefore had taken to using her maiden and married name alternately. This occasioned consternation, as Collier related:

> with reference to [Paton's] real and supposed name, we must say that we could not relish the fulsome compliment stuffed into the mouth of KEELY [sic, as servant Pedro] – that 'whatever name she bore, she would be an honour and an ornament to it' … if she still appears in the bills as Miss PATON, it would have been much better to have … omit[ted] the compliment, as we are sure it put the person to whom it was paid in a very awkward and painful situation – not the less so in consequence of the vociferous and repeated applauses of a very full house.[52]

These lines are not in contemporary sources for the libretto and were most likely added for these performances and their extra-theatrical meaning only.[53]

As Paton perhaps knew, her vocal prowess helped offset her perceived moral transgressions. Reviews of *La gazza ladra* and *La cenerentola* – which admittedly appeared before her elopement with Wood – described the exceptional voice that helped her weather scandal. Lifting Paton's art to the realm of Dryden, *The Age* raved of her Ninetta, 'The notes she breathed forth were so liquid, that they were worthy of a St Cecilia and would raise any "mortal to the skies".' Critics found that she equalled and even surpassed Malibran who, as mentioned earlier, sang Cinderella at the King's Theatre at the same time. Playing on divisions of both class and nationality, *The Age* claimed that 'though the votaries of Fashion may throng to the Opera to hear Lalande or Malibran, the lovers of melody will go to hear Lady William, and have the additional gratification of patronizing national talent'.[54] Several reviewers even suggested a close connection between singer and composer that blurred the line between adaptation and original. The *Morning Post* enthused that 'she might have been taken for the *prima donna* for whose peculiar excellencies of voice, execution, and feeling [*La cenerentola*] had been expressly written'.[55] The continued importance of an event-oriented model is evident. Even as controversy swirled around Paton and even as the adaptions in which she sang diverged from a work-oriented model, such concerns could fall away in the face of the sheer vocal and visual pleasure she offered audiences.

ADAPTATION INTERRUPTED: *LA GAZZA LADRA*

In the first two Rossini adaptations that featured Paton – *Ivanhoé* and *La cenerentola* – adapter Lacy freely altered the originals to suit his star performer. This was possible because both were pastiches; *Ivanhoé* was already a pastiche and Lacy drew from multiple Rossini operas for his adaptation of *La cenerentola*. In contrast, Bishop's adaptation of *La gazza ladra* marked an important shift in attitudes to adaptation. Bishop initially made numerous changes to both libretto and score and wrote several additional numbers, most intended to showcase Paton. He was obliged, however, to discard his added numbers before the première – for reasons unknown – leaving a score confined to Rossini's original opera. The resulting mixture of fidelity and alteration demonstrates the changing but still permeable boundaries for adaptation in the early 1830s.

One area still considered open for alteration was the libretto. This was particularly true since Giovanni Gherardini's libretto was itself an adaptation of a tale Londoners knew well: J. M. T. Badouin D'Aubigny and Louis-Charles Caigniez's *La pie voleuse*, which premièred in Paris in 1815 and was followed by three separate London adaptations in the same year. Several parodies ensued and the play continued as a stock piece in London through the 1820s. The *Literary Gazette* therefore greeted *La gazza ladra* as 'our old acquaintance'. Less diplomatically, Sterling referred to it in *The Times* as 'that most hacknied of all theatrical subjects'.

Both 'originals' clearly served as sources for Bishop's adaptation.[56] The *Morning Post* described it as 'Rossini's *Gazza Ladra*, or rather *The Maid and the Magpie* [the title of one of the British adaptations of the French play], with the greater portion of the music to Rossini's Opera, arranged by Bishop'. Given that the translations of the French play were more ubiquitous 'originals' for Bishop's audience than the opera, they informed virtually all of his changes to the Italian libretto. Bishop divided *La gazza ladra* into three acts rather than two, shifted culpability more to the corrupt and lecherous mayor than Ninetta's employers (who are also the parents of her beloved), made the Jewish peddler character more sympathetic and eliminated a vain attempt by Ninetta's father, Fernando, to save her. Bishop also excluded a gun shot towards the end of the opera, fired in celebration but mistaken as Ninetta's deathblow. The latter was in neither the British adaptations nor the King's Theatre production of *La gazza ladra* in 1821; even the King's Theatre may therefore have been influenced by the British versions. Audiences often received stories like this through multiple lenses, each distorting, augmenting or restoring some elements in a dispersed web of retellings.

Bishop initially intended to alter the score as freely. This can be seen in the unusually rich source materials for the adaptation. A French full printed score of Rossini's original exists, with Bishop's cuts and annotations written directly onto it. There is also an autograph score, which contains only those numbers Bishop altered too much to be able to write into the French score. This autograph score is separate from Bishop's autograph scores of three additional pieces, all of which he composed for the adaptation.[57] These separate autograph scores may stem from a collision between old and new approaches to adaptation. According to the manuscript libretto, Bishop intended to continue past practices by adding six pieces: one ballad each for Giannetto and Fernando and a simple lovers' duet in place of more complex pieces in the original;

and three new ballads for Paton in the leading role. Only three of these are extant, contained in Bishop's separate autograph score, but all six were probably by Bishop.[58]

In a novel move, however, all of these numbers disappeared by the première, for reasons still unclear. A letter from Bishop to stage manager George Bartley shows that it was not his choice. Covent Garden manager Charles Kemble, struggling in the wake of near bankruptcy the previous year, apparently persuaded Bishop to waive his usual payment of £30 for the first night and £5 for each subsequent night. Bishop spent £30 for Rossini's score and Fitzball's assistance with the poetry. Only a little over a week before the première, he found that his original pieces had been cut, which significantly decreased his potential income:

> From what source did I hope that my sacrifice of time and labour and money would be in any way returned to me? Why, from that source which by the arrangements made after the rehearsal of yesterday, in your room, is now entirely cut off from me! I mean the profit likely to accrue from my own music in that opera. That music is now taken away, and the chance of its profit to me destroyed.[59]

Why these arrangements were made is uncertain; perhaps there were protests from the performers, a desire to shorten the work or internal politics. At least one of Bishop's songs reached print, but none were performed onstage, which deprived them of the stage popularity necessary for profitable sheet music sales.[60] Theatre managers would not normally have asked Bishop to waive his fee, but his letter reveals that – as protestors of 'I've been roaming' feared – adapters added pieces for commercial as well as aesthetic reasons.

It is with some irony, then, that Bishop must have read Ayrton's praise in *The Harmonicon*: 'We are indebted to Mr. Bishop, who, though circumstances would not allow him to give the music of [*La gazza ladra*] in an entire state, has added no one thing to it: no temptation of a pecuniary kind has induced him to depart from that strict line of duty, both to the composer and the public, which justice and good taste equally dictated.' Ayrton's comment shows the difficult balance adapters had to maintain, between the financial gain of sheet music sales and the less tangible commodity of a reputation for fidelity. An easy equation between interpolated songs and profits from their sale eroded as adapters were rewarded instead for a discreet, almost 'invisible' approach.

Bishop's changes to *La gazza ladra* were, however, hardly invisible. He replaced recitative with spoken dialogue, cut four solos and one duet and substantially altered the larger ensembles.[61] He also continued established practices of splitting roles into two characters, one spoken and one sung; both Ninetta's employer, Fabrizio, and her friend Pippo were handled this way. Such splits spoke to the continued divergence on the playhouse stage between action and music. This divergence also prompted Bishop to make significant changes to Rossini's ensembles, particularly the most action-based sections.

A striking example is 'Tremate o populi'. Rossini's ensemble, which stretches to 700 measures, depicts a crucial dramatic moment – Ninetta's death sentence – with a loose version of the multi-partite ensemble format or 'solita forma'. Bishop retained approximately half of the ensemble, reshaped into a reflective number. Plot alterations helped him trim the longest, most kinetic portions. Bishop eliminated the entire opening scena (mm. 1–167), in which judges find Ninetta guilty and pronounce her death sentence, by having Ninetta's father, Fernando, enter before the ensemble and inform her of the sentence in spoken dialogue. Bishop also cut fifty-five measures from the tempo d'attacco (mm. 226–373) by having Fernando learn of his pardon before the piece begins; he therefore does not rush on to try to save Ninetta, only to be himself incarcerated.[62] This also allowed Bishop to eliminate the entire tempo di mezzo (mm. 409–61), in which guards try to drag Ninetta and Fernando away. In contrast, Bishop retained both 'static' pezzi concertati with minimal trimming (mm. 168–225 and 374–408).[63] He also retained most of the exciting concluding stretta (mm. 462–704), though he did eliminate 104 measures of repetition. Here, he addressed what Bacon called Rossini's 'great fault', namely 'a disposition to spin out his pieces, by repetition, to too considerable length'.[64] While Bishop therefore drastically abridged the ensemble, he kept more of the music than he had originally intended; the manuscript libretto shows that he had initially planned to skip the entire tempo d'attacco as well. And including even a portion of such a long, dramatically crucial ensemble still stepped beyond his listeners' usual tolerance for such numbers.

Bishop therefore hardly presented *La gazza ladra* in complete form. Compared with his initial plans, however, he diverged significantly from past adaptation practice. His adaptation is not only remarkably free of interpolation, but faithful at the expense of ingrained playhouse ideals. Bishop's proposed additions and substitutions would have infused the sweet, sentimental solo ballads cherished at the playhouses into an opera Bacon characterised as 'remarkable for the almost entire absence of airs'.[65] Bishop's numbers would have accommodated weak performers and showcased superlative ones. Without them, the adaptation allowed leading lady Paton only one solo, forced tenor Wood (the Giannetto) into music by all accounts too difficult for him and weighted the work more heavily towards ensembles than solos; *La gazza ladra* offered nine ensembles and eight solos, Bishop's adaptation eight and four, respectively. The adapted *La gazza ladra* encapsulates how London adapters lurched towards fidelity, sometimes able to alter without remark, sometimes chastised, à la Vestris and 'I've been roaming', for crossing shrinking boundaries for adaptation.

ROSSINI IN TYROL: *GUILLAUME TELL* AS *HOFER*

Adaptations of works like *La gazza ladra* challenged the King's Theatre's virtual monopoly on Rossini. The same year, *Hofer* went a step further, for it was the operatic

London première of Rossini's latest work, *Guillaume Tell*. The King's Theatre had performed *Tell* a few months earlier, but as a ballet, mimicking the success of a balletic *La muette de Portici* a season earlier. Reviewers unanimously approached the Drury Lane adaptation as the true London première of *Guillaume Tell*. Bishop and his publisher, Goulding and D'Almaine, capitalised on this status. Bishop did not add any numbers to Rossini's score, and Goulding and D'Almaine – who may have commissioned the adaptation – published a word book, a libretto and an ambitiously complete piano–vocal score.[66] Here, then, the potential profit to publishers of bringing out the adaptation of an important new work relatively whole seemed to outweigh the profit from adapters' interpolations. Neither Bishop nor his librettist James Robinson Planché felt, however, that they could transfer *Guillaume Tell* to London without significant alteration. Bishop cut much of the score and radically recomposed the rest, while Planché rewrote the libretto to replace Tell with the story of Tyrolean Andreas Hofer. Diverse concerns of politics, casting, musical convention and boundaries for change transported *Guillaume Tell* to the Tyrol.

Planché's most immediate motivation for changing the plot was the saturation of Tell dramatisations on the London stage. Allardyce Nicoll lists nine different dramatic pieces with 'William Tell' in the name between 1794 and 1829.[67] One version in particular concerned Planché, as he explained in his preface:

> The story of William Tell having been so often placed upon the English stage, and latterly by one of our first living dramatists, Mr Sheridan Knowles . . . induced the writer of this opera to venture on the transplantation of Rossini's celebrated composition to a subject, which, while new to the theatre, should at the same time bear sufficient analogy to that of the French Drama, and be in keeping with the peculiar character of the original music.[68]

Proliferating versions had not stopped London adapters in the past, but Knowles' play gave Planché and Bishop pause for several reasons.[69] Not only was it the same story as *Guillaume Tell*, it also embodied the native, legitimate drama that many contemporaries saw as the true purpose of the British stage. To supersede this respected play with an operatic treatment might activate critical rhetoric about the decline of native drama. Already in 1825, the *London Magazine* worried that 'some rackety melodrama or gaudy opera [would] . . . banish [Knowles' play] from the boards at a night's notice'.[70] Bishop had also written the incidental music for Knowles' play and may not have wished to pit his own compositions against Rossini's on the same subject. Finally, Phillips, who sang the leading role, would have faced comparison with superstar tragedian William Macready. Macready not only played Tell in Knowles' version but had suggested the subject to Knowles and in essence 'owned' the role.[71] Planché's choice of Hofer sidestepped clashes between legitimate and illegitimate, native and foreign, actor and singer.

Hofer offered a fresh tale that was both congruent with Tell's and of personal interest to Planché. Hofer and Tell's locales and stories resonated strongly with each other.

Tyrol, a region of Austria bordering Switzerland, shared many of the same mountainous vistas and folk music traditions. Hofer's history also echoed Tell's.[72] In 1809, Hofer led uprisings against Bavaria and Napoleonic France, who wished to oust Austria as rulers of the Tyrol. Initially surprisingly successful against their more experienced foe, the Tyroleans were defeated in 1810 and Hofer was executed by Napoleon's order. Despite the Tyroleans' loss, their courage captured the public imagination. British readers learned details of the revolt against their mutual Napoleonic foe in newspapers, monographs and several poems by William Wordsworth.[73] Some, including Planché, visited the historic sites of battle and Hofer's tomb.

Despite its popularity, Hofer's tale had yet to be dramatised in London and Planché clearly saw an opportunity to fuse past and present patriots. Known for his attention to historical accuracy, Planché imbued his libretto with actual events. True to historical accounts, the Tyroleans rise to arms when women and children distribute pieces of paper with 'S'ist zeit', or 'It's time' written on them, defeat the Bavarians before Austrian troops arrive and joyfully welcome the belated Austrian troops as they march into Innsbruck. Historical personages Joachim Haspinger, a Capuchin monk instrumental in the revolt, and Josephine Negretti, 'a girl of eighteen [who] assumed the dress of a man ... [carried] a rifle and [used] it with considerable dexterity', assisted Hofer.[74] Hofer, distinct enough to merit staging in his own right, similar enough to Tell to meld easily with his story, thus provided a convenient way both to evoke and to replace Tell.

Planché may also have judged Hofer more suitable for the current political climate. Austria was more ally than enemy in 1830 and therefore better filled the role of Hofer's ruler than Tell's opponent. Hunt, in *The Tatler*, did voice a lone protest that Austria's repressive policies undermined the message of freedom:

> The House of Austria cut a poor figure in a story about freedom, – they who are celebrated as partitioners of Poland, and despots of Italy, and who now this minute are keeping hundreds of Italian patriots in their citadels and dungeons ... purely for wishing to see their country independent. What would the Hofers of Lombardy say to this opera?

Few critics seem to have shared this concern, perhaps because Hofer's allies were less compelling than his enemies: Bavaria and, especially, France. The bitterness of the still recent Napoleonic Wars must have made Hofer's stunning, if temporary, defeat of Napoleon's Bavarian allies particularly satisfying.

The current situation in France, as the tensions that led to the 1830 July Revolution mounted, may also have motivated the substitution. Scholars have recently questioned an easy connection between *Tell* and revolution, yet the potential of the opera to stir revolutionary feelings could not be ignored.[75] This was certainly true in Britain, given the incendiary atmosphere that would lead to the Swing riots in the summer of 1830, the Irish Tithe war the following spring and widespread unrest in London after the

House of Lords initially rejected the Reform Bill in 1831. Edward Taylor's review of *Past and present* – a play that followed several characters from the French Revolution through 1829 and that Drury Lane premièred a little over a month before *Guillaume Tell* – voiced the discontent that seethed in some quarters of the audience:

> Let us advise our readers to remark the undisturbed air of the aristocratic company in the first scene, [during] the . . . destruction of the Bastille . . . The history of all revolutions proves the apathy and willful ignorance of the nobles, even to the last moment of the crisis; and whether we see *Guillaume Tell*, *Rienzi*, *Masaniello*, or *Past and Present*, the stage presents the same lesson, without much chance of enlightening the future. The walls of palaces are as thick as ever . . . and ministers will still talk of the overwhelming force of mercenary troops, and the unavailing resistance of an exasperated people.[76]

In this context, Hofer's mixture of rebellion and loyalty broadened his appeal. Hunt observed that Hofer differed from Tell in one important particular: 'Hofer did not throw off a yoke like the greater patriot [Tell]. He only hindered its being changed for another.' One contemporary history of Hofer seized on this to fashion Hofer as anti-revolutionary: 'in every country in Europe the poison of revolutionary principles has more or less contaminated and corrupted national character; but the Tyrolese still retain all their native energy and simplicity'.[77] More radical audience members may of course have ignored this message and focused on the oppressive behaviour of the Bavarian officers, Hofer's stirring speeches – 'It is the cause of Liberty! The holiest in which man can draw his sword' – and the thrilling scenes of revolt.[78] At the same time, as Katharine Newey writes of an 1832 melodrama about Hofer for the Surrey, proponents of reform often framed their desires not in terms of a radical new world, but of a return to 'traditional English values of fairness, loyalty, and tolerance'.[79] Hofer could offer the appeal of an idyllic, rural past. One must approach such political connections cautiously, for the Tell story was widely staged in Britain at this time and its alteration was therefore not required. In the tumultuous early 1830s, however, Hofer offered a potent combination of revolt, fealty and nostalgia.

A final reason for the new story was musical, for it allowed Bishop greater freedom in adapting the music. To attempt *Guillaume Tell* complete was not feasible. The opera was long and difficult, especially since Bishop, having moved to Drury Lane, no longer had Paton to shoulder Mathilde's demanding music. Massive cuts and rearranging were therefore required, yet Bishop had to reconcile these with increasing demands for fidelity. Bishop introduced no new numbers, but the new story allowed him to cut and recompose freely. Planché eliminated the romance between Austrian princess Mathilde and Swiss patriot Arnold. Instead, the love interest devolved on Tyrolean villagers Walter (the Arnold character) and a new role, Bertha. Bishop therefore cut Mathilde's 'Sombre forêt' and Arnold and Mathilde's duet and used only portions of Mathilde's 'Pour notre amour' (transposed for Hofer) and Arnold's 'Asil héréditaire'. Plot elements specific to the Tell story that were dropped, such as the iconic apple-shooting scene and Gesler's death, lost their music; Bishop cut 'Sois immobile' and the entire act four finale. Historical details of the Hofer story also enabled alterations. Bishop combined the famous all-male oath scene that concludes Rossini's act two with the mixed-chorus finale of act three. The female voices in the latter could be explained as the women who historically joined Hofer's uprising.

While cutting numbers, extracting portions of others and even conflating several numbers were standard practices in adaptations, Bishop followed an additional, more novel approach. He took long ensembles or instrumental pieces from *Guillaume Tell*, many already popular in London, and crafted new numbers from their tunes. For instance, Bishop used the overture for melodramatic music before the act three finale and for both of Josephine's solos. As described earlier, Josephine Negretti was a historical personage who fought alongside her male counterparts in the revolt. Planché must have been delighted to find such a character. She was virtually made for Vestris, well known for displaying her alluring figure in trouser roles. In his review for the *Morning Chronicle*, Collier explained how Vestris' identity had become inextricable from the subversion and titillation of gender reversal: 'Madame Vestris was quite in her element, in breeches; and they always fit her so well, in every sense, that it is a pity she should ever put on petticoats.' While Vestris' figure proved fascinating, she also possessed considerable musical skill. Yet, *Guillaume Tell* had few female solos in general – *The Athenaeum* felt it displayed a 'want of any predominant female interest' – and none that would suit Josephine's character.[80]

Given that Vestris had been so chastened for her interpolation of 'I've been roaming', Bishop did not add new solos, but instead culled two from the overture. The second one, 'Strike for Tyrol and liberty', exemplifies his approach (see Ex. 5.3). As readers will immediately perceive, Bishop used one of the most famous melodies of the overture for this solo. Given that tunes from an overture frequently reappeared later in an opera, some listeners may have assumed the solo was original. Nor was Bishop's procedure unique; Rossini himself utilised this melody for the finale of his 1831 abridged version. Bishop clearly saw the overture as raw melodic material to be reshaped into the necessary format. He slowed the tempo from Allegro vivace to Allegro marziale, since a vocalist cannot articulate notes as quickly as a trumpet. Perhaps to compensate for this, or to augment the martial tone, he dotted the rhythm of the opening brass fanfare. The manuscript score shows that Bishop further underlined the military sound by adding a side drum. He also slimmed repetitive measures and fabricated a more definitive ending loosely based on Rossini's cadential material. The vocal stanza follows a simple ABA format, using Rossini's melodies but eliminating repetitions and intervening material.[81] Ayrton predicted in *The Harmonicon* that it 'will soon be heard in every quarter' and it did proliferate in sheet music publications in both Britain and the United States. One might say that the song was itself a product of sheet music culture. Arrangements, excerpts and variations of popular operas

Example 5.3 'Strike for Tyrol and liberty', Bishop, arr., *Guillaume Tell*, mm. 1–53

flourished, freely extracting the most admired melodies and morphing them into new shapes, timbres and media. 'Strike for Tyrol and liberty' did much the same.

The adapted *Guillaume Tell* demonstrates how only the most crucial elements of plot and score constituted a work. As long as the plot concerned an insurrection against unjust oppression, Hofer could stand in for Tell. As long as the score remained all Rossini, Bishop could cut, transpose, conflate and arrange. Core elements retained, Planché and Bishop could craft a version of *Guillaume Tell* that accommodated playhouse convention, musical ability and political climate. Still, their adaptation was more faithful to the score than the balletic version at the King's Theatre and thus constituted the London première of one of Rossini's most significant operas.[82] While the

Example 5.3 (cont.)

playhouses may not have been equal to *Guillaume Tell* entire, increasingly inventive and subtle methods of adaptation allowed them to compete with the King's Theatre even for its most popular composer.

THE PIPPIN AND THE PINEAPPLE REVISITED

In some ways, reactions to these adaptations solidified the dichotomy, noted in Chapter 2, between Mozart as a rare and valuable 'pineapple' and Rossini as a workaday 'pippin'. Holmes even alluded to the trope in *The Atlas*, proclaiming that

Example 5.3 (cont.)

Così fan tutte, 'in comparison to other theatrical music, is as a feast of pine-apples and grapes to a raw turnip'.[83] Changes to Mozart – especially the extensive ones in *Die Entführung* – received harsh rebuke. *John Bull* linked adaptation to commercial scams: '[*Die Entführung*] has been doctored up ... for the London market, as wine merchants manage their claret.' Meanwhile, Hazlitt saw the notable fidelity to *Così fan tutte* as a triumph of improved taste, particularly as contrasted with Bishop's adaptation of *Le nozze di Figaro*:

> An opera of MOZART's has at length been heard in an English theatre: he has been allowed to stand upon his own merits; he has not been smuggled in under the wares of Mr BRAHAM, Mr WATSON, or Mr A. LEE; he has been tried alone, and it is found that a London audience can, in a national theatre, endure him for one evening ... Some years ago the *Figaro* was introduced ... omitting the best airs and almost the whole of the concerted pieces, substituting, however, an Irish melody, a more common-place ballad, and a drinking song ... Since that period the national taste has improved, although the above disgrace is still tolerated; another such profanation, however, would now, in all probability, be quickly scouted and silenced.

Rossini evoked less reverential rhetoric. Despite the substantial changes to both *La gazza ladra* and especially *Guillaume Tell*, both were specifically praised for fidelity.

Taylor hailed the former in *The Spectator* as 'not a thing of shreds and patches, *ma veramente "La Gazza Ladra" da Rossini* – curtailed indeed, but still preserving all its brilliant and striking features'. Ayrton commended Bishop's free rewrite of *Guillaume Tell*, since he had 'very judiciously . . . admitted nothing but the original compositions into this piece'. Change appeared less egregious to Rossini, who did not seem to wed music and text indissolubly. Reviewing *La gazza ladra* at the King's Theatre, the *Literary Chronicle* felt that 'Rossini does not appear to have considered the character of the piece when he applied his music to it; a great portion of it would have suited any other subject quite as well'.[84] Accordingly, several critics advocated further alterations, elevating effective performance above strict fidelity. Writing for *The Times*, Sterling felt *Guillaume Tell* should have been lightened with comedy 'even if a part of the music had been omitted for the purpose; an ample sufficiency would have remained'. Taylor, while praising *La gazza ladra* for not being 'a thing of shreds and patches', stated 'we have heard that Mr. BISHOP wrote a song in this opera for WOOD; and if it be necessary that he have one, we had rather hear him sing one of Bishop's *well* than one of Rossini's *ill*'.

Yet, as more of both composers' oeuvre appeared on the London stage, fissures appeared in this dichotomy. Reactions to Mozart's less popular, more problematic operas, *Die Entführung* and *Così*, demonstrated that his canonical status was still in flux. Many critics struggled to reconcile a picture of perfect genius with perceived deficiencies. These issues came to the fore in assessments of *Die Entführung*'s score and *Così*'s libretto. Some clearly did not know *Die Entführung* well. Collier, for example, claimed that 'good judges will be able, without much difficulty' to discern which pieces Kramer added, but later in the review, he suggested that 'Martern aller Arten' was a new aria, 'written expressly for Miss HUGHES'. The lesser status of this opera diminished the stigma of change and several reviewers approved of Kramer's alterations and additions. Kramer's compression of the lengthy orchestral introduction of 'Martern aller Arten' from sixty measures to seventeen drew praise from Ayrton in *The Harmonicon* that even today might find sympathetic echoes: 'its long, and to say the truth, rather tiresome symphony [was] judiciously abridged'. While Bacon disliked Kramer's cuts in *Die Entführung*, he felt that some of his additions were 'quite as melodious, quite as well instrumented, and quite as effective as any pieces in the opera'. Overwhelmingly, reviewers levelled the same criticism against *Die Entführung* as they had at other German opera adaptations of the time, as explored in Chapters 3 and 4. *The Examiner* utilised common tropes of German music as lacking the spontaneity expected of genius:

> We meet with nothing that is not correct, scientific and appropriate; but those decided marks of characteristic genius do not abound, the expectation of which is necessarily associated with the name of MOZART. The melodies, although occasionally impressive, seem not to be such as linger on the ear.

Some critics clearly felt uncomfortable passing negative judgment on a composer 'with the name of MOZART' and attempted to explain and excuse the perceived failings. Bacon offered two rationalisations for the relative failure of *Die Entführung*'s score. First, he maintained that it was 'frequently asserted' that 'it was beneath the genius of Mozart to write comic music'. This tied into the prevalent Romantic picture of Mozart as a tragic composer. *The Atlas*, for example, likening Spohr to Mozart, wrote approvingly that both had a 'dominant passion for music of a strongly expressive and mournful cast'.[85] Second, Bacon suggested that 'When the opera was written, [Mozart] had not ... attained the excellence he afterwards reached, and therefore ... in the immature state of his powers, much was left undone that in his riper age he would have accomplished.' Such arguments adroitly maintained an unblemished picture of Mozart. Flaws were explained by a narrative of steadily maturing abilities and an admirable inability to lower a lofty style to comedy.

As a late Mozart work, *Così* did not draw the same criticism. Most writers agreed that Mozart had achieved the desired balance of science and melody. In his review for the *Morning Chronicle*, Collier encapsulated the prevailing view of genius: 'MOZART has been prodigal of melody, and the concerted pieces are not mere efforts of art ... but are interspersed with most exquisite airs, as if they flowed from his mind without limit or restraint, and he could not check their course.' The only criticism of the score points to an important facet of fidelity. Ayrton censured Hawes for cutting 'Il core vi dono' but then was equally critical of Hawes' fidelity; he was 'not over-rejoiced to find two airs retained, which, on the Italian stage, have generally been omitted'.[86] As Philip Gossett observes about audiences even today, fidelity to tradition can become more important than fidelity to the original.[87]

The plot, however, found few proponents. Intriguingly, I have not found any reviewers other than Ayrton who even mentioned the plot change. While the adaptation's more prurient plot prevented strong moral objections, many found it unrealistic and flimsy. *The Age* even suggested that 'there should have been an under plot introduced between *Despina* ... and some comic male servant, which would have greatly increased the interest'. Only Taylor defended Mozart, in a relentlessly positive review for *The Spectator*. Taylor felt Mozart's plots were all superior to 'the spiritless and vapid *libretti* of the ordinary Italian Opera' and that Mozart could not have written such 'beautiful melodies and polished designs' for any libretto unworthy of him. For Taylor, at least, canonical status could not brook any defect.

Rossini, meanwhile, surprised critics with *Guillaume Tell*. Ayrton confessed that 'Had this work been placed before us without any intimation of the composer's name, we certainly should not have fixed upon Rossini as its author.' Overwhelmingly, critics viewed *Guillaume Tell* as a new turn towards a Germanic style. Such was the prevalence of the Italian–German divide that few critics mentioned France or viewed *Guillaume Tell* as a grand opera. A minority still found Rossini's style at odds with his Germanic aspirations. Tapping into prevalent views of German music as meagre in melody and complex in orchestration, Taylor explained in *The Spectator*:

> [Rossini] has endeavoured to copy the more elaborate school of Germany, but this is a road on which he will never travel to fame . . . of the complicated process by which a German develops his score, he has no notion. His best songs and concerted pieces are struck off at a heat, and for his instrumental effects he usually trusts to a mere increase of noise and speed. Of noise we have plenty in *Hofer*, of good orchestral writing, but little. It contains hardly a single melody which lingers upon the ear, except the Tyrolean dance.

Most critics, however, hailed *Guillaume Tell* as a new and admirable path. In his review for *The Atlas*, Holmes thought Rossini had discarded many of his most maligned habits by combining the present German style with an older Italian school:

> Rossini has entirely forborne in this opera from imitating himself . . . there are no traces of the same hasty pen which his writings often betray . . . Many parts of this music are in the earlier and purer style of Italian dramatic composition, while the instrumentation has a richness unknown to . . . any composer who has not studied the German discoveries of combination.

Ayrton insisted, however, on distancing these developments from Italy: '[Rossini] has had abundant opportunities, during his residence in Paris and London, of hearing really good music . . . and this evidently has been gradually influencing his style. He has been drinking at the Tedescan spring, the true Hippocrene of musicians'. *Guillaume Tell* was thus hailed as a breakthrough work, a rare mediation of the Italian–German divide. With more of both Rossini's and Mozart's oeuvre regularly staged in London, critics began to finesse their view of the two composers, recognising, if sometimes unwillingly, that they were not quite as dissimilar 'fruits' as initially imagined.

NO MORE ROAMING

When audiences booed Vestris and 'I've been roaming' in 1827, they gave a tangible signal that boundaries of adaptation, class and repertoire had changed from a decade before. Certainly, the Mozart and Rossini adaptations of the late 1820s demonstrate how different playhouse adaptations had become in one decade. Adapters were far more faithful to the originals, the playhouses sometimes presented important London premières and singers like Paton rivalled foreign stars. This new landscape encouraged viewers to assess adaptations as *the* originals, despite often significant changes. As such, the new slate of Mozart and Rossini operas at the playhouses re-ignited comparisons between the two composers. Familiar tropes of Mozart as substantial and rare and Rossini as flighty and quotidian resurfaced. This dichotomy became more complex, however, as critics struggled to reconcile perceived deficiencies in *Die Entführung* and *Così fan tutte* with a canonical view of Mozart. Likewise, Rossini's *Guillaume Tell* prompted critics to rethink his relationship to Italian opera, 'ancient music' and the German style.

The increased quantity and fidelity of playhouse adaptations evoked mixed reactions. Some saw them as a sign of improving musical taste. The *Literary Gazette* thought *La cenerentola* demonstrated that John Bull 'is "progressing" . . . in his taste for music, and will no longer hiss a splendid scena because it would be impossible to dance an Irish jig to the air'.[88] Ayrton even felt that playhouse audiences surpassed their higher-class counterparts at the King's Theatre: 'the taste for music has been improving [on the English boards] in the ratio of its decline at the King's Theatre'.[89] Adapters like Bishop, however, saw their role shift away from composition towards adaptation and arranging. As Bishop found with *La gazza ladra*, this had significant implications for adapters' income. The influx of foreign opera narrowed opportunities for native works. In a review of *Guillaume Tell*, the *Dramatic Magazine* commented: 'Native talent either no longer exists, or is so completely buried by the present monopoly, that it is dead to us.' In demonstrating audiences' interest in relatively complete imported opera, these adaptations exacerbated questions of how beneficial – or harmful – this development was for the native stage.

In 1828, *The Athenaeum* exclaimed, 'Whenever . . . any thing rises to the rank of being accounted a lively and entertaining piece, it is a moral certainty that it is a translation from the French.'[1] While the London stage had long relied on France for new pieces in every genre, the saturation became especially dense in the late 1820s and early 1830s.[2] As Appendix 1 shows, almost half of the operas imported to the London stage during these decades were French, both opéras comiques and the new genre of grand opera. Such a flood of French imports, fiercely fought over at multiple venues, raised troubling questions about the value and nature of fidelity, the legality and morality of adaptation and the effect of imported opera on the native stage.

Fidelity became both more prevalent and more problematic. Adapters included more music, with a more integral dramatic role. When playwright James Robinson Planché adapted Auber's *Le maçon* in 1828, he demanded payment not only for his libretto but also musical publications of the adaptation that used his poetry, since so much of the drama now took place in music: 'The lyrical drama . . . assuming gradually a more strictly operatic form, "the book of the songs" [word book] no longer consisted of a few ballads and duets, a glee and two or three choruses. It contained the greater part of the whole piece.'[3] While some critics saw this as an advance in taste, others attributed it to less noble motives. Both opera house and major theatres used fidelity – and the greater resources that enabled it – to vaunt their versions over each other and their minor theatre competitors. Fidelity became an advertising strategy to lure audiences to yet another version. Fidelity could also be a liability, however, given the greater time and resources required. More faithful versions often brought up the rear in the race to the London première, such that audiences only gradually formed a picture of the original through successively more faithful renditions – if they even attended all of them. Comparisons among competing versions were inevitable and not always to the advantage of the most faithful one, which weakened any direct link between fidelity and worth. An abundance of multiple versions also seemed to erase a work's artistic value, to render it a commodity to be reworked into multiple profitable shapes. The *Literary Gazette* complained of the adaptations of Auber's *La fiancée* in 1830: 'the real worth of the foreign original signifies nothing. It is played at all houses, only because it has happened to suit the purposes of one.'[4] This was especially true if adapters ignored efforts by the original composer and publisher to limit access to the score, which tended to encourage more unscrupulous adaptation rather than greater fidelity.

Fidelity was also worth only as much as the original. Some critics saw French operas as at best undeserving of careful preservation, at worst an accelerant of the decline of native drama. Fidelity to French operas – which had long been maligned in Britain as showy and superficial – did not carry the same cachet as to German composers or even to Rossini. Edward Taylor told Henry Bishop not to adapt such works as Boieldieu's *Les deux nuits*, but to write his own or else, 'if . . . you must needs turn "importer of music," traffic, we beseech you, with Germany or Italy, and not with France'.[5]

Adapting French opera, far from raising musical taste, seemed to be part of the major theatres' degradation into minor theatre fare. Reviewing Planché's adaptation of *Le maçon*, *The Age* railed at

> the cheap and degrading practice of foisting the flimsy trash of the Parisian minor theatres
> upon the British public through the medium of our patent monopolies, to the utter
> extermination of original native dramatic genius, and the corruption of every moral
> and refined purpose for which the higher order of dramatic exhibition is licensed and
> intended. We know that these things are manufactured at so much per line or per act;
> are cut, clipped, adapted, and contrived, by certain literary mechanics to managers,
> at as cheap a rate as Long-lane songs.[6]

In this view, Parisian imports were another symptom of the patent theatres' abandonment of their 'moral and refined purpose' in favour of the commercialised, mechanised reproduction of minor theatre sensationalism. Adaptation thus took on a new, less salubrious aspect. Few critics had imagined that greater dedication to complete operatic performances would result in a flood of light *opéras comiques* and sensational grand operas. This was an unexpected and problematic outcome, and one that resulted in conflicted attitudes towards adapted French opera.

These issues can be seen especially well in adaptations of two of the most influential early examples of grand opera: Auber's *La muette de Portici* and Meyerbeer's *Robert le diable*.[7] Both entranced London audiences in versions at all types of theatre: major theatre, minor theatre and opera house. Such fierce competition weakened already embattled repertoire boundaries. The major theatres were increasingly well equipped to compete equally with the King's Theatre, particularly as the latter struggled to find a place for French opera within its Italianate repertoire. Meanwhile, minor theatres often bested the major theatres because their looser approach allowed them to adapt with greater speed and often with better results. Such proliferating versions benefited theatres but not the original composer, as copyright did not yet extend across national borders. Composers nevertheless sometimes attempted to control the dissemination of their works. This was especially true of Meyerbeer. His highly publicised outrage at unauthorised versions of *Robert*, newly orchestrated from piano–vocal sources, raised issues of copyright, fidelity and the relative importance of orchestration that had rarely been considered so closely before. Even as critics argued for greater fidelity to original operas, however, they began to wonder whether operas like *La muette* and *Robert* were truly worth such consideration, or whether the rage for grand opera simply overran the native stage with sensational effect, political agitation and lurid immorality.

MUTATIONS OF *LA MUETTE*

In February 1828, *La muette de Portici*, by Auber, Scribe and Delavigne, created a sensation in Paris. Generally considered the first grand opera, it thrilled audiences with its historical tale of the revolt of Neapolitan fisherman Tomas Aniello ('Masaniello') against the Spanish in 1647, its intriguing mute character, Fenella, and the stunning eruption of Vesuvius. Several London theatres raced to bring out *La muette* the following season. The King's Theatre was first, not with the opera but with a ballet version on 24 March 1829. This was a clever move. The theatre typically did not perform opera in French, but they did offer ballets and these were virtually all imported from France. Given the significant role of dance in *La muette*, it morphed easily into this new format and the ballet was a success.[8] Three playhouse adaptations followed: the Coburg and Drury Lane mounted competing versions on the same evening, 4 May, and Astley's followed a week later. Unfortunately, Astley's adaptation is documented only by a playbill, but the Coburg and Drury Lane adaptations offer an intriguing comparison between imported opera at the major and minor theatres in the late 1820s.

The density of competing versions was by now typical, as the *Literary Gazette* wittily described when reviewing the Drury Lane adaptation (see Appendix 2 for review citations):

> According to long-established practice, the managers of our Theatres-Royal having deliberated upon the policy of producing a piece which has created a great sensation abroad . . . and, finally, abandoned all idea of its performance; some clearer-sighted speculator dashes at once into the arena with it – makes what the Fancy call a 'smashing hit,' and the whole town having flocked to the fortunate establishment . . . out it comes at last, a copy, when it might have been (here at least) an original . . . the proprietors, if by good luck they escape the shame of defeat, find themselves but gleaners where they might have been reapers – smothered with 'odorous comparisons'.

The major theatres thus found themselves increasingly outwitted by their more nimble minor theatre competitors. Fidelity played an important role. Other than the English Opera House, whose operatic pretensions were discussed in Chapter 4, the minor theatres continued to treat foreign opera as they had *Der Freischütz*; they focused on the plot, maximising its melodramatic potential, and offered only a handful of the most popular, accessible musical numbers. Meanwhile, the major theatres were expected to produce a more faithful and hence time-consuming version, with superior scenery and better-drilled musicians.

This is the case with the Coburg and Drury Lane versions of *La muette*. The adaptation for the Coburg by H. M. Milner, T. Hughes and Montague Philip Corri contained only a handful of musical numbers, while the version for Drury Lane by James Kenney, Thomas Cooke and Barham Livius remained much closer to the French original.[9] In both cases, however, adapters focused changes on the opera's two most troublesome and novel features. Both softened the potentially incendiary revolutionary message and both wrote new melodramatic music for the miming Fenella, although only Drury Lane's survives. The two aspects, therefore, on which modern assessments of the opera hinge received a different reading in London.[10]

AVERTING REVOLUTION

La muette posed problems for the delicate political situation of the late 1820s and early 1830s. As detailed in Chapter 5 with *Guillaume Tell* (see pp. 136–7), potential revolts stirred across Europe. *La muette* has been famously linked to the 1830 Revolution in Belgium and some Londoners may have worried that the opera might prompt a similar reaction in Britain.[11] This was of particular concern given a previous, highly publicised version of the tale, by George Soane for Drury Lane in 1825, which Sarah Hibberd suggests may have influenced Scribe and Delavigne.[12] Soane ran afoul of the censor for pointedly political speeches, such as when Masaniello insists that 'noblemen are nothing' and calls statesmen 'state-cankers, who come between us and our monarch's love'.[13] Although the censor excised these lines, they appeared in Soane's printed libretto, available at the doors of the theatre, and presumably in performance as well.[14]

Contemporaries clearly viewed the story in general as incendiary. Leigh Hunt, witnessing a performance of Drury Lane's *La muette* in 1830, related that he 'almost shook in the box [he] sat in' when he saw Masaniello and thought of 'poor men going to their chill beds' while others 'prepar[ed] for a table full of luxuries'.[15] Shortly before, the *Penny Paper for the People* had urged its readers to attend a royal command performance of the adaptation for the newly crowned King William IV on 28 October. 'In "Massaniello" when you hear the spirit stirring songs of liberty, let the roof shake ... with your terrible chorus; and when you see the Neapolitan *'rabble'* rise against and triumph over their tyrant, let your bursts of applause convince his Majesty that you too would hurl any tyrant from his throne who neglected or abused the interests of his people.'[16] The adaptation was withdrawn for the royal command performance in favour of *Le nozze di Figaro*, but it was still performed throughout the early 1830s. Jacky Bratton argues that it was deliberately mounted on 17 May 1832, the day that King William quelled opposition in the House of Lords to the Reform Bill.[17]

The story of Masaniello does not, however, support revolution unequivocally. Masaniello's rebellion goes awry when the rebels turn tyrant. Masaniello loses his senses and in the end is betrayed and killed by his own countrymen. When Drury Lane librettist Kenney was questioned by the Select Committee on Dramatic Literature in 1832 about whether *La muette de Portici* had 'rather a revolutionary tendency', he responded, 'I apprehend quite the contrary. I was rather fearful that it might be considered a Tory play, for it has a Tory moral decidedly ... The revolutionary fisherman is humiliated, and a lesson is taught very opposite to a revolutionary one.'[18] While Kenney doubtless exaggerated to satisfy his questioners, Hunt pointed out that Scribe and Delavigne had deflected the political thrust of the story: 'We used to wonder how it was, that a piece so radically formidable could have been produced under the old French government. But it is as innocent of offence as can be, considering there is such a gunpowder word in it as "Masaniello." The author has introduced a story of seduction to neutralize the politics.'[19] Modern scholars have also noted that the opera's political message is more ambiguous than is typically recognised. As Hibberd remarks, it maintains an 'uneasy balance between authoritarian legitimacy and heavy revolutionary symbolism'.[20]

Both Kenney at Drury Lane and Milner at the Coburg sought to tip this balance in a more conservative direction.[21] While Milner did so in a more overtly melodramatic mode, the similar approaches of major and minor theatre librettists demonstrate the narrowing gap between these theatres' repertoires. Milner shifted blame from the Spanish rulers to their army. A sergeant proclaims, 'I hate this Neapolitan scum; I should like to string them up, till the trees were loaded with them.'[22] The Spanish viceroy's son Alphonse, however, despite presumably directing his subordinates' actions and seducing Masaniello's sister Fenella, evinces deep regret. In the opening scene he thinks of Fenella, 'whose chilling influence ... strikes an ice-bolt on my guilt-stained heart'.[23] Milner also added a comic character, Masaniello's cousin Giuseppe, whose cowardly, drunken but ultimately good-natured antics lighten the libretto. Masaniello does initially incite his fellows to rebellion with words that would have stirred potential revolutionaries: 'Vengeance! The worm that is so scornfully trod under foot, perchance, may turn and sting ... his proud oppressor.'[24] Once the rebellion starts, however, Masaniello recoils at his compatriots' atrocities. At Fenella's urging, he spares the life of Alphonse and his intended, Elvire. Milner also heightened the already sensational ending by having Masaniello die onstage rather than off, as in the opera, after saving Elvire from a violent mob. In his death speech, he delivers a moral of restraint: '[I] was mad enough to think that liberty could take into her ranks those whose abject souls stamps [*sic*] them eternally base slaves ... never can fair liberty unfold her banner, but where bright virtue stands to uphold the sacred standard.'[25]

At Drury Lane, Kenney made similar modifications. He also moved the cause of the revolt away from specific leaders and towards the Spaniards in general. Masaniello refers more specifically to the Spaniards' tax as the cause for unrest: 'Go to the market-place, and read the new tax-table; that's my weather-glass. Who'll set that to rights?'[26] Again as in Milner, Alphonse appears in a more positive light. He shoulders the blame for the people's discontent, musing, 'The natives have little cause to love us, and griefs like theirs, it should have been my office rather to have relieved than aggravated.'[27] Once the revolt took place, Kenney was quick to highlight its drawbacks. Masaniello speaks harshly of how the revolt went amiss: 'Seeking to rouse men to their rights, I have unkennelled bloodhounds to their prey.'[28] Kenney also slimmed the role of Pietro, who begins as Masaniello's colleague but later betrays him. He and his fellow adapters, Cooke and Livius, cut Masaniello and Pietro's rousing duet, whose patriotic expression and quotation from the Marseillaise made it a popular rallying point for revolution.[29] When Pietro poisons Masaniello at the end, Kenney added a stern rebuke from colleague Borella: 'The punishment should have waited the offence. 'Tis a black deed – a rash deed – and you'll repent it.'[30] In both major and minor theatre manifestations of *La muette*, adapters strove to imbue the story with a similar note of caution, setting boundaries beyond which revolutionary thoughts should not go.

MUSIC AND MUTENESS

As became common in the 1820s and 1830s, major and minor theatre adaptations often took similar approaches to the libretto, but musically they contrasted vividly. Although the Coburg libretto advertised the piece as 'a musical drama', Hughes and Corri retained only a handful of Auber's pieces. These were virtually all choral, shielding the minor theatres' lack of stellar solo singers. While a score is not extant, the libretto and playbill suggest that they kept the overture, the most prominent choruses and the barcarolle.[31] The playbill also states that Hughes wrote the melodramatic music, which presumably means that he wrote fresh accompaniments for Fenella's mimed communication. Minor theatres still therefore took the approach that major theatre adapters had a decade previously – opera became melodrama, a core of speech supplemented with a liberal use of instrumental accompaniment and leavened by a few choice vocal pieces.

At Drury Lane, the surviving sources paint an intriguing picture of the score. The libretto demonstrates that Cooke and Livius kept virtually all of Auber's music, rearranged into three acts rather than five. Only the duet for Masaniello and Pietro, mentioned earlier, and Alphonse and Elvire's duet were cut. Cooke and Livius added three pieces: a Neapolitan dance for Oscar Byrne and his daughter Rosa, which replaced Auber's Bolero after the first night; a shorter, flashier duet for Alphonse and Elvire by Livius; and a solo for celebrated tenor John Braham as Masaniello, based on 'Pourquoi pleurer' from Auber's *Le concert à la cour*.[32] Cooke and Livius also rewrote the overture to include one of the most popular tunes of the opera, the barcarolle. This both tied the overture more closely to the ensuing score and rendered it even more attractive for sheet music purchasers. Finally, they made internal cuts that even today scholars such as Robert Letellier say are 'requir[ed] ... since [Auber's] musical sections can become repetitive'.[33]

The printed score, however, contains only a fraction of this material. Although such a division between how a piece was performed and what was published had always existed in adaptations, it is especially stark here. The printed score leaves out five numbers that are retained in all libretto sources: the chorus 'Du prince objet de notre amour'; Masaniello's solo in act four; and three of the five finales. Seven numbers are included in the score only in a truncated version, frequently for solo voice without the choral parts that are clearly indicated in the libretto. Adapters may have pushed audiences to accept longer, more dramatically involved musical numbers in the theatre, but they continued to accede to more traditional musico-dramatic expectations in the home.

In one respect, however, the printed score is unusual: it includes the melodramatic music for Fenella's miming. Such music was rarely published, so its presence speaks to fascination with this mute role. It also underlines the correlation between Fenella's reliance on mute gesture and the prevalent melodramatic aesthetic, which accompanied such movement with instrumental accompaniment. Finally, it reveals that Cooke and Livius replaced virtually all of Auber's music for Fenella, which fundamentally alters how Fenella converses musically.[34] In her first appearance in the opera, for example, Auber's Fenella communicates with Elvire in gestures as Elvire responds in recitative. Cooke and Livius placed all recitative in dialogue. The instruments accompany only Fenella, pausing for Elvire's speech, although Elvire may have spoken during some instrumental sections.[35] The British Fenella therefore emerges as both more isolated from normal human communication and less needful of it. She is not as dependent on Elvire to conclude her thoughts, both musically and textually, and her interjections are longer, more fully thought through and more musically conventional.

When Fenella enters in Auber, for example, a frantic, repetitive musical motive represents her futile attempt to escape the guards (see Ex. 6.1a). Elvire interjects, Fenella continues the motive briefly to signal her muteness and Elvire promises to aid her. Cooke and Livius, by contrast, provided standard 'hurry' music for Fenella's entrance, with rising semiquavers (Ex. 6.1b). A firm cadence after a dramatic descending scale paints Fenella's supplication at Elvire's feet more obviously and ends her 'sentence' more decisively. Her explanation of her muteness, which the stage directions in the libretto combine with her supplication to Elvire for protection, is considerably longer than Auber's urgent single measure.[36] The repetitive form and calming sarabande rhythm suggest that Fenella more formally and calmly presents her identity.

Fenella's explanation of Alphonse's betrayal is likewise more measured. Auber provides two separate mimed sections: Fenella's declaration of love with pulsing triplets and sighing appoggiaturas; and a few longing gestures that Elvire 'finishes' by explaining 'you were abandoned by this ingrate' (Exx. 6.1c–d). Cooke and Livius

Example 6.1a No. 4 *scène et chœur*, Auber, *La muette de Portici*, mm. 17–33

(Fenella entre avec effroi et court se jeter aux genoux de la Princesse)

offered only one section, a lyrical, almost aria-like set piece that concludes with a resigned cadence (Ex. 6.1e). Again, Fenella seems more self-sufficient; she relates her tale from start to finish rather than obliging Elvire to finish her thought.

Auber's next section, an extended musical depiction of Fenella's imprisonment and escape (mm. 88–160), Cooke and Livius retained verbatim, although they did cut Elvire's one line of recitative, confirming that Fenella was 'en prison'. Cooke and Livius probably felt less need to change Auber here, as he provided the self-contained,

Example 6.1b Melodramatic music, Cooke and Livius, arr., *La muette de Portici*

Fenella rushes on wildly, and throws herself at Elvira's feet imploring protection.

Fenella signifies that she is dumb.

musically literal depiction that characterised their rewritten sections. They lost, however, Auber's repetition of Fenella's opening music, which Anselm Gerhard describes as a 'cinematic flashback', since they had replaced its first appearance.[37] Fenella's final instrumental cue closes the conversation in a markedly different way than Auber. In the French original, Fenella still appears agitated, supplicating to Elvire with sudden ascending leaps and ending with a rising, dotted repetition of an unstable chord (Ex. 6.1f). Cooke and Livius, while still employing sighing figures and large leaps, contained these within a clear parallel period, piano and dolce (Ex. 6.1g).

Example 6.1c No. 4 *scène et chœur*, Auber, *La muette de Portici*, mm. 54–60

Allegro vivace ([Fenella] exprime que l'amour s'empara de son cœur et qu'il a causé tous ses maux.)

Example 6.1d No. 4 *scène et chœur*, Auber, *La muette de Portici*, mm. 77–85

Allegro ([Fenella] fait signe qu'elle l'ignore, il jurait qu'il l'aimait, il la pressait contre son cœur

mais il partit et ne revint plus.) Par cet in - grat tu fus a - ban - don - né - e

Overall, while the French Fenella mimes to fluid music that requires the comple-
tion of Elvire's recitative, the British Fenella offers more self-contained moments
with predictable forms, lyrical melodies and complete cadences. Even within the most
dramatically responsive music of all – melodramatic accompaniment – Cooke and

Example 6.1e Melodramatic music, Cooke and Livius, arr., *La muette de Portici*

Fenella describes the falsehood of Alphonso.

Example 6.1f No. 4 *scène et chœur*, Auber, *La muette de Portici*, mm. 170–7

Livius sought to compartmentalise music and drama. In the process, Fenella became both more conventional, a kind of aural counterpart to Kenney's softening of the revolutionary content, and more radical, an even more isolated figure, ensconced in a musical world that contrasts starkly with others' spoken communication.

Example 6.1g Melodramatic music, Cooke and Livius, arr., *La muette de Portici*

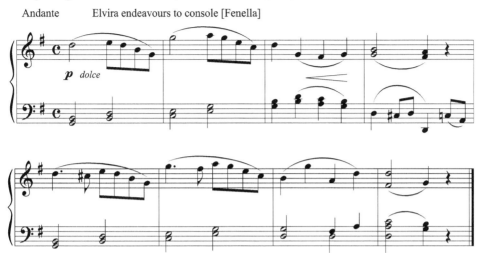

Andante   Elvira endeavours to console [Fenella]

FOREIGNERS AND VOLCANOES

La muette achieved resounding popular success. It enjoyed a solid three-week run at the Coburg and was revived throughout the early 1830s at Drury Lane. The music entranced. *The Athenaeum* quipped, 'If the barrel-organs haven't enough of [*La muette*] by and by, then is "Der Freyschutz" no longer a precedent.'[38] Writing in *The Harmonicon*, William Ayrton bestowed perhaps the highest praise by comparing France favourably with the countries that dominated musical discourse, Italy and Germany. Although some pieces were 'a little à la Rossini', the opera was 'a convincing proof of the rapid advance made in the dramatic music of our neighbours, who bid fair to surpass the Italian school, and even rival that of Germany'. The scenic wonders dazzled. The Coburg playbill identified visual splendour as the main draw of grand opera and melodrama alike: 'Presenting the most Sublime & Awful Spectacle of that Terrific Convulsion of Nature, And produced by entirely Novel Scenic Contrivances, excelling all former efforts to realize that TREMENDOUS PHENOMENON, THE EXPLOSION OF A VOLCANO!' Of Drury Lane's production, despite some initial technical difficulties with Vesuvius' eruption, *The Athenaeum* wrote, '"Johnson, the mechanist of former Drury," would die of fright, could he be resuscitated only to view the desperate showers of lava, the red tides down the mountain, the illuminated buildings, the red sheet tossed up and down in the middle distance, and the people dying in pairs beneath the fire-bolts from the boiling crater! Massaniello for ever!'

Despite *La muette*'s obvious appeal, a few critics chafed at the reliance on the foreign, musical and sensational on the patent theatre stage. Concerns coalesced around the Fenella, a Mademoiselle Alexandrine from Paris. While foreign performers regularly appeared at the King's Theatre, this was one of the few instances of a foreign performer assuming a starring role on the playhouse stage. Arrayed, as the *Dramatic Magazine* described, 'like a French milliner just popped out of a band-box' – in stark contrast to the characteristic costumes of the rest of the cast – Alexandrine proclaimed her difference. Her muteness held special significance, since she did not, in fact, speak the same language as her fellow performers. Edward Sterling thought Alexandrine communicated clearly through gesture, writing in *The Times* that she made her 'sorrows and sufferings perfectly intelligible'. The *Dramatic Magazine*, however, claimed that if the actors had not 'kindly interpreted' her motions, 'we should exclaim, with Mungo, "me see, but me no understand"'.[39] This may signal an early instance of what Maribeth Clark describes as a gradual separation of pantomime from opera and the privileging of song over gesture.[40] It also may speak to latent unease with a performer so unversed in the native tongue that she could only gesture mutely. Alexandrine's foreignness was further emphasised by a close comparison with the Fenella at the King's Theatre, French ballerina Pauline Leroux. *The Athenaeum* felt Alexandrine 'accords so closely with the model of Mademoiselle Pauline Leroux, that we cannot but consider one or the other a mere plagiarist'. Such overlap between the houses activated concerns about the decline of the native drama. *The Examiner* protested that 'surely there was no lack of native talent ... to render the engagement of a foreigner at all necessary'. Different in her dress, nationality and muteness, Alexandrine signalled an unsettling conflation of opera house and playhouse, foreign and native.

Overall, reviewers were divided on whether *La muette* represented an important step forward for native audiences or a further descent into illegitimate territory. Although Sterling stated that 'As a drama, the piece has no great pretensions', he viewed the visual splendour as unusual and meritorious: 'as a scenic representation it has a peculiar merit, and one which has hitherto been almost unknown to the English stage'. Writing a few years later in *The Harmonicon*, an 'amateur' thought that the success of *La muette,* along with *Der Freischütz*, *Guillaume Tell*, *Il barbiere di Siviglia* 'and several other works of first-rate genius, is sufficient to prove that the musical taste, even of the galleries, has been misrepresented'.[41] The *Dramatic Magazine*, however, emphasised how such spectacle overran sense: 'This piece altogether so well answers to Voltaire's description ... that we cannot refrain from inserting it. An opera is a spectacle as wild as it is magnificent, where the ears are more gratified than the mind, and where its subservience to music renders the most ridiculous faults indispensable.' In this light, fidelity to Auber's opera seemed of questionable value. John Payne Collier, for example, preferred the most drastically altered version, at the King's Theatre. In his review of the Drury Lane adaptation for the *Morning Chronicle*, Collier gave the palm to the King's Theatre production because it offered superior dancing and the 'choicest specimens' of the music, 'while it was relieved of the dialogue and solo pieces, which are not much to be regretted, when the story can be otherwise conveyed'. When a piece was so dependent on the ephemeral, devalued arena of spectacle and movement, its text and score appeared less important to preserve faithfully.

THE RACE TO *ROBERT LE DIABLE*

Competition for the latest Parisian hit reached extreme proportions with one of the most sensational, highly anticipated operas of the early 1830s: Meyerbeer's *Robert le diable*. No fewer than six London versions appeared within six months, with all types of theatre – minor, major and opera house – vying for precedence. The *Literary Gazette*, reviewing the patent theatre adaptations, recounted:

> At Paris, where they go regularly mad at certain periods about something or other, the last … fit has been brought on by … *Robert the Devil*. Now, we in London being equally addicted to be crazy at second hand, and insane by imitation, have had a glorious theatrical race, who should be first and foremost in importing, travestying, hashing up, and dishing the said opera.

The race became particularly acrimonious because Meyerbeer tried to control this proliferation.[42] These adaptations therefore brought into especial focus questions of what constituted fidelity, how desirable it was and what obligations – financial and moral – theatres had to the original composer.

Robert's path to London was mired in intrigue. Already several weeks before the opera appeared in Paris on 21 November 1831, rumours circulated that Drury Lane manager Frederick Polhill had 'empowered an agent to treat for the music, that it may be produced at Drury Lane without delay'.[43] This was Henry Bishop, whom *The Age* reported had departed for Paris shortly after the première, Polhill having purchased the score.[44] In fact, King's Theatre manager Monck Mason had beaten Polhill to the purchase, apparently securing what he thought were exclusive rights to the score from Meyerbeer and his publisher Schlesinger for £500.[45] Meyerbeer was to come to London to supervise the production, along with most members of the original French cast. Rather than giving up their plans, however, other theatres circumvented Meyerbeer's control. In a review of the patent theatre versions, *The Age* suggested that bribery could overcome such obstacles: 'money will procure the loan of a score, even if it *be* locked up in the musical bureau of Monsieur Schlesinger'. John Small has noted how much musical culture still depended on manuscript copies and adapters could also have found someone willing to make them a copy.[46] In the event, though, analysis below will demonstrate that the playhouses probably did not have access to a full score, but instead reconstructed the orchestration from available piano–vocal sources and the adapters' remembrance of performances in Paris.[47] The *Theatrical Observer* reported that Bishop was 'recompos[ing] the whole score' as he 'could not procure the orchestral accompaniments'.[48] Presumably, agents from Covent Garden and the various minor theatres followed a similar course or copied each other.

Strictly speaking, this was legal, but numerous commentators denounced this approach. A 'dilettante' in *The Harmonicon* protested: 'if to seize an opera, under such circumstances, be contrary to established notions of justice, how much more so would it be to tear off by violence a part of it, then patch up what had thus been obtained, in direct opposition to the will of the legal, and also equitable, owners'.[49] More succinctly, *The Athenaeum* quipped that the patent theatres, 'failing to procure a copyright, returned to try what they could do with a copywrong'. Contemporaries clearly had a sense that copyright did or at least should govern such interactions.

The battle for chronological precedence was equally intense. The Adelphi captured the London première on 23 January and additional minor theatre productions followed at Sadler's Wells and the Royal Pavilion on 13 February and 12 March, respectively. The major theatres engaged in a particularly acrimonious standoff. After Drury Lane had advertised their version for months, Covent Garden suddenly revealed their own adaptation and announced the same première date, 21 February. Drury Lane hastily accelerated their production to 20 February and Covent Garden countered by reviving a different piece called *Robert the devil* on that date.[50] The King's Theatre, though first in the race to Meyerbeer's score, was last to produce it, on 11 June.

In a letter to the editor of *The Tatler*, Telesforo de Trueba y Cosio decried this system, which prized speed over quality or ethics:

> in this *musical race* . . . the question is, not who will produce the *best* adaptation, but who will bring out the *first* . . . The mischief of the system is obvious. The Minor Theatres, which incur no responsibility by the crime of mutilating operas . . . possess an immense advantage over their superiors in the article of velocity – they can *maim*, curtail, add, transplant, omit, dovetail . . . without fear of reproach, for they are *Minors*, and consequently the legitimate drama is nothing to them. The *Majors*, on the contrary, being obliged to spend more time, capital, and care, arrive only second in the field, and when the charm of novelty is gone![51]

As seen with *La muette*, a double standard thus applied to adaptation in the late 1820s and 1830s. The minor theatres, already on the fringes of the law, perpetuated the kind of thoroughgoing adaptation that the major theatres had practised a decade earlier. The majors were increasingly held to a higher standard of fidelity, but then often found fidelity trumped by speed. The addition of the King's Theatre to this mix was novel. Never before had the King's Theatre vied so directly with the playhouses for an important new opera, particularly a French opera outside their usual focus on Italianate works.[52] The King's Theatre had always been separate in the past, a clear leader in opera where the playhouses were only dabblers. Now, the increasing amount of imported opera at the playhouses, in increasingly faithful form, shifted the playing field. Foreign opera became fair game at all theatres and all productions had to be taken seriously, even if critics still tried to separate minor from major, playhouse from opera house.

Mason, Meyerbeer and Schlesinger desperately tried to forestall this state of affairs through recourse to the law and the media. When the patent theatres mounted their productions in February, Mason threatened them with an injunction to stop their performances, claiming that they had no legal right to the score and citing the copyright act of 1710, the Statute of Anne. As described in the introduction, no law in fact protected Mason's copyright in a foreign work and the move backfired. Polhill called his bluff, replying that 'you are in error, as to your alleged rights; and if it be your intention to appeal to a legal tribunal for redress, I am ready to meet you'.[53] The press printed Mason's threat and Polhill's response, which only heightened interest in the patent theatres' adaptations. Meyerbeer, perhaps aided by his publisher, Schlesinger, tried to sway public opinion through letters to the London press: 'I have had nothing to do with the instrumentation of the operas [at the playhouses]... some of the most prominent vocal pieces produced in them do not belong to me ... The entire opera, arranged for the pianoforte, has not yet been published in Paris; therefore your adapters have been able to procure only a few detached pieces.'[54]

Although such efforts did galvanise critical rhetoric against the playhouse adaptations, they did not stop the playhouses, nor did they necessarily help the King's Theatre's production. When Meyerbeer arrived, he found Mason 'a good but crazy man who is close to bankruptcy'.[55] Numerous delays plagued the production and Meyerbeer had to leave to supervise a production in Berlin before *Robert* finally appeared. Problems continued after the première when the performers' contracts ran out and some refused to continue without further pay.[56] In total, *Robert* lasted only six performances at the King's Theatre, certainly not enough to recoup the £6000 reportedly lavished on it.[57] Unfortunately for Meyerbeer and other composers who wished to control foreign performances of their work, exclusive rights to a score did not always prove of practical or financial value.

THE 'COPYWRONGS'

Charles Gruneisen, in his 1848 *Memoir of Meyerbeer*, stated that 'in no country, not even amongst the savage Algerine, or Mexican tribes, has *Robert le diable* undergone worse treatment, than in London'.[58] Gruneisen here clearly perpetuated the negative hyperbole that Meyerbeer and Mason had generated to vaunt their production. Yet, an examination of the three extant adaptations – at the Adelphi, Drury Lane and Covent Garden – reveals a more complex mixture of departure and fidelity. Their spectrum of re-workings demonstrates the relationship between major and minor theatres, the narrowing divergences between continental and British taste and the sometimes doubtful payback for fidelity.

At the Adelphi, Edward Fitzball, John Buckstone and an anonymous composer did not attempt to present the opera in complete form. At most minor theatres, adapters did not start with the complete score and winnow it to a more acceptable shape. Rather, theirs was a process of selection, looking not for what to cut but for which handful of pieces to retain. Although no score is extant for the Adelphi version, piecing together newspaper notices and the libretto suggests this handful was Raimbaut's opening solo, one of Alice's solos (possibly 'Quand je quittai la Normandie'), the opening of the act two finale, with its eerie accompaniment of four timpani and pizzicato double bass, and the final chorus of act three.[59] The critic for *The Atlas*, Edward Holmes, also suggested that they may have drawn from Meyerbeer for the melodramatic music.

Minor theatre librettists took a similarly free approach to the libretto, divining those elements closest to their melodramatic fare and expanding them. *Robert*'s libretto already fitted well with popular 'German horrors'. As Collier described in his review of the Adelphi version for the *Morning Chronicle*, 'The story is a sort of *Faust – Freischutz – Don Juanised* production.' Fitzball and Buckstone increased these melodramatic tendencies. They augmented the stunning visual display with a new tableau in which Robert sees a vision, conjured by Bertram, of his rival winning Isabelle's hand at the tournament. The Adelphi's unique descending stage heightened the visual experience. The *Literary Gazette* explained: 'from great capacity below, [the stage] has a power and alacrity of sinking *in toto*, which the largest theatres might covet in vain'. This proved especially effective for the ghostly nuns, whom the *Morning Post* described '[sink], with the stage, while fire-brandishing fiends soar in air above them'. Fitzball and Buckstone also made the female roles more conventional by increasing the importance of love interest Isabelle and decreasing that of Robert's *soeur de lait*, Alice. They enlarged comic character Raimbaut, embellished ad libitum by beloved comedian John Reeve.[60] Finally, their Robert vacillated less. As Letellier observes, Robert is 'saved more by grace than personal decision'; he delays signing Bertram's demonic contract long enough for midnight to sound and Bertram to sink into the earth.[61] At the Adelphi, Robert not only makes the decision not to sign, but serves as the melodramatic mouthpiece of morality. Addressing Isabelle, he proclaims, 'Perish the magic which to make thee mine I have so dearly bought, what is't to me? If in possessing thee, I lose thy heart.'[62] True to the melodramatic aesthetic, *Robert* at the Adelphi thus became not only more sensational, but more clearly divided into male and female, serious and comic, good and evil.

The major theatre librettists offered more faithful versions, but many of their changes ran along analogous – sometimes even identical – lines to the Adelphi. This illustrates not only the narrowing gap between major and minor theatre repertoire but also the influence that the first adaptation had on its successors, regardless of its fidelity. As Julie Sanders describes, 'Adaptation and appropriation ... provide their own intertexts, so that adaptations perform in dialogue with other adaptations as well as their informing source.[63] At Covent Garden, for example, Michael Rophino Lacy also augmented scenic display, expanded the comedic role of Raimbaut and fashioned Bertram into a clearer melodramatic villain. His Bertram conjures a new character, Astoroth, the 'Spirit of Fire', who 'rises, his head surrounded by a circle of blue flame, his wings extended, and in his hand a blazing spear'.[64] Bertram spells out his evil intentions to Astoroth – 'this very night I will allure him to a sacrilegious deed of fatal temptation' – and also clarifies why, despite his powers, he has to work to capture Robert's soul: 'Robert must be lost to me for ever, unless, *of his own free will*, he yield himself mine this very night.'[65]

At Drury Lane, Samuel Beazley and Frank Mills followed the Adelphi even more closely by copying Fitzball and Buckstone's new scene of Robert's vision of the tournament. The stage directions read almost identically and the scene was inserted in the libretto later, which suggests that it was hastily added because of its success at the Adelphi.[66] Anyone who saw both productions could not have missed the resemblance, which suggests that Drury Lane's adapters either banked on their audience not overlapping considerably with the Adelphi or on patrons imagining that the scene derived from the original. In fact, *The Age* and the *Theatrical Observer* did just that, going so far as to chastise Covent Garden for not including the scene. Even with the aggressive insistence on fidelity that Meyerbeer and Mason fostered among critics, the 'original' was still not so much the opera in Paris as the first London adaptation.

Musically, the major theatres had no need to rely on the Adelphi. Reviewers painted a sorry picture of the minor theatre's musical efforts. As Holmes described, 'the band has been enlarged, and it does its best to impress that fact upon the public. Of tearing and rasping there is more than sufficient to show that the piece is a great musical effort for the Adelphi.' While prevalent class prejudice against the minor theatres seems to colour this review, the major theatres were far more capable of performing Meyerbeer. The only score remaining is Bishop's for Drury Lane – in which he was assisted in the re-orchestration by Thomas Cooke, R. Hughes and Montague Philip Corri – but an examination of it and Lacy's libretto for Covent Garden suggests that they kept a substantial portion of the French opera. Much of the lengthy score had to be slimmed to fit on a double bill and recitative was replaced with spoken dialogue. Both, however, kept interpolations and completely omitted numbers to a minimum.[67] And, while some internal cuts were designed to avoid Meyerbeer's most adventurous modulations and fluid forms, adapters kept many challenging features. Bishop, for example, retained Meyerbeer's entire denouement, in which Alice and Bertram vie for Robert's soul. Only a few years earlier, Bishop would undoubtedly have reworked such a fusion of action and music. Rupert Ridgewell even feels that Bishop's work 'cannot be thought of as an adaptation in the strong sense of the word.'[68]

Some contemporaries agreed. Adelphi adapter Fitzball even marked Meyerbeer adaptations as a turning point in fidelity:

> My principal credit, in those early days of concerted music [was] the *larding* up of abstruse passages with stage effects, to render them digestible to unsophisticated listeners . . . The people, during twenty years, especially since the works of Meyerbeer, have become wonderfully astute to music of the deepest dye, although I think even that great and judicious master by no means spurns the *light* of other days, to assist his chromatic passages; "Robert the Devil," for instance.[69]

Although it was still wise to palliate musical complexity with scenic horror, the divide between continental and native taste appeared to have contracted.

Meyerbeer's claims that the playhouses had added many 'prominent vocal numbers' and had included only 'detached pieces' were therefore simply false. The full orchestral score of Drury Lane's adaptation does show that the work was re-orchestrated, but Bishop stayed as close to his memory of the production as possible and Drury Lane specially built a new organ to recreate Meyerbeer's timbral effects. Did re-orchestration mar the effect as much as Meyerbeer claimed? Examining the scene of the resuscitated nuns that ends act three, whose orchestration numerous commentators have earmarked as exceptional, suggests it may have, but only subtly.[70]

First of all, Bishop retained only portions of the almost 800 measure finale, so listeners could not always have compared original and adaptation directly. The opening recitative and evocation – scored by Hughes – followed Meyerbeer's basic material, though with changes in orchestration, as described below. Bishop's hand then took over in the manuscript score and more substantial changes ensued. He shortened many sections, substituted similar material for others and cut the first ballet of seduction. The first published full score – to which London adapters did not have access – suggested that this ballet, along with several other numbers, could be cut.[71] The score also indicated numerous places where the orchestration could be altered if the requisite instruments were not available. This suggests that *Robert* was not as fixed as Meyerbeer let on and that Bishop simply followed this spirit of change. Given how violently Meyerbeer protested adapters' re-orchestration, however, it might imply the opposite: that Meyerbeer wanted to control not only the original performance, but how future ones were altered.

Bishop and Hughes did not have access to the suggestions in this score, however, and therefore changed the instrumentation in ways other than those Meyerbeer dictated. In several cases, this would have mitigated Meyerbeer's originality. In m. 9, for example, Hughes replaced the striking, exposed triplets for bassoon and clarinet with pizzicato strings. During the evocation, the descending arpeggio, blared ominously on the trombones and ophicleide in Meyerbeer (mm. 26–7 etc.), Hughes rescored for full orchestra. The *pianississimo* timpani rolls in the nuns' procession (m. 70 etc.) were absent in Bishop. The arresting combination of winds and triangle to depict the nuns' horrifying revels in the bacchanale was replaced by Bishop, first with strings, then with full orchestra, supplemented with cymbals and long drum (bass drum). In other instances, however, Hughes and Bishop retained memorable features of Meyerbeer's orchestration. They kept the peculiar accompaniment of bassoons in the procession of nuns, for instance, and the solo cello in the third ballet of seduction. In a few cases, they even made the instrumentation more unusual. In mm. 48–52, Meyerbeer features strings, accompanied by winds and horns; Hughes created a more lugubrious sound with only bassoons, horns and trombones. Likewise, one of Bishop's added sections featured a passage for three trombones alone.[72]

Did these changes alter Meyerbeer's timbral intentions? Undoubtedly. Could they have completely ruined the effect of *Robert*? It appears unlikely. In some cases, Bishop and Hughes may have forestalled poor effect. While Meyerbeer's passage for trombones and ophicleide alone is impressive, for example, it could falter without strong players; the full orchestra ensured an impressive sound. Meyerbeer's orchestration was not adhered to strictly, but Bishop and his colleagues did endeavour to recapture its most striking aspects.

SHIFTING STANDARDS FOR FIDELITY

The popularity of *Robert* in Paris, combined with its scandal-ridden entrance into London, challenged the parameters and worth of fidelity. Given that re-orchestration was the primary change that the major theatre adapters made, orchestration gained sudden significance. Critics confronted rarely discussed issues: how much instruments contributed to a score's worth; and whether instrumentation was an integral part of a musical work. Many critics backed themselves into a rhetorical corner by advocating a previously unknown sensitivity to instrumental timbre. Reviewing Drury Lane's adaptation for *The Atlas*, Holmes proclaimed:

> There cannot be a doubt, but that the sum total of the effect of any great dramatic work depends materially upon the use of particular instruments; and that though the arranger may have in a pianoforte copy the motion of the parts before him, yet let him hear the original as often as he may, and with the most patient attention, something . . . will escape him . . . while the orchestral parts are spurious, a critical opinion must be received with reservation.

Holmes even tried to redefine the term adaptation: 'this word . . . is . . . generally understood, to refer only to the arrangement of a new language, and to the trifling alteration of the music which that operation renders necessary, while the original score remains intact . . . But the term *adaptation* has never . . . been applied to the total rescoring of a composition.'

Previous chapters have, of course, proved that alterations were hardly 'trifling' and Christian Kramer even received praise for his added obbligato parts in *Die Entführung aus dem Serail*. Hypocrisy also arose when reviewers who advocated a new level of fidelity found their own knowledge unable to meet such demands. Collier, for example, in his review of the Drury Lane version for the *Morning Chronicle*, chastised Bishop for numerous changes in orchestration, including using 'the rough bass instead of the flute' in the seduction scene. Yet, as detailed earlier, this was a place where Bishop had preserved Meyerbeer's instrumentation.

Some reviewers recognised that the situation was not clearcut. Reviewing the King's Theatre production, *The Age* stated, 'It is impossible that a man of Mr. Bishop's eminence, or of Mr. Lacy's industry, could hear any opera three or four times running, and be mistaken in its main bearings.' And, although Ayrton thought it would be 'rank injustice to the author' to judge his work by the Drury Lane adaptation, he admitted that 'the piano-forte copy of the *Freischütz* convinced us, long before we had seen the score, or heard a note of it, except in our own chamber, that it was the work of a great and original mind. An impression from the piano-forte copy of *Robert le Diable* is not equally favourable.' In a musical culture so enmeshed in adaptation, arrangement and transcription, Meyerbeer's insistence that only a staged production with the original orchestration could be considered his work seemed unrealistic.

Whether orchestral timbre truly constituted an unalterable, crucial aspect of a work remained debatable. This was especially true when the King's Theatre production, whose fidelity had been so vaunted, finally appeared. Had orchestration been as central to success as Meyerbeer claimed, when listeners finally heard this correctly scored performance they should have reacted accordingly. A few critics maintained that this was so. The *Morning Post* insisted that 'all was content, delight, and rapture ... The great difference found in the music as it was heard last night was necessarily in the orchestra, and it is there, according to the opinions of the most eminent judges, that its highest merit is found.' Most, however, felt that matters were not quite so obvious. Holmes, whose scathing condemnation of the patent theatres was quoted earlier, admitted that 'however the injustice with which M. MEYERBEER has been used by two of the metropolitan theatres may have predisposed us in his favour ... we found, on trial, that the former copies had been but too faithful'. The easy connection that Meyerbeer and Mason insisted on between fidelity and worth thus disintegrated for many writers.

Fidelity even became a liability. Drury Lane's version, though more faithful than Covent Garden's, pleased less. *The Athenaeum* felt that in the Drury Lane version, 'restricted by the succession of the music, to a close adherence to the dull original, the ... authors ... have attempted little more than a translation, and, therefore, the result is only what might have been expected'. Reviewing Covent Garden, *The Tatler* agreed that the rival production was marred by haste, which 'blinded the management to some defects in this opera which might have been pruned away' and to the 'inefficiency of some of the performers'. The latter was especially detrimental to the success of Drury Lane's version. Mary Ann Wood (née Paton) and Henry Phillips drew plaudits as Alice and Bertram, respectively. Ayrton, however, in his review for *The Harmonicon*, found Wood's husband 'utterly incompetent . . . to do justice to such a part' as Robert and Sterling reported in *The Times* that Fanny Ayton, as Isabelle, 'sang most wickedly out of tune, and was hissed accordingly'. Bishop may have wished for the greater freedom of past adaptations, when he could have shielded these weaknesses.

Even the King's Theatre production, whose fidelity was so vaunted, seemed in need of alteration. The *Literary Gazette* professed 'high gratification to have heard the whole of the opera in a complete state' but in the same breath 'confess[ed] that, to please the taste of an English audience, the opera should be curtailed'. Ayrton went so far as to say that had Meyerbeer been able to stay for the full rehearsal period 'he would most likely have profited by the advice of his experienced friends, and reduced it to dimensions calculated for [London]'. Ayrton therefore claimed that Meyerbeer himself would have understood the crucial role of adaptation, would have understood that in some cases, change produced a better effect than fidelity or, rather, that change was necessary to produce the same effect in a new context.

Fidelity also seemed less valuable when the value of the original itself was questionable. Neither Meyerbeer's vaunted originality nor his innovative melding of scenic and musical effect, central to grand opera, garnered unanimous praise. The spectre of Weber's influence ran through assessments. Reviewing the King's Theatre performance, the *Theatrical Observer* gave the scene of the resuscitated nuns a rather roundabout compliment: 'without the least resemblance to the incantation music of *Der Freischutz*, the composer has not been less successful than Weber'. Others were less generous. Reviewing the patent theatre versions in *The Spectator*, Taylor stated, 'We trace the pupil of WEBER throughout, but we trace only a pupil', while the *New Monthly Magazine* called *Robert* a 'French emasculation of a piece of German *diablerie*'. Many also felt that Meyerbeer failed to achieve Weber's balance between scenic splendour and musical worth. Reviewing the King's Theatre version for *The Atlas*, Holmes contemptuously compared *Robert* to *Fidelio* and *Der Freischütz*, which were 'charming the town' despite not having 'a sixpenny worth of new scenery, or dress'. In contrast, Meyerbeer was 'obliged to compound with mechanics and showmen . . . to support the five drowsy acts of his bad opera'. Holmes urged Mason to 'divorc[e] [music] from exhibitions of pageantry and dancing' and let 'They who wish to see the Diorama . . . go to the Regent's-park'. As with *La muette*, many critics felt that *Robert* veered too close to a minor theatre aesthetic to belong at either opera house or patent theatre.

Perhaps most damningly for *Robert*, the most striking scene did not transfer well to London: the famous scene of the resuscitated nuns, replete with eerie orchestration, lavish scenic display and otherworldly terrors. In a joint review of the two patent adaptations, the *New Monthly Magazine* lectured:

> This scene ... produces a very powerful and striking effect; but this effect is purchased at a price which should not have been paid for it ... there are bounds even to stage-licence in these cases, and who shall say those bounds are not passed when three or four score of cowled nuns are changed – by devils' magic, and to do a devil's work – into as many half-naked dancing-girls – *the scene a church*, and the object lascivious blandishment – for a profane and evil purpose? ... at an *English* theatre, the scene in question is an outrage on public decency – the most gross and mischievous that was ever yet offered to it.

Attempts to soften the shocking subject matter, however, backfired. Collier expressed relief that the nuns at Drury Lane did not, like their Parisian sisters, 'exhibit one bosom naked in the Amazonian style'. Thomas Love Peacock, however, reviewing the King's Theatre production for *The Examiner*, felt changes ruined the scene:

> In Paris, the nuns throw off their robes on the stage, and proceed ... to a Bacchanal dance, in which they appear, as far as stage propriety allows, somewhat in the fashion of Tam O'Shanter's *Cutty Sark*. Here, they glide behind the scenes in their ghostly apparel, and re-appear in the most common-place ballet-dresses; so that the resurrection is one, not of nuns, but of dancing-girls. If there be any thing in our taste, or in our manners, that prevents the representation of this scene, according to its original intention, why, then, we have no business with the performances of the *Académie Royale*.

Caught between the original shocking display and a modest reworking, most theatres found it difficult to maintain the treacherous balance between the lurid and the ludicrous. This was especially true at Drury Lane. Collier noted that 'an illuminated gigantic skeleton' provoked laughter, Sterling that the dancers looked 'as if they had got out of bed in a hurry instead of having just quitted their tombs'. Peacock resisted the notion of feminine display as inherently unnationalistic. Reviewing the patent theatre versions for *The Examiner*, he stated that while the scene may be 'pleasant in the warm climate of Sicily,' where the story was set, it was 'certainly wrong according to our northern notions, especially for those who have thick legs or gummy ancles'. On the surface, this statement cast aspersions on British beauty, but the deeper message seems to be that British women were intrinsically too moral to be able to display themselves as immodestly as their looser continental sisters. The central draw of *Robert* in Paris thus failed to transfer to London, incompatible with 'northern' talents, scruples and taste.

Robert le diable had generated so much anticipation that *The Age* joked it would 'soon banish all nonsensical ideas' of the cholera epidemic that had just struck London.[73] Ultimately, such expectation proved too weighty for the opera to sustain in London, despite its success across Europe. Fidelity played an especially ambiguous role. Meyerbeer and Mason's protests foregrounded the idea of fidelity, extending it even to orchestration. Yet, fidelity to a foreign opera dependent on scenic and sonic effect resonated uncomfortably with the perceived decline of drama into illegitimate fare. In addition, fidelity did not ensure success. At the Adelphi, Fitzball and Buckstone were able to plumb the scenic effects without mastering the difficult music. The patent theatre adapters were caught between extremes, unable to adapt as freely as the Adelphi, yet condemned for not producing the 'true' work reserved for the King's Theatre. Ironically, they did produce remarkably faithful versions, but the special circumstances surrounding *Robert* elevated standards of fidelity to such an impossible height that they still fell short. Most damningly, the King's Theatre's scrupulously faithful version was the least successful. *Robert* demonstrates on the one hand the dangers of adapting and incurring protests from the original composers and on the other the dangers of *not* adapting to suit the new context.

CONCLUSION

French opera at once fascinated and troubled Londoners. As playhouse managers turned aggressively to Paris for imported opera and as French opera moved to the forefront of musical developments, the King's Theatre began to compete more directly with the playhouses for important London premières. This sometimes involved the original composer, as with Meyerbeer, which heightened debates over copyright, ethics and fidelity. London theatres' battles over opera further blurred repertoire lines and challenged distinctions between opera house and playhouse, major theatre and minor theatre, foreign and native. This was especially true with grand opera, whose melding of drama, music, gesture and spectacle sparked prevalent concerns about the decline of the drama. As Telesforo de Trueba y Cosio wrote to *The Tatler* about *Robert le diable*, 'this rage for *adaptation* is as great an obstacle to the possession of a National Opera, as the *French vaudeville* is an impediment to the regeneration of the English Drama'.[74] Ironically, the goal that had seemed so desirable only a few years earlier – of an increased taste for music and an increased focus on fidelity – created a problematic result. Some originals did not seem worthy of fidelity, and adaptation appeared to breed not a more elevated taste or greater respect for the original composer's wishes, but simply more adaptation.

In 1833, William Ayrton proclaimed, 'WHAT properly is called the *English* stage is at its last gasp.'[1] A year after the bill to abolish theatrical patents failed in the House of Lords, it appeared that it may as well have passed. Both patent theatres seemed to have abandoned the legitimate drama, felled by managerial incompetence and greed. The *Literary Gazette* expostulated that the 1832 bill 'appears to have been a pretty consider-able d — ridiculous waste of time; since, had the members only waited till the present season, they would have discovered that there was, in reality, no regular, legitimate, or national drama to inquire about'.[2] At Drury Lane, Frederick Polhill, struggling finan-cially, relinquished his lease to manager Alfred Bunn in spring 1833, although he did not formally withdraw until 1834. Pierre-François Laporte, a Frenchman who had run the King's Theatre from 1828 to 1831, turned his hand to Covent Garden in 1832–3 with disastrous results. He reassumed the directorship of the King's Theatre early in 1833 and abruptly closed Covent Garden in May, leaving the performers to continue the season at the Olympic.[3] Shortly thereafter, Laporte ceded Covent Garden to Bunn, who became the first to lease both theatres simultaneously; the decried monopoly of two theatres became an even more maligned monopoly of one.

As Edmund Cox recalled, this state of affairs was intimately linked with foreign imports: 'A kind of mania for operatic performances seemed to have seized upon the managers of the patent theatres during this very remarkable year.'[4] This mania encompassed foreign and musical performances of all kinds. The patent theatres offered ballerinas from France, operas performed by a German company in their native language, concerts by Nicolò Paganini, a new, more faithful adaptation of *Don Giovanni* with Joséphine de Méric as Donna Anna, adaptations of Bellini's *La sonnambula* and Chélard's *La table et le logement* starring Maria Malibran and a wildly successful adaptation of Auber's *Gustave III*.

The year 1833 thus provides a fitting close to this study. In some ways, it proves the triumph of adapted foreign opera at the playhouses. Continental operas were now performed with scrupulous fidelity (*Don Giovanni*), the most celebrated foreign stars (Malibran) and staggering success (*Gustave III*). This is strikingly different from only two decades earlier, when foreign operas were heavily altered experiments on the fringes of playhouse repertoire. The fact that many of the same performers, audiences and operas now travelled among major theatres, minor theatres and the King's Theatre shows how much the gap of musical taste and skill had narrowed among these venues. The result was not always the refined musical landscape critics desired. Fidelity was more prominent, but freedoms were still accepted depending on the perceived worth of the original and the effectiveness of the adaptation. The focus on foreign stars and works at times seemed to indicate improved musical taste, at others invidious exclusion of native talent. This was especially true when resources were lavished indiscriminately on what contemporaries saw as revered Mozart opera, flimsy Bellini works and the superficial scenic attractions of *Gustave III*. The year 1833 demonstrates the fruits of some twenty years of efforts to accustom playhouse casts and audiences to more faithful renditions of foreign operas. Foreign opera was now firmly entrenched in the playhouse repertoire, with aesthetic and financial rewards that were sometimes great, sometimes dubious.

DON GIOVANNI REVISITED

On 5 February 1833, two events occurred at Drury Lane. First, a new adaptation of *Don Giovanni* appeared, adapted by Henry Bishop and Samuel Beazley. This was touted as a newly complete version of the opera and featured French soprano de Méric as Donna Anna. She had made her London debut the previous year at the King's Theatre and also performed there in 1833. In addition, playbills proudly advertised that 'eminent Professors are added to the strength of the band', whom Ayrton in *The Harmonicon* identified as 'principal instruments of the King's Theatre and Philharmonic band'. (See Appendix 2 for review citations.) The second event that night was a riot. Polhill and Bunn, mimicking the King's Theatre and Covent Garden, eliminated some of the pit in favour of private stalls at half a guinea (or ten shillings sixpence) each, as compared to three shillings sixpence for the pit. The *Morning Post* related 'this innovation excited the ire of a large portion of the audience. Shouts, cries, groans, hisses, and exclamations of almost every kind, continued with increasing violence.' As several critics noticed, the event was reminiscent of the O.P. riots of 1809, in which the audience protested against Covent Garden's raised prices, increased numbers of private boxes and hiring of Italian soprano Angelica Catalani at an exorbitant salary. The concurrent events of a new *Don Giovanni* and a riotous disturbance encapsulate the ambivalent effects of imported opera.

Drury Lane's private stalls were the last straw in an increasing trend of exclusivity. As Bunn protested when he addressed the rioting audience, Drury Lane only followed what the King's Theatre and Covent Garden had already done. At Covent Garden in October 1832, Laporte had gone even further by installing four new private boxes, in direct violation of the O.P. 'arrangement'.[5] Bunn leveraged nationalistic sentiment to chastise the Drury Lane audience for their hypocrisy, pointedly referencing Laporte: 'we should not have ventured to place these stalls in the pit but in the conviction that you would not deny to Drury-Lane that which you had already allowed to a foreigner at another Theatre'.[6] At first, the *Morning Post* reported that some members of the galleries applauded the idea of their own liberality. Others seem to have caught the craftiness of Bunn's rhetoric, as he used nationalistic pride to sanction class exclusivity, and the riot resumed. What Bunn failed to mention was that the added stalls at Covent Garden had not been accompanied by a rise in prices. Bunn and Polhill's obvious pecuniary motive especially rankled protestors and when Bunn insisted that Polhill had not erected the stalls with 'any expectation of enriching his pocket', the *Morning Post* related that he was met with *'Cries of "Oh, oh!" mingled with laughter'*. Clearly, both Bunn and his patrons knew that direct appeals to the elite could generate more income. The *Morning Post* reported that Bunn's new stalls were 'fully occupied' and Ayrton observed that *Don Juan* had 'draw[n] persons into the public boxes, who, on any other occasion, would have been shocked at a proposal to visit the theatre without the consolation of a more private and exclusive retreat'.

Such clear catering to the privileged backfired, however, and Bunn and Polhill were obliged to remove the stalls. The root of the problem for many critics was the attempt to turn a public, national theatre towards the private and the foreign. *The Athenaeum* wrote:

> if the public is not content with the arrangements [Bunn] thinks fit to make, it has nothing to do but to stay away. There can be no doubt of the justness of this argument, if a free trade existed in theatricals; but while monopoly is claimed and allowed, we suspect that it does not hold good, seeing that there cannot be a contract without two parties to it.

Increasingly, the 'second party', i.e. the majority of the audience, rebelled against the use of exclusive patents to pander to exclusive patrons.

Tellingly, however, the rioters did not remonstrate against either Mozart or de Méric, as they had in the 1809 O.P. riots against the high salary paid to Catalani. Once their concerns had been addressed, they settled quietly to hear *Don Giovanni*, which ran almost every evening for two months. The bifurcated protest – incensed at exclusive seating but accepting of foreign works and stars – points to the ambiguous position that foreign opera occupied at the playhouses. On one hand, Mozart was foreign, part of an influx that *Figaro in London* complained '[threw] upon the town a bevy of hungry natives, who can no longer find employment in our national theatre'. This critic was the only one to protest the new *Don Giovanni*, dismissing it as 'hacknied'. On the other, Mozart was a revered composer whose presence on the British stage demonstrated elevated native taste. The *Theatrical Observer* linked Mozart to the prized legitimate drama by calling him 'the presiding genius of harmony and the Shakespeare of composers'. Edward Holmes in *The Atlas* even enfolded *Don Giovanni* into nationalistic pride. Speaking of the Drury Lane cast as if it consisted only of native singers – conveniently ignoring de Méric – Holmes boasted 'we possess resources adequate to the production of the best foreign works in the best style; if the public can be brought to enjoy good music for its own sake, without the sauce of strange names, faces, and language, there is not the least necessity that its pleasure should depend upon aid from abroad'.

Fidelity played an important role in this rhetoric. At Drury Lane, Polhill and Bunn vaunted fidelity as both advertising draw and point of pride and several critics echoed their tactics. The *Morning Post* enthused, 'In previous arrangements the Opera had to undergo curtailment and alteration, but we have at last had the pleasure of enjoying the whole of the exquisite music of this delightful work, performed in a manner worthy of its excellence, and arranged by Mr. Bishop with the most scrupulous fidelity to the original score.' Not only was Bishop and Beazley's *Don Giovanni* far more faithful than the heavily adapted version Bishop had prepared in 1817, but they also offered more of Mozart's score than the King's Theatre's London première of 1817 (in Italian), the English Opera House's adaptation in 1830 (in English) and the travelling German troupe's production at the King's Theatre in 1832 (in German).[7] Bishop accomplished this through a kind of excess of fidelity. Only libretto sources remain, but they suggest that Bishop preserved every piece from both Prague and Vienna versions except the final ensemble, although Leporello and Zerlina's duet was dropped by the time the word book was printed. While previous productions mixed Mozart's two versions, as is still common today, they did not include as many numbers as Bishop. Interestingly, some areas still remained fluid; 'scrupulous fidelity' could be asserted even when Bishop had eliminated the final ensemble, transposed the title role for tenor John Braham and replaced secco recitative with brief spoken dialogue.

Beazley remained even closer to Da Ponte, despite Ayrton's erroneous assertion that he had 'depart[ed] in no way from [the] translation' of *Don Giovanni* in 1817. Beazley had wanted to depart, as he explained in the preface to the word book, and substitute 'a new drama on the subject, founded on the adapter's recollections of the Ballet which he had seen . . . in Spain'.[8] He found, however, that 'Mozart's music . . . follows the march of the piece to which it has been composed so closely as to preclude the possibility of any change in the action without marring the composition'. The contrast with only a few years earlier, when William Dimond felt free to transport *Die Entführung aus dem Serail* to Greece and James Robinson Planché to substitute Andreas Hofer for William Tell, is significant. As fidelity became more expected, the parameters for change shrank. The previous double standard, which had allowed more literary departures than musical ones, began to fade. Overall, Beazley and Bishop presented their audience with an adaptation that would have been impossible one or two decades earlier: music predominated over spoken dialogue; every character sang difficult music; numerous lengthy, intricate ensembles appeared; and music was integral to understanding the plot.

Fidelity did not, however, garner unequivocal praise. While virtually all critics lauded Mozart's music and Bishop's fidelity to it, there were a few dissenting voices. These critics were careful, however, not to implicate Mozart directly in any reproach. Thomas Love Peacock wrote in *The Examiner* that

> There never has been any thing perfect under the sun except the compositions of Mozart, but there are circumstances which may make even them tedious, such as sitting, as people do in our theatres, in more uneasiness than in the stocks. The newly performed music, added, as it is, to much that is more strikingly excellent and established in popular favour, has no effect other than tediousness.

Failings of the production are cleverly diverted to Polhill and Bunn, who forced most of the audience into uncomfortable seats while increasing the luxury of wealthy visitors. Peacock does imply, however, that the added pieces are not 'strikingly excellent'. Maligned as adaptation might be, adapters did select the parts most suited to 'popular favour'. Fidelity did not necessarily add significant value if it resurrected weaker portions.

Ayrton – who had overseen the 1817 King's Theatre production – made a similarly sophisticated argument. Clearly defending his own production against Bishop's, particularly his decision not to include all of the Prague and Vienna pieces, he denounced the Vienna interpolations as 'added ... to gratify particular performers, and to induce them to accept characters, which, in their vanity, they thought not good enough'.[9] These may have been written by Mozart, but only under pressure from egotistical performers. Ayrton himself had not, however, presented the Prague version complete, without any Vienna interpolations, and turned to aesthetic arguments to defend his own departures. He agreed that the final ensemble should be cut (as he had done in his own production) since it was 'splendid' but 'injurious to the effect of the opera as a whole'. He also admitted that Ottavio's Vienna aria, 'Dalla sua pace', was 'lovely' and heaped most scorn on an aria in fact part of the Prague score, 'Ho capito, signor sì' – he had initially kept both pieces but then cut them in performance.[10] As fidelity became an important tool in theatrical competition, its nature came under close scrutiny. When a work existed in different versions, arguments surrounding fidelity became strikingly modern. Contemporaries debated whether the most faithful adaptation was one that performed only the first version, performed all pieces from both or offered a selected amalgam of the two.

Few critics felt comfortable critiquing such an admired composer as Mozart, however, and most instead directed any displeasure to the text. The *Morning Herald*, one of the few to criticise the opera, did so by way of the libretto. 'Its drama is notoriously ill contrived, and its music, however fine, is deficient in connection. Its various components do not fit well together, or succeed each other in a developement [*sic*] naturally progressive. They must be estimated individually.' Beazley's translation received even more pointed condemnation. Leigh Hunt, writing in the *True Sun*, condemned the 'wretched words of the English adapter – the dead carcase that has been attached, Mezentius-like, to [*Don Giovanni's*] ever-living spirit'. *The Athenaeum* counselled that meaning be privileged over rhyme. This would avoid lines like Leporello's 'That's from Figaro – *Mozart's immortal note*', meant to rhyme with 'Just this little bit of Pheasant / Slily I'll slip down my throat'.[11] Others blamed the English language itself. The *New Monthly Magazine* colourfully characterised Beazley's task as 'uniting a gay, bounding, graceful Italian greyhound in the bounds of unlawful matrimony with a stiff, cross, crabbed English bull-dog'. Beazley anticipated such protests in his preface, asking that the 'hypercritical gentlemen of the press' consider the difficulty of his task before 'they vent the bitterness of their critical acumen' on him.[12] He excused himself with a common trope, stating that 'music is the grand object of the Opera, and the poetry a very minor consideration'. Through all these concerns runs a persistent thread of distaste at the combination of music and drama, and particularly at the combination of foreign music and native drama. When, in these critics' minds, foreign music necessitated poor poetry, the patent theatres had truly abandoned the legitimate drama. Adapters had been maligned in the past for changing foreign opera to suit national drama, but they now found it difficult to preserve foreign opera while maintaining the literary focus of the legitimate stage.

Ambiguity continued in comparisons between playhouse and opera house. With their *Don Giovanni*, Drury Lane's managers and adapters directly challenged the King's Theatre in repertoire, performers and fidelity. This overlap invited comparison. A few critics insisted on giving Drury Lane the edge. Holmes boasted, 'The public, who desire to hear the *Don Juan* that MOZART wrote, and not the mutilated, ineffective copy of it, which is given generally at the latter end of the Italian Opera season, may now have their wish.' How different from 1817, when it was Bishop's adaptation of *Don Giovanni* that was seen as the 'mutilated' copy of the King's Theatre production. Most critics, however, echoed Edward Sterling's sentiment in *The Times*: 'The opera, as played here, would suffer by any comparison with the performances of the Italian Theatre; but if compared with any of the performances at the English theatre it is justly entitled to great praise and warm encouragement.' Even though the leading playhouse performers were engaged – Braham in the title role, Henry Phillips as Leporello and Mary Ann Wood, née Paton, as Zerlina – it was the foreigner, de Méric, who received the most copious praise. *The Athenaeum* felt that of the cast, only she 'represented to perfection' her character, particularly because she 'evinc[ed] a proper contempt for everything but a genuine delivery of the music as written by a great master'. While a proposed casting of Pierre Begrez as Ottavio had fallen through because he 'could not talk English enough', de Méric apparently managed the language well.[13] With the self-deprecation so common when discussing sung English, the *New Monthly Magazine* wrote that 'Her enunciation of our guttural English is admirable.'

Increasing fidelity therefore confronted playhouse managers with a problem. If nothing but language and singers distinguished their production from the King's Theatre, what could be done if this language was not considered suitable for music and these singers not equal to their foreign counterparts? If the playhouses wished to compete with the King's Theatre on equal footing, foreign performers became an almost inevitable corollary.

'A LITTLE *INFRA DIG*': MALIBRAN IN *LA SONNAMBULA*

And, indeed, foreign performers surfeited the patent stage for the remainder of the 1832–3 season. French ballerina Pauline Duvernay appeared at Drury Lane in performances of Hérold's *La belle au bois dormant* and Auber's *Le dieu et la bayadère* in February and March, respectively. A German company featuring Wilhelmine Schröder-Devrient performed in June and July at both patent theatres, offering *Fidelio*, *Der Freischütz*, *Euryanthe* and *Die Zauberflöte* in their original language. Most sensationally, Maria Malibran sang at both theatres from May to July. She starred in Bellini's *La sonnambula* and Chélard's *La table et le logement* and also appeared briefly in Bishop's adaptation of *Le nozze di Figaro* and Charles Horn and Braham's *The devil's bridge*.

Malibran's engagement, like de Méric's, signalled a new place for foreign opera stars at the playhouses. In the past, such singers had only infrequently appeared at the patent theatres to sing a few isolated arias; Malibran had done so at Drury Lane in 1829–30. Now, they sang in full productions, in English, alongside native casts. Hiring a singer like Malibran went one step further and signalled a new function for adaptation. Malibran was not engaged, like de Méric, to fill one specific role. Rather, as a more celebrated international star, she brought operas with her; she insisted on singing both the Bellini and the Chélard operas and had performed the other works before.[14] She and the operas were therefore imported as a kind of package. In some ways, these were no longer adaptations but new productions, in English, of the latest foreign hits with the biggest foreign stars.

Bishop and Beazley again worked together to prepare *La sonnambula* for the London stage, but an especially convoluted source situation makes it difficult to assess their work. The manuscript libretto, printed libretto, printed word book and printed score all diverge substantially from each other and were virtually all published well after the première. The manuscript libretto is the only source that dates from 1833, but it may not accurately represent the première, since there were typically many changes between submitting the manuscript libretto for censorship and mounting the première. The word book is relatively close to the première, since it lists the cast for 1835, but word books contain only the texts for the musical numbers and therefore cannot give us a sense of the dialogue. The libretto dates from 1849 at the earliest and was published jointly in London and the United States, where the adaptation also enjoyed popularity.[15] The printed score, which appeared between 1839 and 1842, was clearly designed for domestic use; it cut several numbers, as well as *pertichini* within numbers, that are in all libretto sources.[16] It also included an aria for Elvino based on 'L'amo tanto' from Bellini's *I Capuleti e i Montecchi* that no other source contains. Such variance among sources was typical, as the adaptation moved from rehearsal, to performance, to subsequent performances, changing each time. It is rare, however, to have so few sources stemming from the première date.

While such discrepancies preclude a definitive knowledge of what London audiences heard in 1833, three broad observations can be made: Beazley increased comedy; Bishop retained musical features that his audience and performers had resisted in the past; and the adaptation was intimately linked to Malibran. As with all London adaptations, Beazley utilised spoken dialogue in place of recitative. Perhaps to shield Malibran as a non-native English speaker, little of this dialogue devolved to Amina. Instead, Beazley focused primarily on Lisa and Alessio, expanding and adding to their comic exchanges. This continued a common thread in these adaptations: reconfiguring comedy to the specific type that playhouse audiences relished. Banter between the two as Alessio naively presses his suit and Lisa rejects it contains plenty of the quips and puns that playhouse audiences enjoyed. For example, Alessio tells Lisa 'make up your mind and buckle too with me – but; heigho! There's no buckle without a tongue'.[17]

Bishop also made only modest changes, despite a lingering scholarly perception that he drastically altered the work. It appears that he may, as with *Robert le diable*, have worked only from a vocal score. A full score was not yet published and the *Sunday Times* stated that Bishop had 'arranged' the work from 'a pianoforte copy'. Bellini complained bitterly of pirated publications of his score and it is possible that Bishop based his adaptation on one of these.[18] Unfortunately, no manuscript score of the adaptation exists to confirm or deny this. The *Morning Herald* also stated that Drury Lane had neither contacted nor paid Bellini: 'we cannot form a conclusive opinion of the merits of the original. This fact it is necessary to bear in mind, in justice to the author, who has not been consulted in this speculation upon the productiveness of his work.' Bellini himself was in London at the time, but apparently was not involved with the adaptation and kept a low profile. Malibran complained to Bunn that Bellini, unrecognised, had to pay to attend her performance.[19] Bellini appears to have condemned the adaptation as 'murdered and hacked about … the more because it was sung in the language that, with reason, was called the language of birds'.[20] The authenticity of this letter, however, is questionable and Bellini could have meant the quality of the performance and translation rather than any alterations.[21] Persistent ideas that Bishop changed Bellini drastically may stem from this letter, or from Bishop's printed score, which, as noted earlier, does not accurately represent what was performed onstage.

In fact, however, Bishop's version was remarkably faithful to Bellini's opera, particularly in the context of London adaptation as a whole. He transposed some numbers, replaced some recitative with spoken dialogue and made some internal cuts, but he retained all numbers and the only interpolation, as discussed above, appears only in the printed score and did stay within Bellini's oeuvre. Writing of the adaptation's popularity in the United States, Katherine Preston observes that 'Bishop apparently left the original composer's music intact whenever possible'. Despite separating numbers for sheet music purchasers and transposing some numbers, 'the melody is all Bellini's; it is not "simplified" at all'.[22]

Bishop practised this fidelity even when it meant challenging both his cast and his patrons. He retained substantial amounts of recitative, lengthy numbers, internal repetition and involved ensembles that mixed song and action, all features he had altered in the past. The act one finale exemplifies his approach. The original stretches to 450 measures and well over the first half (mm. 1–256) is devoted to the scena and tempo d'attacco. A delicate pizzicato accompaniment heralds Amina's somnambulant entrance. Rodolfo, uncertain how to react, interjects with hesitant bits of recitative. Amina fluidly expresses her feelings for Elvino, by turns tentative, lyrical, tender and passionate. A passage of recitative follows, in which Rodolfo continues to struggle with his conscience and Lisa, shocked, departs. A kind of duet between Amina and Rodolfo emerges, Allegro moderato, in which he determines to respect her honour, but it offers only isolated passages of full-fledged lyricism. After a transition from F major to D major, the chorus enters to hail Rodolfo as the count. They proceed haltingly, now mimicking a pizzicato, now sustaining chords, now breaking into jaunty dotted rhythms. A sudden shift in mode, from D major to D minor, and an accelerated tempo usher in Elvino, who has heard of Amina's supposed transgression. Amina's slow, timid phrases, as she gradually awakens, contrast with agitated sections for Elvino and the chorus. The slow movement arrives at m. 257. Amina protests her innocence in a poignant melody, joined by Elvino and then Teresa and Lisa, who express their divergent emotions as Alessio and the chorus quietly accompany them. A brief tempo di mezzo ensues, as Elvino cruelly pronounces that there will be no wedding. Bellini parallels the shock with a sudden move from Sostenuto assai to Allegro and from E♭ major to G major. The cabaletta commences in m. 334, Più vivo. Elvino and Amina join in an impassioned outpouring of grief, as the others sing brief chords and occasional melodies to express their amazement; all join together for the exciting close.

Such a finale offered numerous challenges to Bishop's patrons and performers. First, its length stretched previous boundaries, yet Bishop cut only eight measures, from the orchestral close. The rest he retained, including the repeat of the cabaletta, which even today some performances eliminate. Second, the chorus frequently sings like an instrument, with brief chords on important beats. This requires rhythmic precision and confidence in pitch. Several reviewers noted that Drury Lane's chorus struggled to meet these demands. Holmes remarked 'the choruses, which are in a style not very familiar to English performers, seemed to cause some embarrassment, and to be delivered with timidity'. Third, until the slow movement, the finale offers little of the sustained lyricism that playhouse audiences prized. One thought gives way quickly to another, as Bellini follows the characters' changing emotions. Finally, a significant portion of the action takes place in music: Amina's sleepwalking; Rodolfo's decision not to take advantage of her; the discovery of Amina by the villagers and Elvino; and Elvino's rejection of her. Of course, this is not as challenging as some ensembles. The plot trajectory is clear and much of it relies on the visual spectacle of Amina's somnambulism. Still, Bishop had rarely before retained such a long, fluid and dramatically crucial ensemble.

Bishop and his publisher, Boosey, did, however, alter the finale for domestic consumption. The printed score split it into six separate numbers, each with a price for individual sale. To facilitate the separation, Bishop cut transitional material. From the slow movement on, he also cut all vocal lines except Amina and Elvino's. This would have allowed for easier domestic performance, but it does not accord with the staged version, since all the libretti sources contain lines for the chorus and other characters. Nothing better demonstrates the divergence between what was performed onstage – remarkably faithful productions with lengthy ensembles intact – and the older aesthetic still required for domestic sale – briefer, extractable numbers focused on lyricism.

The faithful version that Bishop prepared for the stage, if not for the home, clearly stemmed from Malibran's presence. Malibran would soon sing Amina across Europe and doubtless wished the adaptation to be as close to her future appearances as possible. Yet, Malibran was the impetus for alteration as well as fidelity. Bishop's score shows that he transposed Malibran's solos to suit her lower tessitura and is apparently the only source that documents what is sometimes referred to as a 'Malibran version'.[23] Malibran's other changes are more ephemeral, the extemporaneous embellishment expected from opera stars. By all accounts, Malibran was particularly fond of this method of 'adapting' and some records of her choices remain. Bishop sometimes offered an alternate, more ornamented version in an added staff above the vocal line that probably records Malibran's notes. Malibran's contemporary biographer, Countess de Merlin, also provides an instance of Malibran's embellishment of 'Ah! non giunge uman pensiero' in her Italian performances.[24]

A comparison of Bellini's original (transposed in Merlin from B♭ major to G major), Merlin's account of Malibran's rendition, also in G major, and Bishop's alternate version, in F major, elucidates Malibran's practice (see Exx. 7.1a–b). If the divergent keys are accurate, they suggest that Malibran felt free to choose whichever transposition suited her voice at the moment. The embellishments in Bishop and Merlin are also similar but not identical. This implies that Malibran had a framework that she followed for her ornaments, which she freely altered depending on the performance and the key. These ornaments highlight what many commentators found especially thrilling about her voice: her flexibility, her astonishing lower range and the ease with which she moved between registers. The example also underlines how much singers acted as additional 'adapters' and how much audiences valued their alterations, willing to purchase in sheet music an echo of their stage performance. Fidelity was therefore in

Example 7.1a 'Ah! non giunge', Bellini, *La sonnambula*, as sung by Maria Malibran

The phrase, as Bellini wrote it, is as follows.

Madame Malibran sang it thus:

some ways the opposite of celebrity, as audiences cherished the changes unique to their favourite singers. Merlin described the effect of Malibran's embellishments as 'electrifying', and even those critics opposed to plentiful ornament, such as Ayrton in *The Harmonicon*, had to cede the point: 'following the fashion of the day ... [Malibran's] ornaments are so redundant as often to be ridiculous. These however, are so nicely executed, that they seduce even the best critics.'

Ayrton encapsulates critical reactions to Malibran: her dazzling performance excused multiple ills. Review after review heaped accolades on her. Holmes enthused in *The Atlas*, 'what a hold on the public admiration has this lady, when we consider her personal beauty, the intellectual character of her acting, and her miraculous extent of voice, accompanied by the most polished execution and the highest degree of invention and taste'. Even her English bested her native colleagues. The *Morning Post* declared: 'by none of our native vocalists is the language pronounced in singing with a tithe of her distinctness and expression'. Although the opera stretched to over twenty performances, however, first at Drury Lane, then at Covent Garden and finally at the King's Theatre, where Malibran sang it at her benefit in August, it was considered something of a failure. In his memoirs, Bunn recalled that the opera 'prov[ed] so inattractive' that he had to find other pieces in which Malibran could appear.[25] While Holmes described a 'tumult of applause, which brought to mind the old and glorious days of KEAN', audiences were only full at the beginning and end of Malibran's engagement.

Example 7.1b 'Do not mingle', Bishop, arr., *La sonnambula*, mm. 63–70.

Partially, this was because Bellini's opera did not seem as worthy of praise as Malibran. Here was an instance where the 'original' libretto was viewed as an adaptation, and a poor one. Romani based his tale on Scribe, Aumer and Hérold's 1827 ballet *La somnambule*, which appeared as a play at Covent Garden in 1828 and as a ballet at the King's Theatre in

1829.[26] The latter proved so popular that, when the original Amina and Elvino (Giuditta Pasta and Giovanni Battista Rubini) performed the opera at the King's Theatre in 1831, numerous critics found it inferior to the ballet. The *New Monthly Magazine* observed,

> This opera labours under the two-fold disadvantage, of being founded on a most hacknied subject, and of the latter being ill-calculated for a musical drama. The story had told well in a melodramatic form, and had also made a very interesting ballet, which, unfortunately for the success of the opera, had been an everlasting standing-dish last year ... First impressions are every thing! On seeing 'La Sonnambula,' we could not divest ourselves of "La Somnambule".[27]

While some stories supported multiple adaptations, many reviewers thought this one too slight and too well formulated for ballet to do so. Holmes, for example, found it 'grossly absurd' for Amina to sing 'long scenas, some of them requiring considerable vocal effort, which take place while [she] is asleep'. Others cited Bellini's music as the main drawback. Edward Taylor declared in *The Spectator*, 'We have heard many stupid operas in the course of our lives, but *La Sonnambula* is the most stupid of all.' Bellini, like Rossini before him, seemed derivative, insubstantial and not as worthy of close preservation as Mozart and *Don Giovanni*.

La sonnambula may also have faltered because Bunn and Polhill misread their potential audience. Class played a central role. Reviewers clearly linked Malibran with a more refined clientele than typically frequented the playhouses. Writing in the *Morning Chronicle*, John Payne Collier found 'something a little *infra dig*, in the appearance of so eminent a vocalist on the English boards, and in a merely English performance'. By hiring Malibran and mounting *La sonnambula*, therefore, Bunn and Polhill in essence tried to do with repertoire what they had not been allowed to do with more exclusive seating areas a few months earlier: attract the moneyed clientele of the King's Theatre. The *Globe and Traveller* even reported that they moved the start time one hour later than usual, to half past seven, to accommodate the later dinner hour of such patrons. It is unclear whether such tactics worked. The *Globe and Traveller* observed that the 'dress circle [was] studded with ladies of rank in the manner of the Opera House on a grand night' but *Bell's Life in London* reported that the 'fashionables' stayed away because they could not tear themselves away from Hyde Park or 'dine early' enough, even with the later starting time. Regardless, it does not seem that upper class attendance was enough to make up for sparse turnout from other classes. The *Theatrical Observer* related that, other than the dress circle, the house rarely filled until later in the evening, when half-price tickets were sold; *La sonnambula* was the first piece on the programme, so these patrons missed all or most of it. *The Age* remarked that the house filled only once Malibran's engagement was ending: 'What a funny set of people the cocknies are! ... Malibran has, during the earlier part of her engagement, played in this very identical piece, many nights to less than 200*l*.; and now she is going ... the whole population are leaving their homes to follow her chariot wheels.' As with the ill-advised, high-priced stalls, Bunn and Polhill miscalculated.

They were unable to attract either enough of their regular patrons or enough new, wealthier clients to sustain a lengthy run of *La sonnambula*.

The failure of Malibran to support either Drury Lane or Covent Garden – even as she pocketed some £3000 – seemed endemic of the widely predicted collapse of the patent theatres.[28] Noting the departure of Mary Ann Wood for the United States in the same period, Ayrton sighed, 'If we are to have only foreigners as first vocal women in our English theatres, her place may be filled certainly; but will the public long endure this? We believe they will, for they are grown apathetic.' *Figaro in London* warned that 'small Bunn's management' would throw native performers 'upon the wide world by the intrusion of foreigners ... unless we and the two or three other leviathans of the critical press interfere to snatch the *corpse de theatre* from the yawning jaws of the poor house'. As *The Age* – of which Polhill owned half – pointed out, however, cost-conscious managers were unlikely to pay heed to these 'leviathans'. 'It is all vastly fine to talk of tragedy, comedy, and old Drury ... Polhill tried that, with the finest company in the world, and played to a *loss* of £100 per night; while Laporte ... with two third-rate, and three fifth-rate French dancers, has played to a nightly *gain* of as much.'[29] In 1835, a letter to the editor of *The Examiner* pointed to works such as *La sonnambula* as 'promising an improved state of affairs' for musical taste and 'completely revolutionis[ing]' English opera.[30] In 1833, however, the outcome of foreign operas and foreign stars seemed more questionable.

THE TRIUMPH OF FOREIGN OPERA: *GUSTAVE III*

In October 1833, Bunn launched his first full season in his unprecedented role as manager of both patent theatres. Broadly speaking, Bunn split his resources. Drury Lane he focused on legitimate drama, Covent Garden on light, spectacular and musical fare. In November, this quasi-contest between legitimate and illegitimate drama was decided convincingly in favour of the latter. Bunn reportedly lavished £2000 on an adaptation of *Gustave III* by Auber and Scribe.[31] Despite having been scooped by the Victoria (formerly the Coburg) a few days earlier, the Covent Garden *Gustave* ran for a staggering 101 performances in the first season, double the usual longest-running work. It reputedly recouped and even exceeded Bunn's financial outlay within the first few weeks.[32] In contrast to *Don Giovanni* and *La sonnambula*, neither foreign performers nor fidelity were the main attraction. Rather, grand opera's alluring combination of politics and visual display captured audiences.

Gustave III concerns the assassination of King Gustav III of Sweden in 1792, the same event that would inspire *Un ballo in maschera*.[33] Scribe departed from history by replacing the political motivation of the assassin, Count Ankastrom, with a personal one: Gustave's illicit love for Ankastrom's wife. Adapters for the Victoria and Drury Lane took divergent approaches, both in order to mitigate the potentially troubling staging of a regicide and to suit the musical requirements of their theatres. Ultimately, however, concerns of politics and fidelity alike were swept aside in enthusiasm for the lavish ball during which Gustave is assassinated. This scene captivated audiences with lively dance music, extravagant sets and costumes, and the appearance of 'fashionables' onstage as ball guests. Bunn had finally found a work that would draw the broad spectrum of classes necessary for sustained success. Whether for good or ill, *Gustave* effectively silenced protests about the abandonment of legitimate drama and indisputably established adapted foreign opera at the core of the playhouse repertoire.

In the unsettled political atmosphere of the early 1830s, producing an opera about King Gustave's death required care. Covent Garden librettist James Robinson Planché recalled in his memoirs that censor George Colman 'had some qualms of conscience' about the plot, since 'The assassination of a monarch was an incident none the less objectionable because it was an historical fact.'[34] After some 'correspondence', which unfortunately appears to be lost, Colman agreed to permit the opera. In the circumstances, fidelity to history proved tricky, and Planché and the Victoria librettist, Thomas James Thackeray – a cousin of the famous author – took differing approaches.

Thackeray mitigated the central assassination by remaining close to Scribe, i.e. by making the assassination personally rather than politically motivated. He added, however, political barbs on the fringes of the libretto. A new comic character, Sbiegel, master of revels, banters with officials about their costumes for the ball. When the Chancellor asks what his disguise should be, Sbiegel responds, 'You would like to appear in a *new* character, of course, my lord, what think you of justice?' He later remarks, 'The collector of the royal taxes has taken the character of the devil.'[35] Thackeray, who had authored *On theatrical emancipation and the rights of dramatic authors* the previous year, also utilised Gustave as his mouthpiece. When the director of Gustave's opera *Gustavus Vasa* petitions for an 'exclusive patent', Gustave refuses: 'Monopoly! fit word for *barbaric* ages. No; whilst Gustav[e] lives, science and liberty shall walk hand in hand, unshackled by the chains of prejudice or the trammels of cupidity.'[36] Cheers probably greeted this statement from partisans of a free theatrical market and the quotation is displayed prominently on the title page of the printed libretto. The Victoria's *Gustave* thus ameliorated the most incendiary facet of the plot, the assassination, but found other routes to condemn corruption and monopoly.

In contrast, Planché attempted to move Scribe's libretto back towards historical accuracy. He did this not to highlight the historical regicide, however, but to depoliticise the plot further. First, he noted in his introduction to the published libretto that he had 'plac[ed] . . . Ankastrom in his proper situation as an ex-captain of the guards, instead of exhibiting him . . . the prime minister and bosom friend of Gustav[e]'[37] Sarah Hibberd argues that with Planché's change of Ankastrom from political insider to disaffected outsider, 'the political thrust of the opera is . . . diffused'.[38] Planché also cleansed Gustave of the implication of adultery. Ankastrom still kills Gustave because he believes he is having an affair with his wife, Amélie, but it is a new character, historical figure Colonel Lillienhorn, who is guilty. As Planché noted in his libretto, this both accorded better with fact and presented the monarchy in a more moral light. He 'avoid[ed] the error of making Gustav[e] ... entertain a criminal passion' since, quoting Sir John Carr's *Northern summer* (1805), the king had 'an almost monkish continence'.[39]

Lillienhorn absolved Gustave not only of moral stain but also of music. Planché and composer Thomas Cooke reverted to the by then rare practice of splitting one role – Gustave – into two, spoken and sung. In his memoirs, Planché complained of this split, protesting that 'actors who could not sing compelled [me] to cut my coat more in accordance with my cloth than with my inclination'.[40] He even expressed a retrospective wish that he could have substituted another tale altogether, as did Somma in *Un ballo in maschera*. But, he sighed, Somma 'had the advantage of furnishing a libretto for another composer, and I was compelled to adhere to Gustavus III and Sweden'.[41] Planché may have ascribed blame to the music because of the criticism he received for mixing historical fact and theatrical fabrication – Lillienhorn had not had an affair with Amélie, after all, nor had Ankastrom shot Gustave because of adultery. Planché, who built a reputation for historically accurate staging, clearly wished to excuse his departures from fact.

The situation, however, was not quite so straightforward. Cooke treated the score freely enough that Planché could have introduced further changes. Planché had also successfully replaced the story of Guillaume Tell with Andreas Hofer, and could have taken a similar tactic here. In addition, the Gustave (James Warde) did not seem such a fine actor nor the Lillienhorn (John Templeton) such a poor one that the split was inevitable. Warde, who had also played the spoken Ibrahim in the adaptation of *Die Entführung aus dem Serail*, aspired to high tragic acting but received mixed reviews and moved more to the minor theatres in the 1830s.[42] Templeton had played several important operatic roles, including Elvino in *La sonnambula* and Ottavio in the newly adapted *Don Giovanni*, although a few critics had remarked negatively on his acting.[43] It seems more likely that Planché himself desired the split, for only this way could he absolve the king from blame while still adhering to Scribe's basic outline. The absence of music for the king also points to continued links between speech and power on the native stage, as song still appeared unsuitable for a regal leader.

The Victoria also featured a completely spoken Gustave, but for different reasons. At the Victoria, as at most minor theatres, composer John Barnett kept only a fraction of the foreign score. The available sources – the libretto and newspaper reviews – indicate that Barnett used only four of Auber's numbers: the overture; Oscar's couplets from the act one and five finales; and a song and chorus for Christian, possibly drawn from the act two finale.[44] Barnett supplied two additional solos, one for a conspirator and one for Sbiegel. As seen in previous chapters, the minor theatres did not have the musical resources to attempt full operas, nor did critics place the same weight of expected fidelity on them as on the patent theatres. Minor theatre adapters thus often treated the opera as a core plot accompanied by highlights from the score. This was in fact how much of London operatic culture operated. The libretto was published, or a summary of its plot given in newspaper reviews, and then a handful of its more popular numbers appeared as sheet music, often altered to suit the domestic market or fitted with variations or fantasias.

In Cooke's adaptation for Covent Garden, one can see the conflict between this model and burgeoning expectations of fidelity. Cooke retained the majority of Auber's lengthy, five-act score, but compressed it to fit three acts and accommodate a spoken Gustave. He slimmed several numbers substantially and cut both of the trios that included Gustave, Gustave's duet with Amélie, Amélie's duet with Ankastrom and the *morceau d'ensemble* in act two. Gustave's remaining music devolved primarily to Lillienhorn.[45] It is unclear whether Cooke kept all of Auber's dance music, since the printed score does not include it. As with *La sonnambula* and so many other adaptations, however, the printed score is not an accurate record of the stage performance. Aimed at sheet music sales, the score of Cooke's *Gustave* leaves out sections of recitative, *pertichini* and several ensembles or portions of them, all of which the libretto sources include. Reviewers and scholars also feel that some of the transpositions were for domestic use only.[46] The score is complete enough, however, to show that Cooke's changes were more extensive than those to *Don Giovanni* or *La sonnambula*. Reacting to the paucity of appealing solos in the original, he expanded and regularised the form of Amélie's aria and crafted a new solo for Ankastrom from Auber's tunes. Cooke's *Gustave* and its printed materials thus represent a mixture of fidelity, alteration and repackaging for the domestic market.

The change that drew most attention was the aria Cooke created for Ankastrom. Henry Phillips, who sang the role, recalled, 'Here again occurred that most extraordinary circumstance of having a song written for me, which till then had been utterly unconnected with the opera . . . I had a duet, concerted music, and little solos, but no scena or ballad. What was to be done? One I must have.'[47] This illustrates the continued importance of performers' desires in adaptation, but it was not simply an egotistical demand for a showpiece. As Phillips notes, this was an 'extraordinary circumstance' that stemmed both from the original and the shift to a spoken Gustave. Unusually, there is no stand-alone aria for the vital character of Ankastrom in Auber's opera. In fact, there are only three arias not embedded in ensembles, one for Amélie and two for Gustave. This lopsided arrangement made sense in the original, since Gustave was both the main character and sung by celebrated tenor Adolphe Nourrit. When Cooke reassigned Gustave's arias to Lillienhorn, however, he gave a disproportionate number of arias to a secondary character, sung by relative newcomer Templeton. Meanwhile, the more important character, Ankastrom (and the far more celebrated singer Phillips) had no extended solo.

To rectify this, Phillips described, Cooke 'most ingeniously composed a short recitative, and adopted the melody of the overture as the foundation of his subject'.[48] In other words, Cooke followed Bishop's procedure in *Guillaume Tell* and crafted a kind of fantasia on a melody from the overture. The melody he chose begins the overture and recurs in the act three finale, in which Ankastrom attempts to lead a disguised Amélie to safety. Cooke retained the melody in both of these places, but added a third appearance in Ankastrom's new solo. Ankastrom, wounded by Amélie's apparent infidelity, ruminates on how she will regret her actions later when, her beauty faded and her days tortured, she remembers his love. This solo furthers Planché's agenda of downplaying the political thrust of the story, since it focuses on Ankastrom's personal motivations for the assassination. It also accords with the function of the classic British stage ballad, which was reflective, static and general enough to transfer to the parlour and to any jilted lover.

Cooke's music is commensurately accessible. Unfortunately, the printed score does not give the entire piece. The opening recitative, which Phillips says Cooke composed and which is included in the libretto, is not present, nor are a total of ten lines in the middle of the text. Reviewing the printed score, the *Morning Post* indicated that these lines comprised the 'second movement', which was marred by a 'want of fitness and indefinite character' in performance and omitted from the published version. Whether this means that they were cut only for the printed score or also later cut in performance is unclear.

What remains in print are two strophic stanzas that utilise the overture melody in a rondo-like fashion (see Ex. 7.2a). The first four measures of the overture melody appear, in a significantly altered character. Auber's melody is Allegro non troppo, in E♭ major, with wedges on the pickup notes (see Ex. 7.2b). A ceremonial, regal effect results, which the grace notes lighten with a hint of joviality. Cooke slowed the tune to Andante, raised the key to F major and eliminated the wedges. This completely altered the effect. The *Morning Post* considered it 'almost the single example of deep pathos among AUBER'S compositions'. After three repetitions of the tune – once for orchestra, twice for voice – Cooke inserted a longing, rising line moving to the dominant before repeating the opening melody. Another new melody, with an impressive leap of an eleventh and a brief cadential flourish, concludes the stanza. The strophic form repeats the entire stanza to new text, save the last two lines, which serve as a refrain. A few moments subvert the usually straightforward harmonic language of British ballads. In the final melody, Cooke mildly paints the word 'madness' by preceding it with dissonant anticipation notes in mm. 25 and 27; the leap of an eleventh also occurs on this word in both stanzas. Additionally, some critics found Auber's use of a raised fifth in the dominant chord in the pickup beats unpleasant; the *Morning Post* thought it was 'not particularly agreeable to persons of musical taste'. Overall, though, the solo provided the kind of simple accompaniment, predictable form, modest vocal line and striking emotional effect that listeners relished in ballads. Phillips' performance, which he made the unusual choice to deliver seated, was a highlight.[49] The *Theatrical Observer* judged it 'the most beautiful thing in the Opera'.

Little outrage greeted either Cooke's or Barnett's changes to Auber. Writing for *The Spectator*, Taylor even expressed a sense of national pride that Cooke had been able to pass himself off as Auber. Erroneously attributing both Ankastrom and Amélie's arias to Cooke, the critic 'hope[d] this disclosure of their English parentage w[ould] not operate to their prejudice either with hearers or purchasers' Amélie's aria was in fact

Example 7.2a 'When Time Hath Bereft Me', Cooke, arr., *Gustave III*, mm. 1–36

by Auber, although Cooke rearranged it significantly. As with so many adaptations, less well-known originals could more easily brook change; alteration could not offend if it could not be detected. And, as Phillips rather condescendingly remarked, an audience ignorant of the original could blissfully pay for the privilege of imagining

Example 7.2a (cont.)

they heard that original: 'none of the audience, not one of whom, perhaps, had heard it when first produced, knew better, and took all for granted like the little children, who at the peep-show, asking which was Daniel, and which were the lions, were told they might make their choice, as they had paid their money'.[50] Even when changes were obvious, few critics objected. Nobody, for example, took the Victoria to task for inserting songs by Barnett. Collier in the *Morning Chronicle* even judged that these were 'not injudiciously substituted for others by Auber not likely to please in London more than in Paris'. Minor theatres were held to lower standards of fidelity, but such outright praise for interpolation had become rare by the 1830s.

Example 7.2b Overture, Auber, *Gustave III*, mm. 1–4

This tolerant attitude, so different from the rhetoric of strict fidelity surrounding Mozart and already-hallowed works such as *Don Giovanni*, highlights how much the value of fidelity rested on the value of the original. Few critics found Auber worthy of careful preservation. In his review for *The Atlas*, Holmes noted that 'Successful airs are not the prominent feature of this opera; its strength lies in its well-conceived and characteristic concerted music.' Virtually all critics agreed with this statement and Cooke's reworked and added solos are in a sense another version of this criticism. Auber also seemed to lack the originality crucial to genius. The *Sunday Times* remarked, 'The fact is, Auber heard once, his after works are Auber *in perpetuum*, without variations.' The crux of the criticism was Auber's French style. Hunt, employing prevalent dichotomies of French flightiness vs. German depth, argued in the *True Sun* that the plot was 'most singularly unfitted . . . for the illustration of [Auber's] sparkling, light, and laughing music'. Such a tale should be 'sustained by the fancifulness and passion of Beethoven, or some of the masterly composers of his country'. Light and agreeable but lacking depth and originality, Auber's music did not seem to warrant faithful replication.

Fidelity was, however, the focus of animated debate over the libretto. Critics struggled with which 'original' – history or opera – demanded greater reverence. Some condemned Planché's alterations to Scribe. Collier, reviewing the adaptation for the *Morning Chronicle*, found the added role of Count Lillienhorn 'rather an excrescence than a necessary character in the piece', whose appearance was 'unavoidable' only because of the 'supposition that the music given to the King in the original must be retained'. Fidelity to the music was thus a drawback that necessitated poor dramatic decisions. Hunt argued that Planché had taken the worst of both worlds: he had kept the 'absurdity' of the regicide being motivated by Ankastrom's jealousy while 'infinitely lessen[ing] the dramatic interest' by shifting the crime of adultery to Lillienhorn. Ultimately, 'the plot is the same as . . . [at the] Victoria . . . save that the latter has more reason for itself, and is, therefore, far more interesting'.

Others, however, lauded Planché for ingeniously surmounting the difficulty of a spoken Gustave by infusing the story with greater historical accuracy. Sterling, in his review for *The Times*, added a nationalistic slant:

Our more lively neighbours may be less inclined than the people of this country to scrutinize very closely the historical accuracy of theatrical representations; but it would have been felt here, that to represent a monarch of pure morals and exalted character as engaging eagerly in a disgraceful amour ... was too glaring a falsehood to be endured.

While infidelity to history and disrespect to monarchy intertwined dangerously on French soil, Sterling implies, the British demanded both historical accuracy and deferential treatment of monarchy. The incendiary act of regicide is contained through the strictures of historical fact. The monarchy is shielded by a moral purity that renders assassination unnecessary, prompted only by mistaken assumptions.

Still, the opera was about an assassination and that assassination was represented onstage. Here again, historical accuracy and theatrical effect clashed. Planché, following historical record, had the king shot in the loins.[51] In an 'absurd mistake', however, Taylor related that the Gustave, Warde, 'disclose[d] a vest with the *breast* coloured with red ink ... Warde and the property-man, we suppose, were so used to blood-stained waistcoats, that they could not think of violating the good old custom.' While only a few may have noticed this error, all were certainly struck by what Taylor called the 'ostentatious display of sanguinary stains'. Several critics recorded slight disturbances in the audience and Holmes counselled 'it is a superfluous exactness in a point in which the imagination supplies all that is necessary to interest or effect'. At once too faithful and too theatrical, the display of blood made some in the audience uncomfortably aware of the one historical fact that Scribe and Planché could not alter: the king's assassination.

In the end, though, neither fidelity nor its absence was the primary draw of *Gustave III*. Peacock summarised in *The Examiner*: 'As a drama, *Gustavus the Third* falls far short of mediocrity; as an opera, it does not appear to rise much higher; but as a show it has more than ordinary pretentions.' This show culminated in the stunningly lavish spectacle of the masked ball. Holmes raved, 'We shall not attempt to describe the gay and brilliant appearance of the stage in the masquerade scene, the depth of the illuminated hall, its countless numbers of masquers, their endless variety of dress, the rich effect of the carpeted floor, Mrs. VINING's pretty dancing, nor the whimsical drolleries of Madame CELESTE.' As Holmes noted, *Gustave* achieved the merging of theatrical elements central to grand opera: 'Sound and show do not compensate in it for the want of dramatic interest – they are united with it.' Fashionable society became part of the spectacle as noblemen and politicians appeared onstage as masqueraders. The audience was itself a draw, as Covent Garden finally attracted the fashionable clientele it had so long courted. Elite patrons, unable to see the opera at the King's Theatre, where it did not appear complete until 1851, flocked to the patent theatre.[52] As the *Theatrical Observer* remarked, it became 'quite *mauvais ton*' not to have attended and listed nobles such as the Princes Esterhazy, the Duke of Gloucester and a young Princess Victoria among the audience.[53] *Gustave*'s dazzling scenic display, combined with the voyeuristic pleasure of seeing nobility onstage and off, captivated viewers.

Critics felt less uniformly optimistic about the first fruit of Bunn's union of the patent theatres. Some recognised that theatrical monopoly was almost a necessity for such productions. Holmes perceived that only with 'the force of both houses' could 'works which require the assistance of large bodies of performers on the stage and in the orchestra, – and almost the whole of the modern musical drama is to be ranked in this class[–] . . . be assured from loss, and the interests of the musical art consulted'. As genres such as grand opera came to the forefront, the 'musical art' seemed to become further removed from legitimate drama, ensconced instead in the lavish scenic adjuncts so closely linked to illegitimate theatre on the London stage. This aroused a few vigorous protests. Taylor penned a caustic critique, claiming that numerous native composers could have done better, deriding Bunn for not being able to find one singer in two houses to play Gustave, giving the only negative review of the ball scene and declaring that the opera was a failure. Of course, the opera was hardly a failure, and most reviews evince a tone of resignation. *The Athenaeum* sighed, 'We are no advocates for the eternal system of producing foreign operas to the exclusion of the works of English composers, but once in a blue moon such a thing may be allowed. At all events, whether we allow it or not, it has been done . . . and so admirably done, that objection . . . is effectually silenced.' *Gustave*'s success moved imported foreign opera firmly to the centre of the native stage.

A NEW LANDSCAPE

The three case studies in this chapter delineate three prevalent features of London operatic life that continued in succeeding decades: increased reliance on foreign stars; an influx of often lavishly produced but not always strictly faithful foreign operatic adaptations; and greater fidelity to revered works. Both foreign stars and foreign operas continued to proliferate at the playhouses. Managers sought what Susan Bennett has termed '"safe" production selections' in order to remain solvent in an intensely competitive theatrical environment in which major theatre, minor theatre and opera house fought for the same repertoire and performers. As Bennett notes, however, in this model, 'theatres must rely on dazzling productions and/or the involvement of stars to sell seats. Paradoxically both approaches are expensive and overall costs inevitably rise.'[54] This was certainly true as the playhouses continued to feature expensive stars such as Malibran and to race after the latest operatic hits, especially lavish grand operas. These productions did not necessarily repay the outlay, garner critical acclaim or feature strict fidelity. As with *Gustave*, fidelity remained less crucial for less well-known and artistically valued works, particularly when the original offended audiences' sensibilities too far. Planché, for example, reluctantly noted that 'truth, power, and poetical justice . . . [were] all sacrificed' to avert the starkly tragic endings of both Marliani's *Il bravo* and Halévy's *La juive*.[55]

Still, alterations, particularly to the score, were less ubiquitous than in the past. This was especially true for works that were gaining canonical status, as is exemplified by reactions to a final event of interest in 1833: a performance of Bishop's adaptation of *Le nozze di Figaro* at Covent Garden in June 1833, with Malibran as Susanna, de Méric as the Countess and Lucia Vestris as Cherubino. A performance of *Fidelio* by the touring German company followed, in German. Several critics reported that the audience expressed dissatisfaction with Malibran's interpolated songs – 'Should he upbraid' and 'The light guitar' – as well as Bishop's comic song for the gardener. Holmes remonstrated:

> it is evidently time to lay this record of our bad taste on the shelf . . . What has been gained by defacing, mutilating, and vulgarizing so perfect an opera as *La* [sic] *Nozze di Figaro*? . . . while the musical directors of theatres have been wrapped up in the notion of the unimprovable condition of the public, the knowledge of MOZART has been silently in progress . . . The public are beginning to instruct the *kapellmeister*, and his sophistications are abhorred alike by the pit and the two shilling gallery. The boxes murmur silently, but all agree that . . . a great deal of trouble has been taken to make a bad piece of a good one. Mr. BISHOP is absolutely destitute of judgement . . . He does not yet seem to know that a great work, pure and well performed, is almost sure to make its way.[56]

Class clearly informs the issue, as Holmes implies that only the least well-off patrons – the one shilling gallery – might still welcome Bishop's adaptations. Meanwhile, the 'public' (presumably the middle class) has been admirably increasing its musical knowledge. Nationalism is also at play, since Holmes states 'if such things were well received, and *Fidelio*, too, applauded to the echo on the same evening, the contradiction would have annihilated our belief in any thing like public taste'.

As the patent theatres increasingly relied on foreign performers along with foreign operas, the contrast between altered British adaptation and faithful continental performance deepened. Holmes' blistering condemnation became standard, representative of the rhetoric that, for well over a century afterwards, sought to silence and erase these adaptations. In succeeding years, managers heeded such sentiments and the adaptations discussed in this book gradually slipped from view, replaced with new, more faithful versions.

The change from the 1810s to the 1830s is striking. Fidelity, while still fluid and dependent on the artistic worth of both original and adaptation, was far more prevalent; the boundaries for change had narrowed significantly. Foreign operas, foreign stars and touring foreign companies proliferated at the playhouses. Although the bill to dissolve theatrical patents had been defeated in 1832, the patents' practical value had all but evaporated. Major theatre, minor theatre and opera house competed for the latest foreign operatic hits with increasingly similar productions and casts. When the patents were officially rescinded in 1843, it was a small step for Covent Garden to become the opera house it is today. The ideal of a native stage devoted to and supported exclusively by spoken, legitimate drama had not proved viable for many reasons, one of which was opera's popularity. Similarly, although native opera enjoyed renewed activity in the 1830s and 1840s with the works of composers such as Michael Balfe and Edward Loder, it ultimately neither overshadowed nor staunched the steady flow of imported opera now firmly embedded in London theatrical repertoire. While the most striking aspect of these adaptations might initially be the changes adapters made to foreign operas, ultimately the importation of foreign opera prompted equally far-reaching changes in London's musical and theatrical life.

Nineteenth-century efforts to eliminate adaptation still influence operatic culture. Modern scholars and performers have continued the trajectory away from such adaptations and these practices have remained relegated to the past. What would happen if we returned to this culture of adaptation, if we revived some of these early nineteenth-century efforts? There seems to be a lurking concern that, were Bishop's *Figaro* to be performed today or numerous nineteenth-century versions of *Der Freischütz* to flood theatres again, the original would somehow be injured, be seen in an unflattering light, be conflated with these adapted forms, perhaps even be discarded in favour of them. The harsh language still employed to describe these adaptations – Thomas Bauman refers to the 'gross disfigurement' of *Die Entführung aus dem Serail*, Cyril Ehrlich calls Bishop a 'despoiler of Mozart and Rossini' – suggests as much.[57]

Such an outcome, however, seems unlikely. Reviving nineteenth-century adaptations would not only allow for a greater understanding of operatic culture of the past, it might also achieve some of the same aims that motivated them in the first place. Hearing these adaptations again might, for example, bring operas closer to their non-operatic roots. We might again experience operas not as isolated works, but as part of a continuum of multiple retellings of popular stories. Or, these adaptations might allow a mixed cast of accomplished singers, modest singers and actors to produce operas at venues and for audiences normally closed to the genre. Reviving these adaptations might, in other words, reveal them as constructive rather than destructive. Linda Hutcheon argues, 'an adaptation is not vampyric: it does not draw the life-blood from its source and leave it dying or dead . . . It may, on the contrary, keep that prior work alive, giving it an afterlife it would never have had otherwise.'[58] London adapters have often been denigrated for 'mutilating' operas, but their work was more akin to mutation, to the continual changes necessary to bring works to new venues, listeners and time periods.

Operas adapted for the London playhouses, 1814–1833

Opera	Date of première	Composer	English Title	Date of adaptation	Theatre[1]	Adapter(s)[2]
Jean de Paris	1812	Boieldieu	Jean de Paris	1 November 1814	DL	Samuel James Arnold (L), Charles Edward Horn (M)
Don Giovanni	1787	Mozart	John of Paris	12 November 1814	CG	Isaac Pocock (L), Henry Bishop (M)
			The libertine	20 May 1817	CG	Isaac Pocock (L), Henry Bishop (M)
			Don Juan	5 July 1830	EOH	William Hawes (M)
			Don Juan	5 February 1833	DL	Samuel Beazley (L), Henry Bishop (M)
Il barbiere di Siviglia	1816	Rossini	The barber of Seville	13 October 1818	CG	John Fawcett and Daniel Terry (L), Henry Bishop (M)
Le petit chaperon rouge	1818	Boieldieu	Rose d'amour	3 December 1818	CG	James Kenney (L), John Addison (M)
Le nozze di Figaro	1786	Mozart	The marriage of Figaro	6 March 1819	CG	Henry Bishop, assisted by Isaac Pocock and Louise Costello (L), Henry Bishop (M)
La lettre de change	1815	Bochsa	The promissory note	29 June 1820	EOH	Samuel James Arnold and Samuel Beazley (L), Nicholas Bochsa (M)
Der Freischütz	1821	Weber	Der Freischütz; or, the seventh bullet	22 July 1824	EOH	W. McGregor Logan and Samuel James Arnold (L), William Hawes (M)
			Der Freischütz; or, the seven charmed bullets	30 August 1824	RA	J. H. Amherst (L), Montague Philip Corri (M)
			Der Freischütz; or, Zamiel the spirit of the forest and the seventh bullet	c. August 1824[3]	WL	John Kerr (L)
			Der Freischütz; or, the demon of the wolf's glen and the seven charmed bullets	6 September 1824	S	Edward Fitzball (L)
			Dr. Freischütz	2 October 1824	O	Charles Dibdin (L)[4]
			The Freyschütz; or, the wild huntsman of Bohemia	14 October 1824	CG	Barham Livius, James Robinson Planché and Washington Irving (L), Barham Livius (M)
			He fries-it; or, the seventh charming pancake!	c. 25 October 1824[5]	RC	
			Der Freischütz	10 November 1824	DL	George Soane (L), Henry Bishop (M)

Original title	Year	Composer	English title	Date	Venue	Adapters
La neige	1823	Auber	The frozen lake	3 September 1824	EOH	James Robinson Planché (L), G. W. Reeve and Mr Watson (M)
			The frozen lake	26 November 1824	CG	Same as above
Abu Hassan	1811	Weber	Abon Hassan	4 April 1825	DL	William Dimond (L), Thomas Cooke (M)
Preciosa[6]	1820	Weber	Preciosa	28 April 1825	CG	William Ball W. McGregor Logan, and George Soane (L), William Hawes (M)[7]
Tarare	1787	Salieri	Tarrare	15 August 1825	EOH	Samuel James Arnold (L), William Hawes (M)
Die Schweizerfamilie	1809	Weigl	Lilla	21 October 1825	CG	James Robinson Planché (L), Barham Livius (M)
Léocadie	1824	Auber	Leocadia	17 December 1825	DL	Barham Livius (L, M)
Das unterbrochene Opferfest	1796	Winter	The oracle	7 August 1826	EOH	Hampden Napier (L), William Hawes (M)
			The oracle	20 February 1827	CG	Same as above
La dame blanche	1825	Boieldieu	The white lady	9 October 1826	DL	Samuel Beazley (L), Thomas Cooke (M)
			The white maid	2 January 1827	CG	John Howard Payne (L), George Herbert Rodwell (M)
Il Turco in Italia	1814	Rossini	The Turkish lovers	1 May 1827	DL	Michael Rophino Lacy (L, M)
I fuorusciti di Firenze	1802	Paer	The freebooters	20 August 1827	EOH	Hampden Napier (L), William Hawes (M)
Die Entführung aus dem Serail	1782	Mozart	The seraglio	24 November 1827	CG	William Dimond (L), Christian Kramer (M)
Die Nachtigall und der Rabe	1818	Weigl	Die Nachtigall und der Rabe	8 May 1828	S	Charles A. Somerset (L)
Così fan tutte	1790	Mozart	Tit for tat	29 July 1828	EOH	Samuel James Arnold and Hampden Napier (L), William Hawes (M)
Der neue Paris	1826	Maurer	Not for me	23 August 1828	EOH	Hampden Napier (L), William Hawes (M)
Silvana	1810	Weber	Sylvana	2 September 1828	S	Charles A. Somerset (L), Jonathan Blewitt (M)
L'amor marinaro	1797	Weigl	The pirate of Genoa	5 September 1828	EOH	Hampden Napier (L),[8] William Hawes (M)
Le maçon	1825	Auber	The mason of Buda	21 October 1828	A	James Robinson Planché (L), George Herbert Rodwell (M)
			The French spy	4 April 1831	Q	John Thomas Haines (L)
La vieille	1826	Fétis	Love in wrinkles	4 December 1828	DL	Michael Rophino Lacy (L, M)
			My old woman	14 January 1829	S	George Macfarren (L), Jonathan Blewitt (M)
Ivanhoé	1826	Rossini	The maid of Judah	7 March 1829	CG	Michael Rophino Lacy (L, M)

(cont.)

Opera	Date of première	Composer	English Title	Date of adaptation	Theatre[1]	Adapter(s)[2]
La muette de Portici	1828	Auber	The dumb girl of Portici	4 May 1829	RC	H. M. Milner (L), T. Hughes and Montague Philip Corri (M)
			Masaniello	4 May 1829	DL	James Kenney (L), Thomas Cooke and Barham Livius (M)
			Masaniello	11 May 1829	RA	J. H. Amherst (L), Mr Callcott (M)
Die Räuberbraut	1828	Ries	The robber's bride	15 July 1829	EOH	Edward Fitzball (L), William Hawes (M)
Der Vampyr	1828	Marschner	Der Vampyr	25 August 1829	EOH	James Robinson Planché (L), William Hawes (M)
Les deux nuits	1829	Boieldieu	The night before the wedding and the wedding night	17 November 1829	CG	Edward Fitzball (L), Henry Bishop (M)
La fiancée	1829	Auber	The national guard	4 February 1830	DL	James Robinson Planché (L), Thomas Cooke (M)
La gazza ladra	1817	Rossini	Ninetta	4 February 1830	CG	Henry Bishop and Edward Fitzball (L), Henry Bishop (M)
La cenerentola (and others)	1817	Rossini	Cinderella	13 April 1830	CG	Michael Rophino Lacy (L, M)
Guillaume Tell	1829	Rossini	Hofer	1 May 1830	DL	James Robinson Planché (L) and Henry Bishop (M)
Fra diavolo	1830	Auber	Fra diavolo	24 November 1830	Q	
			Fra diavolo	13 January 1831	O	
			The devil's brother	1 February 1831	DL	Charles Shannon (L), Alexander Lee (M)
			Fra diavolo	3 November 1831	CG	Michael Rophino Lacy (L, M)
Zemire und Azor	1819	Spohr	Azor and Zemira	5 April 1831	CG	William Ball (L), George Smart (M)[9]
Le colporteur	1827	Onslow	The emissary	13 May 1831	DL	Barham Livius (L, M)
Le philtre	1831	Auber	The love spell	27 October 1831	O	Charles Edward Horn (M)
			The love charm	3 November 1831	DL	James Robinson Planché (L), Henry Bishop (M)
Robert le diable	1831	Meyerbeer	Robert le diable	23 January 1832	A	John Buckstone and Edward Fitzball (L)
			Robert le diable	13 February 1832	SW	

Original title	Year	Composer	English title	Date	Venue	Adapters
Der Alchymist (and others)	1830	Spohr	The demon	20 February 1832	DL	Samuel Beazley and Frank Mills (L), Henry Bishop, assisted by Thomas Cooke, Montague Philip Corri, and R. Hughes (M)[10]
			Robert the devil or the fiend-father	21 February 1832	CG	Michael Rophino Lacy (L, M)[11]
			The demon father	12 March 1832	RP	
			Der Alchymist	20 March 1832	DL	Thomas Haynes Bayly and Edward Fitzball (L), Henry Bishop (M)
Le dieu et la bayadère	1830	Auber	The maid of Cashmere	16 March 1833	DL	Edward Fitzball (L), Henry Bishop (M)
Le serment	1832	Auber	The coiners	23 March 1833	CG	Michael Rophino Lacy (L, M)
La sonnambula	1831	Bellini	La sonnambula	1 May 1833	DL	Samuel Beazley (L), Henry Bishop (M)
La table et le logement	1829	Chélard	The students of Jena	4 June 1833	DL	James Robinson Planché (L)
Zampa	1831	Hérold	The bridal promise	10 June 1833	CG[12]	John Oxenford (L)
Le pré aux clercs	1832	Hérold	The court masque	9 September 1833	A	James Robinson Planché (L), William Hawes (M)
Gustave III	1833	Auber	Gustavus of Sweden	7 November 1833	RC	Thomas James Thackeray (L),[13] John Barnett (M)
			Gustavus the third	13 November 1833	CG	James Robinson Planché (L), Thomas Cooke (M)

APPENDIX 2

Reviews of adaptations[1]

REVIEWS OF *JEAN DE PARIS* ADAPTED AS *JEAN DE PARIS*,
DRURY LANE

London Times, 2 November 1814
Monthly Theatrical Reporter, December 1814, 101–6
Morning Post, 2 November 1814
New Monthly Magazine, 1 December 1814

REVIEWS OF *JEAN DE PARIS* ADAPTED AS *JOHN OF PARIS*, COVENT
GARDEN

The Examiner (Leigh Hunt), 6 November 1814
London Times, 14 November 1814
Monthly Theatrical Reporter, December 1814, 101–6
Morning Chronicle (William Hazlitt), 14 November 1814
New Universal Magazine, November 1814, 411
Theatrical Inquisitor, November 1814, 340

REVIEWS OF *DON GIOVANNI* ADAPTED AS *THE LIBERTINE*, COVENT
GARDEN

British Stage (Thomas Kenrick), June 1817, 132
The Examiner (Leigh Hunt), 2 December 1821
Morning Chronicle, 22 May 1817
New Monthly Magazine, 1 July 1817
Theatrical Inquisitor, May 1817, 390

REVIEWS OF *IL BARBIERE DI SIVIGLIA* ADAPTED AS *THE BARBER
OF SEVILLE*, COVENT GARDEN

British Stage (Thomas Kenrick), November 1818, 249
London Times (Edward Sterling), 14 October 1818
Morning Chronicle, 14 October 1818

Quarterly Musical Magazine and Review (Richard Mackenzie Bacon), 1820, 66–80
Theatrical Inquisitor, October 1818, 309–11

REVIEWS OF *LE NOZZE DI FIGARO* ADAPTED AS *THE MARRIAGE OF FIGARO*, COVENT GARDEN

British Stage (Thomas Kenrick), April 1819, 119
Journal of Music and the Drama, 22 March 1823
Theatrical Inquisitor, March 1819, 228–32
Theatrical Observer, 21 December 1825

REVIEWS OF *DER FREISCHÜTZ* ADAPTED AS *DER FREISCHÜTZ*, ENGLISH OPERA HOUSE

European Magazine, August 1824, 177
The Harmonicon (William Ayrton), August 1824, 167–8
Literary Gazette, 24 July 1824
Quarterly Musical Magazine and Review (Richard Mackenzie Bacon), 1824, 391–404
Theatrical Observer, 29 July and 7 August 1824

REVIEW OF *DER FREISCHÜTZ* ADAPTED AS *DER FREISCHÜTZ*, SURREY

The Drama, September 1824, 398–9

REVIEWS OF *DER FREISCHÜTZ* ADAPTED AS *THE FREYSCHÜTZ*, COVENT GARDEN

The Drama, October 1824, 42–3
The Examiner, 17 October 1824
Morning Chronicle, 15 October 1824

REVIEWS OF *DER FREISCHÜTZ* ADAPTED AS *DER FREISCHÜTZ*, DRURY LANE

European Magazine, November 1824, 461–2
The Examiner, 14 November 1824
The Harmonicon (William Ayrton), December 1824, 233–4
Literary Gazette, 13 November 1824
London Magazine, December 1824, 647–8
Morning Chronicle, 11 November 1824

REVIEWS OF *DIE ENTFÜHRUNG AUS DEM SERAIL* ADAPTED AS *THE SERAGLIO*, COVENT GARDEN

The Atlas (William Hazlitt), 2 December 1827
The Examiner, 2 December 1827
The Harmonicon (William Ayrton), December 1827, 249–50
John Bull, 2 December 1827
Morning Chronicle (John Payne Collier), 26 November 1827
New Monthly Magazine (Thomas Noon Talfourd), 1 January 1828, 16–17
Quarterly Musical Magazine and Review (Richard Mackenzie Bacon), 1827, 520–9
Theatrical Observer, 3 December 1827

REVIEWS OF *COSÌ FAN TUTTE* ADAPTED AS *TIT FOR TAT*, ENGLISH OPERA HOUSE

The Age, 3 August 1828
The Atlas (Edward Holmes), 3 August 1828
The Examiner (William Hazlitt), 3 August 1828
The Harmonicon (William Ayrton), September 1828, 214
Morning Chronicle (John Payne Collier), 30 July 1828
The Spectator (Edward Taylor), 2 August 1828

REVIEWS OF *LA MUETTE DE PORTICI* ADAPTED AS *MASANIELLO*, DRURY LANE

The Athenaeum, 6 May 1829
Dramatic Magazine, 1 June 1829
The Examiner, 10 May 1829
The Harmonicon (William Ayrton), September 1829, 225–6
Literary Gazette, 9 May 1829
London Times (Edward Sterling), 5 May 1829
Morning Chronicle (John Payne Collier), 5 May 1829

REVIEWS OF *DIE RÄUBERBRAUT* ADAPTED AS *THE ROBBER'S BRIDE*, ENGLISH OPERA HOUSE

Dramatic Magazine, 1 August 1829
The Examiner, 19 July 1829
The Harmonicon (William Ayrton), August 1829, 205–6
London Times (Edward Sterling), 16 July 1829

Morning Chronicle (John Payne Collier), 16 July 1829
Morning Post, 16 July 1829
The Spectator (Edward Taylor), 18 July 1829

REVIEWS OF *DER VAMPYR* ADAPTED AS *DER VAMPYR*, ENGLISH OPERA HOUSE

La Belle Assemblée, October 1829, 178
The Examiner, 30 August 1829 and 6 September 1829
The Harmonicon (William Ayrton), October 1829, 261
Morning Chronicle (John Payne Collier), 26 August 1829
Morning Post, 26 August 1829
Quarterly Musical Magazine and Review (Richard Mackenzie Bacon), 1829, 507–17
The Spectator (Edward Taylor), 29 August 1829

REVIEWS OF *LA GAZZA LADRA* ADAPTED AS *NINETTA*, COVENT GARDEN

The Age, 7 February 1830
The Harmonicon (William Ayrton), March 1830, 135
Literary Gazette, 6 February 1830
London Times (Edward Sterling), 5 February 1830
Morning Post, 5 February 1830
The Spectator (Edward Taylor), 6 February 1830

REVIEWS OF *GUILLAUME TELL* ADAPTED AS *HOFER*, DRURY LANE

The Atlas (Edward Holmes), 9 May 1830
Dramatic Magazine, 1 June 1830
The Harmonicon (William Ayrton), June 1830, 268 and September 1830, 389
London Times (Edward Sterling), 3 May 1830
Morning Chronicle (John Payne Collier), 3 May 1830
The Spectator (Edward Taylor), 8 May 1830
The Tatler (Leigh Hunt), 12 November 1830[2]
Theatrical Observer, 3 May 1830

REVIEWS OF *ZEMIRE UND AZOR* ADAPTED AS *AZOR AND ZEMIRA*, COVENT GARDEN

The Age, 10 April 1831
The Athenaeum, 9 April 1831

The Examiner, 10 April 1831
The Harmonicon (William Ayrton), May 1831, 129–30
Literary Gazette, 9 April 1831
Morning Chronicle (John Payne Collier), 6 April 1831
The Spectator (Edward Taylor), 9 April 1831

REVIEWS OF *ROBERT LE DIABLE* ADAPTED AS *ROBERT LE DIABLE*, ADELPHI

The Atlas (Edward Holmes), 29 January 1832
Literary Gazette, 28 January 1832
Morning Chronicle (John Payne Collier), 24 January 1832
Morning Post, 24 January 1832
Theatrical Observer, 25 January 1832

REVIEWS OF *ROBERT LE DIABLE* ADAPTED AS *THE DÆMON*, DRURY LANE

The Atlas (Edward Holmes), 26 February 1832
The Harmonicon (William Ayrton), March 1832, 69–70
London Times (Edward Sterling), 21 February 1832
Morning Chronicle (John Payne Collier), 22 February 1832

REVIEWS OF *ROBERT LE DIABLE* ADAPTED AS *ROBERT THE DEVIL*, COVENT GARDEN

The Tatler, 22 February 1832
Theatrical Observer, 22 February 1832

JOINT REVIEWS OF *ROBERT LE DIABLE* AT COVENT GARDEN AND DRURY LANE

The Age, 26 February and 4 March 1832
The Athenaeum, 25 February 1832
The Examiner (Thomas Love Peacock), 26 February 1832
Literary Gazette, 25 February 1832
New Monthly Magazine, 1 March 1832
The Spectator (Edward Taylor), 25 February 1832

REVIEWS OF *ROBERT LE DIABLE*, THE KING'S THEATRE

The Age, 25 June 1832
The Atlas (Edward Holmes), 17 June 1832
The Examiner (Thomas Love Peacock), 17 June 1832
The Harmonicon (William Ayrton), July 1832, 159–60
Literary Gazette, 16 June 1832
Morning Post, 12 June 1832
Theatrical Observer, 14 June 1832

REVIEWS OF *DER ALCHYMIST* ADAPTED AS *DER ALCHYMIST*,
DRURY LANE

The Athenaeum, 24 March 1832
The Atlas (Edward Holmes), 25 March 1832
Figaro in London, 31 March 1832
Morning Chronicle (John Payne Collier), 21 March 1832
The Spectator (Edward Taylor), 24 March 1832
Theatrical Observer, 26 March 1832
True Sun (John Forster), 21 March 1832

REVIEWS OF *DON GIOVANNI* ADAPTED AS *DON JUAN*, DRURY LANE

The Athenaeum, 9 February 1833
The Atlas (Edward Holmes), 10 February 1833
The Examiner (Thomas Love Peacock), 10 February 1833
Figaro in London, 9 and 16 February 1833
The Harmonicon (William Ayrton), April 1833, 92
London Times (Edward Sterling), 6 February 1833
Morning Herald, 7 February 1833
Morning Post, 6 and 8 February 1833
New Monthly Magazine, 1833, pp. 377–8
Theatrical Observer, 6 February 1833
True Sun (Leigh Hunt), 7 February 1833

REVIEWS OF *LA SONNAMBULA* ADAPTED AS *LA SONNAMBULA*,
DRURY LANE

The Age, 16 June 1833
The Atlas (Edward Holmes), 5 May 1833

Bell's Life in London, 5 May 1833

Figaro in London, 5 May 1833

Globe and Traveller, 2 May 1833

The Harmonicon (William Ayrton), June 1833, 139–40

Morning Chronicle (John Payne Collier), 2 May 1833

Morning Herald, 2 May 1833

Morning Post, 2 May 1833

The Spectator (Edward Taylor), 11 May 1833

Sunday Times, 5 May 1833

Theatrical Observer, 10 May 1833

REVIEW OF *GUSTAVE III* ADAPTED AS *GUSTAVUS OF SWEDEN*, VICTORIA

Morning Chronicle (John Payne Collier), 8 November 1833

REVIEWS OF *GUSTAVE III* ADAPTED AS *GUSTAVUS THE THIRD*, COVENT GARDEN

The Athenaeum, 16 November 1833

The Atlas (Edward Holmes), 17 November 1833

The Examiner (Thomas Love Peacock), 17 November 1833

London Times (Edward Sterling), 14 November 1833

Morning Chronicle (John Payne Collier), 14 November 1833

Morning Post, 14 November and 18 December 1833

The Spectator (Edward Taylor), 16 November 1833

Sunday Times, 17 November 1833

Theatrical Observer, 15 November 1833

True Sun (Leigh Hunt), 14 November 1833

NOTES

INTRODUCTION

[1] Only a few recent scholars devote attention to these. See, for example, Beard, 'Figaro in England'; Carnevale, '"... That's the barber!"'; Carter, 'Mozart in a "land without music"'; Cowgill, 'Re-gendering the libertine' and 'Mozart's music in London'; Dideriksen, 'Repertory and rivalry'; Fend, 'Zur Rezeption von Mozarts Opern in London'; Fenner, *Opera in London*; and Stuart W. Rogers, 'Cenerentola a Londra'.

[2] Goehr, *The imaginary museum of musical works* and Weber, *The rise of musical classics*. These ideas have stirred controversy, especially over the date when this concept was introduced. See Talbot, ed., *The musical work*. For an examination of how these concepts impacted opera, see Till, 'The operatic work'.

[3] Temperley, 'Bishop, Sir Henry R.' and Ehrlich and McVeigh, 'Music', p. 243.

[4] Everist, *Giacomo Meyerbeer and music drama* and *Music drama at the Paris Odéon*; Gossett, *Divas and scholars*; Levin, *Unsettling opera*; Parker, *Remaking the song*; and Poriss, *Changing the score*.

[5] See, for example, Dyer, *Pastiche* and Hutcheon, *A theory of adaptation*.

[6] Tracy C. Davis, *The economics of the British stage*; Moody, *Illegitimate theatre in London*; Cowgill, 'Mozart's music in London'; Dideriksen, 'Repertory and rivalry'; Mero, 'The quest for national musical identity'; and Rohr, *The careers of British musicians*.

[7] See, for example, Ahlquist, *Democracy at the opera* and Preston, *Opera on the road*.

[8] Operatic change hardly ended completely, of course, as scholars such as Roberta Marvin have shown. See 'The Victorian Violetta' and 'The censorship of Verdi's operas in Victorian London'.

[9] For the repertoire for these theatres, I have utilised playbills, newspaper advertisements and reviews and several ledgers: Diary of Covent Garden Theatre; Ledgers of Covent Garden Theatre; and Receipts of performances at Drury Lane Theatre.

[10] See Marsden, *The re-imagined text*.

[11] Hutcheon, *A theory of adaptation*, p. 4.

[12] Hutcheon, *A theory of adaptation*, p. 5.

[13] Hutcheon, *A theory of adaptation*, p. 87.

[14] Hutcheon, *A theory of adaptation*, p. 92.

[15] Levin, *Unsettling opera*, pp. 45–6.

[16] Taruskin, 'Setting limits', p. 460.

[17] See Ganzel, 'Patent wrongs and patent theatres' and Tracy C. Davis, *The economics of the British stage*.

[18] Samuel Foote obtained this patent in recompense for a riding accident on the Duke of York's horse. Burling, *Summer theatre in London*, p. 119.

19 See Thomas, 'The 1737 licensing act and its impact'.

20 Boaden, *Memoirs of the life of John Philip Kemble*, vol. 1, p. 81; the Yorke quotation is from the *Political review*, 16 September 1809, quoted in Baer, *Theatre and disorder*, p. 199.

21 Leppert, *Music and image*, p. 25.

22 Great Britain Parliament, *Report from the select committee*, p. 38.

23 See my 'Between opera and musical'.

24 See Pisani, *Music for the melodramatic theatre*.

25 Ahlquist, 'Masculinity and legitimacy'.

26 Contracts for Covent Garden in 1818–20 indicate a small but serviceable orchestra, which was typically led by a violinist and/or keyboardist and contained twelve violins, two violas, two cellos, two double basses, one flute, two oboes, one clarinet, two bassoons, two horns, two trumpets, one trombone, timpani and one player responsible for bells, castanets, tambourine, etc. The exact orchestration for each piece was fluid, since several musicians played multiple instruments. 'Memoranda of agreements'. Bruce Carr notes that theatre orchestras grew in size during this time. Drury Lane, for example, employed twenty-four musicians in 1775, thirty-four in *c.* 1825 and sixty-six by 1847. 'Theatre music: 1800–1834', pp. 289–90. For more on the orchestra, see Vanessa L. Rogers, 'Orchestra and theatre music'. Occasional playbills and libretti that list chorus members indicate that the chorus, in a standard soprano, alto, tenor and bass arrangement, averaged seven to twelve singers per part. Both orchestral and choral ensembles were often augmented for particularly challenging works, as was proudly advertised on playbills.

27 Tracy C. Davis, *The economics of the British stage*, p. 8.

28 Macarthy, *A letter to the King*, p. 10.

29 Tracy C. Davis, *The economics of the British stage*, p. 8.

30 Many of these authors did write 'closet dramas' not intended for the stage. See Carlson, *In the theatre of Romanticism*.

31 Mathias, *The shade of Alexander Pope*, pp. 56–7.

32 Great Britain Parliament, *Report from the select committee*, p. 25.

33 The dimensions of theatres given in Great Britain Parliament, *Report from the select committee*, in a foldout sheet between pp. 122 and 123 and in appendix no. 12, demonstrate that the King's Theatre, as well as several continental houses, were larger than the patent theatres.

34 Brantlinger, *Fictions of state*, p. 123.

35 *London Times*, 22 September 1817.

36 Planché, *Olympic revels*, vol. 1, p. 60.

37 Jim Davis, 'Spectatorship', p. 57. In-depth studies of audiences exist for earlier and later periods, but not the early nineteenth century. See Hughes, *The drama's patrons* and Davis and Emeljanow, *Reflecting the audience*.

38 Unidentified newspaper clipping of 1821, quoted in Booth, *Prefaces to English nineteenth-century theatre*, p. 55.

39 See Morgan, *Manners, morals, and class in England*.

40 Great Britain Parliament, *Report from the select committee*, p. 173.

41 For more on the 'old price riots', see Baer, *Theatre and disorder in late Georgian London* and Hadley, *Melodramatic tactics*.

42 *British Stage*, April 1819, 119 and *London Times*, 20 April 1848.

43 *Oxberry's dramatic biography*, vol. IV, p. 11.

44 Bratton, *New readings in theatre history*; Cowgill, 'Mozart productions and the emergence of *Werktreue*'; and Hall-Witt, *Fashionable acts*.

45 For more on the press, see Brake and Demoor, *Dictionary of nineteenth-century journalism*; Connors and MacDonald, *National identity in Great Britain*; Fenner, *Opera in London*; Langley, 'The English musical journal'; and Vann and VanArsdel, eds., *Victorian periodicals*.

46 Hunt, *The autobiography of Leigh Hunt*, p. 155.

47 Appendix 2 lists the reviews cited for each adaptation as well as the likely reviewers when known. Although we cannot be certain of these identities in all cases, this avoids awkward wording such as 'the reviewer we believe to be Leigh Hunt'.

48 See, for example, Fenner, *Leigh Hunt and opera criticism* and Wood, *Romanticism and music culture in Britain*.

49 9 April 1831.

50 For more on Collier, see Bratton, *New readings in theatre history*, pp. 83–8.

51 Bratton, 'Miss Scott and Miss Macauley', 59.

52 See Cowgill, 'Mozart productions and the emergence of *Werktreue*' and Hall-Witt, *Fashionable acts*.

53 Weber, 'The history of music canon', p. 352.

54 See Cooper, *The house of Novello*, pp. 103–4; Deazley, 'Commentary on *international copyright act 1838*'; Rose, *Authors and owners*; and Stephens, *The profession of the playwright*.

55 2 January 1828.

56 Moody, *Illegitimate theatre in London*, p. 111.

57 Quoted in Northcott, *The life of Sir Henry R. Bishop*, p. 123.

58 Parker, *Remaking the song*, p. 8.

59 23 June 1833.

60 *The Harmonicon*, December 1827, 250.

61 22 March 1823.

62 *Morning Chronicle*, 3 January 1827.

63 8 August 1826.

64 Dobson, *The making of the national poet*, pp. 4–5.

65 Everist, 'Lindoro in Lyon', 85.

66 See Connolly, *The censorship of English drama, 1737–1824* and Stephens, *The censorship of English drama, 1824–1901*.

67 *The Harmonicon*, August 1832, 180.

1 A TALE OF TWO BOIELDIEUS

1 Robinson, 'Two London versions of *The deserter*', p. 240. See also Armondino, 'The opéra comique in London'.

2 Girdham, *English opera in late eighteenth-century London*, pp. 137–53.

3 Price, 'Unity, originality, and the London pasticcio', 25.

4 Marsden, *The re-imagined text*, p. 46.

5 For more on copyright, see Rose, *Authors and owners*; Small, 'The development of musical copyright'; and Stephens, *The profession of the playwright*.

6 Burden, 'Opera in the London theatres', p. 215.

7 *London Times*, 6 October 1814.

8 For discussions of court cases surrounding adaptation, arrangement, abridgement and translation, see Lockhart, 'Trial by ear'; Rose, *Authors and owners*; and Small, 'The development of musical copyright'.

9 Kassler, ed., *Charles Edward Horn's memoirs*, p. 39.

10 *Flora Tristan's London journal*, 1840, p. 176.

11 Washington Irving, who acted in this freelance capacity, wrote to John Howard Payne in 1821 that Drury Lane manager Robert William Elliston 'has an agent in Paris at a weekly salary'. Luquer, 'Correspondence of Washington Irving', p. 467

12 Bishop kept a travel diary of his visit, now unfortunately lost. Quotations from it are in Northcott, *The life of Sir Henry R. Bishop*, pp. 16–18.

13 Nicoll, *Early nineteenth century drama*, p. 79.

14 24 October 1814.

15 Rachel Cowgill notes the King's Theatre's proclivity for opera seria, which lasted longer than in other European centres. '"Wise Men from the East"', p. 44.

16 To avoid confusion, throughout this book I refer to characters and operas by their original names and titles, even when these have been changed in the adaptation. If general nouns rather than proper names are used, I use the English translation, i.e. seneschal, not sénéchal.

17 Horn, *Jean de Paris: a favorite divertimento*. There are also later, American publications of a ballad by Horn, 'Farewell to my harp', but this was not included in the 1814 adaptation.

18 Arnold, *Jean de Paris, a comic drama*, pp. 24, 26, 34, 43.

19 For more on the stage Irishman, see Truninger, *Paddy and the paycock*.

20 See Cowgill, 'Regendering the libertine'; Senelick, 'Boys and girls together'; and Straub, *Sexual suspects*.

21 See Straub, *Sexual suspects* and Tracy C. Davis, *Actresses as working women*.

22 Arnold, *Jean de Paris, a comic drama*, p. 29.

23 Langbaine, *An account of the English dramatick poets*, p. 94.

24 Pocock, 'Advertisement' to *John of Paris; a comic opera*, n.p.

25 Bishop cut the following pieces by Boieldieu: the overture; the airs for Olivier, the seneschal and Jean; the duets for Olivier and Lorezza and for Jean and the princess; the chorus 'De monsieur Jean'; and the concluding chorus. He added: his own overture; solos for Olivier, the seneschal, the princess and Lorezza; two solos for Jean; melodramatic music for the seneschal's entrance; a few instrumental pieces for the ballet; a duet for John and the princess; and a concluding finale. Lorezza's solo appears only in the manuscript libretto and therefore probably was not performed onstage. Jean's first solo, the duet for Jean and the princess and the last finale were placed in quotation marks in the printed libretto, which indicates they were omitted in performance.

26 1816 travel journal of Henry Rowley Bishop, quoted in Northcott, *The Life of Sir Henry R. Bishop*, pp. 31–2.

27 Lockhart, 'Trial by ear', 209.

[28] Pocock, 'Advertisement' to *John of Paris; a comic opera*, n.p.

[29] Everist, 'Lindoro in Lyon', 53.

[30] Fischlin and Fortier, 'General introduction', p. 3.

[31] Planché, *Recollections and reflections*, p. 176.

[32] Preston, *Opera on the road*, p. 2.

[33] Saunders, *Adaptation and appropriation*, pp. 18–19.

[34] Dibdin, *The reminiscences of Thomas Dibdin*, vol. ii, p. 65.

[35] *Morning Chronicle*, 14 November 1831.

[36] *London Times*, 16 May 1821.

[37] Carr, 'The first all-sung English 19th-century opera'.

[38] Ahlquist, 'Masculinity and legitimacy'.

[39] *Quarterly Musical Magazine and Review*, 1820, p. 67.

[40] Planché, *Recollections and reflections*, p. 55.

[41] *Oxberry's dramatic biography*, vol. i, p. 23.

[42] See Gossett, 'Gioachino Rossini and the conventions of composition' and Powers, '"La solita forma"'.

[43] *Quarterly Musical Magazine and Review*, 1821, p. 62.

[44] For more on the ballad, see Biddlecombe, *English opera*, pp. 36–37, 40–41 and Temperley, 'Ballroom and drawing-room music', pp. 121–34.

[45] Phillips, *Musical and personal recollections*, vol. i, p. 192.

[46] Throughout this book, statistics for performances are drawn from playbills or, when these are not available, advertisements in *The Times*. Unusually, the two competing versions of *Jean de Paris* were merged into a new adaptation in 1827.

[47] Hutcheon, *A theory of adaptation*, p. xvii.

[48] *The Harmonicon*, December 1829, pp. 299–300. Fétis' accusation appeared within a series of letters on the state of music in London, first published in the *Revue Musicale* and then translated and published in *The Harmonicon*. The specific reference to Bishop is in *The Harmonicon*, November 1829, 277.

[49] Hutcheon, *A theory of adaptation*, p. xvii.

[50] Roe, 'Hunt, (James Henry) Leigh'.

2 THE PIPPIN AND THE PINEAPPLE: ROSSINI AND MOZART

[1] For the reception of Mozart's operas in early nineteenth-century London, see Cowgill, '"Wise Men from the east"'; Cowgill, 'Mozart's music in London'; and Fend, 'Zur Rezeption von Mozarts Opern in London'.

[2] Hogarth, *Memoirs of the opera*, vol. ii, pp. 368–9.

[3] *The Harmonicon*, October 1823, 137. Ayrton took this from *Blackwood's Edinburgh Magazine*, October 1822, 447, which stated that the distinction was between a 'fozy turnip and a pineapple'. Walton, 'Rara avis or fozy turnip', p. 95.

[4] Numerous contemporary reviewers stated that Pocock based his libretto on Thomas Shadwell's *The libertine*. Although the adaptation was also titled *The libertine*, the two are only loosely connected.

5 Ahlquist, 'Masculinity and legitimacy'.

6 7 October 1822.

7 *Memoirs of the opera*, vol. II, p. 351.

8 *Theatrical Inquisitor*, July 1819, 9.

9 Katharine Ellis notes that tenor Adolphe Nourrit sang Don Giovanni in an 1834 Paris version. 'Rewriting *Don Giovanni*', p. 214. British tenor John Braham also sang the role in a new adaptation for Drury Lane in 1833, discussed in Chapter 7. Braham was apparently not available to sing the role in spring 1817. He had been embroiled in a criminal conversation case in 1816 that led to tensions with the audience and he apparently withdrew from the stage for a time. *London Times*, 7 March 1816 and 24 October 1817.

10 Hadden, 'Sinclair, John'; *British Stage*, December 1817, 279; *The Examiner*, 15 February 1824.

11 *British Stage*, January 1819, 30.

12 *The autobiography of Leigh Hunt*, p. 128.

13 A large literature explores melodrama. See, for example, Brooks, *The melodramatic imagination*; Hibberd, ed., *Melodramatic voices*; and Pisani, *Music for the melodramatic theatre*.

14 Rushton, *W. A. Mozart: Don Giovanni*, pp. 73–6.

15 23 October 1813.

16 Pocock, *The libertine: an opera*, pp. 41–6.

17 *Literary Gazette*, 8 February 1817.

18 All translations from Mozart operas are from McClatchy, trans., *Seven Mozart librettos*.

19 Pocock, *The libertine: an opera*, p. 33.

20 Pocock, *The libertine: an opera*, p. 34.

21 Pocock, *The libertine: an opera*, p. 25.

22 Pocock, *The libertine: an opera*, p. 43.

23 Pocock, *The libertine: an opera*, p. 7.

24 14 April 1817.

25 Pocock, *The libertine: an opera*, p. 13.

26 For a discussion of Bishop's adaptation, see Carnevale, '"... That's the barber!"'

27 *The Spanish barber, or fruitless precaution* (Philadelphia: M. Carey, 1811) and *The Spanish barber; or, the fruitless precaution*, Plays submitted to the Lord Chamberlain, Huntington Library, Larpent Collection, Larpent 436. See Hoskins, 'Samuel Arnold's *The Spanish barber*'.

28 Preston, *Opera on the road*, p. 285.

29 *The Examiner*, 22 March 1818.

30 Poriss, *Changing the score*, pp. 135–68 and Gossett, *Divas and scholars*, p. 217.

31 Gossett, 'Rossini and authenticity', 1009.

32 Bishop reworked Paisiello's aria for the Count, 'Saper bramante', as a duet for Rosina and Fiorello in place of the Count's 'Se il mio nome'. From Rossini, Bishop retained: the introduction, minus the Count's serenade; the duet for Figaro and the Count and the trio for Figaro, Rosina and the Count, with Fiorello singing the Count's part in both; Rosina's 'Una voce poco fa'; Bartolo's 'Quando mi sei vicina'; and the finales of acts one and two. He retained part of the quintet 'Don Basilio!' in the manuscript sources, but cut it in the printed sources. Bishop added: a new overture; solos for Bartolo and for Fiorello; and two solos for Rosina.

33 Rossini added 'Ah se è ver' for an 1819 Venetian production. Gossett, *Divas and scholars*, p. 563.

34 Bishop's was the first published score of Rossini's opera. See Patricia B. Brauner, 'Critical commentary' in Gioachino Rossini, *Il barbiere di Siviglia . . .*, ed. Patricia B. Brauner (Kassel: Bärenreiter, 2008), pp. 29–34.

35 *Oxberry's dramatic biography*, vol. ii, p. 45.

36 *The autobiography of Leigh Hunt*, p. 130.

37 Bacon said that Bartolo's solo – though marked as 'composed by Henry R. Bishop' – was based on a trio in Paisiello's *I zingari in fiera*, used by Storace in *Mahmoud* and Bishop in *Zuma*. I have not found any numbers in these operas that correlate to Bartolo's solo.

38 1823, 4.

39 *The Harmonicon*, July 1830, 290.

40 *Morning Chronicle*, 13 March 1818.

41 *The Harmonicon*, April 1823, 47.

42 *Morning Chronicle*, 14 November 1831.

43 *Morning Chronicle*, 14 November 1814.

44 For a modern edition of Bishop's adaptation, see my *Henry Rowley Bishop, Mozart's 'The marriage of Figaro'*.

45 Although Bishop was the official librettist, he states that he received assistance from 'a friend, whose Dramatic works have long since obtained. . . applause' and 'a *juvenile* Author', whom Richard Northcott identifies as Isaac Pocock and Louise Costello, respectively. Bishop, 'Advertisement' in *The marriage of Figaro . . .* (London: John Miller, 1819), p. v and Northcott, *The life of Sir Henry R. Bishop*, p. 49. Tim Carter suggests that Bishop probably used the most recent edition of the Holcroft, an 1811 publication of John Philip Kemble's slimmed version. Thomas Holcroft, *The follies of a day; a comedy, in three acts . . .* (London: J. Barker, 1811). Carter, 'Mozart in a "land without music"', vol. i, p. 198

46 Bishop cut: Figaro and Susanna's second duet; both trios; all of Mozart's arias for Bartolo, the Count, the Countess, Barbarina, Marcellina and Basilio; Susanna and Cherubino's duet; the sextet; the chorus 'Ricevete, oh padroncina'; the act three finale; and Figaro and Susanna's arias in act four. He added: four instrumental pieces; arias for Susanna, the Countess, Antonio and Fiorello (brought in from *Il barbiere di Siviglia*); and a duet for Susanna and the Countess based on the popular Italian song, 'O pescator dell' onde'. He also replaced the overture with a new one; replaced Figaro's 'Non più andrai' with an act one finale that drew from this aria, 'Di scrivermi ogni giorno' and the act one finale from *Così fan tutte*; replaced Susanna and Marcellina's duet with one for Susanna and Barbarina; and used the finale of Rossini's *Tancredi* (Venice version) to close the work.

47 Quoted in Northcott, *The life of Sir Henry R. Bishop*, p. 33.

48 See *Le nozze di Figaro. A comic opera, in two acts, as represented at the King's Theatre . . . the 18. of June*, 1812, Plays submitted to the Lord Chamberlain, Huntington Library, Larpent 1722 and *Le nozze di Figaro; or, The wedding of Figaro . . . as represented at the King's Theatre* (London: W. Winchester and Son, 1818). See also Cowgill, 'Mozart productions and the emergence of *Werktreue*'.

49 Hutcheon, *A theory of adaptation*, pp. 91–2.

50 Poriss, *Changing the score*, pp. 66–99.

51 Ebers, *Seven years*, p. 102.

52 See *Cosi fan tutte, ossia la scuola degli amanti . . . as represented at the King's Theatre* (London: J. Brettell, 1811) and *Le nozze di Figaro. A comic opera, in two acts, as represented at the King's Theatre . . . the 18. of June,* 1812, Plays submitted to the Lord Chamberlain, Huntington Library, Larpent 1722.

53 *London Times*, 14 January 1822.

54 McClatchy, trans., *Seven Mozart librettos*, p. 303 and Bishop, *The marriage of Figaro . . .* (London: John Miller, 1819), p. 8.

55 Quoted in Cowgill, 'Mozart productions and the emergence of *Werktreue*', p. 166

56 1827, 326.

57 *The Examiner*, 28 October 1821.

58 Genest, *Some account of the English Stage*, vol. VIII, p. 701.

59 *London Times*, 19 January 1818.

60 *The Harmonicon*, October 1823, 135.

3 'THE FLOOD-GATES OF FOREIGN MUSIC': *DER FREISCHÜTZ*

1 Annegret Fauser documents these rumours in 'Phantasmagorie im deutschen Wald?', pp. 246–7. A score with an Italian translation was published in London by Ewer & Co. and the *Allgemeine Musikalische Zeitung* carried a report in December 1824 that 'After all the suspicions, the Italian opera will not come to pass next year; perhaps the fault should be attributed more to the bankruptcy of Chamber's Bank than any particular aspects of the opera.' Translation mine, with assistance from Amanda Ennis. The King's Theatre did occasionally perform the overture to *Der Freischütz*, starting in 1828.

2 Everist, *Music drama at the Paris Odéon*, p. 282.

3 *A letter to the musicians of Great Britain* (1833), quoted in Rohr, *The careers of British musicians*, p. 14.

4 *The Atlas*, 23 June 1833.

5 See Tracy C. Davis, *The economics of the British stage*.

6 See Peterson, '"The best the house could afford"', p. 137.

7 See Kennerley, '"Flippant dolls"', pp. 169–72.

8 See Nicoll, *Early nineteenth century drama*, pp. 92–5 and Bolton, *Scott dramatized*. Scott did not publicly acknowledge authorship of his novels until 23 February 1827, but his identity was widely known before then. Scott, *The journal of Sir Walter Scott*, p. 319.

9 'On the supernatural in fictitious composition; and particularly on the works of E. T. A. Hoffmann (1827)', in Clery and Miles, eds., *Gothic documents*, pp. 285–6.

10 Butler, 'Antiquarianism', pp. 335–6.

11 Fauser details several English translations of German works in the 1820s. 'Phantasmagorie im deutschen Wald?', pp. 251–2. The Adelphi, Coburg and Drury Lane all offered versions of Faust in 1823–5.

12 Tusa, 'Cosmopolitanism and the national opera', 500.

13 May 1823, 65–6, signed 'Tedesco' and 'A collection of vocal and instrumental music', 1823, vol. 1 part 2, nos. 6, 28, 48 and 64.

14 The original tale was from the *Gespensterbuch* (1811–17) by Johann August Apel and Friedrich August Schulze (under the pen name F. Laun) and appeared translated in *Popular tales and romances of the northern nations* (London: W. Simpkin and R. Marshall, 1823). Only a playbill for the Coburg performance remains, but it appears to have been a dramatisation of this tale. There is no indication that Weber's music was used and the playbill advertises 'the New Music by T. Hughes'. I have not found contemporary reviews of this performance and critics unanimously referred to the English Opera House adaptation as the London première. I have therefore not included this as a *Der Freischütz* adaptation in Appendix 1.

15 Cox, *Musical recollections*, vol. 1, p. 88 and *The Harmonicon*, March 1824, 53.

16 Washington Irving was initially involved in the work, but by December 1823 had given up on seeing his version produced. Luquer, 'Correspondence of Washington Irving', 461–82. Irving was adamant that his name should not be involved with the adaptation. Only Livius' and Planché's names were publicly mentioned, although in the preface to his printed libretto Livius did thank 'another friend, whose name, were he permitted, it would be his pride and his pleasure to declare, for various valuable hints and emendations'. Livius, 'Prefatory remarks' in *The Freyschütz*, n.p. The relative involvement of Livius, Irving and Planché cannot be known precisely and is debated in Kirby, 'Washington Irving' and George R. Price, 'Washington Irving's librettos', 348–55. See also Jones, 'Romantic opera in translation', 29–30. Planché himself felt he was the main author. He described Livius as 'an amateur author and composer, who arranged the music of *Der Freischütz* for my version of that opera'. *Recollections and reflections*, p. 54.

17 Phillips, *Musical and personal recollections*, vol. 1, p. 81.

18 Ayrton wrote 'we hear that the *Freichütz* [sic] is translated and adapted, and may be expected very shortly' at Covent Garden. *The Harmonicon*, January 1824, 12. In the preface to the printed libretto, Livius stated that the opera had been slated for February, but had encountered 'unexpected and unavoidable delays'. Livius, 'Prefatory remarks' in *The Freyschütz*, n.p. Later, Ayrton reported that 'The Covent Garden management has engaged the celebrated German composer, Von Weber, to supply the place of Mr. Bishop, who goes to Drury-Lane.' *The Harmonicon*, June 1824, 119.

19 *The Harmonicon*, October 1824, 192.

20 For more on the English Opera House, see Tracy C. Davis, *The economics of the British stage* and Hume and Jacobs, 'London'.

21 In the score published by the Royal Harmonic Institution, Logan is listed as the poet for all the pieces adapted from the original, Arnold as the poet for all interpolated numbers.

22 Hawes did cut Agathe and Aennchen's duet once Catherine Stephens assumed the role of Agathe in mid-August, 1824.

23 As indicated in Table 3.1, one of the duets was probably cut before performance and some of the new numbers were added after the première.

24 For differing views on Weber's models, see Stephen C. Meyer, *Carl Maria von Weber*, pp. 81–5, 109–15; Tusa, 'Cosmopolitanism and the national opera', 483–6; and Warrack, *Carl Maria von Weber*, pp. 213–18.

25 *The Harmonicon*, February 1824, 14.

[26] Thomas Moore published several volumes of 'popular national airs' from 1818 to 1828 and many similar publications appeared. For a discussion of the role of such tunes in the wider European context, see Gelbart, *The invention of 'folk music' and 'art music'*.

[27] One of the new solos for Agathe is loosely based on Weber's 'Lied der Hirtin'. The other added numbers are advertised as 'founded on an original German melody'. I have not been able to locate the original tunes.

[28] Tusa, 'Cosmopolitanism and the national opera', 490.

[29] Phillips, *Musical and personal recollections*, vol. I, pp. 82–3.

[30] *The biography of the British stage*, p. 16.

[31] Jones, 'Romantic opera in translation', 40.

[32] For theatre lighting, see Rosenfeld, *Georgian scene painters*.

[33] For the staging of the Wolf's Glen scene and its resonances with the phantasmagoria, see Burden, 'The writing and staging of Georgian Romantic opera', pp. 434–39; Fauser, 'Phantasmagorie im deutschen Wald?', p. 256; and Newcomb, 'New light(s) on Weber's wolf's glen scene'.

[34] Two other minor theatre productions appeared as well, at the Olympic and at the Coburg, both in October. See Appendix 1. These are parodies of the opera rather than adaptations of it, however, and therefore fall outside the scope of this book. For a discussion of them, see my 'Continental opera Englished'.

[35] For information on the composition of the Surrey orchestra, see Knight, *A major London 'minor'*.

[36] Doerner, 'German Romantic opera?', 16–19.

[37] Amherst, *Der Freischutz*, p. 14.

[38] [Fitz]Ball, *Der Freischutz*, p. 31.

[39] Amherst, *Der Freischutz*, p. 9.

[40] Kerr, *Der Freischutz* . . . (London: John Lowndes, n.d.), p. 36.

[41] [Fitz]Ball, *Der Freischutz*, p. 15.

[42] Amherst, *Der Freischutz*, p. 5.

[43] Amherst, *Der Freischutz*, p. 18.

[44] The sentence about the increased orchestra is identical to the wording in the English Opera House playbill.

[45] [Fitz]Ball, 'Advertisement' in *Der Freischutz*, n.p.

[46] At Covent Garden, George Bennett continued his reign as a spoken Caspar, Mr Baker as Cuno, and Mary Ann Paton and William Pearman, who had replaced Miss Noel and John Braham at the English Opera House by September, respectively, reprised the romantic leads. Paton herself had replaced Catherine Stephens, who sang the role from mid-August to early September. Drury Lane featured the same performer in the role of Aennchen, Miss Povey.

[47] As noted earlier, Washington Irving was involved in the Covent Garden libretto in the beginning stages. Since the extent of his contribution is open to debate, however, and since only Livius and Planché were officially mentioned, I use their names in this discussion.

[48] Diary of Covent Garden Theatre.

[49] 14 November 1824.

[50] Livius, 'Prefatory remarks' in *The Freyschütz*, n.p.

51 Livius, *The Freyschütz*, p. 17.

52 Livius, 'Prefatory remarks' in *The Freyschütz*, n.p.

53 Soane, *Der Freischütz: a romantic opera*, pp. 33, 35.

54 Stephens, *The censorship of English drama*, pp. 22–5.

55 Soane, *Der Freischütz: a romantic opera*, pp. 33–5.

56 Colman noted in the manuscript libretto on 9 November that the piece had been revised and that, pending a few more changes that he had pencilled in, it could be performed. The piece appeared at Drury Lane one day later. Soane, *Der Freischutz*.

57 See Fitzball, *Thirty-five years of a dramatic author's life*, vol. 1, p. 161.

58 Livius, 'Prefatory remarks' in *The Freyschütz*, n.p.

59 'Critical remarks' in *Der Freischütz; or, the seventh bullet* . . . (London: Thomas Dolby, 1825), p. vi.

60 Ahlquist, 'Masculinity and legitimacy', 11–12.

61 Walton, 'Looking for the revolution in Rossini's *Guillaume Tell*', 134.

62 See Fauser, 'Phantasmagorie im deutschen Wald?', pp. 250–1.

63 *The Harmonicon*, April 1823, 52.

64 'D. — G', 'Remarks' in *Der Freischutz; or, the seventh bullet* . . . (London: G. H. Davidson, c. 1849–60), p. 5. 'D. —G' is probably George Davidson.

65 *The Harmonicon*, April 1825, 70.

66 E. Douglas Bomberger suggests that the Berlin première also drew 'the ordinary person'. 'The Neues Schauspielhaus in Berlin', p. 169.

67 *Quarterly Musical Magazine and Review*, 1825, 204.

68 Moody, '"Fine word, legitimate!"', 234.

69 *John Bull* reported 'by way of novelty the FREISCHUTZ is in active preparation [at Drury Lane], as well as an equestrian melo-drama, with MR. DUCROW and his troop, who have been exhibiting for the space of one hundred and forty-four consecutive nights at Astley's'. 24 October 1824.

70 December 1824, 554.

71 Moody, *Illegitimate theatre in London*, pp. 48–9.

72 Gamer, 'Marketing a masculine romance', 526.

73 31 July 1824 and 18 November 1824.

74 See Doerner, 'German Romantic opera?'

75 *The Harmonicon*, September 1824, 172 and *Literary Gazette*, 13 November 1824. For a discussion of various other versions of the original tale, some of which also altered the ending, see Warrack, *Carl Maria von Weber*, p. 206.

76 See Carter, 'Mozart in a "land without music"', vol. 1, p. 203 and Maycock, 'Weber's operas in England', 40–1.

77 Hogarth, *Memoirs of the opera*, vol. 11, p. 369.

78 For a discussion of the British context for *Oberon*, see Fischler, 'Oberon and odium'.

79 In a letter of 28 December 1823, Livius directed Carl August Böttinger, a museum director in Dresden, to 'reimburse [Weber] for the manuscripts he had the goodness to supply'; perhaps Böttinger did not follow his directive. Quoted in Reichart, 'Washington Irving's friend and collaborator', 523.

80 Cox and Cox, *Leaves from the journals of Sir George Smart*, p. 71.

[81] Since Covent Garden rarely offered foreign commissions, it is hard to assess how typical this sum was. Certainly, it was less than Rossini reportedly received when he visited around the same time – £2500 from the King's Theatre, £50 per private concert, £100 per lesson. *Literary Gazette*, 14 February 1824 and Michael Scott, 'Rossini in England: part 1' and 'Rossini in England: part 2'. It was more, however, than the £300 Hawes paid Ferdinand Ries for the copyright of *The sorceress* at the English Opera House. Hill, ed., *Ferdinand Ries*, pp. 518–19.

[82] He also received £191 for various miscellaneous compositions and appearances in the city. Cox and Cox, *Leaves from the journals of Sir George Smart*, p. 250. Oxberry's dramatic biography stated that 'Hawes [who published the work] is said to have given £1000 for the copyright of the music' for *Oberon*, but no further evidence substantiates this sum. Vol. v, p. 18.

[83] Bedford, *Recollections and wanderings*, pp. 65–6.

[84] Letter to his wife, 30 May 1826, quoted in Reynolds, *Weber in London*, p. 35.

[85] Letter to his wife, 18 April 1826, quoted in Reynolds, *Weber in London*, pp. 32–3.

[86] *Quarterly Musical Magazine and Review*, 1826, 145.

[87] Ehrlich and McVeigh, 'Music', p. 244.

[88] Letter from Weber to Planché, 19 February 1825, quoted in Planché, *Recollections and reflections*, p. 52.

[89] 6 December 1835.

[90] Quoted in Reynolds, *Weber in London*, p. 14.

[91] Biddlecombe, *English opera from 1834 to 1864*.

4 THE SEARCH FOR WEBER'S SUCCESSOR

[1] The theatre did perform Italian operas by German composers such as Meyerbeer, Mayr and Winter.

[2] For more on the Reform Bill, see Colley, *Britons: forging the nation*.

[3] Newey, 'Reform on the London stage', p. 244. See also Newey, 'The 1832 select committee'.

[4] For theatre management in this period see Tracy C. Davis, *The economics of the British stage*.

[5] See Grafe, 'Un français'.

[6] See Cowgill, '"Wise men from the east"'; Cowgill 'Mozart productions and the emergence of *Werktreue*'; and Hall-Witt, *Fashionable acts*.

[7] Garlick, *To serve the purpose of the drama*, p. 96.

[8] Review of *I fuorusciti di Firenze*, 25 August 1827.

[9] Review of *L'amor marinaro*, 13 September 1828.

[10] Langley, 'Arnold, Samuel James'.

[11] The patent theatres apparently also attempted to commission works from German composers. Drury Lane planned to commission an opera from Meyerbeer in 1825, Covent Garden from Mendelssohn in 1831. Neither came to fruition. *The Harmonicon*, April 1826, 86 and *The Athenaeum*, 24 December 1831.

[12] Hawes apparently promised Marschner £600 for a new opera as well as payment for conducting it, but this miscarried owing to the death of the composer's daughter and a fire at the English Opera House in 1830. Palmer, *Heinrich August Marschner*, pp. 91–2.

[13] Ries originally intended to write an opera for London with George Soane in the late 1820s, but diverted his efforts to *Die Räuberbraut* when Soane dallied too long. He again thought of

Soane for the project that turned into *The sorceress*, but Edward Fitzball wrote this libretto. In the late 1830s he worked with Soane on another project that was eventually dropped. See Hill, ed., *Ferdinand Ries*, especially letters 127, 144, 147, 167, 170–1, 230, 445, 468 and 480. Letter numbers in the following footnotes refer to this source.

[14] See especially letters 218 and 220.

[15] Letter 218, Harriet and Ferdinand Ries to Joseph Ries, 3 January 1828.

[16] See, for example, letters 343 and 346. Ries may have antagonised these theatres already in 1825, when he pressed for his planned opera with Soane to be performed at both. Letter 147, Ferdinand Ries to Joseph Ries, 30 August 1825.

[17] For more on copyright and publishing across international lines, see Rowland, 'Clementi as publisher' and Small, 'The development of musical copyright'.

[18] Letter 240, Ferdinand Ries to Joseph Ries, 24 September 1828.

[19] Letter 254, Ferdinand Ries to C. F. Peters, 6 December 1828.

[20] Letter 269, Ferdinand Ries to Joseph Ries, 7 March 1829.

[21] Letter 259, Ferdinand Ries to Joseph Ries, 23 December 1828.

[22] A similar situation happened with *The sorceress*. Ries asked Joseph to impress upon Hawes that Simrock's name had to appear as a publisher 'otherwise he cannot at all claim here his property right'. Letter 345, Ferdinand Ries to Joseph Ries, 6 November 1831. The contract with Hawes for *The sorceress* appears as letter 31. In it, Hawes is to pay £300 for the copyright of the opera in the 'United Kingdom of Great Britain and Ireland' only, with Ries retaining the copyright of both text and music 'in Germany and elsewhere'.

[23] Bert Hagels, 'Vorwort' in Ferdinand Ries, *Die Räuberbraut*, ed. Bert Hagels (Berlin: Ries & Erler, 2011), p. iii.

[24] *Dramatic Magazine* and the *Morning Chronicle*. See also Burwick, *Playing to the crowd*.

[25] Allardyce Nicoll mistakenly equates *The robber's wife* with the adaptation of *Die Räuberbraut*, which was titled *The robber's bride*. See Nicoll, *Early nineteenth century drama*, p. 385.

[26] See Stuart, *Stage blood* and Twitchell, *The living dead*.

[27] *The Examiner*, 13 August 1820. In his memoirs, Planché blamed Arnold, who had 'set his heart on Scotch music and dresses – the latter, by the way, were in stock'. Planché, *Recollections and reflections*, p. 26

[28] 'Advertisement' in *Songs, duets, glees, chorusses, &c. in Der Vampyr*, n.p.

[29] Stuart, *Stage blood*, p. 118.

[30] Grey, 'The Gothic libertine', pp. 87–94.

[31] Although the stage direction clearly indicates that Emmy 'dies', in the following scene she is referred to only as wounded. *The vampire, a grand romantick opera*, ff. 523r, 524v.

[32] Hawes added an aria in *Die Räuberbraut*, discussed later, and cut two duets from *Der Vampyr*, one for Ruthven and Emmy and the other for Aubry and Malwina.

[33] Hawes, 'Hah! yet one and thirty days'.

[34] Phillips sang both bass and baritone roles, according to current designations. Contemporaries primarily referred to him as a bass, but occasionally as a baritone.

[35] Although this solo, 'Can I bear this affliction?', is not in either the manuscript libretto or the printed score, it is in the word book and was mentioned in several reviews. It does not appear to correlate to any numbers in Ries' score and its model is unclear. It appears that Hawes cut the act three duet for Laura and Fernando to accommodate the new solo.

[36] Quoted in Howard Irving, 'William Crotch on borrowing', 250.

[37] A. Dean Palmer situates Marschner's chorus within the Gesangverein tradition. 'Vampyr, Der (i)'.

[38] Here, Bartley quotes Arthur Murphy's similar statement in the prologue to *The apprentice* (1756): 'To-night no smuggled scenes from France we shew, 'Tis English, English, Sirs, from top to toe.' Nicoll, *Late eighteenth century drama*, p. 121. My thanks to Eric Saylor for assistance in locating this quotation. Quotations from Bartley's address are taken from *The Examiner*, 4 October 1829.

[39] 26 November 1859. For Spohr's reception in London, see J. C. A. Brown, 'The popularity and influence of Spohr in England'.

[40] November 1823, 159–61 and December 1824, 215–16.

[41] 9 April 1831.

[42] Smart indicates in his diary that he purchased a score for approximately £25. Spohr apparently was already in negotiation with a London theatre to perform this work, which may explain why Smart did not pursue it. Smart writes that Spohr 'told me he had just sent, or was going to send, the score for a theatre in London, he did not know which'. Cox and Cox, *Leaves from the journals of Sir George Smart*, p. 209. Smart apparently did not purchase the score for *Zemire und Azor* at this time, as the *Literary Gazette* reported that 'it is not above six weeks since the foreign opera [i.e. *Zemire und Azor*] was procured for the purpose of this arrangement'.

[43] In 1825, the *Literary Gazette* stated that Spohr's *Faust* was to be performed at Drury Lane. 9 April 1825. *Faustus* did appear at the theatre in May, but with music by Henry Bishop. Spohr's *Faust* did not appear in London until 1840. Loewenberg, *Annals of opera*, p. 648.

[44] There had been two London productions of the Grétry: at Drury Lane in 1776, translated into English and intermixed with music by Thomas Linley, and at the King's Theatre in 1779. *The Athenaeum*, *The Examiner* and *The Harmonicon* mentioned these productions in their reviews of *Zemire und Azor*.

[45] Clive Brown, 'Zemire und Azor'.

[46] Bishop, *Songs, duets, trios, &c. &c. in the new grand opera entitled Der Alchymist*.

[47] J. C. A. Brown, 'The popularity and influence of Spohr in England', p. 27.

[48] Collier noted in the *Morning Chronicle* that Azor's aria was dropped.

[49] *The Harmonicon*, May 1830, 224.

[50] Ellis, *Music criticism in nineteenth-century France*, p. 71.

[51] Fisher, 'Twiss, Horace (1787–1849)'.

[52] See Meyer, *Carl Maria von Weber*, p. 168 and Warrack, *German Opera*, pp. 339, 342–3.

5 MOZART AND ROSSINI REVISITED

[1] Charles Edward Horn composed 'I've been roaming' to a text by George Darley that appeared in the *London Magazine* in 1824. By 1826, Richard Mackenzie Bacon remarked 'by the help of Madame Vestris [it] has become one of the most popular songs of the day'. *Quarterly Musical Magazine and Review*, 1826, 117

2   The letter appeared in the *Morning Post* and the *London Times* on 31 December 1827.

3   Paton sang 'I've been roaming' in *Love in a village* and both she and Love sang the number in *The lord of the manor*.

4   2 January 1828.

5   Vestris sang 'I've been roaming' and 'The light guitar' in *Giovanni in London* in February 1828. For a benefit performance of *Figaro* in May, she sang Cherubino and interpolated a song from *The loves of the butterflies*.

6   Kennerley, '"Flippant dolls"', pp. 173–4.

7   15 December 1827.

8   *Quarterly Musical Magazine and Review*, 1827, 356.

9   Letter to the editor, *Morning Post*, 2 January 1828. Later in the Victorian period, this practice became standardised in the 'royalty ballad', in which publishers paid star performers to sing their ballads. Porter et. al., 'Ballad'.

10   February 1828, 35.

11   *Morning Chronicle*, 15 December 1827.

12   *The Examiner*, 16 January 1820.

13   See Einstein, 'The first performance of Mozart's *Entführung* in London'.

14   See Cowgill, '"Wise Men from the East"'.

15   Stephanie based the libretto on Bretzner's *Belmont und Constanze, oder die Entführung aus dem Serail* (1781). For discussions of the opera's exoticism, see, for example, Al-Taee, *Representations of the orient in Western music*; Bauman, *W. A. Mozart: Die Entführung aus dem Serail*; and Meyer, '*Turquerie* and eighteenth-century music'.

16   'Preface' in *The seraglio: an opera*, pp. iv–v.

17   Locke, 'Cutthroats and casbah dancers', p. 109.

18   Al-Taee, *Representations of the orient in Western music*, p. 126.

19   Bauman, *W. A. Mozart: Die Entführung aus dem Serail*, p. 28.

20   See Brewer, *The flame of freedom*.

21   Kramer, *The seraglio: an opera*, p. 5.

22   Meyer, '*Turquerie* and eighteenth-century music', 487–8.

23   Kramer, *The seraglio, the celebrated opera by Mozart*.

24   See, for example, *Quarterly Musical Magazine and Review*.

25   See Truninger, *Paddy and the paycock*.

26   Kramer, *The seraglio: an opera*, p. 20.

27   'Preface' in *The seraglio: an opera*, p. iv.

28   Waters, 'A statement of matters', p. 291.

29   Everist, 'Lindoro in Lyon', 85.

30   These adaptations are described in Hortschansky, 'Gegen Unwahrscheinlichkeit und Frivolität'. See also Zenck, '"Ach wir alle sind von Flandern"'.

31   All translations from Mozart operas are from McClatchy, trans., *Seven Mozart librettos*.

32   Ian Woodfield describes how this process began already with Mozart and Da Ponte's revisions. *Mozart's Così fan tutte*, pp. 95–6.

33   Arnold, *The tables turned*, f. 179v.

34   Arnold, *The tables turned*, f. 200v.

35 Arnold, *The tables turned*, f. 199v.

36 See *Cosi fan tutte, . . . as represented at the King's Theatre . . .* (London: J. Brettell, 1811). Woodfield traces the transmission of this version back to a Dresden libretto of 1791. *Mozart's Così fan tutte*, p. 190.

37 See Cowgill, 'Mozart productions and the emergence of *Werktreue*'.

38 See Peterson, '"The best the house could afford"', p. 137 and Walton, 'Rara avis or fozy turnip'.

39 According to Ayrton, the score included five Rossini pieces, drawn from *Matilde di Shabran, La donna del lago, Il Turco in Italia* and *Zelmira*. *The Harmonicon*, June 1824, 111–12.

40 *La cenerentola* is one of the more thoroughly researched adaptations of the period. See Graziano, *Italian opera in English*; Stuart W. Rogers, 'Cenerentola a Londra'; and Smith, 'An English transformation'.

41 *Quarterly Musical Magazine and Review*, 1825, 86.

42 *Morning Chronicle*, 3 May 1827.

43 Vestris did not sing Pippo in the Covent Garden adaptation, as she was not employed there at the time.

44 *London Times*, 24 August 1833.

45 The *Theatrical Observer* (4 May 1827) noted the fashionable audiences who attended *Il Turco in Italia*, *The Harlequin* (11 July 1829) those at *Ivanhoé*.

46 *London Times*, 9 March 1829.

47 *Bell's Life in London*, 29 March 1829 and *Morning Post*, 13 April 1830. Bishop dedicated the libretto of *La gazza ladra* to Paton under her married name of Lady William Lennox.

48 *The York musical festival of 1828. A comedy, in five acts.* (London: Hirst, Chance, & Co., 1828). I am grateful to Charles McGuire for this reference. See also *The public and private life of Lady William Lennox*.

49 *Memoir of Mr. and Mrs. Wood*, p. 13.

50 *Memoir of Mr. and Mrs. Wood*, p. 18.

51 20 June 1830.

52 *Morning Chronicle*, 14 April 1830.

53 See *Cinderella: or, the fairy queen and the glass slipper* (London: J. Dicks, 1830) and *Cinderella: or, the fairy queen and the glass slipper* (London: T. H. Lacy, 1850).

54 2 May 1830.

55 14 May 1830.

56 Bishop adapted both the score and the libretto, but received some assistance on the latter from Edward Fitzball. The printed libretto indicates that Fitzball wrote the 'poetry', or the song texts only. Bishop, 'Advertisement' in *Ninetta; or, the maid of Palaiseau . . .* (London: J. Ebers, [1830]). Fitzball's memoirs, however, include a letter from Bishop discussing changes that needed to take place in the dialogue and urging speed in writing the finale. Although Fitzball stated simply that Bishop 'engaged [him] to write the words', he may have given more comprehensive assistance. Fitzball, *Thirty-five years of a dramatic author's life*, vol. II, pp. 195–6.

57 These are a ballad for Ninetta, 'Still mem'ry paints the humble vale', a solo for Giannetto, 'In the cold stilly night', and a solo for Fernando, 'Like the hunter-stricken deer'.

[58] *The Athenaeum* suggested that Bishop used numbers from *Guillaume Tell* and *Otello*, but I have not been able to correlate Fitzball's poetry to these operas. 16 January 1830, 31.

[59] Henry Rowley Bishop to George Bartley, 27 January 1830, quoted in Northcott, *The life of Sir Henry R. Bishop*, p. 84.

[60] Northcott states that all Bishop's numbers for his adaptation of *La gazza ladra* were published. I have only located one, 'Still mem'ry paints the humble vale'. *The life of Sir Henry R. Bishop*, p. 82.

[61] Bishop cut Pippo's brindisi, Ninetta and Giannetto's duet, Gottardo's second aria, Lucia's aria and Fernando's aria. The latter had also been cut in the King's Theatre production. The King's Theatre had further altered the original by using a different aria for Lucia, discarding part of Pippo's brindisi, cutting Gottardo's first aria and adding an aria for Pippo. *La gazza ladra … first performed at the King's Theatre on Saturday, March 10, 1821 …* (London: Printed for John Ebers, n.d.).

[62] Bishop apparently fluctuated here, for he wrote to Fitzball 'You will find that the *dialogue* which brings on [Fernando] directly before the *Quintetto*, No. 14, must *now* be *restored*, as he does not come on *in* the Quintet, but before it'. Fitzball, *Thirty-five years of a dramatic author's life*, vol. I, p. 196.

[63] 'Solita forma' typically did not contain two pezzi concertati. Instead, it usually progressed directly from scena to tempo d'attacco. Powers, '"La solita forma"', 69. I have chosen to separate mm. 168–225 as an 'extra' pezzo concertato since this passage involves a change in tempo, characters and subject matter. This section also evinces the slow tempo, static text in *versi lirici* and lyrical music of a pezzo concertato. Finally, dividing the ensemble in this way brings out the thematic connection between the tempo d'attacco and the tempo di mezzo, which begin with the same material.

[64] *Quarterly Musical Magazine and Review*, 1820, 79.

[65] *Quarterly Musical Magazine and Review*, 1821, 254.

[66] Bishop was in Paris in 1829, where he apparently met Rossini and attended performances of *Guillaume Tell*. Northcott, *The life of Sir Henry R. Bishop*, pp. 81–2. Northcott mistakenly dates the visit 1828, but must mean 1829 since *Guillaume Tell* was not premièred until that year. Bishop also viewed Boieldieu's *Les deux nuits* at this time and adapted it with librettist Fitzball. Fitzball makes clear in his memoirs that Goulding and D'Almaine commissioned the adaptation of *Les deux nuits*. *Thirty-five years of a dramatic author's life*, vol. I, pp. 182–3. It seems likely that Goulding and D'Almaine also commissioned Bishop to adapt *Guillaume Tell*, since they published all printed sources for the adaptation. It also appears that Bishop had access to the 1829 Troupenas edition of *Guillaume Tell*. In the cabaletta section of Arnold's 'Asil héréditaire', Bishop included a portion that had been cut in performance, but was in the Troupenas edition. See Gioachino Rossini, *Guillaume Tell*, ed. M. Elizabeth C. Barlet (Milan: Ricordi, 1992), vol. III, pp. 1366–77.

[67] Nicoll, *Alphabetical catalogue of plays 1660–1900*, p. 550. See also Burwick, *Playing to the crowd*, pp. 101–16.

[68] Planché, Preface to *Hofer, the Tell of the Tyrol*, p. v.

[69] Knowles' play may have influenced the opera, as it was performed in France in 1828.

[70] June 1825, 300.

[71] Saunders, 'Knowles, James Sheridan'.

[72] For a recent study of Hofer, see Cole, *Andreas Hofer*. For reports that would have been available in early nineteenth-century London, see, among others, Hormayr zu Hortenburg, *Memoirs of the life of Andreas Hofer* and Muller, *An account of the sacrifices made.*

[73] Wordsworth wrote 'Hoffer', 'Advance – come forth from thy Tyrolean ground', 'Feelings of the Tyrolese' and 'On the final submission of the Tyrolese'. William Wordsworth, *Complete poetical works* (Cambridge: Riverside Press, 1932).

[74] Hormayr zu Hortenburg, *Memoirs of the life of Andreas Hofer*, p. 42.

[75] See, for example, Walton, 'Looking for the revolution in Rossini's *Guillaume Tell*'.

[76] *The Spectator*, 27 February 1830.

[77] Hormayr zu Hortenburg, *Memoirs of the life of Andreas Hofer*, p. xvii.

[78] Planché, *Hofer, the Tell of the Tyrol*, p. 17.

[79] Newey, 'Reform on the London Stage', p. 250. Benjamin Walton also argues that nostalgia played a crucial role in the original opera. 'Looking for the revolution in Rossini's *Guillaume Tell*'. Allardyce Nicoll mistakenly conflates the Surrey version by Edward Fitzball with Planché's. *Early nineteenth century drama*, p. 584.

[80] 13 July 1839.

[81] The manuscript score for this song represents an earlier version in which both the vocal and instrumental conclusions were extended in the second stanza. This version is also in the same key as Rossini's original: E major. The printed version is in G major, either to accommodate Vestris or amateur performers. Bishop, 'Cast we our weaker hearts away'.

[82] For the King's Theatre version, see *Songs from Guillaume Tell . . .*, Plays Submitted to the Lord Chamberlain, British Library Additional Manuscript 42900.

[83] Holmes here refers to the original comparison, which was between a 'fozy turnip and a pineapple'. Walton, 'Rara avis or fozy turnip', p. 95.

[84] 17 March 1821.

[85] 10 April 1831.

[86] He may have meant Don Alfonso's 'Vorrei dir, e cor non ho', any of Guglielmo or Fiordiligi's arias, or Ferrando's last two arias, none of which the King's Theatre's 1811 London première included. *Cosi fan tutte, . . . as represented at the King's Theatre . . .* (London: J. Brettell, 1811). The 1811 version also eliminated Dorabella's 'Smanie implacabili che m'agitate' and Despina's 'Una donna a quindici anni', but these were restored in the 1817 libretto. *Cosi fan tutte, . . . as represented at the King's Theatre . . .* (London: John Twigg, 1817).

[87] Gossett, *Divas and scholars*, pp. 329–30.

[88] 24 April 1830.

[89] *The Harmonicon*, July 1830, 290.

6 GRAND OPERA: COMPETITION AND COPYRIGHT

[1] 2 January 1828.

[2] Gabriella Dideriksen marks 1831–2 as the decisive season when French opera adaptation surpassed Italian at Covent Garden. 'Repertory and rivalry', p. 153. For a discussion of the adaptation of *La dame blanche*, see my 'Scott repatriated?'

[3] Planché, *Recollections and reflections*, p. 107.

4 9 January 1830. *La fiancée* was adapted by both Drury Lane and Covent Garden, but the latter did not use Auber's score.

5 *The Spectator*, 21 November 1829.

6 26 October 1828. Long-lane songs is probably a reference to the family business of John Evans, a broadside printer located on Long Lane. My thanks to Oskar Cox Jensen for assistance with this reference.

7 Other examples of grand opera are discussed in Chapters 5 (*Guillaume Tell*) and 7 (*Gustave III*). For more on adapted French operas, see my 'In enemy territory?'

8 A few vocal numbers were included. The libretto contains Italian translations for four choruses and one solo with chorus. *Songs from Masaniello ou le Pêcheur de Portici*, Plays Submitted to the Lord Chamberlain, British Library, Additional Manuscript 42985. Newspaper reports suggest, however, that only two choruses were included in performance. *The Harmonicon*, May 1829, 122.

9 Milner had previously written a separate melodrama for the Coburg entitled *Massaniello, the fisherman of Naples and deliverer of his country*, with music by T. Hughes, which appeared in February 1825. See *Masaniello, the fisherman of Naples* (London: J. Lowndes, n.d.). Nicoll erroneously lists the date of its revival, 5 June 1826, as the première. *Early nineteenth century drama*, p. 501.

10 Modern studies include Clark, 'The body and the voice'; Hibberd, *French grand opera*; Hibberd, '*La muette* and her context'; and Newark, 'Interpreting *La muette*'.

11 See, for example, Leeuwe, 'Revolution durch Oper?'

12 Hibberd, '*La muette* and her context', p. 152.

13 *Masaniello, the fisherman of Naples* (London: John Miller, 1825), p. 8.

14 For the censor's marks, see *Masaniello*, Plays Submitted to the Lord Chamberlain, British Library Additional Manuscript 42870. *The Times* noted that the published libretto was available on the night of the performance. 18 February 1825.

15 *The Tatler*, 27 November 1830.

16 18 February 1831; this reprints excerpts from the previous year's papers of 26 and 31 October and 3, 5 and 6 November.

17 Bratton, *New readings in theatre history*, p. 75.

18 This question appears during a discussion of Drury Lane's lack of proper payment to Kenney for the libretto. Great Britain Parliament, *Report from the select committee*, p. 227.

19 *The Tatler*, 27 November 1830.

20 Hibberd, '*La muette* and her context', p. 166.

21 For a discussion of how various Italian adaptations either augmented or palliated the revolutionary element, see Rosen, 'A tale of three libretti'.

22 Milner, *Masaniello*, p. 24.

23 Milner, *Masaniello*, p. 9.

24 Milner, *Masaniello*, p. 16.

25 Milner, *Masaniello*, p. 40.

26 Kenney, *Masaniello*, p. 20.

27 Kenney, *Masaniello*, p. 8.

28 Kenney, *Masaniello*, p. 35.

[29] Schneider, 'Scribe and Auber', pp. 179–80.

[30] Kenney, *Masaniello*, pp. 49–50.

[31] They probably retained the introduction, the *scène et chœur de la chapelle*, the *chœur des pêcheurs*, the famous barcarolle, the *chœur du marché* and the finales to acts two and four; two dances are also indicated that probably used Auber's dance music, but this is unclear. The libretto says a 'song [was] introduced' for the comic character Giuseppe, but no words are given. Milner, *Masaniello*, p. 15. The playbill states that the overture was included.

[32] The bolero had been danced by Miss Byrne and a M Gilbert from the King's Theatre on the first evening but was replaced with this dance thereafter. The *Theatrical Observer* suggested that this was due to a substantial height difference between Gilbert and Byrne. The score does not list a composer for this piece.

[33] Letellier, *Daniel-François-Auber*, p. 354.

[34] For virtually all numbers, the score indicates whether Cooke or Livius adapted it. The melodramatic music is, however, unattributed.

[35] There are more stage directions for Fenella in the libretto than the score. Kenney, *Masaniello*, pp. 10–12. It is therefore unclear whether Fenella did some of her miming without music, whether Elvire spoke during some of her music or whether some of the music was repeated between the dialogue.

[36] 'Expresses by signs that she is dumb, but that nothing will equal her gratitude: and by her supplicating gestures implores her protection against her pursuers'. Kenney, *Masaniello*, p. 10.

[37] Gerhard, *The urbanization of opera*, p. 146.

[38] All reviews cited in this section are of Drury Lane. See Appendix 2.

[39] Mungo was a popular blackface character from *The padlock* (1768), revived throughout the early nineteenth century.

[40] Clark, 'The body and the voice', pp. 118, 125, 127–9.

[41] May 1831, 109.

[42] For Meyerbeer's connections with London, see Everett, 'Meyerbeer in London'.

[43] *Theatrical Observer*, 29 October 1831.

[44] 11 December 1832. Rupert Ridgewell reports a rumour that Polhill had been offered the rights to perform *Robert* but had hesitated to follow through. Ridgewell, '"Meyerbeer's best intentions"', p. 7.

[45] See *The Harmonicon*, March 1832, 69. *The Athenaeum* indicated that Polhill had planned to offer only £400, so it appears he was outbid. 24 December 1831.

[46] Small, 'The development of musical copyright', p. 286.

[47] The complete edition of *Robert le diable* indicates that a piano–vocal score was published already in 1831. Wolfgang Kühnhold and Peter Kaiser, 'Kritischer Bericht' in Giacomo Meyerbeer, *Robert le diable*, ed. Wolfgang Kühnhold and Peter Kaiser, vol. x of *Giacomo Meyerbeer Werkausgabe* (Munich: G. Ricordi, & Co., 2010), p. 33.

[48] 24 January 1832.

[49] February 1832, 43.

[50] *Robert the devil* has a different plot, but Nicoll erroneously lists it as an adaptation of *Robert le diable*. *Early nineteenth century drama*, pp. 340, 592. Covent Garden manager Charles Kemble's side of the story was reported by the *Theatrical Observer*: 'We have heard that Mr Kemble

says that so far from wishing to out-jockey the rival theatre, he sent to them to know when they intended to produce their Opera, as he wished to start fair, the answer was sent that Tuesday was the night fixed on, when Mr Kemble, though his Opera was so far advanced that he might have done it on Saturday, announced it for Tuesday, upon which the Drury Lane manager immediately changed his night to Monday.' 23 February 1832.

51 26 December 1831.

52 Mason also apparently engaged Auber to write an opera for the King's Theatre, but this did not materialise. *The Athenaeum*, 24 December 1831.

53 *The Age*, 26 February 1832.

54 On 28 February 1832, *The Times* and the *Theatrical Observer* published this letter, of 24 February, from Meyerbeer to 'a friend'. Heinz Becker notes that Meyerbeer wrote in his Taschenkalender for 21 February 1832 'Schlesinger englische Zeitung', which may indicate that Meyerbeer's publisher, Schlesinger, was behind the letter. Meyerbeer, *Briefwechsel und Tagebücher*, vol. II, pp. 164 and 623.

55 Letellier, ed., *The diaries of Giacomo Meyerbeer*, p. 440.

56 The *Theatrical Observer* reprinted the handbill Mason distributed in the theatre regarding this. 21 June 1832.

57 *Literary Gazette*, 16 June 1832.

58 Gruneisen, *Memoir of Meyerbeer*, 11. This appears to be rhetorical, as Alfred Loewenberg does not list any performance in Mexico before 1848. The closest was a performance in Valparaiso, Chile in 1847. Loewenberg, *Annals of opera*, pp. 737–38.

59 Other numbers may have been used, but the libretto fits poorly with most potential equivalents and was written in such haste that some of the numbers (including Alice's solo) have only a blank space left for the text. Fitzball and Buckstone, *Robert le diable*.

60 Collier and the *Theatrical Observer* referred to Reeve's improvised jokes.

61 Letellier, *Meyerbeer's 'Robert le diable'*, p. 29.

62 Fitzball and Buckstone, *Robert le diable*, f. 143v.

63 Sanders, *Adaptation and appropriation*, p. 24.

64 Lacy, *Robert the devil*, p. 16.

65 Lacy, *Robert the devil*, pp. 23, 29.

66 Ridgewell, '"Meyerbeer's best intentions"', p. 41.

67 Bishop cut the overture, the *chœur dansé* and *pas de cinq* in act two and the choruses 'Frappez les airs' and 'Gloire à la providence'. The King's Theatre also cut the latter, as well as the opening chorus of act four, which both Bishop and Lacy dropped. Bishop and Lacy included a few numbers in their manuscript libretti that were then cut or abridged in the printed sources. Reviewing the Drury Lane version for *The Atlas*, Holmes noted that additional pieces were discarded after the Drury Lane première as well.

68 Ridgewell, '"Meyerbeer's best intentions"', p. 43.

69 Fitzball, *Thirty-five years of a dramatic author's life*, vol. II, pp. 378–9.

70 Hector Berlioz felt this scene deserved 'the prize for instrumentation'. *Gazette Musicale de Paris*, 12 July 1835.

71 Giacomo Meyerbeer, *Robert le diable* (Paris: Maurice Schlesinger, [1832]; reprint, New York: Garland, 1980).

[72] Bishop, Cooke and Hughes, *The demon!*, vol. II, ff. 23r–v.

[73] 19 February 1832.

[74] 26 December 1831.

7 OF FOREIGNERS AND FIDELITY

[1] *The Harmonicon*, June 1833, 139.

[2] 9 February 1833.

[3] See Grafe, 'Un français'.

[4] Edmund Cox, *Musical recollections*, vol. I, p. 271.

[5] *Morning Chronicle*, 2 October 1832.

[6] *Morning Post*, 6 February 1833.

[7] See *Il Don Giovanni . . . as represented for the first time in this country April 1817 at the Kings Theatre*, Plays submitted to the Lord Chamberlain, Huntington Library, Larpent 1966; *Don Giovanni . . . represented for the first time in London, at the King's Theatre* (London: Winchester & Son, 1817); *Don Giovanni . . .*, Plays submitted to the Lord Chamberlain, British Library Additional Manuscript 42903; and *Don Juan . . . as performed for the first time at the King's Theatre* (London: G. Schulze, 1832).

[8] Beazley, 'Preface' in *Songs, duets, recitative, &c. &c. in Don Juan*, p. i.

[9] Rachel Cowgill discusses Ayrton's production and the edition of *Don Giovanni* that he probably used. 'Mozart productions and the emergence of *Werktreue*', p. 166.

[10] The pieces are in the manuscript and printed libretti, but are placed in quotation marks in the latter, which indicated omission in performance. Rachel Cowgill notes that 'Dalla sua pace' was apparently reinstated in later performances. 'Mozart's music in London', p. 227.

[11] Beazley, *Don Juan*, f. 338r.

[12] Beazley, 'Preface' in *Songs, duets, recitative, &c. &c. in Don Juan*, pp. i–ii.

[13] Apparently, Wood's husband had initially turned down the role of Ottavio and when Begrez refused it as well, John Templeton was cast. *Morning Chronicle*, 4 February 1833.

[14] A long tradition states that Malibran first sang Amina at the Teatro del Fondo in Naples in the spring of 1833. In their critical edition of *La sonnambula*, however, Luca Zoppelli and Alessandro Roccatagliati note that no primary sources confirm this claim, which appears to be an error on the part of Bellini's notoriously incorrect biographer, Francesco Florimo. Therefore, although the *Morning Post* stated that Malibran had already 'delighted Italy' as Amina, it appears that she debuted in the role in London. I am grateful to Fabrizio Della Seta for his assistance with this matter. Roccatagliati and Zoppelli, 'Introduzione' in Vincenzo Bellini, *La sonnambula; melodramma in due atti di Felice Romani*, ed. Alessandro Roccatagliati and Luca Zoppelli, vol. VII of *Edizione critica delle opere di Vincenzo Bellini* (Milan: Ricordi, 2009), p. xlii.

[15] The libretto was published jointly by John Perry in New York and Thomas Hailes Lacy in London. Philip A. H. Brown indicates that Lacy did not begin publishing until 1849. *London publishers and printers*, p. 109.

[16] The score was published by Boosey & Co. at 28 Holles Street. Philip A. H. Brown indicates that the publisher used this name and address from 1816 to 1854. *London publishers and printers*, p. 21. The score lists the adapter as 'Henry R. Bishop, Mus. Bac. Oxon'. Bishop did not earn

this degree until 1839. In 1842, he was knighted and most likely would have been referred to as 'Sir' after that date.

17 *La sonnambula. A grand opera*, p. 5.

18 Roccatagliati and Zoppelli, 'Introduzione', p. xl.

19 Bunn, *The stage*, vol. I, p. 245.

20 Florimo, ed., *Bellini*, p. 138. Translation in Galatopoulos, *Bellini*, p. 289.

21 Philip Gossett indicates that Florimo 'is known to have invented or rewritten many a letter from Bellini' and that this one is probably fabricated. *Divas and scholars*, p. 355.

22 Preston, *Opera on the road*, pp. 286–7.

23 Gossett, *Divas and scholars*, p. 355. Bishop also followed contemporary convention by lowering Elvino's high tessitura. In addition, he transposed Lisa's solos down for Miss Betts. Transpositions are always suspect, however, as they may have been made for domestic sale only.

24 Merlin, *Memoirs of Madame Malibran*, vol. I, pp. 192–3.

25 Bunn, *The stage*, vol. II, p. 114.

26 For a discussion of the ballet, see Hibberd, 'Dormez donc'.

27 September 1831, 403.

28 Bunn states that he paid her £2000 for fifteen performances in May, then signed another agreement for £1000 for twelve nights in June. *The stage*, vol. II, pp. 112–17.

29 10 February 1833.

30 6 December 1835.

31 *Theatrical Observer*, 19 November 1833.

32 *Theatrical Observer*, 19 November and 3 December 1833. Only Drury Lane's coronation pageant in 1821–2 had run longer, for 105 nights.

33 Scribe relied mainly on J. Cohen's *Les cours du Nord* . . . (Paris: Arthus Bertrand, 1820), an expanded translation of John Brown, *The Northern courts* . . . (Edinburgh: Archibald Constable and Co. and London: Rest Fenner, 1818). For a comparison of Scribe and Cohen, see Schneider, 'Scribe and Auber', p. 181. For a discussion of the political context of Auber's opera, see Hibberd, *French grand opera*.

34 Planché, *Recollections and reflections*, p. 179.

35 Thackeray, *Gustavus of Sweden*, p. 29.

36 Thackeray, *Gustavus of Sweden*, pp. 7–8.

37 Planché, *Gustavus the third, or the masked ball* (London: D'Almaine & Co. [1833]), p. v.

38 Hibberd, 'Grand opera in Britain and the Americas', p. 408.

39 Planché, *Gustavus the third, or the masked ball* (London: D'Almaine & Co. [1833]), p. v.

40 Planché, *Recollections and reflections*, p. 148.

41 Planché, *Recollections and reflections*, p. 149.

42 Seccombe, 'Warde, James Prescott'.

43 In a review of *La sonnambula*, *The Athenaeum* praised Templeton's strides in singing, but wished he could 'make a corresponding improvement in his acting'.

44 'Hail to our monarch!' has the same meaning and placement as the opening of Auber's finale and the libretto indicates it is by Auber, but the text does not fit smoothly. The *Morning Post* stated that Auber's overture was used.

45 Lillienhorn sings Gustave's two arias, his duet with Ankastrom, and several passages in large ensembles. Ribbing sings his part in the *chœur et ronde* in act two.

46 The *Morning Post* indicated that one portion of the overture had been transposed 'to make it more easy for the pianoforte player'. Dideriksen feels that Templeton was able to sing the high original keys and that transpositions were for domestic consumption. 'Repertory and rivalry', p. 312.

47 Phillips, *Musical and personal recollections*, vol. 1, p. 240.

48 Phillips, *Musical and personal recollections*, vol. 1, p. 241.

49 Phillips, *Musical and personal recollections*, vol. 1 pp. 241–2.

50 Phillips, *Musical and personal recollections*, vol. 1, p. 240.

51 See Planché, *Gustavus the third, or the masked ball* (London: D'Almaine and Co., [1833]), p. viii and Cassirer, 'Gustaf III', p. 39.

52 Taylor suggested that the King's Theatre was planning a production. This never materialised, but the last act was performed for a benefit in June 1834.

53 12 December 1833 and 22 November 1833.

54 Bennett, *Theatre audiences*, p. 115.

55 Planché, *Recollections and reflections*, p. 173.

56 *The Atlas*, 23 June 1833.

57 Bauman, *W. A. Mozart: Die Entführung aus dem Serail*, p. 111 and Ehrlich, *First philharmonic*, p. 67.

58 Hutcheon, *A theory of adaptation*, p. 176.

APPENDIX I OPERAS ADAPTED FOR THE LONDON PLAYHOUSES, 1814–1833

1 The following abbreviations are used: A = Adelphi Theatre; CG = Covent Garden Theatre; DL = Drury Lane Theatre; EOH = English Opera House; O = Olympic Theatre; RA = Royal Amphitheatre, also known as Astley's; RC = Royal Coburg Theatre (known later as the Royal Victoria Theatre); RP = Royal Pavilion; Q = Queen's Theatre, known under several names, including the New Royal West London Theatre and the Tottenham-street Theatre; S = Surrey Theatre; SW = Sadler's Wells; WL = West London Theatre.

2 L indicates the adapter of the libretto, M the adapter of the music. Listings left blank are unknown. This information is drawn from Nicoll, *Early nineteenth century drama* as well as *The Oxford dictionary of national biography*, playbills, libretti, scores and newspaper reviews.

3 A playbill for 25 November 1824 announces the seventy-first performance of the work. Extrapolating backwards and assuming a performance virtually every evening would place the première in late August or early September.

4 The *Theatrical Observer* attributed this parody to the author of *Dr Syntax*. Allardyce Nicoll lists two plays of that name, one anonymous (SW, 31 March 1823), the other by Charles Dibdin (RA, 5 May 1823). *Theatrical Observer*, 1 October 1824 and Nicoll, *Early nineteenth century drama*, pp. 295, 451.

5 A playbill for 29 October 1824 announces the fifth performance of the work, which would place the première on Monday 25 October if the work were performed every evening.

6 The *London Magazine* announced that both patent theatres were preparing *Preciosa*, but DL never performed it. May 1825, 145. The EOH had apparently planned the London première in

1824, submitting a libretto to the Lord Chamberlain on 18 August. For as yet unknown reasons, the theatre abandoned *Preciosa*. Their libretto diverges from both the original and CG's adaptation.

7 These attributions stem from Nicoll but are tentative. It is possible that Hawes was involved with the adaptation of the score, since the *London Magazine* noted that 'After the failure of *Preciosa*, Mr. Hawes had well nigh cut the throat of his benefactor.' June 1825, 271. Soane, Ball and McGregor Logan all appear as translators of the text in published score excerpts, but none of these excerpts correlates to the extant text of the CG adaptation.

8 John Payne Collier suggested that the librettist might be Napier. *Morning Chronicle*, 6 September 1828.

9 Some of the later printed score sources indicate that William Henry Kearns 'newly adapted' the opera.

10 While the librettist is not officially named in the surviving source material, a letter from Washington Irving states, 'Frank Mills has caught a dramatic mania, and aided in cooking up the piece for Drury Lane. He wrote the songs, and a Mr Beasley [*sic*] (not Reuben) the dialogue.' Letter to Peter Irving, 16 March 1832, in Irving, *The life and letters of Washington Irving*, vol. II, p. 483. The *Theatrical Observer* also referred to Beazley and Mills as the librettists. 21 February 1832.

11 Lacy is the only adapter listed for CG, but *The Spectator* mentioned a Kearns (possibly William Henry) as a fellow adapter. 25 February 1832. Clive Brown also states that John Barnett was involved in this production and composed music for it, but I have been unable to corroborate this. 'Barnett, John (1802–1890)'.

12 The CG company performed this at the O.

13 Two divergent libretti exist for the RC adaptation, one by Thackeray, one by Milner. Newspaper reports make clear that Thackeray's version was the one debuted in 1833. It is unclear under what circumstances Milner's was performed.

APPENDIX 2 REVIEWS OF ADAPTATIONS

1 Only reviews cited within the book are listed here. Identifications of reviewers rely primarily on Fenner, *Opera in London*; Kent, 'Periodical critics of drama, music, and art, 1830–1914'; and Leanne Langley, 'The English musical journal'.

2 The newspaper mistakenly labels this 11 November.

BIBLIOGRAPHY

SOURCES FOR ADAPTATIONS

Jean de Paris adapted as *Jean de Paris*, Drury Lane, 1814

Arnold, S[amuel] J[ames], *Jean de Paris, a comic drama* ... (London: Whittingham and Arliss, 1814)
  Jean de Paris, a farce ..., Plays submitted to the Lord Chamberlain, Huntington Library, Larpent 1829
Horn, Charles Edward, *Jean de Paris: a favorite divertimento, arranged for the piano forte* ... (London, W. Horn, c. 1817–24)

Jean de Paris adapted as *John of Paris*, Covent Garden, 1814

Bishop, Henry R[owley], *John of Paris*, vol. xiii of *Sir H. R. Bishop's works* (London: Goulding, D'Almaine and Potter, c. 1814–20)
  John of Paris, opera ..., Boston Public Library, M.230.26
Pocock, I[saac], *John of Paris; a comic opera* ... (London: John Miller, 1814)
  John of Paris. Comic opera ..., Plays submitted to the Lord Chamberlain, Huntington Library, Larpent 1830

Don Giovanni adapted as *The libertine*, Covent Garden, 1817

Bishop, Henry R[owley], *Don Juan, or the libertine, a grand operatic drama* ... (London: Goulding, D'Almaine, Potter & Co., c. 1817–20)
Pocock, I[saac], *The libertine: an opera* ... (London: John Miller, 1817)
  The libertine; an operatick drama ..., Plays submitted to the Lord Chamberlain, Huntington Library, Larpent 1973

Il barbiere di Siviglia adapted as *The barber of Seville*, Covent Garden, 1818

Airs, trios, choruses, etc. etc. in the comick opera in two acts called The barber of Seville ... (London: E. Macleish, 1818)
The barber of Seville, 1818. Chiefly adapted from Rossini ..., British Library Additional Manuscript 36950
The barber of Seville; a comic opera ... (London: J. Roach, 1818)
The barber of Seville a comick opera ..., Plays submitted to the Lord Chamberlain, Huntington Library, Larpent 2046

Bishop, Henry R[owley], *The overture and music (complete) to the comic opera called The barber of Seville . . .* (London: D'Almaine & Co., c. 1838–48)

Le nozze di Figaro adapted as *The marriage of Figaro*, Covent Garden, 1819

Bishop, [Henry Rowley], *Airs, duets, trios, choruses, etc. etc. in the new comick opera . . . called The marriage of Figaro . . .* (London: E. Macleish, 1819)
   The marriage of Figaro; a comic opera . . . (London: Goulding, D'Almaine, Potter, c. 1819–23)
   The marriage of Figaro; a comic opera . . . (London: John Miller, 1819)
The marriage of Figaro a comic opera . . ., Plays submitted to the Lord Chamberlain, Huntington Library, Larpent 2077
The marriage of Figaro; comic opera . . ., British Library Additional Manuscript 27712

Der Freischütz adapted as *Der Freischütz*, English Opera House, 1824

Der Freijschutz, the wild hunter or the seventh bullet . . ., Plays submitted to the Lord Chamberlain, British Library Additional Manuscript 42867
Der Freischütz; or, the seventh bullet . . . (London: G. H. Davidson, c. 1849–60)
Der Freischütz; or, the seventh bullet . . . (London: Thomas Dolby, 1825)
Der Freyschutz, romantische Oper in drei Akten . . ., Royal College of Music Manuscript 4348
Hawes, William and W. McGregor Logan, *Weber's celebrated opera Der Freischutz or the seventh bullet . . .* (London: Cramer, Addison & Beale, [1841])
'Oh fortune we hail thee', Royal College of Music Manuscript 1038
Songs, duets, incantation, concerted pieces, choruses, etc. in the new musical performance of Der Freischütz; or, the seventh bullet . . . (London: John Lowndes, n.d.)
The whole of the music . . . in the celebrated melodrame, called Der Freischütz; or the seventh bullet . . . (London: Royal Harmonic Institution, 1824)

Der Freischütz adapted as *Der Freischütz*, Royal Amphitheatre, 1824

Amherst, J. H., *Der Freischutz, or the seven charmed bullets . . .* (London: Duncombe, c. 1824–36)

Der Freischütz adapted as *Der Freischütz*, West London Theatre, 1824

Kerr, J[ohn], *Der Freischutz; or, Zamiel the spirit of the forest . . .* (London: J. Dicks, n.d.)
   Der Freischutz; or Zamiel the spirit of the forest, and the seventh bullet . . . (London: John Lowndes, n.d.)

Der Freischütz adapted as *Der Freischütz*, Surrey Theatre, 1824

[Fitz]Ball, Edward, *Der Freischutz; or, the demon of the wolf's glen, and the seven charmed bullets . . .* (London: John Lowndes, n.d.)

Der Freischütz adapted as *The Freyschütz*, Covent Garden, 1824

'Each sorrow repelling a duet ... sung ... in the grand operatic romance of Der Freischutz or the wild huntsman' (New York: E. Riley, n.d.)

'Heart wilt thou rest thee never ... in the romantic opera of Der Freischutz, or the black huntsman of Bohemia' (London: W. Eavestaff and Lavenu & Co., n.d.)

Livius, Barham, *The Freyschütz; or, the wild huntsman of Bohemia* ... (London: John Miller, n.d.)

Planché, J[ames] R[obinson] and Barham Livius, *Songs, duets, choruses, incantations, etc. in the romantic opera of Der Freïschutz; or, the black huntsman of Bohemia* ... (London: John Miller, 1824)

Planché, J[ames] R[obinson] and Washington Irving, *Der Freischutz* ..., Plays submitted to the Lord Chamberlain, British Library Additional Manuscript 42868

'Wine, wine, rich and rosy wine. The celebrated drinking song ... in the romantic opera of Der Freischutz, or the black huntsman of Bohemia' (London: Lavenu & Co. and W. Eavestaff, n.d.)

Der Freischütz adapted as *Der Freischütz*, Drury Lane, 1824

Bishop, Henry R[owley], *The overture, & the popular music in Carl Maria von Weber's celebrated romantic opera of Der Freischütz* ... (London: Goulding, D'Almaine & Co., [1824])

Soane, G[eorge], *Der Freischutz*, Plays submitted to the Lord Chamberlain, British Library Additional Manuscript 42869

  Der Freischütz: a romantic opera ..., 3rd edn (London: Simpkin & Marshall, 1825)

Die Entführung aus dem Serail adapted as *The seraglio*, Covent Garden, 1827

Kramer, [Christian], *Airs, duets, choruses, &c. in the new grand opera ... called The seraglio* ... (London: W. Reynolds, n.d.)

  The seraglio, the celebrated opera by Mozart, with additional music ... (London: Clementi and Co. and S. Chappell, [1828])

The seraglio: an opera ... (London: R. S. Kirby, 1828)

The seraglio, Plays submitted to the Lord Chamberlain, British Library Additional Manuscript 42885

Così fan tutte adapted as *Tit for tat*, English Opera House, 1828

Arnold, S[amuel] J[ames] *The tables turned (tit for tat or the tables turned)*, Plays submitted to the Lord Chamberlain, British Library Additional Manuscript 42891

'Be sure you write and often; the favorite quintet ... in the opera called Tit for tat or the tables turn'd' (London: W. Hawes, n.d.)

Hawes, [William], *Recitative, Songs, duets, chorusses, &c. in Tit for tat; or, the tables turned.* (London: S. G. Fairbrother, [1828])

'One word from my angel ... in the popular opera, called Tit for tat or the tables turn'd' (London: W. Hawes [1827])

'What my Dorabella, the favorite trio, ... in the popular opera, called Tit for tat or the tables turn'd' (London: W. Hawes, n.d.)

La muette de Portici adapted as *The dumb girl of Portici*, Coburg Theatre, 1829

Milner, H. M., *Masaniello; or, the dumb girl of Portici* (London: John Cumberland, n.d.)

La muette de Portici adapted as *Masaniello*, Drury Lane, 1829

Auber, [Daniel François Esprit], 'Ah! why that tear ...', Cambridge University Library, Additional Manuscript 9045, ff. 71–2

Auber, [Daniel François Esprit], arr. T[homas] Cooke, 'Take heed, whisper low, barcarole in Masaniello', Cambridge University Library, Additional Manuscript 9045, ff. 34v–37v

Kenney, James, *Masaniello: a grand opera* ... (London: Edward Moxon, 1831)

Masaniello or the dumb girl of Portici ... Plays submitted to the Lord Chamberlain, British Library Additional Manuscript 42895

Masaniello or the dumb girl of Portici: a grand opera, written for the English stage by James Kenney ... (London: I. Willis and Co., [1829])

Songs, duets, &c. in the new grand opera of Masaniello; or, the dumb girl of Portici (London: published at the theatre, 1829)

Die Räuberbraut adapted as *The robber's bride*, English Opera House, 1829

Hawes, W[illiam], *Recitative, songs, duets, &c. in the grand serio-comick opera, called The robber's bride!* ... (London: S. G. Fairbrother, [1829])

The robber's bride, a grand opera (London: W. Hawes, 1829)

The robber's bride, or, the outlaws of the Appenines ... Plays submitted to the Lord Chamberlain, British Library Additional Manuscript 42896

Der Vampyr adapted as *Der Vampyr*, English Opera House, 1829

'A few vocal parts from "The dice of death" ... and "Der Vampyr" ...' British Library Additional Manuscript 36573

Hawes, W[illiam], 'From the ruin's topmost tow'r, cavatina ... in Marschner's grand opera Der Vampyr ...' (London, W. Hawes, [1829])

'Hah! yet one and thirty days, scena ... in Marschner's grand opera Der Vampyr ...' (London, W. Hawes, [1829])

'In autumn we should drink boys, the favorite drinking glee ... in Marschner's grand opera Der Vampyr ...' (London, W. Hawes, [1829])

'Like a cloudless summer morning, grand scena ... in Marschner's grand opera Der Vampyr ...' (London, W. Hawes, [1829])

'Oh! my father, duet ... in Marschner's grand opera Der Vampyr ...' (London, W. Hawes, [1829])

'See mother dear, romance ... in Marschner's grand opera Der Vampyr ...' (London, W. Hawes, [1829])

'Oh fortune, we hail thee', Royal College of Music Manuscript 1038

'Oh! my father! must tomorrow ...', British Library Royal Philharmonic Society Manuscript 99

Songs, duets, glees, chorusses, &c. in Der Vampyr; a grand romantick opera ... (London: S. G. Fairbrother, [1829])

'The parts of Michael Zips and Johan Brosky (printed), and a few instrumental parts, from Marschner's "Der Vampyr" ...', British Library Additional Manuscript 33811

The vampire, a grand romantick opera ..., Plays submitted to the Lord Chamberlain, British Library Additional Manuscript 42896

'Vocal parts of Marschner's "Der Vampyr," adapted to the English stage by William Hawes ...', British Library Additional Manuscript 33810

La gazza ladra adapted as *Ninetta*, Covent Garden, 1830

Bishop, Henry R[owley], 'In the cold stilly night ... written for "Maid & magpie" when revived ... as an opera, but not used', Royal College of Music Manuscript 64, no. 10

'Like the hunter-stricken deer ... written for "Maid & magpie" when revived, as an opera, ... but not used', Royal College of Music Manuscript 64, no. 12

Ninetta; or, the maid of Paliscan [sic], (n.p., n.d.), Library of Congress M1500.B615 N4

Ninetta; or, the maid of Palaiseau ... (London: J. Ebers, [1830])

The songs, duetts, choruses, &c. &c. in the opera entitled Ninetta; or, the maid of Palaiseau (London, [Balne, 1830])

'Still memory paints the humble vale ... composed for the opera of Ninetta ...' (London: Goulding & D'Almaine, [1830])

'Still mem'ry paints the humble vale ... written for "Maid & magpie" when revived, as an opera, but not used', Royal College of Music Manuscript 64, no. 9

'Joy inspires my bounding heart ... in the opera of Ninetta ...' (London: Goulding & D'Almaine, [1830–43])

Fitzball, E[dward], *Ninetta, or the maid of Palaiseau,* Plays submitted to the Lord Chamberlain, British Library Additional Manuscript 42898

Ninetta ..., mostly adapted from Rossini ..., British Library Additional Manuscript 36965

Guillaume Tell adapted as *Hofer*, Drury Lane, 1830

Bishop, H[enry] R[owley], 'Cast we our weaker hearts away', Royal College of Music Manuscript 64, no. 23

Songs, duets, choruses, &c. in the historical opera of Hofer, the Tell of the Tyrol ... (London: Goulding and D'Almaine, [1830])

'Dear happy Tyrol', Royal College of Music Manuscript 64, no. 11

'Fast from the lake', Royal College of Music Manuscript 64, no. 15

Hofer, the Tell of the Tyrol. A grand historical opera adapted from the grand opera of Guillaume Tell (London: D'Almaine & Co., n.d.)

Planché, J[ames] R[obinson], *Hofer, the Tell of the Tyrol* (London: Goulding and D'Almaine, [1830])

Hofer ..., the Tell of the Tyrol!, Plays submitted to the Lord Chamberlain, British Library Additional Manuscript 42901

Zemire und Azor adapted as *Azor and Zemira*, Covent Garden, 1831

The magic rose or beauty and the beast (Azor and Zemira or the magic rose), Plays submitted to the Lord Chamberlain, British Library Additional Manuscript 42909

Smart, Sir George, *Airs, duets, choruses, &c. in the new grand opera ... called Azor and Zemira; or, the magic rose* ... (London: W. Reynolds, 1831)

Smart, Sir George and W[illiam] Ball, *Grand opera of Azor & Zemira* ... (London: D'Almaine & Co., [1831])

Robert le diable adapted as *Robert le diable*, Adelphi Theatre, 1832

Fitzball, E[dward], and J[ohn] B. Buckstone, *Robert le diable, the devil's son* ..., Plays submitted to the Lord Chamberlain, British Library Additional Manuscript 42914

Robert le diable adapted as *The dæmon*, Drury Lane, 1832

Bishop, Henry R[owley], T[homas] Cooke, [Montague Philip Corri] and R. Hughes, *The demon! Grand opera from "Robert le Diable"* ..., 2 vols., Royal College of Music Manuscript 382

The demon duke or the mystic branch ..., Plays submitted to the Lord Chamberlain, British Library Additional Manuscript 42914

The dæmon; or, the mystic branch ... (London: John Miller, 1832)

Robert le diable adapted as *Robert the devil*, Covent Garden, 1832

Lacy, M[ichael] R[ophino], *The fiend-father or Robert of Normandy*, Plays submitted to the Lord Chamberlain, British Library Additional Manuscript 42914

Robert the devil or the fiend-father ... (London: Thomas Hailes Lacy, n.d.)

Songs, duets, and concerted pieces of music in the new celebrated opera of Robert le Diable ... (Boston: John H. Eastburn, 1835)

Der Alchymist adapted as *Der Alchymist*, Drury Lane, 1832

Bayly, T[homas] H[aynes] and E[dward] Fitzball, *Der Alchymist*, Plays submitted to the Lord Chamberlain, British Library Additional Manuscript 42915
Bishop, H[enry] R[owley], *Songs, duets, trios, &c. &c. in the new grand opera entitled Der Alchymist* ... (London: J. Mallett, [1832])

Don Giovanni adapted as *Don Juan*, Drury Lane, 1833

Beazley, S[amuel], *Don Juan*, Plays submitted to the Lord Chamberlain, British Library Additional Manuscript 42920
Songs, duets, recitative, &c. &c. in Don Juan ... (London: John Miller, 1833)

La sonnambula adapted as *La sonnambula*, Drury Lane, 1833

Beazley, S[amuel], *La sonnambula*, Plays submitted to the Lord Chamberlain, British Library Additional Manuscript 42921
Bishop, H[enry] R[owley], *The celebrated opera La sonnambula* ... (London: T. Boosey & Co., [1839–42])
  Songs, Duets, Recitative, &c. &c. in the grand opera of the sonnambula ... (London: John Miller, [1835])
La sonnambula. A grand opera ... (New York: John Perry and London: Thomas Hailes Lacy, [1800s])

Gustave III adapted as *Gustavus of Sweden*, Victoria Theatre, 1833

Thackeray, Thomas James, *Gustavus of Sweden* ... (London: R. Wilkes, 1833)

Gustave III adapted as *Gustavus the third*, Covent Garden, 1833

Celebrated opera of Gustavus the third or the masked ball ... (London: D'Almaine & Co., [1830s])
Cooke, T[homas], *Songs, duets, choruses, etc. etc. in the grand opera of Gustavus the third, or the masked ball* ... (London: J. Mallett, [1833])
Planché, J[ames] R[obinson], *Gustavus the third, or the masked ball* (London: D'Almaine and Co., [1833])
  Gustavus the third, or the masked ball, Plays submitted to the Lord Chamberlain, British Library Additional Manuscript 42924

PRIMARY SOURCES

Bedford, Paul, *Recollections and wanderings* (London: Routledge, Warne & Routledge, 1864)
The biography of the British stage ... (London: Sherwood, Jones & Co., 1824)

Boaden, James, *Memoirs of the life of John Philip Kemble, Esq. Including a history of the stage, from the time of Garrick to the present period*, 2 vols. in 1 (Philadelphia: Robert H. Small and New York: Wilder & Campbell, 1825)

Bunn, Alfred, *The stage: both before and behind the curtain*, 3 vols. (London: Richard Bentley, 1840)

Charlton, David, ed., *E. T. A. Hoffmann's musical writings: Kreisleriana, the poet and the composer, music criticism*, trans. Martyn Clarke (Cambridge University Press, 1989)

Clery, E. J. and Robert Miles, eds., *Gothic documents: a sourcebook 1700–1820* (Manchester University Press, 2000)

Cox, Edmund, *Musical recollections of the last half-century*, 2 vols. (London: Tinsley Brothers, 1872)

Cox, H. Bertram and C. L. E. Cox, *Leaves from the journals of Sir George Smart,* 1st edn 1907 (Da Capo Press: New York, 1971)

Diary of Covent Garden Theatre, 7 vols., British Library Additional Manuscripts 23156–62

Dibdin, Thomas, *The reminiscences of Thomas Dibdin . . .*, 2 vols. (New York: J & J Harper, 1828)

Ebers, John, *Seven years of the King's Theatre* (Philadelphia: Carey, Lea and Carey, 1828)

Fisher, Burton D. ed., *The barber of Seville: opera classics library* (Miami: Opera Journeys Publishing, 2005)

Fitzball, Edward, *Thirty-five years of a dramatic author's life*, 2 vols. (London: T. C. Newby, 1859)

Flora Tristan's London journal, 1840: Promenades dans Londres, trans. Dennis Palmer and Giselle Pincetl, orig. edn Paris 1840 (Charlestown, MA: Charles River Books, 1980)

Florimo, Francesco, ed., *Bellini: memorie e lettere* (Florence: G. Barbèra, 1882)

Genest, John, *Some account of the English stage: from the Restoration in 1660 to 1830*, 10 vols. (Bath: H. E. Carrington, 1832)

Graziano, John, *Italian opera in English: Cinderella (1831) adapted by M. Rophino Lacy from Gioacchino Rossini's La cenerentola* (London and New York: Garland Publishing, 1994)

Great Britain Parliament, House of Commons, *Report from the select committee on dramatic literature . . .* (London: n.p., 1832)

Gruneisen, Charles Lewis, *Memoir of Meyerbeer; with notices, historical and critical, of his celebrated operas . . .* (London: T. Brettell, 1848)

Hogarth, George, *Memoirs of the opera in Italy, France, Germany, and England*, 2 vols., orig. edn 1851 (New York: Da Capo Press, 1972)

Hormayr zu Hortenburg, Josef, *Memoirs of the life of Andreas Hofer; containing an account of the transactions in the Tyrol during the year 1809*, trans. Charles Henry Hall (London: John Murray, 1820)

Hunt, Leigh, *The autobiography of Leigh Hunt*, ed. J. E. Morpurgo (London: Cresset Press, 1948)

Irving, Pierre Munroe, *The life and letters of Washington Irving*, 4 vols. (New York: G. P. Putnam, 1862)

Kassler, Michael, ed., *Charles Edward Horn's memoirs of his father and himself* (Aldershot and Burlington: Ashgate and London: Society for Theatre Research, 2003)

Langbaine, Gerard, *An account of the English dramatick poets . . .* (Oxford: George West and Henry Clements, 1691)

Ledgers of Covent Garden Theatre, British Library Egerton Manuscripts 2209–19 and Additional Manuscript 23167

Letellier, Robert Ignatius, ed., *The diaries of Giacomo Meyerbeer. I: 1791–1839* (Madison, NJ: Fairleigh Dickinson University, 1999)

Macarthy, Eugene, *A letter to the King on the question now at issue between the major and minor theatres* (London: Effingham Wilson, 1832)

Mathias, Thomas James, *The shade of Alexander Pope on the banks of the Thames* ..., 3rd edn (London: T. Becket, 1799)

McClatchy, J. D., trans., *Seven Mozart librettos* (New York and London: W. W. Norton and Co., 2011)

Memoir of Mr. and Mrs. Wood (Boston: James Fisher, 1840)

Memoranda of agreements between the proprietors of the Theatre Royal, Covent Garden, and various musicians ..., British Library Additional Manuscript 29365

Merlin, Countess de, *Memoirs of Madame Malibran* ..., 2nd edn, 2 vols. (London: Henry Colburn, 1844)

Meyerbeer, Giacomo, *Briefwechsel und Tagebücher*, ed. Heinz Becker, 8 vols. (Berlin: Walter de Gruyter, 1959)

Muller, Major C., *An account of the sacrifices made, and the sufferings experienced by, the valiant inhabitants of the Tyrol and Vorarlberg* ... (London: R. Juigné, 1810)

Oxberry, [Catherine and William, eds.], *Oxberry's dramatic biography*, 6 vols. (London: George Virtue, 1825–27)

Phillips, Henry, *Musical and personal recollections during half a century*, 2 vols. (London: Charles J. Skeet, 1864)

Planché, James Robinson, *Olympic revels; or, prometheus and pandora* ... *first performed at the Olympic Theatre, 3rd January, 1831* in T. F. Dillon Croker and Stephen Tucker (eds.), *The extravaganzas of J. R. Planché* ... 5 vols. (London: Samuel French, 1879), vol. I, pp. 37–60

  Recollections and reflections: a professional autobiography, new and revised edn (London: S. Low, Marston & Co., 1901)

The public and private life of Lady William Lennox, alias, Miss Anne Paton, alias Mr Wood's chum-chum ... ([London: W. P. Chubb, 1831])

Receipts of performances at Drury Lane Theatre, British Library Additional Manuscripts 29709–11

Scott, Walter, *The journal of Sir Walter Scott*, ed. W. E. K. Anderson (Edinburgh: Canongate, 1998)

Waters, Edmund, 'A statement of matters, relative to the King's Theatre' in Michael Burden (ed.), *London opera observed, 1711–1844* (London: Pickering & Chatto, 2013), vol. IV, pp. 283–302

SECONDARY WORKS

Ahlquist, Karen, *Democracy at the opera: music, theater, and culture in New York City, 1815–60* (Urbana: University of Illinois Press, 1997)

  'Masculinity and legitimacy on the English musical stage: the mature male, 1800–1845', *Women and Music: a Journal of Gender and Culture*, 8 (2004), 1–21

Al-Taee, Nasser, *Representations of the orient in Western music: violence and sensuality* (Burlington: Ashgate, 2010)

Armondino, Gail, 'The opéra comique in London, or transforming French comic opera for the English stage, 1770–1789', unpublished PhD thesis, Catholic University of America (2000)

Baer, Marc, *Theatre and disorder in late Georgian London* (Oxford: Clarendon Press, 1992)

Bauman, Thomas, *W. A. Mozart: Die Entführung aus dem Serail* (Cambridge University Press, 1987)

Beard, Harry R., 'Figaro in England', *Maske und Kothurn*, 10 (1964), 498–513

Bennett, Susan, *Theatre audiences: a theory of production and reception* (London and New York: Routledge, 1997)

Biddlecombe, George, *English opera from 1834 to 1864 with particular reference to the works of Michael Balfe* (New York and London: Garland, 1994)

Bolton, H. Philip, *Scott dramatized* (London and New York: Mansell, 1992)

Bomberger, E. Douglas, 'The Neues Schauspielhaus in Berlin and the première of Carl Maria von Weber's *Der Freischütz*' in Mark A. Radice (ed.), *Opera in context: essays on historical staging from the late Renaissance to the time of Puccini* (Portland, OR: Amadeus Press, 1998), pp. 147–69

Booth, Michael, *Prefaces to English nineteenth-century theatre* (Manchester University Press, 1980)

Brake, Laurel and Marysa Demoor, *Dictionary of nineteenth-century journalism in Great Britain and Ireland* (Ghent: Academia Press and London: The British Library, 2009)

Brantlinger, Patrick, *Fictions of state: culture and credit in Britain, 1694–1994* (Ithaca, NY: Cornell University Press, 1996)

Bratton, J. S., 'Miss Scott and Miss Macauley: "genius comes in all disguises"', *Theatre Survey*, 37 (1996), 59–74

Bratton, Jacky, *New readings in theatre history* (Cambridge University Press, 2003)

Brewer, David *The flame of freedom: the Greek war of independence, 1821–1833* (London: John Murray, 2001)

Brooks, Peter, *The melodramatic imagination: Balzac, Henry James, melodrama, and the mode of excess* (New Haven: Yale University Press, 1976)

Brown, Clive, 'Zemire und Azor' in *The new Grove dictionary of opera. Grove music online. Oxford music online*. Oxford University Press, accessed 11 August 2014, http://proxy.ashland.edu:2227/subscriber/article/grove/music/O003600

'Barnett, John (1802-1890)' in H. C. G. Matthew and Brian Harrison (eds.), *Oxford dictionary of national biography* (Oxford University Press, 2004); online edn, ed. Lawrence Goldman, October 2009, www.oxforddnb.com/view/article/1478 (accessed 7 April 2015)

Brown, J. C. A., 'The popularity and influence of Spohr in England', unpublished PhD thesis, Exeter College, University of Oxford (1980)

Brown, Philip A. H., *London publishers and printers, c. 1800–1870* (London: British Library, 1982)

Burden, Michael, 'Opera in the London theatres' in Jane Moody and Daniel O'Quinn (eds.), *The Cambridge companion to British theatre, 1730–1830* (Cambridge University Press, 2007), pp. 205–18

'The writing and staging of Georgian Romantic opera' in Julia Swindells and David Francis Taylor (eds.), *The Oxford handbook of the Georgian theatre, 1737–1832* (Oxford University Press, 2014), pp. 424–41

Burling, William J., *Summer theatre in London, 1661–1820, and the rise of the Haymarket Theatre* (Madison, NJ: Fairleigh Dickinson University Press and London: Associated University Presses, 2000)

Burwick, Frederick, *Playing to the crowd: London popular theatre, 1780–1830* (New York: Palgrave Macmillan, 2011)

Butler, Marilyn, 'Antiquarianism (popular)' in Iain McCalman (ed.), *An Oxford companion to the Romantic age: British culture, 1776–1832* (Oxford University Press, 2001), pp. 328–38

Carlson, Julie Ann, *In the theatre of Romanticism: Coleridge, nationalism, women* (Cambridge University Press, 1994)

Carnevale, Nadia, '"... That's the barber!" Henry Rowley Bishop e l'adattamento del *Barbiere Rossiniano*' in Francesco Izzo and Johannes Streicher (eds.), *Ottocento e oltre: scritti in onore di Raoul Meloncelli* (Rome: Editoriale Pantheon, 1993), pp. 99–112

Carr, Bruce, 'The first all-sung English 19th-century opera', *Musical Times*, 115 (1974), 125–26
   'Theatre Music: 1800–1834' in Nicholas Temperley (ed.), *Music in Britain: the Romantic age, 1800–1914* (London: The Athlone Press, 1981), pp. 288–306

Carter, Tim, 'Mozart in a "land without music": Henry Bishop's *The marriage of Figaro*' in Kathrin Eberl and Wolfgang Ruf (eds.), *Musikkonzepte – Konzepte der Musikwissenschaft: Bericht über den Internationalen Kongreß der Gesellschaft für Musikforschung Halle (Saale) 1998* (Kassel: Bärenreiter, 2000), vol. 1, pp. 196–206

Cassirer, Peter, 'Gustaf III – the theatre King: librettist and politician' in Inger Mattson (ed.), *Gustavian opera: an interdisciplinary reader in Swedish opera, dance and theatre 1771–1809* (Stockholm: Royal Swedish Academy of Music, 1991), pp. 29–44

Charlton, David, *French opera 1730–1830: meaning and media* (Aldershot and Brookfield, VT: Ashgate, 2000)

Clark, Maribeth, 'The body and the voice in *La muette de Portici*', *19th-Century Music*, 27 (2003), 116–31

Cole, Laurence, *Andreas Hofer: the social and cultural construction of a national myth in Tirol, 1809–1909* (San Domenica: Badia Fiesolana, 1994)

Colley, Linda, *Britons: forging the nation, 1707–1837*, rev. edn (New Haven: Yale University Press, 2009)

Connolly, Leonard W., *The censorship of English drama, 1737–1824* (San Marino: The Huntington Library, 1976)

Connors, Linda E. and Mary Lu MacDonald, *National identity in Great Britain and British North America, 1815–1851: the role of nineteenth-century periodicals* (Burlington and Surrey: Ashgate, 2011)

Cooper, Victoria, *The house of Novello: practice and policy of a Victorian music publisher, 1829–1866* (Aldershot and Burlington: Ashgate, 2003)

Cowgill, Rachel, 'Mozart's music in London 1764–1829: aspects of reception and canonicity', unpublished PhD thesis, King's College, University of London (2000)
   'Mozart productions and the emergence of *Werktreue* at London's Italian opera house, 1780–1830' in Roberta Montemorra Marvin and Downing A. Thomas (eds.), *Operatic migrations: transforming works and crossing boundaries* (Aldershot and Burlington: Ashgate, 2006), pp. 145–86
   'Re-gendering the libertine; or, the taming of the rake: Lucy Vestris as Don Giovanni on the early nineteenth-century London stage', *Cambridge Opera Journal*, 10 (1998), 45–66
   '"Wise men from the east": Mozart's operas and their advocates in early nineteenth-century London' in Christina M. Bashford and Leanne Langley (eds.), *Music and British culture, 1785–1914: essays in honour of Cyril Ehrlich* (Oxford University Press, 2000), pp. 39–64

Davis, Jim, 'Spectatorship' in Jane Moody and Daniel O'Quinn (eds.), *The Cambridge companion to British theatre, 1730–1830* (Cambridge University Press, 2007), pp. 57–69

Davis, Jim and Victor Emeljanow, *Reflecting the audience: London theatregoing,* 1840–80 (Iowa City: University of Iowa Press, 2001)

Davis, Tracy C., *Actresses as working women: their social identity in Victorian culture* (London and New York: Routledge, 1991)

   The economics of the British stage, 1800–1914 (Cambridge University Press, 2000)

Deazley, Ronan, 'Commentary on *international copyright act* 1838' in L. Bently and M. Kretschmer (eds.), *Primary Sources on Copyright (1450–1900)*, www.copyrighthistory.org

Dideriksen, Gabriella, 'Repertory and rivalry: opera at the second Covent Garden Theatre, 1830 to 1856', unpublished PhD thesis, King's College, University of London (1997)

Dobson, Michael, *The making of the national poet: Shakespeare, adaptation, and authorship,* 1660–1769 (Oxford: Clarendon Press, 1992)

Doerner, Mark F., 'German Romantic opera? A critical reappraisal of *Undine* and *Der Freischütz*', *Opera Quarterly,* 10 (1993–4), 10–26

Dyer, Richard, *Pastiche* (London and New York: Routledge, 2007)

Ehrlich, Cyril, *First philharmonic: a history of the Royal Philharmonic Society* (Oxford: Clarendon Press and Oxford University Press, 1995)

Ehrlich, Cyril and Simon McVeigh, 'Music' in Iain McCalman (ed.), *An Oxford companion to the Romantic age* (Oxford University Press, 2001), pp. 242–9

Einstein, Alfred, 'The first performance of Mozart's *Entführung* in London' in *Essays on music* (New York: W. W. Norton, 1956), pp. 206–16

Ellis, Katharine, *Music criticism in nineteenth-century France: La Revue et Gazette musicale de Paris,* 1834–80 (Cambridge University Press, 1995)

   'Rewriting *Don Giovanni*, or "The thieving magpies"', *Journal of the Royal Musical Association,* 19 (1994), 212–50

Everett, Andrew, 'Meyerbeer in London: an account of his visits to London from 1815 to 1862' in Sieghart Döhring and Arnold Jacobshagen (eds.), *Meyerbeer und das europäische Musiktheater* (Laaber: Laaber-Verlag, 1998), pp. 386–406

Everist, Mark, *Giacomo Meyerbeer and music drama in nineteenth-century Paris* (Aldershot and Burlington: Ashgate, 2005)

   'Lindoro in Lyon: Rossini's *Le barbier de Séville*', *Acta Musicologica,* 64 (1992), 50–85

   Music drama at the Paris Odéon, 1824–1828 (Berkeley: University of California Press, 2002)

Fauser, Annegret, 'Phantasmagorie im deutschen Wald? Zur *Freischütz*-Rezeption in London und Paris 1824' in Hermann Danuser and Herfried Münkler (eds.), *Deutsche Meister – böse Geister? Nationale Selbstfindung in der Musik* (Schliengen: Argus, 2001), pp. 245–73

Fend, Michael, 'Zur Rezeption von Mozarts Opern in London im frühen 19. Jahrhundert' in Ingrid Fuchs (ed.), *Internationaler Musikwissenschaftlicher Kongreß zum Mozartjahr 1991, Baden – Wien,* 2 vols. (Tutzing: Hans Schneider, 1993), vol. II, pp. 601–14

Fenner, Theodore, *Leigh Hunt and opera criticism: the 'Examiner' years,* 1808–1821 (Lawrence: University Press of Kansas, 1972)

   Opera in London: views of the press 1785–1830 (Carbondale and Edwardsville: Southern Illinois University Press, 1994)

Fischler, Alan, '*Oberon* and odium: the career and crucifixion of J. R. Planché', *Opera Quarterly,* 12 (1995), 5–26

Fischlin, Daniel and Mark Fortier, 'General introduction' in Daniel Fischlin and Mark Fortier (eds.), *Adaptations of Shakespeare* (London and New York: Routledge, 2000), pp. 1–22

Fisher, David R., 'Twiss, Horace (1787–1849) ...', www.historyofparliament.org, accessed 11 November 1814

Fuhrmann, Christina, 'Between opera and musical: music in early nineteenth-century London playhouses' in Robert Gordon and Olaf Jubin (eds.), *The Oxford handbook of the British musical* (Oxford University Press, forthcoming in 2016)

'Continental opera Englished, English opera continentalized: *Der Freischütz* adapted for the London stage, 1824', *Nineteenth-Century Music Review*, 1 (2004), 115–42

'In enemy territory? Scribe and grand opera in London, 1829–33' in Sebastian Werr (ed.), *Eugène Scribe und das europäische Musiktheater* (Münster: Lit Verlag, 2007), pp. 89–106

'Scott repatriated? La dame blanche crosses the channel' in Gillen Wood (ed.) *Romanticism and opera, Romantic Circles Praxis Series*, www.rc.umd.edu/praxis/opera/fuhrmann/fuhrmann.html

ed., *Henry Rowley Bishop, Mozart's 'The marriage of Figaro': adapted for Covent Garden, 1819* (Middleton, WI: A-R Editions, 2012)

Galatopoulos, Stelios, *Bellini: life, times, music* (London: Sanctuary, 2002)

Gamer, Michael C., 'Marketing a masculine romance: Scott, antiquarianism, and the Gothic', *Studies in Romanticism*, 32 (1993), 523–49

Ganzel, Dewey, 'Patent wrongs and patent theatres: drama and the law in the early nineteenth century', *Publications of the Modern Language Association of America*, 76 (1961), 384–96

Garlick, Görel, *To serve the purpose of the drama: the theatre designs and plays of Samuel Beazley, 1786–1851* (London: Society for Theatre Research, 2003)

Gelbart, Matthew, *The invention of 'folk music' and 'art music': emerging categories from Ossian to Wagner* (Cambridge University Press, 2007)

Gerhard, Anselm, *The urbanization of opera*, trans. Mary Whittall (The University of Chicago Press, 1998)

Girdham, Jane, *English opera in late eighteenth-century London: Stephen Storace at Drury Lane* (Oxford: Clarendon Press, 1997)

Goehr, Lydia, *The imaginary museum of musical works: an essay in the philosophy of music* (Oxford: Clarendon Press, 1992)

Gossett, Philip, *Divas and scholars: performing Italian opera* (The University of Chicago Press, 2006)

'Gioachino Rossini and the conventions of composition', *Acta Musicologica*, 42 (1971), 48–58

'Rossini and authenticity', *The Musical Times*, 109 (1968), 1006–10

Grafe, Etienne, 'Un français, directeur de théâtre à Londres, au commencement du XIXème siècle, Pierre-François Laporte 1799–1841', unpublished PhD thesis, Université de Lyon (1996–7), typescript, Victoria and Albert Museum

Grey, Thomas S., 'The Gothic libertine: the shadow of Don Giovanni in Romantic music and culture' in Lydia Goehr and Daniel Herwitz (eds.), *The Don Giovanni moment* (New York: Columbia University Press, 2006), pp. 75–106

Hadden, J. C., 'Sinclair, John (1791–1857)', rev. Anne Pimlott Baker in H. C. G. Matthew and Brian Harrison (eds.), *Oxford dictionary of national biography* (Oxford University Press,

2004); online edn, ed. Lawrence Goldman, May 2007, www.oxforddnb.com/view/article/
25628 (accessed 14 November 2014)

Hadley, Elaine, *Melodramatic tactics: theatricalized dissent in the English marketplace, 1800–1885*
(Stanford University Press, 1995)

Hall-Witt, Jennifer, *Fashionable acts: opera and elite culture in London, 1780–1880* (Durham:
University of New Hampshire Press and Hanover: University Press of New England, 2007)

Hibberd, Sarah, '"Dormez donc, mes chers amours": Hérold's *La somnambule* (1827) and dream
phenomena on the Parisian lyric stage', *Cambridge Opera Journal*, 16 (2004), 107–32

   French grand opera and the historical imagination (Cambridge University Press, 2009)

   'Grand opera in Britain and the Americas' in David Charlton (ed.), *The Cambridge companion to
   grand opera* (Cambridge University Press, 2003), pp. 403–22

   '*La muette and her context*' in David Charlton (ed.), *The Cambridge companion to grand opera*
   (Cambridge University Press, 2003), pp. 149–67

   ed., *Melodramatic voices: understanding music drama* (Burlington: Ashgate, 2011)

Hill, Cecil, ed., *Ferdinand Ries: Briefe und Dokumente* (Bonn: Röhrscheid, 1982)

Hortschansky, Klaus, 'Gegen Unwahrscheinlichkeit und Frivolität: Die Bearbeitungen im 19.
Jahrhundert' in Susanna Vill (ed.), *Così fan tutte: Beiträge zur Wirkungsgeschichte von Mozarts
Oper* (Bayreuth: Mühl'scher Universitätsverlag, 1978), pp. 54–66

Hoskins, Robert H. B., 'Samuel Arnold's *The Spanish barber*', *Early Music New Zealand*, 4 (1985),
11–14

Hughes, Leo, *The drama's patrons: a study of the eighteenth-century London audience* (Austin:
University of Texas Press, 1971)

Hume, Robert D. and Arthur Jacobs, 'London' in *The new Grove dictionary of opera. Grove music
online. Oxford music online*. Oxford University Press, accessed 30 October 2014, http://
proxy.ashland.edu:2220/subscriber/article/grove/music/O902853pg2

Hutcheon, Linda, with Siobhan O'Flynn, *A theory of adaptation*, 2nd edn (London and New York:
Routledge, 2013)

Irving, Howard, 'William Crotch on borrowing', *The Music Review*, 53 (1992), 237–54

Jones, Catherine, 'Romantic opera in translation: Carl Maria von Weber and Washington
Irving', *Translation and Literature*, 20 (2011), 29–47

Kennerley, David, '"Flippant dolls" and "serious artists": professional female singers in Britain,
c. 1760–1850', unpublished PhD thesis, University of Oxford (2013)

Kent, Christopher, 'Periodical critics of drama, music, and art, 1830–1914: a preliminary list',
Victorian Periodicals Review, 13 (1980), 31–55

Kirby, Percival R., 'Washington Irving, Barham Livius and Weber', *Music and Letters*, 31 (1950),
133–47

Knight, William G., *A major London 'minor': the Surrey Theatre 1805–1865* (London: Society for
Theatre Research, 1997)

Langley, Leanne, 'Arnold, Samuel James' in *Grove music online. Oxford music online*. Oxford
University Press, accessed 2 August 2014, http://proxy.ashland.edu:2220/subscriber/art
icle/grove/music/45656

   'The English musical journal in the early nineteenth century', unpublished PhD thesis,
   University of North Carolina Chapel Hill (1983)

Leader, Zachary, *Revision and Romantic authorship* (Oxford: Clarendon Press, 1996)

Leeuwe, Hans de, 'Revolution durch Oper? Aubers Stumme von Portici 1830 in Brüssel', *Maske und Kothurn*, 30 (1980), 267–83

Leppert, Richard, *Music and image: domesticity, ideology, and socio-cultural formation in eighteenth-century England* (Cambridge University Press, 1993)

Letellier, Robert Ignatius, *Daniel-François-Auber: the man and his music* (Newcastle Upon Tyne: Cambridge Scholars Publishing, 2010)

> *Meyerbeer's Robert le diable: the premier opéra romantique* (Newcastle Upon Tyne: Cambridge Scholars Publishing, 2012)

Levin, David, *Unsettling opera: staging Mozart, Verdi, Wagner, and Zemlinksy* (The University of Chicago Press, 2007)

Locke, Ralph, 'Cutthroats and casbah dancers, muezzins and timeless sands: musical images of the Middle East' in Jonathan Bellman (ed.), *The exotic in Western music* (Boston: Northeastern University Press, 1998), pp. 104–36

Lockhart, William, 'Trial by ear: legal attitudes to keyboard arrangement in nineteenth-century Britain', *Music and Letters*, 93 (2012), 191–221

Loewenberg, Alfred, *Annals of opera, 1597–1940*, 3rd edn (Totowa, NJ: Rowman and Littlefield, 1978)

Luquer, Thatcher T. Payne, 'Correspondence of Washington Irving and John Howard Payne [1821–1828]', *Scribner's Magazine*, 48 (1910), 461–82

Marsden, Jean I., *The re-imagined text: Shakespeare, adaptation, and eighteenth-century literary theory* (Lexington: The University Press of Kentucky, 1995)

Marvin, Roberta, 'The censorship of Verdi's operas in Victorian London', *Music and Letters*, 82 (2001), 582–610

> 'The Victorian Violetta: the social messages of Verdi's *La traviata*' in Rachel Cowgill, David Cooper and Clive Brown (eds.), *Art and ideology in European opera: essays in honour of Julian Rushton* (Woodbridge: The Boydell Press, 2010), pp. 222–40

Maycock, John, 'Weber's operas in England (1822–26)', *The Monthly Musical Record*, 82 (February 1952), 39–42

Mero, Alison, 'The quest for national musical identity: English opera and the press, 1834–1849', unpublished PhD thesis, Indiana University (2014)

Meyer, Eve R., 'Turquerie and eighteenth-century music', *Eighteenth-Century Studies*, 7 (1974), 474–88.

Meyer, Stephen C., *Carl Maria von Weber and the search for a German opera* (Indiana University Press, 2003)

Moody, Jane, '"Fine word, legitimate!": toward a theatrical history of Romanticism', *Texas Studies in Literature and Language*, 38 (1996), 223–44

> *Illegitimate theatre in London, 1770–1840* (Cambridge University Press, 2000)

Morgan, Marjorie, *Manners, morals, and class in England, 1774–1858* (New York: St Martin's Press, 1994)

Newark, Cormac, 'Interpreting *La muette*' in Sebastian Werr (ed.), *Eugène Scribe und das europäische Musiktheater* (Münster: Lit Verlag, 2007), pp. 46–64

Newcomb, Anthony, 'New light(s) on Weber's wolf's glen scene' in Thomas Bauman and Marita McClymonds (eds.), *Opera and the Enlightenment* (Cambridge University Press, 1995), pp. 61–88

Newey, Katherine, 'The 1832 select committee' in Julia Swindells and David Francis Taylor (eds.), *The Oxford handbook of the Georgian theatre, 1737–1832* (Oxford University Press, 2014), pp. 140–55

    'Reform on the London stage' in Arthur Burns and Joanna Innes (eds.), *Rethinking the age of reform: Britain 1780–1850* (Cambridge University Press, 2003), pp. 238–53

Nicoll, Allardyce, *Alphabetical catalogue of plays 1660–1900*, vol. VI of *A history of English drama 1660–1900* (Cambridge University Press, 1959)

    Early nineteenth century drama, 1800–1850, vol. IV of *A history of English drama, 1660–1900*, 2nd edn (Cambridge University Press, 1955)

    Late eighteenth century drama, vol. III of *A history of English drama 1660–1900*, 2nd edn (Cambridge University Press, 1952)

Northcott, Richard, *The life of Sir Henry R. Bishop* (London: Press Printers, 1920)

Palmer, A. Dean, *Heinrich August Marschner, 1795–1861: his life and stage works* (Ann Arbor: University Microfilms International, 1980)

    'Vampyr, Der (i)' in *The new Grove dictionary of opera. Grove music online. Oxford music online.* Oxford University Press, accessed 11 August 2014, http://proxy.ashland.edu:2227/subscriber/article/grove/music/O011161

Parker, Roger, *Remaking the song: operatic visions and revisions from Handel to Berio* (Berkeley: University of California Press, 2006)

Peterson, Megan M., '"The best the house could afford": critical reaction to Rossini's *Il barbiere di Siviglia* at the King's Theatre, 1818–30', unpublished Master's thesis, The University of Western Ontario (1999)

Pisani, Michael, *Music for the melodramatic theatre in London and New York* (Iowa City: University of Iowa Press, 2014)

Plasketes, George, 'Re-flections on the cover age: a collage of continuous coverage in popular music', *Popular Music and Society*, 28 (2005), 137–61

Poriss, Hilary, *Changing the score: arias, prima donnas, and the authority of performance* (Oxford University Press, 2009)

Porter, James, et al., 'Ballad' in *Grove music online. Oxford music online.* Oxford University Press, accessed 2 November 2014, http://proxy.ashland.edu:2220/subscriber/article/grove/music/01879

Powers, Harold S., '"La solita forma" and "the uses of convention"', *Acta Musicologica*, 59 (1987), 65–90

Preston, Katherine K., *Opera on the road: traveling opera troupes in the United States, 1825–1860* (Urbana and Chicago: University of Illinois Press, 1993)

Price, Curtis, 'Unity, originality, and the London pasticcio', *Harvard Library Bulletin* New Series 2 (1991), 17–30

Price, George R., 'Washington Irving's Librettos', *Music and Letters*, 29 (1948), 348–55

Reichart, Walter A., 'Washington Irving's friend and collaborator: Barham John Livius, Esq.', *Publications of the Modern Language Association of America*, 56 (1941), 513–31

Reynolds, David, ed., *Weber in London, 1826: selections from Weber's letters . . .* (London: Oswald Wolff, 1976)

Ridgewell, Rupert, '"Meyerbeer's best intentions utterly destroyed?" Henry Bishop's *Robert le diable* (London, 1832)', unpublished Master's thesis, Royal Holloway, University of London (1993)

Robinson, Michael F., 'Two London versions of *The deserter*' in Daniel Heartz and Bonnie Wade (eds.), *Report of the twelfth congress Berkeley 1977* (Kassel: Bärenreiter and Philadelphia: The American Musicological Society, 1981), pp. 239–45.

Roe, Nicholas, 'Hunt, (James Henry) Leigh (1784–1859)' in H. C. G. Matthew and Brian Harrison (eds.), *Oxford dictionary of national biography* (Oxford University Press, 2004); online edn, ed. Lawrence Goldman, October 2009, www.oxforddnb.com/view/article/14195 (accessed 12 November 2014)

Rogers, Stuart W., 'Cenerentola a Londra', *Bollettino del Centro rossiniano di studi*, 37 (1997), 51–67

Rogers, Vanessa L., 'Orchestra and theatre music' in Julia Swindells and David Francis Taylor (eds.), *The Oxford handbook of the Georgian theatre, 1737–1832* (Oxford University Press, 2014), pp. 304–20

Rohr, Deborah Adams, *The careers of British musicians, 1750–1850: a profession of artisans* (Cambridge University Press, 2001)

Rose, Mark, *Authors and owners: the invention of copyright* (Cambridge, MA: Harvard University Press, 1993)

Rosen, David, 'A tale of three libretti: *La muette de Portici* in Italy' in Maria Ida Biggi et al. (eds.), *L'immaginario scenografico e la realizzazione musicale: Atti del Convegno in onore di Mercedes Viale Ferrero* (Alessandria: Edizioni dell'Orso, 2009), pp. 167–80

Rosenfeld, Sybil, *Georgian scene painters and scene painting* (Cambridge University Press, 1981)

Rosenthal, Laura J., *Playwrights and plagiarists in early modern England: gender, authorship, literary property* (Ithaca and London: Cornell University Press, 1996)

Rowland, David, 'Clementi as publisher' in Michael Kassler (ed.), *The music trade in Georgian England* (Farnham and Burlington: Ashgate, 2011), pp. 159–91

Rushton, Julian, *W. A. Mozart: Don Giovanni* (Cambridge University Press, 1981)

Sanders, Julie, *Adaptation and appropriation* (London and New York: Routledge, 2006)

Saunders, Thomas Bailey, 'Knowles, James Sheridan (1784–1862)', rev. Peter Thomson in H. C. G. Matthew and Brian Harrison (eds.), *Oxford dictionary of national biography* (Oxford University Press, 2004); online edn, ed. Lawrence Goldman, May 2005, www.oxforddnb.com/view/article/25628 (accessed 10 May 2010)

Schneider, Herbert, 'Scribe and Auber: constructing grand opera' in David Charlton (ed.), *The Cambridge companion to grand opera* (Cambridge University Press, 2003), pp. 168–88

Scott, Michael, 'Rossini in England: part 1', *Opera*, 27 (1976), 210–14

   'Rossini in England: part 2', *Opera*, 27 (1976), 434–9

Seccombe, Thomas, 'Warde, James Prescott (1792–1840)', rev. Nilanjana Banerji in H. C. G. Matthew and Brian Harrison (eds.), *Oxford dictionary of national biography* (Oxford University Press, 2004); online edn, ed. Lawrence Goldman, www.oxforddnb.com/view/article/28717 (accessed 21 November 2014)

Senelick, Lawrence, 'Boys and girls together: subcultural origins of glamour drag and male impersonation on the nineteenth-century stage' in Lesley Ferris (ed.), *Crossing the stage: controversies on cross-dressing* (London and New York: Routledge, 1993), pp. 80–95

Small, John, 'The development of musical copyright' in Michael Kassler (ed.), *The music trade in Georgian England* (Farnham and Burlington, VT: Ashgate, 2011), pp. 233–386

Smith, Jan, 'An English transformation: Michael Rophino Lacy's adaptation of Rossini's *La cenerentola* (London, 1830)', unpublished Master's thesis, University of London (2001)

Stephens, John Russell, *The censorship of English drama, 1824–1901* (Cambridge University Press, 1980)
  The profession of the playwright: British theatre 1800–1900 (Cambridge University Press, 1992)
Straub, Kristina, *Sexual suspects: eighteenth-century players and sexual ideology* (Princeton University Press, 1992)
Stuart, Roxana, *Stage blood: vampires of the 19th-century stage* (Bowling Green State University Popular Press, 1994)
Talbot, Michael, ed., *The musical work: reality or invention?* (Liverpool University Press, 2000)
Taruskin, Richard, 'Setting limits' in Richard Taruskin, *The danger of music and other anti-utopian essays* (Berkeley: University of California Press, 2008), pp. 447–66
Temperley, Nicholas, 'Ballroom and drawing-room music' in Nicholas Temperley (ed.), *Music in Britain: the Romantic age 1800–1914* (London: The Athlone Press, 1981), pp. 109–34
Temperley, Nicholas and Bruce Carr, 'Bishop, Sir Henry R.' in *Grove music online. Oxford music online.* Oxford University Press, accessed 14 November 2014, http://proxy.ashland.edu:2220/subscriber/article/grove/music/40027
Thomas, David, 'The 1737 licensing act and its impact' in Julia Swindells and David Francis Taylor (eds.), *The Oxford handbook of the Georgian theatre, 1737–1832* (Oxford University Press, 2014), pp. 91–106
Till, Nicholas, 'The operatic work: texts, performances, receptions and repertories' in Nicholas Till (ed.), *The Cambridge companion to opera studies* (Cambridge University Press, 2012), pp. 225–53
Truninger, Annelise, *Paddy and the paycock: a study of the stage Irishman from Shakespeare to O'Casey* (Bern: Francke Verlag, 1976)
Tusa, Michael C., 'Cosmopolitanism and the national opera: Weber's *Der Freischütz*', *Journal of Interdisciplinary History*, 36 (2006), 483–506
Twitchell, James B., *The living dead: a study of the vampire in Romantic literature* (Durham: Duke University Press, 1981)
Vann, T. Don and Rosemary T. VanArsdel, eds., *Victorian periodicals and Victorian society* (University of Toronto Press, 1994)
Walton, Benjamin, 'Looking for the revolution in Rossini's *Guillaume Tell*', *Cambridge Opera Journal*, 15 (2003), 127–51
  'Rara avis or fozy turnip: Rossini as celebrity in 1820s London' in Tom Mole (ed.), *Romanticism and celebrity culture, 1750–1850* (Cambridge University Press, 2009), pp. 81–102
Warrack, John, *Carl Maria von Weber* (London: H. Hamilton, 1968)
  German opera: from the beginnings to Wagner (Cambridge University Press, 2001)
Weber, William, 'The history of music canon' in Nicholas Cook and Mark Everist (eds.), *Rethinking music* (Oxford University Press, 1999), pp. 336–55
  The rise of musical classics in eighteenth-century England: a study in canon, ritual, and ideology (Oxford: Clarendon Press and Oxford University Press, 1996)
Wood, Gillen D'Arcy, *Romanticism and music culture in Britain, 1770–1840: virtue and virtuosity* (Cambridge University Press, 2010)
Woodfield, Ian, *Mozart's Così fan tutte: a compositional history* (Woodbridge: Boydell, 2008)
Zenck, Claudia Maurer, '"Ach wir alle sind von Flandern": Frühe deutsche Übersetzungen von *Così fan tutte*' in Pierre Béhar and Herbert Schneider (eds.), *Österreichische Oper oder Oper in Österreich?: die Libretto-Problematik* (Hildesheim: Georg Olms, 2003), pp. 231–54

INDEX

'Follow, follow o'er the mountain', 117
'Home sweet home'. *See* Bishop, Sir Henry Rowley
'I've been roaming'. *See* Horn, Charles Edward
'Manca un foglio'. *See* Romani, Pietro
'Should he upbraid'. *See* Bishop, Sir Henry Rowley
'The light guitar'. *See* Barnett, John
'The roast beef of old England'. *See* Leveridge, Richard
'What can a poor maiden do?'. *See* Horn, Charles
      Edward

Abu Hassan. See Weber, Carl Maria von
Addison, John
      Le petit chaperon rouge, adapted, 196
Adelphi Theatre, The, 68, 160–4, 169, 197–9,
      214 n. 11
Aders, Mr and Mrs Charles, 96
Age, 110, 113, 130–1, 143, 147, 159, 163, 166, 168, 182–3,
      203–5, 227 n. 53
Ahlquist, Karen, 40, 86
Alchymist, Der. See Spohr, Louis
Alchymist, Der, adapted. *See* Bayly, Thomas Haynes,
      Bishop, Sir Henry Rowley, Fitzball, Edward
Alexandrine, Mademoiselle, 158
Allgemeine Musikalische Zeitung, 214 n. 1
Alsager, Thomas Massa, 63, 69
Al-Taee, Nasser, 121
Amherst, J. H.
      Der Freischütz, adapted, 80–3, 196
      La muette de Portici, adapted, 147–59, 198
Apel, Johann August
      Gespensterbuch, 73
apprentice, The. See Murphy, Arthur
Armida. See Rossini, Gioachino
Arne, Thomas Augustine
      Artaxerxes, 5, 26
      Love in a village, 221 n. 3
Arnold, Samuel, 74
      Le barbier de Séville, adapted, 47

Arnold, Samuel James, 17, 80, 94–6, 109, 219 n. 27
      Così fan tutte, adapted, 14, 95, 119, 126–8, 140–4, 197
      Der Freischütz, adapted, 73–80, 86–90, 95, 196
      Jean de Paris, adapted, 13, 16, 19–22, 33–8, 74, 196
      La lettre de change, adapted, 196
      Tarare, adapted, 197
Artaxerxes. See Arne, Thomas Augustine
Astley's Theatre. *See* Royal Amphitheatre, The
Athenaeum, 8–9, 109–10, 112, 138, 146, 157–60, 166,
      172, 174–5, 192, 203–6, 218 n. 11, 220 n. 44, 223
      n. 58, 226 n. 45, 227 n. 52, 229 n. 43
Atlas, 10, 143. *See* Hazlitt, William, Holmes,
      Edward
Attwood, Thomas
      The prisoner, 60
Auber, Daniel-François-Esprit, 1, 227 n. 52
      Le concert à la cour, 151
      Le dieu et la bayadère, 176, 199
      La fiancée, 146, 198
      Fra diavolo, 199
      Gustave III, 15, 170–1, 183–92, 199, 225 n. 7
      Léocadie, 197
      Le maçon, 146–7, 197
      La muette de Portici, 14, 135, 147–60, 167, 198
      La neige, 109, 197
      Le philtre, 198
      Le serment, 199
audiences. *See* theatre, London
Augustus Frederick, Prince, duke of Sussex, 92
Aumer, Jean, 181
Aureliano in Palmira. See Rossini, Gioachino
Austria
      relationship to *Guillaume Tell*, adapted, 136
Ayrton, William, 1, 8, 10, 12, 39–40, 57–8, 69, 74,
      86–7, 89–90, 107–8, 112, 128, 133, 138, 142–5,
      157, 166–7, 170–4, 180, 183, 203–6, 215 n. 18,
      222 n. 39, 228 n. 9
Ayton, Fanny, 129, 167

CPSIA information can be obtained
at www.ICGtesting.com
Printed in the USA
LVHW101727040119
602794LV00010B/182/P